# The Holiday Handbook

700+ Storytime Activities
from Arbor Day to Yom Kippur...
from Diwali to Kwanzaa to Ramadan

Barbara A. Scott

Neal-Schuman
An imprint of the American Library Association
Chicago 2012

Published by Neal-Schuman, an imprint of the American Library Association
50 E. Huron Street
Chicago, IL 60611
www.neal-schuman.com

Printed in the United States of America
16  15  14  13  12      5  4  3  2  1

Extensive effort has gone into ensuring the reliability of the information in this book; however, the publisher makes no warranty, express or implied, with respect to the material contained herein.

ISBNs: 978-1-55570-768-2 (paper); 978-1-55570-814-6 (PDF)

**Library of Congress Cataloging-in-Publication Data**
Scott, Barbara A., 1956–
    The holiday handbook : 700+ storytime activities from Arbor Day to Yom Kippur...from Diwali to Kwanzaa to Ramadan / Barbara A. Scott.
        p. cm.
    Includes bibliographical references and index.
    ISBN 978-1-55570-768-2 (alk. paper)
    1. Creative activities and seat work—Handbooks, manuals, etc. 2. Holidays—Handbooks, manuals, etc. 3. Handicraft—Handbooks, manuals, etc. I. Title.

LB1027.25.S35 2012
372.5—dc23
                                                        2012003531

Cover design by Rosie Holderby
Text design in Minion and Avenir by UB Communications

♾ This paper meets the requirements of ANSI/NISO Z39.48-1992 (Permanence of Paper).

This book is dedicated to my family—
Greg, BJ, and Sarah.
I love each of you very much.

# Contents

# Preface

Storytimes or storyhours are an integral part of the job of a children's librarian. Early childhood educators, day care providers, and teachers of elementary grades also often present stories with activities as part of their jobs. These professionals (and sometimes paraprofessionals) are the intended audience for *The Holiday Handbook: 700+ Storytime Activities from Arbor Day to Yom Kippur…from Diwali to Kwanzaa to Ramadan*.

## Holidays and Storytimes

Holidays are usually times of general busyness in the midst of celebration, and libraries, day care centers, and schools are no exception. Just as families hold holiday celebrations in their homes, your library or school may find holidays to be a time for special programming in addition to any regular storytimes that you hold. Depending on the area of the country (or world) in which you live, some holiday celebrations may provide a learning opportunity for everyone involved.

I designed *The Holiday Handbook: 700+ Storytime Activities from Arbor Day to Yom Kippur… from Diwali to Kwanzaa to Ramadan* to be a one-stop source for everything the busy librarian, early childhood educator, or day care worker would need to conduct a holiday storytime or special programming centering around a holiday. I hope this book will give the busy librarian or educator more time to concentrate on presenting the program instead of looking in multiple sources for activities.

I know from experience how nice it was when, while attending workshops as part of my job, presenters would share complete units for storytimes, holiday or not. Thus, over the several years that I became a presenter myself at state summer program workshops, I crafted my presentations as complete storytime units for whatever the theme happened to be that year. I always provided a detailed handout for suggested storytimes (usually six to seven different themes), complete with everything needed, even patterns for crafts! My audience was always very appreciative, and many attendees told me that they looked forward to these handouts year after year.

Many books focus on the major holidays, but *The Holiday Handbook: 700+ Storytime Activities from Arbor Day to Yom Kippur…from Diwali to Kwanzaa to Ramadan* is different in that I have attempted to give even the lesser-known holidays the same treatment as the well-known ones.

## Organization of the Book

*The Holiday Handbook: 700+ Storytime Activities from Arbor Day to Yom Kippur…from Diwali to Kwanzaa to Ramadan* covers 34 different holiday storytimes. Each chapter focuses on a specific holiday or similar holidays and is organized in the same manner:

- **History (introductory material):** Each chapter has a short history of the holiday. You may wish to share this with your participants, or it can simply be for your own benefit. I readily admit that before I did research on any of the chapters concerning Jewish holidays, I had little, if any, idea about what the holidays represented or how they were tied to the Jewish faith. My research entailed searching online, diving into books that were recommended from online sites, and combing through titles that I had available to me both through my library and through interlibrary loan. There is an old adage that says that you are never too old to learn, and how true that is!

- **Poetry:** Following the history of the holiday is a listing of poems that you may use to introduce your storytime. I had the distinct pleasure of hearing Dr. Caroline Feller Bauer speak many years ago when her book *The Poetry Break: An Annotated Anthology with Ideas for Introducing Children to Poetry* came out. It offers many creative ways of introducing poetry to children, and this was one idea that I took and ran with! Rare is the storytime that I do not open with a poem related to whatever the theme may be. As I suggested in my first book, *1,000 Fingerplays and Action Rhymes*, if you can type out and simply illustrate the poem for the benefit of your participants, so much the better. Another alternative that works just as well is to use realia that helps you "tell" the poem (e.g., see the programming idea for "My Mother's Chocolate Valentine" by Jack Prelutsky in the "Valentine's Day" chapter). Remember that poetry is rhythm and rhyme, which are a part of phonological awareness, an integral component of early literacy and prereading skills. Phonological awareness also involves recognizing the sounds of letters and words and the ability to hear and play with the smaller sounds in words. And if anything plays with words, it's poetry! Anywhere from 1 to 24 poems are referenced, depending on the holiday.

- **Books:** What would a storytime be without stories? From the newest copyrights to older titles (dubbed "Older Gems, or Titles Too Good to Pass Up"), each chapter boasts an extensive list of books, including both fiction and nonfiction titles, that will provide simple introductions to the holidays or great stories to share. For the newer titles, depending on the popularity of the holiday, anywhere from 5 to 39 books are listed; for the "Older Gems," anywhere from 1 to 10 titles are listed.

- **Activities:** Activities that engage participants are a staple of storytimes or special programming: coloring pages, cut-and-tell stories, draw-and-tell stories, flannel- or Velcro-board stories, games (matching and otherwise), and so on. Each chapter offers a variety of such activities that could be found for the different holidays. I like to include all of the types listed previously within the parameters of my storytime sessions, with the exception of the coloring pages, an activity I usually reserve for concluding my storytime sessions. Depending on the holiday, chapters may include as few as 5 or 6 activities or as many as 30.

- **Fingerplays:** Each chapter includes fingerplays and action rhymes (rhymes that use the whole body) to use with participants. There may be as few as 1 or 2 fingerplays for some of the lesser-known holidays, but the more common holidays will have 20 or more fingerplays from which to choose.

- **Musical Selections:** Each chapter lists a number of songs that can be used as an additional activity with your participants. Dancing and playing instruments are great large- and small-motor activities for children, and singing also reinforces the same rhythm and rhyme concepts that poetry does, all leading back to those very important literacy and prereading skills. Do you own rhythm band instruments? Bean bags? Scarves? Parachutes? Or do you just want to dance? Young participants are likely to enjoy any of these ways of expressing themselves as well as singing along to the music. The musical selections are listed by the song title, the performer, and the CD on which the song appears. Some songs are available only as downloads and this information is included as well.

- **Crafts:** Participants love to cut and glue and create, and parents love those handmade items that can be hung on the refrigerator at home or used year after year as a special reminder. Each chapter provides descriptions of numerous holiday-related crafts, and pictures are provided for 1 or 2 of the crafts featured. Crafts may number as few as 3 or as many as 10, depending on the chapter.

- **Patterns:** Each chapter includes 1 or 2 (in most cases, 2) pieces of original artwork by artist Earl Musick. This artwork can be used as you see fit: name tag patterns, patterns for flannel/Velcro-board presentations, or matching games.

Included at the end of the book are 2 appendixes: (A) contact information for companies that offer items to enhance your storytimes, from puppets to realia, from crayons to craft kits, and (B) a craft photo gallery.

It is always fun to learn about different cultures, and what a great way to expose participants in your programming to the customs of people from around the world! We may not be able to travel to those countries we talk about, but we can bring a little bit of them to our corner of the world.

As of this writing, I've been doing storytimes and programming for 26 years, and the excitement of seeing little ones react to the books read or the activities done has never grown old. I hope that *The Holiday Handbook: 700+ Storytime Activities from Arbor Day to Yom Kippur…from Diwali to Kwanzaa to Ramadan* inspires you, re-energizes you, and makes your busy work life a little simpler!

# Acknowledgments

I would like to thank all of the authors and librarians who have graciously allowed me to use their fingerplays/action rhymes or craft ideas for this book. They are listed in the following section.

My sincere appreciation goes out to Kathy Buchsbaum, my editor for this project. Not only was she a source of encouragement and an answerer of many questions, she has also provided some original rhymes for a number of the Jewish-themed chapters.

My thanks and appreciation also goes to Charles Harmon of Neal-Schuman for having faith in me and my book proposal and for offering to publish me for a second time.

A big thank-you goes out to Earl Musick, illustrator extraordinaire!

A huge thank-you goes to my daughter, Sarah Scott, who shot the photographs for this book!

Finally, my heartfelt thanks to my family and friends, who have been a great source of encouragement to me!

"Eight Little Candles" and "I'm a Little Latke" are reprinted here with the permission of Dr. Betsy Diamant-Cohen.

"Kisses," "Head and Shoulders, Knees and Toes: A St. Patrick's Day Twist," "Tree," "Plant a Tree," "It Is Purim," "Hamentaschen Dance," "Purim," "I Like Matzah," and "The Matzah Dance," "Apple Dance," "Ramadan Is Here" (two versions), "Here Is My Light," "These Are My Clothes," and "Diwali" are reprinted here with the permission of Kathy Buchsbaum.

"Happy, Happy Hanukkah," "The First Thanksgiving," and "Frozen Thanksgiving Meal" are reprinted here with the permission of Jan Irving and Robin Currie, authors of *Mudluscious: Stories and Activities Featuring Food for Preschool Children* (Libraries Unlimited, 1986).

"Light Bulb Hunt," "Turkey Hide-and-Seek," "What Do I Hear?," "The Basket the Bunny Brought," "In the Company of a Star," and "Santa's Clothes" are reprinted here with the permission of Susan Dailey (http://www.susanmdailey.com/).

"Five May Baskets" and "Dreidl" are reprinted here with the permission of Lynda S. Roberts, author of *Mitt Magic: Fingerplays for Finger Puppets* (Gryphon House, 1985).

"Friendship Stew" is reprinted here with the permission of Kathleen Poznick, Children's Librarian at Weatherford Public Library, Weatherford, Texas.

The latke craft idea for the Hanukkah chapter is reprinted here with the permission of Victoria G. Dworkin, Children's Librarian at Hawaii State Library.

# April Fools' Day

*Celebrated on April 1st of each year, this day gives us all an excuse to play jokes and be silly! Enlarge your theme to include all things silly!*

## History

April Fools' Day is sometimes known as All Fools' Day. The history behind the day, however, is uncertain.

One account says that ancient cultures, including the Romans and the Hindus, celebrated New Year's Day on or around April 1st. In 1582, Pope Gregory XIII instituted the adoption of a new calendar, the Gregorian Calendar, which stated that New Year's Day would be celebrated on January 1st. According to lore, many people either refused to accept this new date or did not learn about it right away, and they continued to celebrate New Year's Day on April 1st. Others made fun of these people, sending them on "fools' errands" or tricking them into believing something that wasn't true. (See Jerry Wilson's "April Fool's Day" at http://www.wilstar.com/holidays/aprilfool.htm.)

Many cultures, however, celebrate days similar to April Fools' Day around the start of the month of April. The Romans had a festival called Hilaria that they celebrated on March 25th. The Hindu calendar has Holi, and the Jewish calendar has Purim. Perhaps it is the time of year, with the season turning from winter to spring that just brings out the silliness in everyone! (See David Johnson and Shmuel Ross's "April Fools' Day: Origin and History" at http://www.infoplease.com/spot/aprilfools1.html.)

## Poetry

"April Fool's Day," from page 70 in *Quick Tricks for Holidays* by Annalisa McMorrow (Monday Morning Books, 2001).

"Curious Questions," from page 52 of *Poems Just for Us! 50 Read-Aloud Poems with Cross-Curricular Activities for Young Children* by Bobbi Katz (Scholastic Professional Books, 1996).

"First of April" by Timothy Tocher, from page 247 in *Celebrate the Seasons: The Best of Holidays and Seasonal Celebrations—Issues 9–12, PreK–3*, edited by Donna Borst (Teaching and Learning Company, 1998).

"I Had a Silly Day," from page 127 in *More Simply Super Storytimes: Programming Ideas for Ages 3–6* by Marie Castellano Boyum (Upstream Productions, 2006).

"If You Believe Me," from page 23 in *Ring Out, Wild Bells: Poems about Holidays and Seasons*, selected by Lee Bennett Hopkins (Harcourt Brace Jovanovich, 1992).

"Mr. Backward," from page 71 of *Bing Bang Boing* by Douglas Florian (Harcourt, Brace, and Company, 1994).

"Padiddle," about a lady whose Dalmatian loses his spots, by J. Patrick Lewis, from page 184 in *The Poetry Break: An Annotated Anthology with Ideas for Introducing Children to Poetry* by Caroline Feller Bauer (H.W. Wilson, 1995).

"Silly Supper Farm," from page 114 in *A Poem for Every Day! An Anthology of 180 Poems with Activities to Enhance Your Teaching* by Susan Moger (Teaching Resources, 2006).

"Vice Versa Verse," from page 48 in *A Little Book of Little Beasts* by Mary Ann Hoberman (Simon and Schuster, 1973).

# Books

Bateman, Teresa. *April Foolishness*. Albert Whitman and Company, 2004. ISBN: 978-0807504055.
Family pranks highlight the gentle, teasing relationships in this amusing tale. Grandpa thinks he's wise to his grandchildren's April Fools' Day tricks and ignores their warnings of animals run amok.

deGroat, Diane. *April Fool! Watch Out at School*. HarperCollins, 2009. ISBN: 978-0061430428.
On April Fools' Day, Gilbert is unhappy that everyone is tricking him and he is unable to get them back. Then he thinks of a great way to fool his best friend!

Haskamp, Steve. *Eight Silly Monkeys*. Intervisual, 2003. ISBN: 978-1581172294.
Young ones will love counting backward as they watch eight monkeys disappear one by one with each turn of the page in this delightful tale.

Hill, Susanna Leonard. *April Fool, Phyllis!* Holiday House, 2011. ISBN: 978-0823422704.
It might be April Fools' Day, but Punxsutawney Phyllis knows that winter isn't over yet. Her infallible instincts tell her a blizzard is brewing, but no one will believe her.

Lamb, Albert. *Tell Me the Day Backwards*. Candlewick Press, 2011. ISBN: 978-0763650552.
Timmy Bear asks his mother to play a game with him at bedtime in which they remember everything he did during the day, but in reverse order. While not an April Fools' Day book, a neat idea!

Lorig, Steffanie. *Such a Silly Baby!* Chronicle Books, 2007. ISBN: 978-0811851343.
The hapless mother in this bouncy rhyming tale just can't keep track of her silly baby: he gets switched with the chimpanzee at the zoo, with the dancing bear at the circus, with a lazy sow at the farm, and with a buffalo at the Wild West show.

McMullan, Kate. *Pearl and Wagner: One Funny Day*. Dial, 2009. ISBN: 978-0803730854.
Friends Wagner and Pearl star in three episodes taking place on April Fools' Day.

Minarik, Else Holmelund. *April Fools!* HarperFestival, 2002. ISBN: 978-0694016945.
It's April Fools' Day, the perfect day for playing tricks. Little Bear wants to have some fun with his friends, but if he's not careful, they might just play a trick on him first!

---

### Older Gems, or Titles Too Good to Pass Up

Brown, Marc T. *Arthur's April Fool*. Little, Brown Books for Young Readers, 1985. ISBN: 978-0316112345.
Arthur worries about remembering his magic tricks for the April Fools' Day assembly and Binky's threats to pulverize him.

Hoberman, Mary Ann. *The Seven Silly Eaters*. Harcourt Children's Books, 1997. ISBN: 978-0152000967.
The combination of food and farce makes for an affectionate rhyming picture book about a family of picky eaters who drive their mother frantic.

Raffi. *Shake My Sillies Out*. Turtleback, 1990. ISBN: 978-0833544759.
Animals and campers join together in the woods one evening and shake their sillies, clap their crazies, and yawn their sleepies out.

Talkington, Bruce. *Disney's: Winnie-the-Pooh's Silly Day*. Disney Press, 1999. ISBN: 978-0786843343.
Every year on April Fools' Day, Winnie the Pooh and his friends are victims of silly pranks and tricks, and they know who's to blame—the April Fool, of course! But this year they're determined to beat the Fool at his own game.

Wood, Audrey. *Silly Sally*. Harcourt Children's Books, 1992. ISBN: 978-0152744281.
Come along and join Silly Sally and her outrageous friends as they parade into town in a most unusual way!

Morton, Carlene. *The Library Pages*. Upstart, 2010. ISBN: 978-16022130456.

Mrs. Heath is horrified when she sees the changes the students have made while she is on maternity leave and wonders if her wonderful library will ever be the same.

Ruelle, Karen G. *April Fool*. Holiday House, 2003. ISBN: 978-0823417803.

Harry loves April Fools' Day. Last year he pulled tricks on his parents with spiders and whoopee cushions. His little sister Emily thinks they should just use those tricks again, but Harry informs her that only new tricks are allowed.

Schiller, Melissa. *April Fool's Day*. Children's Press, 2003. ISBN: 978-0516279424.

Part of the Rookie Read-About Holidays series, this is a great introduction to the holiday.

Spinelli, Eileen. *Silly Tilly*. Marshall Cavendish Corporation, 2009. ISBN: 978-0761455257.

Tilly, a goose, bathes in apple juice, wears a pancake as a hat, and likes to tickle frogs. But her ways raise the ire of the other farm animals, who demand that she cease all silliness.

Taxali, Gary. *This Is Silly!* Scholastic, 2010. ISBN: 978-0439718363.

A very silly boy takes you on very silly adventure where you meet very silly characters who run in silly circles, fly in silly skies, and walk in the silliest parade ever!

Thomas, Jan. *Rhyming Dust Bunnies*. Beach Lane Books, 2009. ISBN: 978-1416979760.

Three dust bunnies, Ed, Ned, and Ted, rhyme all the time. They say that *far*, *jar*, and *tar* rhyme with *car*, but a fourth dust bunny, Bob, just does not seem to get it; he says, "Look!"

Welling, Peter J. *Michael Le Souffle and the April Fool*. Pelican Publishing Company, 2003. ISBN: 978-1589801059.

In the small town of Bakonneggs, France, the grumpy mayor, a pig named Melon de Plume, and a happy red rooster, Michael Le Souffle, battle wits until they learn to enjoy April Fools' Day together.

Ziefert, Harriet. *April Fool!* Puffin, 2000. ISBN: 978-0141305820.

On the way to school one morning, Will regales his friends with a tall tale about an adventurous, acrobatic elephant he once saw along the same route.

## Activities

### Coloring Pages

Consult your favorite pattern books or holiday coloring books for pages to use as coloring sheets. Be sure to search online as well. There's lots of great stuff out there!

### Cut-and-Tell

**"Four"** This story about four sillies is found, complete with text and cutting patterns and instructions, on pages 52–54 of *Storytelling with Shapes and Numbers* by Valerie Marsh (Alleyside Press, 1999). Once you are done with the cutting, it will reveal the number 4!

### Flannel/Velcro Board

**What's Missing?** The instructions and the patterns for this flannel/Velcro-board activity can be found on pages 175–177 of *Felt Board Fun* by Liz and Dick Wilmes (Building Blocks Publications, 1984). Each picture has a part (depicted with dotted lines) that can be cut away. I take these, color them, cut out the dotted line areas, add Velcro to both, and laminate for durability. I first place the incomplete picture on the board and ask participants what is missing. When they identify what is missing, I then add those parts to the picture.

**What's Wrong?**     Patterns for this flannel/Velcro-board activity appear on pages 178–179 of *Felt Board Fun* by Liz and Dick Wilmes (Building Blocks Publications, 1984). These pictures show things that have something wrong with them, such as a truck with square tires or a whale carrying an umbrella. Color these patterns, cut them out, and laminate for durability. Place the patterns on your board and ask participants to tell you what is wrong with them. Then, of course, talk about what would make the pictures right.

**"What Did You Put in Your Pocket?"**     This rhyme by Beatrice Schenk de Regniers, pages 24–29 in *Juba This and Juba That: Story Hour Stretches for Large or Small Groups* by Virginia A. Tashjian (Little, Brown, and Company, 1969), could easily be adapted into a flannel/Velcro-board presentation. It could even be done with realia (box of pudding, plastic water glass, plastic ice cream cone with scoop, a potato, small bottle of molasses, your fingers, and a handkerchief).

**"The Whale and the Elephant"**     The text for this silly story can be found on pages 61–62 of *Festivals Together: A Guide to Multicultural Celebration* by Sue Fitzjohn et al. (Hawthorn Press, 1993). This is a great story to tell using flannel/Velcro-board figures or by dividing your participants up into two groups (one group is the whale, the other the elephant) and having a long rope that they can pull on in opposite directions when prompted.

**Silly Sally Flannelboard**     Audrey Wood's book *Silly Sally* is one of the "Older Gems" books for this chapter. *Storytime Magic: 400 Fingerplays, Flannelboards, and Other Activities* by Kathy MacMillan and Christine Kirker (American Library Association, 2009) provides flannel board figure patterns to turn this book into a flannel/Velcro-board presentation. Larger versions of the patterns are available online from the American Library Association at http://www.ala.org/ala/aboutala/offices/publishing/editions/webextras/macmillan09775/macmillan09775.cfm. Click on the number 340 link.

## Games

**Joker Matching Game**     Use the image search on Google to find a suitable "court jester" piece of clip art to copy twice and reproduce on different colors of paper. You might also wish to use the elf/jester Ellison die. Give each participant one of the copies and keep one for yourself, placing it in either an apron pocket or a container. Begin the matching game by placing one of your jokers on the flannel/Velcro board and invite the participant who has the match to bring it up. Continue until all colors have been matched.

## Miscellaneous

**Silly Hat Parade/Backwards Day**     The week before your April Fools' Day celebration, ask participants to bring something from home that could be worn as a hat, and you can also invite them to wear their clothes backwards for the day. Play some music and parade around your area or library. When you parade through the library, walk backwards. Remind your participants to go slowly while doing this—falls can happen easily—and to stay aware of those walking around them.

**Look Closer!**     Use the image search on Google to find close-up pictures of everyday things, such as shoelaces, yarn, a towel, and so forth. Simply type in "close-up picture of . . ." into the search bar. Print out these close-up pictures and laminate them for durability. Show participants pictures and have them guess what they think they might be. You might want to have a smaller picture on the back of the large picture that shows the item at actual size.

**"Oh Me, Oh My"**     This participatory chant can be found on pages 11–13 of *Crazy Gibberish and Other Story Hour Stretches* by Naomi Baltuck (Linnet Books, 1993). This silly chant has simple motions that you can teach your participants and is perfect for an April Fools' Day theme!

**"The Snooks Family"**    This story can be found on pages 47–50 of *Juba This and Juba That: Story Hour Stretches for Large or Small Groups* by Virginia A. Tashjian (Little, Brown, and Company, 1969). I remember hearing Caroline Feller Bauer tell this wonderfully silly story at a workshop. Use a real candle, if you dare. I have a plastic candle that came with a play set my daughter had when she was young. It has a small lever on the side that, when pushed, makes the flame "drop" to go out.

### April Fools' Day Songs

- "All Around the Town," a piggyback song (new song, sung to a familiar tune), can be found on page 31 of *Holiday Piggyback Songs* compiled by Jean Warren (Warren Publishing House, 1988).
- "The Silly Song" and "Silly Song II" can be found on pages 83–84 of *More Piggyback Songs* compiled by the Totline Newsletter Staff (Warren Publishing House, 1984).
- "I Tried Not to Get the Giggles," "Silly Monkeys," and "Pickle Parade" can be found on page 11 of *The Best of Totline Magazine, Volume 4*, compiled by Gayle Bittinger (McGraw-Hill Children's Publishing, 2004).
- In addition, the song "Backwards" can be found on page 122 of *The Best of Totline Newsletter* compiled by Jean Warren (Warren Publishing House, 1995).

## Fingerplays

### April Trickery

| | |
|---|---|
| The big round sun | *(Form a circle with fingers of both hands.)* |
| In an April sky | *(Raise arms to form circle over head.)* |
| Winked at a cloud | *(Wink.)* |
| That was passing by. | |
| The gray cloud laughed | |
| As it scattered rain. | *(Pretend to scatter rain with fingers.)* |
| Then out came the big, | |
| Round sun again. | *(Form circle with fingers of both hands.)* |

—Author unknown

### April First

| | |
|---|---|
| Little bears have three feet. | *(Hold up three fingers.)* |
| Little bears have four. | *(Use four fingers in same way.)* |
| Little cows have two feet. | *(Use two fingers in the same way.)* |
| And girls and boys have more. | *(Use five fingers in same way.)* |
| Do you believe my story? | *(Point to "you"; point to own self.)* |
| I'll tell it only once a year. | *(Hold up index finger for "one.")* |
| When April comes along. | *(Clap hands to express pleasure.)* |
| APRIL FOOL! | |

—Author unknown

### Wind Tricks

| | |
|---|---|
| The wind is full of tricks today. | *(Make sweeping motion with one hand for wind.)* |
| He blew my daddy's hat away. | *(Pretend to sweep hat off head.)* |
| He chased our paper down the street. | *(One hand chases the other around.)* |
| He almost blew us off our feet. | *(Pretend to almost fall.)* |
| He makes the trees and bushes dance. | *(With raised arms, make dancing motions.)* |
| Just listen to him howl and prance. | *(Cup hand to ear.)* |

—Author unknown

### Silly Sally

| | |
|---|---|
| Silly Sally tried to get dressed. | *(Pretend to pull on clothes.)* |
| Silly Sally had a mess. | |
| Silly Sally put her shirt on her toes. | *(Point to toes.)* |
| Silly Sally put her socks on her nose. | *(Point to nose.)* |
| Silly Sally put her pants on her head. | *(Point to head.)* |
| Silly Sally, just go back to bed! | *(Rest head on hands; snore.)* |

—Susan M. Dailey
*A Storytime Year* (Neal-Schuman, 2001, p. 70)

### What Fun!

| | |
|---|---|
| What fun! Let's make a silly face. | *(Pause and let kids make faces.)* |
| What fun! Let's make a silly pose. | *(Pause and let kids get in silly positions.)* |
| What fun! Let's make a silly sound. | *(Pause and let kids make noises.)* |
| Silly is so fun to be! | |

—Susan M. Dailey
*A Storytime Year* (Neal-Schuman, 2001, p. 70)

### Make a Face

| | |
|---|---|
| Make a face, touch your toes, | *(Match actions to words.)* |
| Now you're being silly! | *(Wiggle index finger, playfully scolding, each time this is repeated.)* |
| | |
| Wiggle your fingers, hold your nose. | |
| Now you're being silly! | |
| Flap your arms, turn around. | |
| Now you're being silly! | |
| Pat your stomach, touch the ground. | |
| Now you're being silly— | |
| Just like me! | *(Point to self.)* |

—Author unknown

---

**More Great Fingerplays**

"I Saw a Sight Today," "Surprise! It's April Fool's!," "Happy April Fool's," and "What April Fools' is For," from page 275 of *1001 Rhymes and Fingerplays for Working with Young Children*, compiled by the Totline Staff (Warren Publishing House, 1994).

---

## Musical Selections

"April Fool" from *Touched by a Song* by Miss Jackie Silberg. Miss Jackie Music. ASIN: B002K74FCK.

"Backwards Day" and "Crazy Shoes Theme" from *Jim Gill Sings Moving Rhymes for Modern Times*. Jim Gill Music. ASIN: B000FKOZRO.

"Big Fun" and "Silly Willies" from *Greg and Steve: Big Fun*. Youngheart. ASIN: B00000AG60.

"Boom, Boom Ain't It Great to Be Crazy" and "Shake My Sillies Out" from *Sing Along with Bob #2*. Bob's Kids Music. ASIN: B00000DAO5.

"Goofy Hat Dance" from *Greg and Steve: Fun and Games*. Greg and Steve Productions. ASIN: B0000A8XP9.

"Laughing in Rhythm" from *Jim Gill's Irrational Anthem and More Salutes to Nonsense*. Jim Gill Music. ASIN: B0007CYBNS.

"Shake My Sillies Out" from *More Singable Songs by Raffi*. Rounder. ASIN: B0000003H7.

"Silly Dance Contest" from *Jim Gill Sings The Sneezing Song and Other Contagious Tunes*. Jim Gill Music. ASIN: B000FKOZQU.

"Silly Sticks" from *Rhythm Sticks Rock* by Georgiana Stewart. Kimbo. ASIN: B000QUU6GM.

## Crafts

**April Fools' Clown**     Instructions and patterns appear on pages 56–58 of *Cut and Create! Holidays: Easy Step-by-Step Projects That Teach Scissor Skills* by Kim Rankin (Teaching and Learning Company, 1997). Gluing simple shapes together and adding features makes a nice-sized clown, complete with hat!

**Largest Tie Ever!**     This craft can be found on TheBestKidsBooksite.com under their "April Fool's Day" section. The base of the craft is a very large piece of colored construction paper or a colored heavier-weight paper. You will also need a hole punch, two pipe cleaners per participant, scissors, and markers or crayons. Take scissors and paper and cut out a very large tie shape. You may wish to have these precut for participants. Punch two holes on either side of the very top of the tie. Take each of the pipe cleaners and affix them to either side of the top of the tie. This will allow participants to wear their ties once they are done. Decorate tie shape with crayons or markers.

**Silly Shakers**     This craft also comes from TheBestKids Booksite.com. Take two paper cups, place dried beans in one, place one on top of the other so that the rims are together, and tape them closed. Make sure they are completely taped so that the beans can't escape. Decorate and shake!

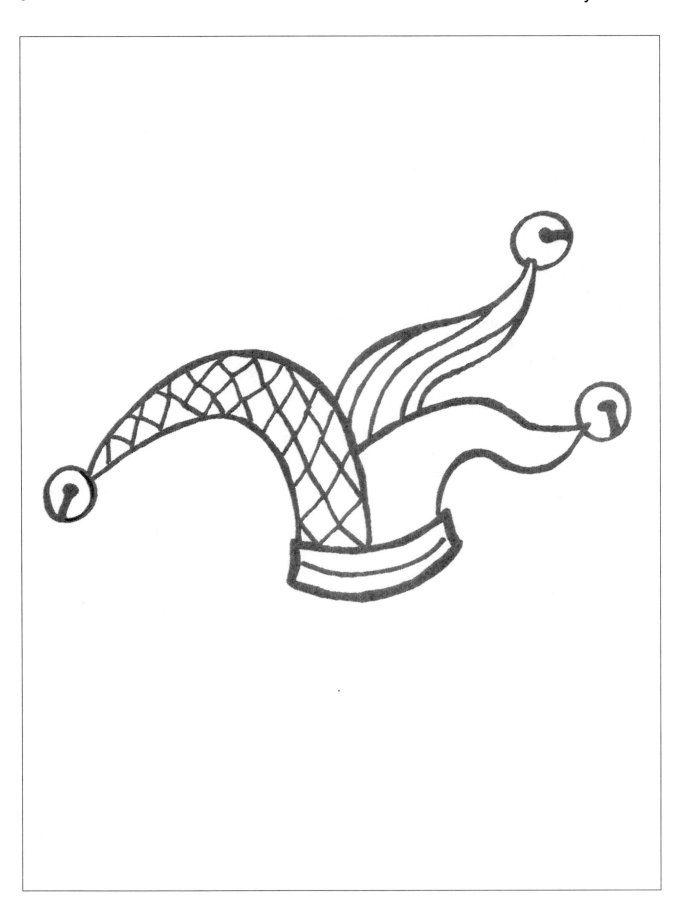

# Arbor Day, Earth Day, and Tu B'Shevat

*Use these programs to help participants appreciate our earth and the trees that supply us with so many things!*

## History

Earth Day is celebrated on April 22nd. It was first celebrated in 1970, and its purpose is to increase awareness of our earth's endangered resources and how they are used. The day was created by Gaylord Nelson, a former U.S. Senator. Nelson realized that there were very few people who were aware of environmental problems. He had seen them firsthand after witnessing the devastation caused by an oil spill off the coast of Santa Barbara, California, in 1969. (See "Earth Day: The History of a Movement" at http://www.earthday.org/earth-day-history-movement.)

Arbor Day is celebrated as a national holiday on the last Friday in April. Julius Sterling Morton started the first Arbor Day in Nebraska on April 10, 1872. He was a settler in the state and was convinced that the planting of trees would help to conserve water and save the prairie topsoil. He convinced the state to set aside a day for tree planting. His effort was very successful, as more than a million trees were planted. As the years passed, the movement grew and many other states adopted Arbor Day as a holiday. People celebrate Arbor Day by planting and caring for trees, and by recognizing the usefulness of the tree in our daily lives. (See Julia Jasmine's *Multicultural Holidays: Share Our Celebrations* [Teacher Created Materials, 1994].)

If you wish to celebrate this type of holiday earlier in the year, the Jewish holiday of Tu B'Shevat normally occurs in the months of January or February. Tu B'Shevat is known as the New Year for Trees and is used for calculating the age of trees. The word "Tu" is the number 15 in the Hebrew language, so the day is the fifteenth day of the Jewish month of Shevat.

Several customs relate to the holiday of Tu B'Shevat. These include eating a new fruit on this day, or one of the fruits of the seven species described in the Bible: wheat, barley, grapes, figs, pomegranates, olives, and dates. Some people plant trees on this holiday. In some places, money is collected to plant trees in Israel. (See Tracey Rich's "Tu B'Shevat" at http://www.jewfaq.org/holiday8.htm.)

## Poetry

"Arbor Day," a perfect simple poem to present, from page 133 in *Fingerplays and Rhymes: For Always and Sometimes* by Terry Lynne Graham (Humanics Ltd. Partners, 1987).

"Arbor Day," from page 222 of *The Poetry Break: An Annotated Anthology with Ideas for Introducing Children to Poetry* by Caroline Feller Bauer (H.W. Wilson, 1995).

"Celebrate the Earth," from page 54 of *Circle-Time Poetry Around the Year* by Jodi Simpson (Scholastic, 2005).

"Everyday Is Earth Day," "Save the Earth" by Betty Miles, "In Tune with Mother Nature," "Earth Day" by Jane Yolen, and "Our Earth," available from http://www.canteach.ca/elementary/songspoems 51.html.

"Tree Hugging" and "If There Were No Trees," available from http://stepbystepcc.com/holidays/ arborday.html.

"Trees" by Harry Behn and "What Do We Plant?" by Henry Abbey, available from http://www.dltk-kids .com/crafts/earth/songs.html.

## Books

Bennett, Kelly. *Arbor Day*. Children's Press, 2003. ISBN: 978-0516277547.
 Part of the Rookie Read-About Holidays series, this book is a simple introduction to Arbor Day.

Brown, Marc. *Arthur Turns Green*. Little, Brown Books for Young Readers, 2011. ISBN: 978-0316129244.
 Arthur's sister D.W. wonders what the Big Green Machine is that Arthur is talking about. And why is he showing up for dinner with green hands?

Bulla, Clyde R. *A Tree Is a Plant.* Collins, 2001. ISBN: 978-0064451963.
 From the Let's-Read-and-Find-Out Science series, this reillustrated book on the science of trees is well designed for preschool and early-primary-grade children.

Capucilli, Alyssa. *Biscuit's Earth Day Celebration*. HarperFestival, 2010. ISBN: 978-0061625145.
 Join Biscuit as he helps take care of our green world.

deGroat, Diane. *Ants in Your Pants, Worms in Your Plants!* (Gilbert Goes Green). HarperCollins, 2011. ISBN: 978-0061765117.
 Gilbert has trouble coming up with ideas. First he couldn't think of a springtime poem, and now he needs an idea for an Earth Day project!

Ernst, Lisa Campbell. *Round Like a Ball*. Blue Apple Books, 2008. ISBN: 978-1934706015.
 This engaging, eco-friendly picture book opens with a child-friendly invitation to "play a guessing game." Through a series of short rhyming clues, children will join in as members of a family "unearth" the mysterious round object little by little.

Formento, Alison. *This Tree, 1, 2, 3*. Albert Whitman and Company, 2011. ISBN: 9780807578916.
 The lone tree behind Oak Lane School tells the story of the animals who call it home.

Gerardi, Jan. *Eco People on the Go!* Random House, 2011. ISBN: 978-0375854134.
 A lift-the-flap story with rhyming text in which a little boy learns seven green ways to travel. Part of the Teenie Greenies series.

Gerardi, Jan. *The Little Composter*. Random House, 2011. ISBN: 978-0375854126.
 A lift-the-flap story with rhyming text in which a little boy goes green by building a compost heap. Another title in the Teenie Greenies series.

Gold-Vukson, Marji. *Grandpa and Me on Tu B'Shevat*. Kar-Ben Publishing, 2004. ISBN: 978-1580131223.
 In a cumulative rhyme à la "The House That Jack Built," a little boy and his grandfather plant a seedling and watch it develop into an apple tree as they grow older, passing on to succeeding generations the tradition of caring for the tree and enjoying its fruit.

Jeffrey, Sean, et al. *Franklin Plants a Tree*. Kids Can Press, 2001. ISBN: 978-1550748789.
 It's Earth Day and Mr. Heron is giving away free trees. Franklin can hardly wait to plant a big climbing tree in his backyard.

Kleinberg, Naomi. *Grouches Are Green*. Random House, 2011. ISBN: 978-0375865500.
 Oscar the Grouch shows his Sesame Street friends how to reduce, reuse, and recycle.

Mayer, Mercer. *It's Earth Day!* HarperFestival, 2008. ISBN: 978-0060539597.
 Little Critter is on a mission! After watching at school a film about climate changes, Little Critter decides to do his part to slow down global warming.

Muldrow, Diane. *We Planted a Tree*. Golden Books, 2010. ISBN: 978-0375964329.
 In two different parts of the world, two families plant a tree. As the trees grow, cleaning the air, enriching the soil, and providing fruit and shade, the families flourish as well.

---

### Older Gems, or Titles Too Good to Pass Up

Fleming, Denise. *Where Once There Was a Wood*. Henry Holt and Company, 1996. ISBN: 978-0805037616.

Fleming's handmade paper collages dramatically illustrate a simple story of a forest replaced by houses and the animals that lost their home.

Glaser, Linda. *Our Big Home: An Earth Poem*. Millbrook Press, 2000. ISBN: 978-0761312925.

Celebrating water, the sun, and wind, this rhythmic story relates how humans share the planet with animals.

Ross, Anna. *Grover's Ten Terrific Ways to Help Our Wonderful Planet*. Sagebrush Education Resources, 1999. ISBN: 978-0785787655.

Grover and his friends on Sesame Street show how we can all do little things that will add up to a cleaner planet.

Rouss, Sylvia A. *Sammy Spider's First Tu B'Shevat*. Kar-Ben Publishing, 2000. ISBN: 978-1580130653.

Sammy watches as the seasons pass and trees blossom, bear fruit, and shed their leaves. When Tu B'Shevat arrives, his spinning skills provide a gift for his favorite tree.

Udry, Janice M. *A Tree Is Nice*. HarperCollins, 1987. ISBN: 978-0064431477.

This Caldecott classic speaks simply and eloquently of the many pleasures a tree provides.

---

O'Conner, Jane. *Fancy Nancy: Every Day Is Earth Day*. Turtleback, 2010. ISBN: 978-0606122948.

After learning about being green at school, Nancy decides to teach her family all about respecting the environment.

Sollinger, Emily. *Dora Celebrates Earth Day!* Simon Spotlight/Nickelodeon, 2009. ISBN: 978-1416975809.

Dora explores the ways we can all make a difference and help save the planet by doing simple things at home.

Trueit, Trudi S. *Earth Day*. Children's Press, 2006. ISBN: 978-0531118368.

Another in the Rookie Read-About Holidays series, this book offers a simple introduction to Earth Day and how it is celebrated.

Zolkower, Edie S. *It's Tu B'Shevat*. Kar-Ben Publishing, 2005. ISBN: 978-1580131278.

This board book provides an introduction to the youngest children about the Jewish New Year for trees.

## Activities ————————————————————————————————

### Coloring Pages

Consult your favorite pattern books for pages to use as coloring sheets. Be sure to search online as well. There's lots of great stuff out there!

- Visit http://dulemba.com/index_ColoringPages.html for author and illustrator Elizabeth O. Dulemba's great collection of holiday coloring pages. Click on the Earth Day link. While there, sign up for her Coloring Page Tuesdays e-mails.
- Go to http://www.dltk-kids.com/crafts/earth/mearthposter.htm to find Earth Day pages that can be printed out in black and white.
- Check out http://www.first-school.ws/theme/cp_h_arbor_day.htm for Arbor Day coloring pages.

## Cut-and-Tell

**"The Tooth-Picking Giants"**    This cut-and-tell story with patterns can be found on pages 26–29 of *Paper-Cutting Stories for Holidays and Special Events* by Valerie Marsh (Alleyside Press, 1994). Trees are the result of the paper cutting.

## Draw-and-Tell

**"Alligator"; "Duck"; "Suzanne, the Pelican"**    All three of these conservation stories can be found on pages 45–50 of *Lots More Tell and Draw Stories* by Margaret J. Oldfield (Creative Storytime Press, 1973).

## Flannel/Velcro Board

**"Three Little Seeds"**    This flannel-board story about trees can be found on pages 66–67 of *The Best of Totline Magazine, Volume 4*, edited by Gayle Bittinger (Totline Publications, 2004).

**"A Special Tree"**    This story, which follows a tree through the different seasons, is found on page 28 of *FlannelGraphs: Flannel Board Fun for Little Ones, Preschool–Grade 3*, by Jean Stangl (Fearon Teacher Aids, 1986). The patterns appear on page 66.

## Games

**Tree Matching Game**    Use an Ellison machine tree die (there are a variety to choose from) to cut out pairs of trees from different colors of construction paper. Laminate shapes for durability and attach Velcro or flannel. To play the matching game, hand out one of the pair of trees/colors to participants, keeping one for yourself and placing them in an apron pocket or container of some sort. Once all pieces are passed out, begin the game by placing on the flannel/Velcro board, one at a time, a tree from your pocket or container. Let participants bring up their matches. Continue until all colors have been matched. You could also do this game with just leaf shapes as well.

**Earth Matching Game**    Use the Ellison Globe #2 die to cut out pairs of Earth shapes from different colors of construction paper. Laminate shapes for durability and attach Velcro or flannel. Follow the instructions listed for the Tree Matching Game.

**Recycle Symbol Matching Game**    Ellison offers a die cut of the recycle symbol that you could cut from different colors of construction paper, laminate, and attach Velcro or flannel. Follow the instructions for the Tree Matching Game.

**Pin the Leaf on the Tree**    The instructions for this game are simple. Have a large tree trunk and green top precut, or you can use just the large trunk. Use one (or more) of the Ellison machine leaf dies and cut your leaf shapes from different-colored paper. Place tape on the backs of the leaves. Blindfold participants and allow them to place their leaves on the tree. There is no wrong place for the leaf to be in this game! Continue as long as there is interest.

**The Litterbug Game**    The rules for this game, played like "Duck, Duck, Goose," can be found on page 40 of *The Storytime Sourcebook* by Carolyn N. Cullum (Neal-Schuman, 1990).

**Recycled Games**    The idea for materials for these games appears on page 39 of *Learning and Caring about Our World: Activities for Helping Young Children Learn and Care about the Environment* by Gayle Bittinger (Warren Publishing House, 1990). It suggests using plastic soft drink bottles and a rubber ball for a bowling game and cutting out the centers of plastic lids to make lids for a ring toss game with plastic soft drink bottles. Have these games set out for your participants to play!

### Miscellaneous

**Arbor Day/Earth Day Nature Walk**    Since these holidays fall in April, weather conditions could be favorable enough for you to take your group outside for a walk. Tell them to use all of their senses! Allow them to take a snack, such as raisins or trail mix! For Arbor Day, observe the different types of trees that make their homes in your area. Talk about the different types of trees and identify them for participants.

**How Old Am I?**    If possible, obtain a cross-section of a tree, showing the age rings. Explain to participants that each ring represents a year of life or age for the tree. Count the rings together.

**What Is Litter?**    This activity can be found on page 29 of *Learning and Caring about Our World: Activities for Helping Young Children Learn and Care about the Environment* by Gayle Bittinger (Warren Publishing House, 1990). Have available items that are obviously litter and other items that are found in nature, such as a pine cone, a leaf, a branch, a rock. Hold up the items and ask participants if the item is litter or not. Have a small garbage can to dispose of the litter as it is identified.

**Tu B'Shevat Items**    The Craft Shop website (http://www.thecraftshoponline.com/) offers a number of sticker, foam, and paper cut-out items that would work well for presenting the concept of this holiday to young participants. Included are trees, leaves, and fruit. You could use these items to create flannel/Velcro-board presentations.

**Guest Speakers**    At this time of year, your county's Soil and Water Conservation District may be giving away free trees. This organization is also a great source for guest speakers for programming!

## Fingerplays ——————————————————————————————————————————

### Tree

| | |
|---|---|
| I am a tree, I am big and strong. | *(Put arms up like branches.)* |
| In the spring, I grow leaves. | *(Sway arms and wiggle fingers as new leaves.)* |
| In the winter, they all fall. | *(Make arms fall or fall down on the ground.)* |

—Kathy Buchsbaum

### Plant a Tree

*(This action rhyme is sung to the tune of "The Wheels on the Bus.")*

| | |
|---|---|
| Now it's time to plant a tree, plant a tree, plant a tree. | *(Pretend to plant a tree.)* |
| Now it's time to plant a tree, it is Tu B'Shevat (Arbor Day/Earth Day). | |
| Now it's time to water that tree, water that tree, water that tree. | *(Pretend to water the tree.)* |
| Now it's time to water that tree, it is Tu B'Shevat (Arbor Day/Earth Day). | |
| Now it's time to watch it grow, watch it grow, watch it grow. | *(Put hands over eyes like goggles.)* |
| Now it's time to watch it grow, it is Tu B'Shevat (Arbor Day/Earth Day). | |
| Now it's time to hug our tree, hug our tree, hug our tree. | *(Arms around yourself for a hug.)* |
| Now it's time to hug our tree, it is Tu B'Shevat (Arbor Day/Earth Day). | |

—Kathy Buchsbaum

---

### More Great Fingerplays

The fingerplays "The Lonely Tree," "Trees," and "Trees in Israel," perfect for the Tu B'Shevat holiday, can be found on pages 32-34 in *Clap and Count! Action Rhymes for the Jewish Year* by Jacqueline Jules (Kar-Ben Copies, 2001).

The book *Learning and Caring about Our World: Activities for Helping Young Children Learn and Care about the Environment* by Gayle Bittinger (Warren Publishing House, 1990) has the following fingerplays and songs:

- "The Trees Are Growing" (fingerplay, page 19)
- "Litter Is Garbage" (song, page 29)
- "Down at the Dump" (song, page 31)
- "People and Plants" (song, page 47)
- "Soot, Soot, Soot" (song, page 52)
- "I'm Not a Water Hog" (song, page 74)

---

## Musical Selections ————————————————————————————————

"Beautiful World" from *Greg and Steve: Kids in Action*. Greg and Steve Productions. ASIN: B0000A8XP8.

"Care of the Earth" from *Debbie's Ditties 2 Much Fun*. Available from http://www.rainbowswithin reach.com/.

"Earth Day" from *Happy Everything* by Dr. Jean. Melody House. ASIN: B000SM3N0E.

"The Earth Is Our Mother" from *The Best of Gemini*, Volume 2, by Gemini. Available from http://www.songsforteaching.com/.

"Every Day an Earth Day" from *All Year* by Intelli-Tunes. Available from http://www.songsforteaching .com/.

"The Good Earth (Earth Day)" from *Rhythms and Rhymes for Special Times* by Jack Hartmann. Available from http://www.songsforteaching.com/.

"Green Grass Grows All Around" from *Abiyoyo and Other Story Songs for Children* by Pete Seeger. Smithsonian Folkways. ASIN: B000001DM6.

"Plant a Seed" from *Sing It! Say It! Stamp It! Sway It!*, Volume 2, by Peter and Ellen Allard. 80-Z Music. ASIN: B000056IIN.

"R-E-C-Y-C-L-E" from *This Pretty Planet* by Tom Chapin. Sony Wonder. ASIN: B00004SCCK. Other great songs on this CD include "Happy Earth Day."

"This Land Is Your Land" from *Greg and Steve: Rockin' Down the Road*. Youngheart. ASIN: B00000DGMU.

"The Tu Bishvat Song" from *Shanah Tovah: A Good Year—Songs for Jewish Holidays* by Debbie Friedman. Available as a download from http://www.amazon.com/.

"Tu B'Shvat" from *Shanah Tovah, Shanah M'tukah* by Joanie Calem. CD Baby. ASIN: B0034PWOXY.

## Crafts ————————————————————————————————————————

**Tissue Leaf**     This simple craft uses a white construction paper leaf pattern as its base. Orange, yellow, and red tissue paper cut into small squares are then glued onto the leaf pattern. Instructions appear on page 21 and the large leaf pattern appears on page 31 of *September Arts and Crafts, Grades 1–3*, edited by Susan Walker (The Education Center, 2000).

**Earth Day Earth Craft**     Instructions and patterns appear on pages 64–66 of *Cut and Create! Holidays: Easy Step-by-Step Projects That Teach Scissor Skills* by Kim Rankin (Teaching and Learning Company, 1997). The base of the craft is a circle (for Earth) and land areas that are glued onto the circle.

**Leaf Pendant**    This craft makes a cool-looking leaf, complete with veins! Instructions appear on page 19 and the leaf pattern appears on page 18 of *Arts and Crafts for All Seasons, Grades 1–3,* by the Mailbox Books Staff (The Education Center, 1999).

**Handprint Tree**    You will need construction paper, brown crayons, fallen leaves, glue, and scissors. Optional items are Easter grass and cotton balls. On the construction paper, trace each participant's arm from the elbow up, including the fingers. This is the trunk of the tree. Color it brown. Glue leaves on the trunk. If you choose to use the Easter grass and cotton balls, glue the grass at the base of the tree and the cotton balls above the tree for clouds.

**Leaf Rubbings**    Great leaf rubbing plates are available from Enasco Early Learning. They are Roylco Leaf Rubbing Plates and come in a set of 16 different leaf and seed plates for $7.55. I personally use these and they are just super! Have enough sets of the plates so that you can place a set at each of your programming tables. Provide white construction paper and crayons for participants to use for the rubbings by placing the plates underneath the construction paper.

**Easy Shapes Tree Craft**    The template is available from http://www.first-school.ws/t/shape treebw.htm. Simple shapes are glued together to form trees. You will want to enlarge the patterns to make them easier for little hands to work with.

**Planet Earth Coffee Filter Craft**   Instructions for this simple craft are available from http://www.dltk-kids.com/crafts/earth/mcoffeefilter.htm. This craft uses washable markers to color coffee filters, which are then sprayed with a water bottle two or three times. This wicks the colors of the markers on the filter!

**Bark Rubbings**   Take your art area outside of your building for this craft! All you need are paper, crayons, and trees! Place the paper against the bark of the tree and use the side of the crayon to do your rubbing. Use different colors of crayons to make the rubbings interesting.

**Earth Day Crown**   Instructions for this craft can be found on page 77 of *Little Hands Fingerplays and Action Songs: Seasonal Rhymes and Creative Play for 2-to-6-Year-Olds* by Emily Stetson and Vicky Congdon (Williamson Publishing, 2001). The simple crown shape is decorated with pictures from old magazines or seed catalogs. You could also use Ellison flower dies, or other recycling-theme dies to decorate it!

**Art with Recyclables**   This idea is found on page 35 of *Learning and Caring about Our World: Activities for Helping Young Children Learn and Care about the Environment* by Gayle Bittinger (Warren Publishing House, 1990). Use items that would normally be thrown away. A list is given. Allow participants to create a piece of recycled art!

**Tu B'Shevat Crafts**   The Craft Shop website (http://www.thecraftshoponline.com/) offers a variety of craft kits for this holiday. Here are some of the items available:

- Velvet Art Coloring/Pack of 12 pictures for $11.99
- Fruit Beads/ Pack of 375 beads for just $1.99—great for making necklaces with lanyards
- Wooden Tree and Wooden Apple Shapes/$.30 each—great base for painting

**Leaf and Fruit/Vegetable Wreath**   Cut the middle from a paper plate, using the remaining circle as the base for your wreath. Use leaf, fruit, and vegetable Ellison dies to make shapes to glue onto your circle in a pleasing presentation. What could be easier?

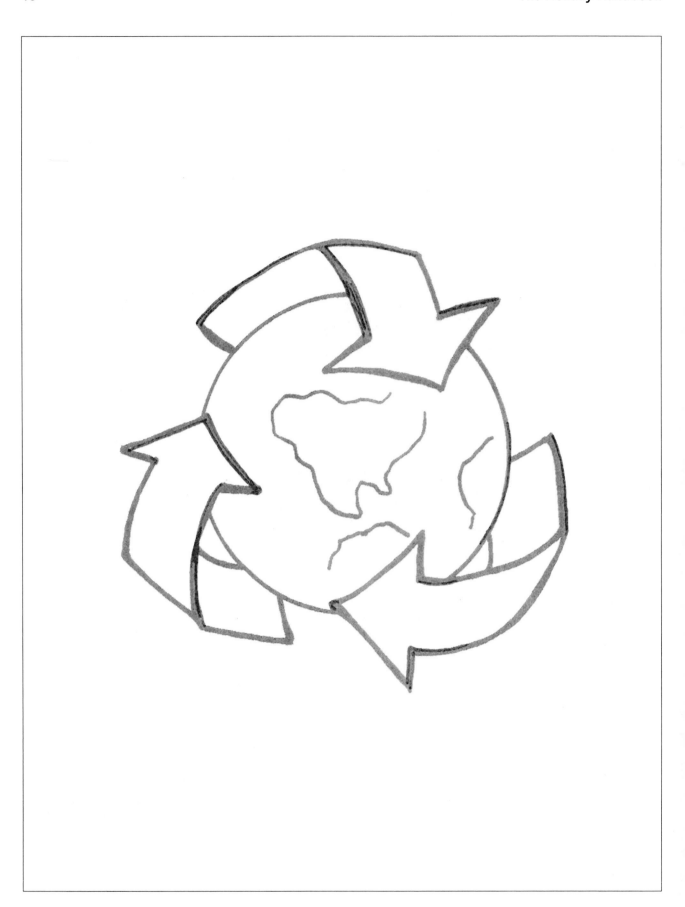

# *Birthdays*

*No matter where we are in the world, we all have birthdays, so why not celebrate them? You can also hold an "unbirthday" program that celebrates everyone's birthday!*

## History

Birthday parties, birthday cakes, birthday candles—did you know that all of these customs that we follow today are ancient in origin?

Thousands of years ago, birthdays were considered a dangerous time of year. People believed that evil spirits would try to do them harm. They thought that if friends and relatives visited the birthday person that person would be protected. So began the concept of the birthday party.

Do you use noisemakers at your parties? In old times, these were probably used to attempt to scare off those evil spirits that were lurking around!

The custom of decorating a birthday cake with candles originated many years ago as well. People believed that many gods lived in the sky, so they lit torches and candles when they prayed. The rising smoke would help send their prayers to the gods. So, when you blow out the candles on your cake (and make a wish), you are following another ancient custom. (See Arlene Erlbach's *Happy Birthday, Everywhere* [Millbrook Press, 1997].)

## Poetry

"Birthday Cake," from page 48 of *Poems Just for Us: 50 Read-Aloud Poems with Cross-Curricular Activities for Young Learners* by Bobbi Katz (Scholastic Professional Books, 1996).

"Birthdays" by Marchette Chute, "Birthdays" by Mary Ann Hoberman, "Between Birthdays" by Ogden Nash, and "In the Cupboard" by Barbara Ireson, from pages 201, 203, 204, and 208, respectively, of *The Poetry Break: An Annotated Anthology with Ideas for Introducing Children to Poetry* by Caroline Feller Bauer (H.W. Wilson, 1995).

"Eddie's Birthday Present," from page 39 of *Read for the Fun of It: Active Programming with Books for Children* by Caroline Feller Bauer (H.W. Wilson, 1992). This would be a great poem to illustrate as she suggests.

"My Birthday Cake Is Acting Strange," from page 38 of *Exploding Gravy: Poems to Make You Laugh* by X.J. Kennedy (Little, Brown, 2002).

"Tomorrow's My Unbirthday," from page 37 of *It's Raining Pigs and Noodles* by Jack Prelutsky (Greenwillow Books, 2000).

"Your Birthday Cake," "Candles," and "Happy Birthday!," from pages 22, 26, and 27, respectively, of *Here's a Little Poem: A Very First Book of Poetry*, collected by Jane Yolen and Andrew Fusek Peters (Candlewick Press, 2007).

## Books

Asch, Frank. *Happy Birthday, Big Bad Wolf*. Kids Can Press, 2011. ISBN: 978-1553373681.
    When the Big Bad Wolf comes knocking at the door of the Pig family, he is in for a real surprise! The family is throwing him a birthday party.

Blackstone, Stella. *Bear's Birthday*. Barefoot Books, 2011. ISBN: 978-1846865169.
 Join Bear as he celebrates his birthday with a party for all his friends.

Capucilli, Alyssa S. *Biscuit's Birthday*. Perfection Learning, 2005. ISBN: 978-0756958824.
 It's Biscuit's birthday and he's having a party! Join his friends in helping him celebrate.

Carter, David A. *Birthday Bugs: A Pop-Up Party*. Little Simon, 2004. ISBN: 978-0689818580.
 It's time to celebrate with the Birthday Bugs—and there's one popping out of each of the bright birthday presents found inside.

deGroat, Diane. *Happy Birthday to You, You Belong in a Zoo*. Perfection Learning, 2007. ISBN: 978-0756981082.
 Gilbert has been invited to the class bully's birthday party—and buys him a frying pan as a gift.

Fernandes, Eugenie. *Big Week for Little Mouse*. Kids Can Press, 2004. ISBN: 978-1553376651.
 Little Mouse spends all week preparing for her birthday party. The concept of opposites is introduced in this book as well.

Hill, Eric. *Spot's Birthday Party*. Turtleback, 2003. ISBN: 978-0613878296.
 Spot and his animal friends play hide-and-seek at his birthday party.

Huget, Jennifer. *The Best Birthday Party Ever*. Schwartz and Wade, 2011. ISBN: 978-0375847634.
 A child plans an elaborate birthday party and eagerly counts the months, days, hours, and minutes before the celebration.

Katz, Karen. *Where Is Baby's Birthday Cake?* Little Simon, 2008. ISBN: 978-1416958178.
 It's Baby's birthday, but where is his cake? Lift the flaps until it's found!

LaReau, Kara. *Rocko and Spanky Go to a Party*. Harcourt, 2004. ASIN: B0007XWN8M.
 Sock monkey siblings Rocko and Spanky spend lots of time preparing to go to the birthday party that they have been invited to attend.

O'Conner, Jane. *Fancy Nancy, Bonjour Butterfly*. HarperCollins, 2008. ISBN: 978-0061235887.
 Looking forward to her friend's Butterfly Birthday, Nancy runs into problems when the party falls on the same day as her grandparents' fiftieth anniversary party.

Patricelli, Leslie. *The Birthday Box*. Candlewick Press, 2007. ISBN: 978-0763628253.
 A child gets a present from Grandma. What is it?

---

### Older Gems, or Titles Too Good to Pass Up

Asch, Frank. *Happy Birthday, Moon*. Perfection Learning, 2000. ISBN: 978-0812448320.
 When a bear discovers that the moon shares his birthday, he buys the moon a beautiful hat as a present. One of my favorite books of all time!

Bunting, Eve. *Happy Birthday, Dear Duck*. Perfection Learning, 1990. ISBN: 978-0812484274.
 As charming friend after friend brings gifts, Duck finds himself with a pile of presents, which he thinks he has no use for until the final present arrives. This book is one that I have used again and again.

Carle, Eric. *The Secret Birthday Message*. Turtleback, 1986. ISBN: 978-0808574422.
 On the night before Tim's birthday, he receives a rebus note, a secret message directing him to his gift.

Hoff, Syd. *Happy Birthday, Danny and the Dinosaur!* Perfection Learning, 1997. ISBN: 978-0590130271.
 Danny returns to the museum to invite his dinosaur friend to his sixth birthday party. As in the original book, the dinosaur does things his own unique way.

Hutchins, Pat. *It's My Birthday!* Greenwillow Books, 1999. ISBN: 978-0688096632.
 Billy the Monster is the birthday boy, but like many human children, he has a hard time sharing his special day.

Rey, Margret. *Curious George and the Birthday Surprise*. HMH Books, 2003. ISBN: 978-0618346882.
When the man with the yellow hat tells George he is planning a surprise, of course George is curious.

Rose, Deborah L. *Birthday Zoo*. Albert Whitman and Company, 2002. ISBN: 978-0807507766.
Rhyming text describes the preparations made for a boy's birthday party by his hosts, the animals at the zoo.

Salas, Laura P. *C Is for Cake! A Birthday Alphabet*. A+ Books, 2010. ISBN: 978-1429639149.
Learn all about birthdays while learning your ABCs too!

Schoenherr, Ian. *Don't Spill the Beans!* Greenwillow Books, 2010. ISBN: 978-0061724572.
A bear tries hard to keep a birthday surprise a secret.

Thomas, Jan. *A Birthday for Cow!* Harcourt Children's Books, 2008. ISBN: 978-0152060725.
Despite the objections of Pig and Mouse, Duck insists on adding a special ingredient to the cake they are making to celebrate Cow's birthday.

Thomas, Shelley Moore. *Happy Birthday, Good Knight*. Dutton Juvenile, 2006. ISBN: 978-0525471844.
The Good Knight tries to help three little dragons make a birthday present for a very special friend.

Watts, Melanie. *Scaredy Squirrel Has a Birthday Party*. Kids Can Press, 2011. ISBN: 978-1554534685.
In this book, Scaredy Squirrel plans his own birthday party...and things get crowded.

Yaccarino, Dan. *The Birthday Fish*. Henry Holt and Company, 2005. ISBN: 978-0805074932.
Cynthia has always wanted a pony for her birthday, but when she blows out the candles on her cake this year, she gets a surprise.

## Activities

---

### Coloring Pages

Consult your favorite pattern books for pages to use as coloring sheets. Be sure to check online as well. There's a lot of great stuff out there!

- Visit http://dulemba.com/index_ColoringPages.html for author and illustrator Elizabeth O. Dulemba's great collection of holiday coloring pages! While there, sign up for her Coloring Page Tuesdays e-mails!
- Also, Diane deGroat has a birthday-themed coloring page on her website, located at http://www.dianedegroat.com/Diane_deGroat_5.html. This would a great follow-up activity after reading her book, located in the Books section of this chapter.

---

### Cut-and-Tell

**"Sammy's Special Present"**   This cut-and-tell story, complete with cutting pattern, can be found on pages 9–10 of *Paper-Cutting Stories for Holidays and Special Events* by Valerie Marsh (Alleyside Press, 1994). The result is a birthday cake complete with candles.

### Draw-and-Tell

**"Birthday Presents"**   This draw-and-tell story can be found on pages 62–64 of *Top Dot Tales* by Valerie Marsh (Alleyside Press, 2001).

**"The Birthday Surprise"**   This draw-and-tell story is found on pages 26–28 of *Stories to Draw* by Jerry J. Mallet and Marian R. Bartch (Freline, 1982).

**"The Birthday Present"**   This draw-and-tell story can be found on pages 10–21 of *Chalk Talk Stories* by Arden Druce (Scarecrow Press, 1993).

### Flannel/Velcro Board

**"Four Pretty Presents"**    This fingerplay is found in the book *First Time Circle Time: Shared-Group Experiences for Three, Four, and Five-Year-Olds* by Cynthia Holley and Jane Walkup (Fearon Teacher Aids, 1993). I have taken the fingerplay and turned it into a flannel board activity. I found a clip-art pattern for a wrapped present that I liked and enlarged it and copied it in the colors mentioned in the rhyme. In order to have four colors to use for the presents, I substituted the color green for the last present and changed the text of the rhyme slightly to reflect that.

### Games

**Birthday Matching Game**    Use the patterns at the end of the chapter and reproduce them on different colors of construction paper. Laminate for durability. Pass out one copy to each participant, keeping one for yourself. Once everyone has a shape, begin matching the pictures by putting them on your flannel or Velcro board. Continue until all pictures/colors have been matched. You may also wish to use Ellison dies for these shapes to produce your matching game.

Another wonderful set of patterns that I use for a storyhour matching game came from the pattern set that came with *Make-Take Games: Easy to Make—Fun to Play* by Liz and Dick Wilmes (Building Blocks Publications, 1990).

**Let's Play a Game!**    Set out an area of your children's room and have a Pin the Tail on the Donkey game set up for participants to enjoy. You may wish to include this as part of your storyhour plan or use it for an activity afterward as participants enjoy their birthday banquet. You may also wish to include other birthday party games, such as Musical Chairs, etc.

**Pass the Balloon**    This simple game is played very similarly to Hot Potato. Pass or toss a balloon around the circle while music is played. When the music stops, freeze! Don't let the balloon touch the ground and the balloon should keep moving from person to person until the music stops.

**Same ... or Different?**    This fun game tests the observation powers of your young participants. The patterns for the cards for this game can be found on pages 229–232 of *Table and Floor Games* by Liz and Dick Wilmes (Building Blocks Publications, 1994). The pictures show different items you might see at a birthday party, such as balloons, hats, candles, and cupcakes. In some pictures, the two objects pictured are exactly the same. In others, there are noticeable differences. Copy and enlarge the pictures if you wish. When coloring them, make sure that you color the exact matches exactly the same. You will have a little more leeway with the ones that are not exactly the same. When we do this game at my library, I tell participants that I am going to show them pictures of things that they might see at a birthday party. I tell them to look closely at the pictures and tell me if they are the same or different. If they are the same, I have them give me a "thumbs-up" gesture; if they are different, a "thumbs-down" sign. If they are different, I also ask to tell me how they are different.

### Miscellaneous

**Unbirthday Party**    I hold an annual "unbirthday" party storyhour each year, usually in spring. It is generally the last storyhour session before we break for the month of May. Prior to the storyhour, I have parent volunteers sign up to bring everything needed for a birthday party: cupcakes (much easier to handle than a cake), individually packaged ice creams, juice (in juice boxes or pouches; much less mess and chance of spillage), birthday hats, plates, plasticware, napkins, and favors. At the conclusion of the storyhour session, all participants are seated and we pass out the goodies. Of course, we always sing "Happy Birthday" and give everyone a round of applause!

A variation on the cupcakes would be to have the parent volunteers leave them unfrosted. Ask them to provide several tubs of ready-made frosting and colored sprinkles. Allow participants to frost and decorate their own cupcakes before eating. You may wish to have a table set aside for this purpose.

**Birthday Party Activity Set**    Use this realia, available from Becker's School Supplies. Includes a six-slice cake on a serving plate, toppings, seven candles, spatula, and storage box. Cost for the set is $19.99. The contact information for Becker's School Supplies can be found in Appendix A at the end of this book.

## Fingerplays ————————————————————————

### Five Brown Pennies

| | |
|---|---|
| Five brown pennies in my purse; | *(Hold up five fingers.)* |
| This one's for some gum; | *(Point to thumb.)* |
| This one's for a lollipop; | *(Point to pointer finger.)* |
| This one's for a drum. | *(Point to middle finger.)* |
| These I'll save inside my purse, | *(Point to ring and little fingers.)* |
| Until your birthday comes! | |

—Author unknown

### Ten Little Candles

*(This rhyme would make a great flannel/Velcro-board presentation as well! All you need is a large cake and ten candles to remove, two at a time.)*

| | |
|---|---|
| Ten little candles on a chocolate cake; | *(Hold up both hands with fingers extended.)* |
| Wh! Wh! Now there are eight! | *(Bend down two fingers.)* |
| Eight little candles on a candlestick; | |
| Wh! Wh! Now there are six! | *(Bend down two fingers.)* |
| Six little candles, and not one more; | |
| Wh! Wh! Now there are four! | *(Bend down two fingers.)* |
| Four little candles, red, white, and blue; | |
| Wh! Wh! Now there are two! | *(Bend down two fingers.)* |
| Two little candles standing in the sun; | |
| Wh! Wh! Now there are none! | *(Close hands into fists.)* |

—Author unknown

### Birthday Candles

| | |
|---|---|
| Today I have a birthday; | |
| I'm six years old, you see; | |
| And here I have a birthday cake, | *(Make circle with thumbs and forefingers.)* |
| Which you may share with me. | |
| First we count the candles; | |
| Count them, every one. | |
| One, two, three, four, five, six. | *(Hold up fingers one by one.)* |
| The counting now is done. | |
| Let's snuff out the candles; | |
| Out each flame will go… | |
| Wh…wh…wh…wh…wh…wh… | *(Bend down fingers one at a time as you blow on them.)* |
| As one by one we blow! | |

—Author unknown

**What Am I Baking?**

*(Suit actions to words.)*

Sift the flour and break an egg.
Add some salt and a bit of nutmeg.
A spoon of butter, a cup of milk.
Stir and beat as fine as silk.
Want to know what I'm going to bake?
Sh—sh, it's a secret!
A birthday cake!

——Author unknown

**My Birthday**

| | |
|---|---|
| When I woke up this morning, | *(Stretch and yawn.)* |
| I clapped and shouted hurray! | *(Clap, then say "hurray.")* |
| I was very excited | |
| For it was my birthday! | *(Point to self.)* |
| I ate what I wanted for breakfast. | *(Pretend to eat.)* |
| I had a friend over to play. | *(Pretend to dribble ball.)* |
| I got three cards in the mail | *(Hold up three fingers.)* |
| For it was my birthday! | *(Point to self.)* |
| We had a cake for supper | *(Make circle with hands for cake.)* |
| With candles on the top. | *(Hold up fingers for candles.)* |
| I blew them out and made a wish— | *(Blow.)* |
| That my birthday would never stop! | *(Shake head "no.")* |

——Susan M. Dailey
*A Storytime Year* (Neal-Schuman, 2001, pp. 327–328)

---

**More Great Fingerplays**

"The Birthday Child" and "Four or Five Candles," from page 16 of *Rhymes for Circle Time* by Louise B. Scott (Instructional Fair/T.S. Denison, 1999).

"Five Birthday Candles," from pages 73–74 of *Picture Book Story Hours: From Birthdays to Bears* by Paula G. Sitarz (Libraries Unlimited, 1987).

"Happy Birthday," from page 42 of *Felt Board Fingerplays* by Liz and Dick Wilmes (Building Blocks Publications, 1997).

"Happy Birthday" and "Making a Birthday Cake," from page 270 of *1001 Rhymes and Finger-plays for Working with Young Children*, compiled by the Totline Staff (Warren Publishing House, 1994).

"My Birthday Cake," "A Birthday," and "Six Little Candles," from page 17 of *Rhymes for Circle Time* by Louise B. Scott (Instructional Fair/T.S. Denison, 1999).

---

## Musical Selections

"Can't Wait to Celebrate" from *Jim Gill's Irrational Anthem and More Salutes to Nonsense* by Jim Gill. Jim Gill Music. ASIN: B0007CYBNS.

"Happy Birthday" from *Party Time Karaoke: Kids Songs*. Sybersound Records. ASIN: B000075A8O.

"Happy Birthday to You" and "The Unbirthday Song" from *Happy Birthday* by Sharon, Lois and Bram. BMG Music. ASIN: B000008KMM.

"A Happy Party" from *Martian Television Invasion* by Thaddeus Rex. Thaddeus Rex Productions. ASIN: B0002J8G1Y.

"It's Your Birthday" from *Rhythms and Rhymes for Special Times* by Jack Hartmann. Available from www.songsforteaching.com.

"Let's Have a Party" from *Joining Hands with Other Lands: Multicultural Songs and Games*. Kimbo Educational. ASIN: B00000DARS.

"Somebody's Birthday" from *Holidays and Special Times* by Greg and Steve. Youngheart. ASIN: B00000DGN5.

"Stinky Cake" from *Stinky Cake* by Carole Peterson. CD Baby. ASIN: B000CAKRTW.

"We're All Together Again/If I Knew You Were Coming, I'd've Baked a Cake" from *Great Big Hits* by Sharon, Lois and Bram. Casablanca Kids. ASIN: B000OSD6QI.

## Crafts

**Party Hats**    This simple craft requires the base of a piece of poster board cut into a 9-inch circle. Cut away one-fourth of the circle. This will allow you to make the hat cone-shaped once it is decorated. Add designs to the poster board, using crayons, markers, or other decorations. This would be a great time to dip into your craft closet and bring out odds and ends, such as ribbon, sequins, stickers, glitter, etc. Once the hat is decorated, make a cone shape by overlapping the edges of the circle. Staple or tape into place. Punch a hole on the bottom of each side of the hat, and add yarn so that it can be tied in place on the head.

**Birthday Crowns**    *Paper Hat Tricks I* by Patt Newbold and Anne Diebel (Paper Hat Tricks, 1994) has some great crown patterns (called King/Queen/Prince/Princess crown in the table of contents) that you can use as a base for this craft. Copy the pattern and trace it onto 11-by-17-inch (or larger) paper. Then, break out the miscellaneous craft supplies to decorate your crown! Once finished, you will most likely need to add a strip of paper in the back to fit the crown to the participant's head. Or, you may wish to buy prepackaged crown kits (which normally come with decorating supplies) from your favorite catalog or online source.

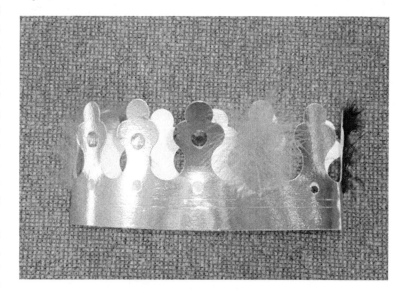

S&S Worldwide offers foam crowns in kits for $12.99 for a package of 12. The price drops to $11.89 if three or more packages are purchased. They also offer crown templates that can be traced onto paper, cut out, and decorated. Eight templates are offered in the set, at a price of $9.25 per set. Contact information for S&S Worldwide can be found in Appendix A at the end of this book.

**Birthday Wrapping Paper**    A simple way to make special wrapping paper is to print a design on tissue paper or brown paper bags (cut open to a large rectangular shape), using sponge pieces or fruit and/or vegetable halves (lemons, limes, onions, etc.) dipped into tempera paint! Allow to dry completely before taking home. If you don't want the mess that paint may bring, use inexpensive stickers that you could purchase at a local dollar store. Another variation would be to use stamps with birthday designs on them and stamp pads.

**Birthday Party Parade Hats**    Let your participants choose what type of hat they'd like. Patterns for three different hats (crown, stars, and triangle-shaped) appear on pages 63–65 of *March Patterns and Projects* (Sundance/Newbridge Educational Publishing, 2000). Instructions appear on page 61. Patterns are glued or stapled to headbands to form the hats.

**Happy Birthday Hat and Button**    Patterns for this craft can be found on page 9 of *Art Projects for All Seasons* by Karen Finch (Carson-Dellosa Publishing, 1993). The "Happy Birthday" part of the hat is colored and then construction paper strips are added to the sides to fit the participant's head. The button is colored and then taped to the participant's clothing.

**Birthday Cake Lacing Card**    The pattern for this craft can be found on page 18 of *Seasonal Cut-Ups* by Marilynn G. Barr (Monday Morning Books, 2005). Provide participants with crayons, yarn, large plastic needles, and a hole punch. Ask participants to color the cake (and background, if desired).

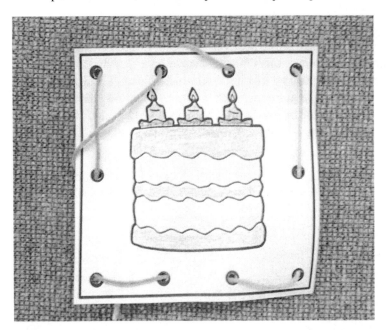

Allow them to either straight-lace or loop-lace their yarn around the picture. These two types of lacing are explained on page 7. They may wish to leave enough yarn so that this picture can be hung on a doorknob. You may wish to enlarge this pattern slightly.

# Chinese New Year

*This holiday is the perfect opportunity to have a guest speaker visit your storyhour session! Our special speaker brought in beautiful clothing from China, as well as everyday items.*

## History

Chinese New Year is a holiday that celebrates the beginning of a new year according to the lunar calendar. It is considered to be one of the most important holidays for Chinese families. Every year is associated with one of the 12 animals of the Chinese zodiac, with each animal being represented once every 12 years. The year (and people born in that year) is believed to have the characteristics of the animal it represents. Chinese New Year is celebrated with parades, dancing, fireworks, and the eating of special foods. The most common customs associated with this holiday are cleaning house (sweeping out the bad fortune of the past year), paying off debts (starting the year with a clean slate), showing respect for older family members, giving and receiving money (children receive money tucked into red envelopes), and sharing special foods with visitors. Pink, orange, and red foods are favored, as they symbolize good luck; fish and pork are eaten to symbolize a good harvest and that wishes come true.

On New Year's Eve, Chinese families prepare a special altar in their homes to pray to their ancestors and a variety of gods, including the Kitchen God, who watches over all families. The Kitchen God is the god who is in charge of reporting to the Emperor Jade about all deeds the families have done, good or bad. Many leave food offerings for him.

On New Year's Day, families visit friends and relatives and may attend community events, such as parades. People may greet each other by saying, "Gung hay fat choy!," which means "Happy New Year!" (See Laura Young's "What Is Chinese New Year?" at http://holidays.kaboose.com/what-is-chinese-new-year.html.)

## Poetry

"Chinese Dragon," from page 39 of *Eric Carle's Dragons, Dragons and Other Creatures That Never Were* compiled by Laura Whipple (Puffin, 2004).

"Chinese Lion Dancers," a short verse that would work well as an opening poem, from page 105 of *Literate Beginnings: Programs for Babies and Toddlers* by Debby Ann Jeffery (American Library Association, 1995).

"Chinese New Year" and "New Year Is Coming," from Mama Lisa's World of Children and International Culture (http://www.mamalisa.com). Click on the Asia link under "Kid Songs from Around the World" on the homepage; then click on the China link.

"Happy Chinese New Year" and "Chinese New Year," from pages 29 and 30 of *Month-by-Month Poetry: December, January, and February* by Marian Reiner (Scholastic Professional Books, 1999).

"The New Year Lanterns," from page 12 of *Dragon Kites and Dragonflies: A Collection of Chinese Nursery Rhymes* by Demi (Houghton Mifflin, 1986).

"Nian Is Coming," from page 24 of *Winter Lights: A Season in Poems and Quilts* by Anna Grossnickle Hines (Greenwillow Books, 2005).

---

**More Great Poems**

An excellent book of poems for presentations about Chinese life in the United States is *My Chinatown: One Year in Poems* by Kam Mak (Harper Children's, 2002). This book also includes two poems that you can use for your Chinese New Year presentation, the second poem from the Summer section, about dragon boats, and the third poem from the Winter Again section, about Chinese New Year.

---

# Books

Bae, Hyun-joo. *New Clothes for New Year's Day*. Kane/Miller Book Publishing, 2007. ISBN: 978-1933605296.

> Simple words and inventively composed pictures depict each step in donning the elaborate, traditional costume, from the wrapped and tied "rainbow-striped jacket" to the silk pouch that brings good luck.

Compestine, Ying Chang. *D Is for Dragon Dance*. Perfection Learning, 2007. ISBN: 978-1606860106.

> In this alphabetical celebration of the Chinese New Year, a boy and a girl prepare for the festivities with their family.

Compestine, Ying Chang. *The Runaway Rice Cake*. Simon and Schuster Children's Publishing, 2001. ISBN: 978-0689829727.

> It is Chinese New Year's Eve, and the Chang family is preparing to celebrate the holiday. Although they have very little food, they have enough rice flour to make one rice cake. When the *nian-gao* is cooked, it comes to life, pops out of the pan, and leads the Changs on a merry chase through the village.

Compestine, Ying Chang. *The Runaway Wok: A Chinese New Year Tale*. Dutton Juvenile, 2011. ISBN: 978-0525420682.

> In this high-spirited original folktale set in yesteryear Beijing, a magical pan becomes a Robin Hood hero.

Demi. *Happy, Happy Chinese New Year!* Crown Books for Young Readers, 2003. ISBN: 978-0375826429.

> With delightful charm and simplicity, Demi offers a lovely look at the Chinese New Year.

Gleason, Carrie. *Chinese New Year*. Crabtree Publishing Company, 2008. ISBN: 978-0778742807.

> Part of the Celebrations in My World series, this title focuses on the holiday that is celebrated in Chinese communities around the world.

Holub, Joan. *Dragon Dance: A Chinese New Year Lift-the-Flap Book*. Puffin, 2003. ISBN: 978-0142400005.

> Introduce the customs of Chinese New Year to even the youngest readers with this festive lift-the-flap book.

Katz, Karen. *My First Chinese New Year*. Henry Holt and Company, 2004. ISBN: 978-0805070767.

> This very simple introduction to the Chinese New Year focuses on food, families, and customs.

Lin, Grace. *Bringing in the New Year*. Knopf Books for Young Readers, 2008. ISBN: 978-0375837456.

> This exuberant story follows a Chinese-American family as they prepare for the Lunar New Year.

Lin, Grace. *Dim Sum for Everyone*. Knopf Books for Young Readers, 2001. ISBN: 978-0375810824.

> Just right for young children, this book celebrates a cultural custom and a universal favorite activity—eating!

Lin, Grace. *Fortune Cookie Fortunes*. Perfection Learning, 2006. ISBN: 978-0756977672.

> This exuberantly illustrated story about every kid's favorite part of a Chinese meal also includes a brief history of the fortune cookie.

Lin, Grace. *The Ugly Vegetables*. Charlesbridge Publishing, 2009. ISBN: 978-0881063363.
Her mother's garden has unusual Chinese vegetables, but mom's soup is wonderful!

Man-Kong, Mary. *Lucky New Year!* Golden Books, 2008. ISBN: 978-0375852244.
Celebrate the Chinese New Year with its magical traditions—from giving gifts to watching parades!

McKissack, Fredrick. *Chinese New Year: Count and Celebrate!* Enslow Publishers, 2009. ISBN: 978-0766031012.
This book counts from 1 to 10, explaining the different aspects of the Chinese New Year to youngsters.

Sanger, Amy Wilson. *Yum Yum Dim Sum*. Tricycle Press, 2003. ISBN: 978-1582461083.
Another of the World Snacks series, this book serves up a scrumptious parade of Chinese delights, from oolong tea and dumplings to sticky rice and pork buns!

Silverhardt, Lauryn. *Happy Chinese New Year, Kai-Lan!* Simon Spotlight, 2009. ISBN: 978-1416985050.
Kai-Lan and her friends are excited to wear the dragon costume in their celebration of the Chinese New Year, but they must be able to work together to make the dragon dance in the parade.

Thong, Roseanne. *Red Is a Dragon*. Chronicle Books, 2008. ISBN: 978-0811864817.
A beautiful Chinese dragon in several shades of red writhes across a double-page spread, accompanied by children carrying drums, cymbals, and strings of firecrackers—a fitting start for a concept book about colors.

Wang, Fang. *Li's Chinese New Year*. Mantra Lingua, 2010. ISBN: 978-1846115813.
It's nearly Chinese New Year and Li can't wait. What animal is he going to be for the special school celebration? Will he be a fierce tiger or a strong ox?

Wong, Janet. *This Next New Year*. Farrar, Straus, and Giroux, 2000. ISBN: 978-0374355036.
A Chinese-Korean boy relates how he and his friends celebrate the "lunar new year, the day of the first new moon."

---

### Older Gems, or Titles Too Good to Pass Up

Chinn, Karen. *Sam and the Lucky Money*. Lee and Low Books, 1997. ISBN: 978-1880000533.
Sam receives four bright red envelopes decorated with shiny gold emblems as part of the traditional Chinese New Year celebration, each containing a dollar.

Thong, Roseanne. *Round Is a Mooncake: A Book of Shapes*. Chronicle Books, 2000. ISBN: 978-0811826761.
In this book about shapes, some of the items identified are from Chinese-American households.

Vaughn, Marcia. *The Dancing Dragon*. Mondo Publishing, 1996. ISBN: 978-1572551343.
In rhymed couplets, a Chinese-American child describes the excitement, preparation, and festivities of the Chinese New Year, culminating in a parade that includes a magnificent dragon carried aloft on sticks.

Wallace, Ian. *Chin Chiang and the Dragon's Dance*. Groundwood Books, 1998. ISBN: 978-0888990204.
Chin Chiang has long dreamed of dancing the dragon's dance, but when the first day of the Year of the Dragon arrives and he is to dance with his grandfather, he is sure he will shame his family and bring bad luck to everyone.

Waters, Kate. *Lion Dancer: Ernie Wan's Chinese New Year*. Scholastic, 1991. ISBN: 978-0590430470.
On the Chinese New Year, six-year-old Ernie will perform his first Lion Dance. An intimate look at a Chinese household as the family shares a proud moment with Ernie.

Young, Ed. *Cat and Rat: The Legend of the Chinese Zodiac*. Turtleback, 1998. ISBN: 978-0613123587.
In this intriguing picture book, Caldecott Medalist Young retells a Chinese folktale about the origins of the zodiac.

Yu, Li Qiong. *A New Year's Reunion: A Chinese Story*. Candlewick Press, 2011. ISBN: 978-0763658816.
Maomao's dad, who works many miles away, comes home for New Year.

Zucker, Jonny. *Lanterns and Firecrackers: A Chinese New Year Story*. Barron's Educational Series, 2003.
ISBN: 978-0764126680.
Follow a family as they set off firecrackers, watch lion and dragon dances, and hang up lanterns to
celebrate the start of their New Year.

## Activities

---

### Coloring Pages

Consult your favorite pattern books for pages to use as coloring sheets. Be sure to search
online as well. There's lots of great stuff out there!

- TheBestKidsBooksite.com offers a great coloring page with Chinese characters at
  http://www.thebestkidsbooksite.com/crafttemp/gunghayfatchoy.pdf.

---

### Cut-and-Tell

Depending on the animal that the new year is associated with, why not search to see if there are
scissors stories available for that particular animal?

### Draw-and-Tell

Depending on the animal that the new year is associated with, why not search to see if there are draw-
and-tell stories available for that particular animal?

**Bo ga Ippon (What Will It Be?)**    The text and drawing instructions for this story from Japan can be
found on pages 56–57 of *The Story Vine: A Source Book of Unusual and Easy-to-Tell Stories from
Around the World* by Anne Pellowski (Macmillan, 1984).

### Flannel/Velcro Board

**Lion Dance Flannel Board**    I adapted "Lion Dance Song" from page 25 in *Small World Celebrations*
by Jean Warren and Elizabeth McKinnon (Warren Publishing House, 1988) into a flannel board
presentation by doing a Google image search for pictures that illustrated the stanzas (Chinese lion
dance, Chinese firecrackers, etc.). I enlarged these pictures, printed them out, taped them to pieces of
construction paper, laminated the pictures for durability, and placed Velcro on the back so they
would adhere to the board.

**"The New Year's Animals: A Chinese Folktale"**    This story explains how each of the 12 animals of
the zodiac were chosen and why Rat is first. The text and patterns can be found on pages 13–21 of
*Multicultural Folktales for the Feltboard and Readers' Theatre* by Judy Sierra (Oryx Press, 1996).

***The Dragon's Tail and Other Animal Fables of the Chinese Zodiac***    This book by Demi (Henry Holt
and Company, 1996) introduces fables about each zodiac animal, which appear in a two-page spread.
Although the age-appropriateness of the stories is listed by Amazon as K–3, with a little ingenuity,
these tales could be adapted for a younger audience. A search through your favorite pattern books
would likely yield all of the patterns needed to tell the tales as flannel/Velcro-board stories.

### Games

**Chinese Zodiac Matching Game**    Small pictures of all 12 zodiac animals can be found at
http://www.abcteach.com/free/m/matching_chinesezodiac.pdf. Enlarge these animals (they are all

drawn in squares for easy cutting out), copying two of each onto different colors of paper. Laminate for durability. Give each participant one of the animal pictures, keeping one for yourself and placing them in an apron pocket or a container. Begin the matching game by pulling one of the animals/colors from your pocket. Allow participants to match them. Continue until all animals/colors are matched.

**Chinese New Year Matching Game**    Patterns for a variety of Chinese New Year symbols (Chinese lantern and lion mask) appear on pages 69–72 of *Holiday Patterns*, compiled by Jean Warren (Warren Publishing House, 1991). The best patterns to use would be the ones that are already enclosed in a square, as this would make cutting them out simple. Follow the instructions for the matching game listed previously in this section. Another way to do this matching game would be to use Ellison dies, such as the handheld fan, the Chinese dragon, fortune cookie, and the die for the animal that represents the current year.

## Miscellaneous

**Wear Red!**    Since red is considered a good luck color, inform participants before they attend your program to be sure to wear something red!

**Dragon Parade**    Use one of the dragon masks that are included in the craft section of this chapter. Allow a participant to be the head of the dragon. Have participants line up, holding one another's waists. Move around the room, pretending to be a Chinese dragon. A variation of this would be to use the dragon mask for the head, but to let the participants play rhythm instruments.

**Ribbon Dance**    Use any of the music listed in the "Musical Selections" section or locate a CD of strictly Chinese music. Equip participants with ribbon sticks (available through Oriental Trading Company or Music in Motion) and allow them to dance, moving their ribbon sticks through the air.

**Tangram Shapes**    Research the story behind the tangram. Make tangram shapes (patterns are readily available online) or purchase a set for use. If you have a magnet board, this would be a great way to use the online patterns. Laminate them for durability and adhere strips of magnet to the backs. There are numerous sites online that show you simple figures. Use the tangrams to make simple shapes and allow participants to guess what the shapes are. Two books that might be helpful in finding figures are *Tangrams: 300 Puzzles* by Ronald C. Read (Dover Publications, 1965) and *The Fun with Tangrams Kit* by Susan Johnston (Dover Publications, 1977). The second book comes with two complete sets of tangram pieces. *Note:* A simple tangram pattern appears on page 63 of *Crafts from World Cultures: Easy-to-Make Multicultural Art Activities* by Janice Veith and Anne Weber (Monday Morning Books, 1995).

**Chinese Language**    Teach participants how to say simple phrases in Chinese. For example, "ni hao" (nee how) means "hello." Or, teach them to count from 1 to 10 in Chinese. Visit EnchantedLearning .com to find pronunciations of Chinese words at http://www.enchantedlearning.com/school/China/numbers/.

**Chinese New Year's Party**    Hold a party as part of your storyhour session. Oranges and apples are traditional refreshments, and fortune cookies are always fun!

**"Here Come the New Years"**    This song, sung to the tune of "Old McDonald," can be found on page 25 of *Small World Celebrations* by Jean Warren and Elizabeth McKinnon (Warren Publishing House, 1988). There is a verse for each Chinese zodiac animal and participants can make the sounds for each. Have illustrations of each of the animals to hold up as that year is mentioned. Use the illustrations from the Chinese Zodiac Matching Game if you desire. Laminate illustrations for durability.

### Chinese New Year Songs

- "Chinese New Year," sung to the tune of "We Are Siamese," appears on page 86 of *More Simply Super Storytimes: Programming Ideas for Ages 3–6* by Marie Castellano Boyum (Upstart, 2006).
- "Chinese Hello Song" and "Chinese Dragon" can be found at http://www.canteach.ca/elementary/songspoems54.html.
- "Dragon Dance Song," "Chinese New Year Dragon," and "Almond Cookies" can be found online at http://www.perpetualpreschool.com/holiday_themes/chinese_newyear_songs.htm.
- "Ni Hao Song (Hello Song") can be found on page 27 of *The Best of Totline Newsletter*, compiled by Jean Warren (Warren Publishing House, 1995).

### Chinese New Year Paper Dolls

Visit Activity Village (http://www.activityvillage.co.uk/paper_dolls.htm) for paper dolls that you can print out (in color!) and then scroll down on the same page to find Chinese New Year clothing and accessories and traditional Chinese clothing that can be printed out and placed on the paper dolls. *Note:* Winston and Lily are the patterns you will need to choose—they are the Asian pair. This would be a great opening activity to introduce participants to the traditional clothing worn during this holiday! I would print these out on card stock and laminate for durability.

### Asian/Japanese Play Foods

Use this realia, available from Becker's School Supplies. The Asian food set includes moon cake, chicken and cashew, rice, two spring rolls, two steamed dumplings, two-piece steamer, and fried dumpling. The Japanese set includes carrot flower, salmon roe, California roll, cucumber roll, hand roll salmon, tuna roll, two shrimp sushi, mackerel sushi, and white rice. Both sets are $14.99 each. The contact information for Becker's School Supplies can be found in Appendix A at the end of this book.

## Fingerplays

### Chinese New Year Rhyme

You'll find whenever the New Year comes,
The Kitchen God will want some plums.    *(Make small circle with one hand for plum.)*
The girls will want some flowers new,    *(Put hands together in prayer position; pull apart, leaving wrists together, to represent opening flower.)*

The boys will want firecrackers, too.    *(Clap hands together.)*
A new felt cap will please papa,    *(Point to head.)*
And a sugar cake for dear mama.    *(Make larger circle in front of body with both hands.)*

—Traditional Chinese rhyme

---

### More Great Fingerplays

"Chinese New Year Dragon" is an action rhyme, from page 266 of *1001 Rhymes and Fingerplays for Working with Young Children*, compiled by the Totline Staff (Warren Publishing House, 1994).

The book *Dragon Kites and Dragonflies: A Collection of Chinese Nursery Rhymes* by Demi (Houghton Mifflin, 1986) can be used to introduce participants to some traditional Chinese nursery rhymes.

"Chinese New Year" and "New Year Is Coming" are two fingerplays that can be found online at Mama Lisa's World of Children and International Culture (http://www.mamalisa.com/). On the homepage, click on the map of Asia under the "Kid Songs from Around the World" section; then click on "China" from the list of countries. This site also contains other Chinese songs and rhymes that you may wish to use for your program.

"Lion Dance Song" and "Chinese Hello Song" are action songs that can be found on page 25 of *Small World Celebrations* by Jean Warren and Elizabeth McKinnon (Warren Publishing House, 1988).

## Musical Selections

"China (Show Ma Mo)" from *Multicultural Rhythm Stick Fun* by Georgiana Stewart. Kimbo. ASIN: B00000DARR.

"Chinese Friendship Dance" from *Educational Activities Dances Around the World* by Henry Buzz Glass and Rosemary Hallum. Educational Activities. ASIN: B0006645KY.

"Chinese New Year" and "Count in Chinese" from *Asia* by Mr. I and Gary Q. Songs for Teaching. Available from http://www.songsforteaching.com/.

"Chinese New Year" from *Joining Hands with Other Lands: Multicultural Songs and Games*. Kimbo. ASIN: B00000DARS.

"Chinese New Year" from *Touched by a Song* by Miss Jackie Silberg. Miss Jackie Music. ASIN: B002K74FCK.

"Chinese New Year" from *A World of Parachute Play* by Georgiana Stewart. Kimbo. ASIN: B00000DAS0.

*Chinese New Years Music* CD by Heart of the Dragon Ensemble. ARC. ASIN: B000MV9N82.

---

### More Great Music

Free downloads of Chinese New Year music and songs are available from TheHolidaySpot .com at http://www.theholidayspot.com/chinese_new_year/music/. I particularly like "Golden Snake Dance." It is a great song to dance to; you can have your participants dance while holding dragon masks or dragon crafts. While the song itself is only just over a minute long, you could possibly loop it for a longer playing time.

Another great music resource is Nancy Stewart's site NancyMusic.com. Go to http://www .nancymusic.com/Gunghayplay.htm to access both sheet music and a downloadable MP3 for "Gung Hay Fat Choy—Chinese New Year Song" by Nancy Stewart. This link provides the text of the song along with motions and also allows you to hear the artist perform this cute song.

---

## Crafts

**Chinese Dragon Mask**    The dragon pattern for this craft can be found on page 54 of *February Patterns, Projects, and Plans to Perk Up Early Learning Programs* by Imogene Forte (Incentive Publications, 1990). Reproduce pattern on construction paper or card stock if using markers. Add a craft stick or paint stick glued to the back to create a mask. A wonderful mask pattern can also be found on page 13 of the May/June 2003 issue of *CopyCat Magazine* (now out of print but often available through interlibrary loan). Another great pattern can also be found at http://www.kidsdomain .com/craft/cegif/newyear/chinesedragon1.gif.

**Chinese New Year Dragon Costume**    This craft allows participants to make not only a dragon mask, but hands, feet, and scales down the back to go with it! You could certainly simplify the craft and make only the mask and hands, or mask and feet if desired. Instructions appear on page 35 and patterns appear on pages 36–38 of *January Patterns and Projects* (Newbridge Educational Publishing, 2000).

**Chinese Lanterns**    Fold a piece of construction paper in half. Cut lines from the fold line. Then unfold and staple the short edge of the paper together. EnchantedLearning.com provides instructions online at http://www.enchantedlearning.com/crafts/chinesenewyear/lantern/.

**Lai See Envelopes**    Although these can be purchased online through vendors such as Oriental Trading Company (type in "Chinese money envelopes" in the search box), the February 2005 issue of *CopyCat Magazine* (now out of print but often available through interlibrary loan) provides a pattern for a Lai

See Envelope in their article "Picture Book Patterns for Lion Dancer." Participants can color and cut out. Provide play money coins for them to place in their envelopes.

**Chinese Zodiac Wreath**     The base of this craft is a large paper plate with the center cut out of it. You can use the patterns from ABCteach.com (http://www.abcteach.com/ free/m/matching_chinesezodiac .pdf) and copy them so that all participants have a copy of all 12. You may have to play with the size of these pictures to make all 12 of them fit around the plate. Allow participants to color these pictures and then glue them around the plate. A similar craft can be found online at http://www.dltk-holidays .com/china/mcalendarwreath.html. A search of Oriental Trading Company's site shows a prepackaged kit available with all of the zodiac animals. Participants can color these and glue them. Search under "Chinese New Year Wreaths" or "New Year craft kits."

**Dragons on Parade Craft**     This wonderful dragon craft is available from Kaboose.com (http:// crafts .kaboose.com/chdragoneasy.html). The instructions say to attach a sturdy piece of paper to the back for a holder. You could also attach a paint stick to the bottom of the dragon's face as well. In

addition, you could cut out the eye areas and participants could hold their masks in front of their faces as they parade or dance! I love this dragon face pattern. It is one of the nicest I've seen.

**Chinese New Year Dragon**     This craft is a dragon that is shown in four sections, which are colored and glued together. The patterns are on pages 172–173 of *The Big All-Year Book of Holidays and Seasonal Celebrations: Preschool/Kindergarten, Issues 14–18*, edited by Donna Borst (Teaching and Learning Company, 2002).

**Chinese New Year Dragon Puppet**     The patterns and instructions for this paper bag puppet from TeacherVision at http:// www.teachervision.fen.com/tv/printables/ TCR/0615_131-132.pdf. They appear as PDFs for easy printing. The head of the dragon is glued to the bag's bottom and the body to the long part of the bag. This same craft appears in the book *Multicultural Holidays: Share Our Celebrations* by Julia Jasmine (Teacher Created Materials, 1994).

# Christmas

*This is a holiday for which your programming can go so many different ways—trees, bells, elves, Santa Claus, presents, gingerbread, and more!*

## History

The word "Christmas" comes from the Old English words "Cristes maesse," meaning "Christ's mass." Christians the world over celebrate the birth of Jesus Christ, God's son, on December 25th. It was Pope Julius I who, in the year 350, proclaimed December 25th the birthday of Christ.

The Christmas celebration actually begins on December 24th, or Christmas Eve. It is said that on this night Mary and Joseph found refuge in the stable in Bethlehem and the angels appeared to the shepherds, heralding the birth of Jesus. Some families attend church, exchange gifts, and have a family meal on the 24th. And of course, Christmas Eve is when Santa Claus makes his trip around the world, delivering presents!

Christmas Day is more often than not the day when most families will celebrate the holiday. Children are up early, opening gifts; families may attend church services; and family dinners are held, sometimes with extended family joining in.

Santa Claus is known around the world. Each country or region has a gift-bringer that is very much like the Santa that Americans know and love. (See Edna Barth's *Holly, Reindeer, and Colored Lights: The Story of the Christmas Symbols* [Seabury Press, 2000].)

## Poetry

"A Box of Socks" by Cheryl Potts, from page 56 of *Poetry Fun by the Ton with Jack Prelutsky* by Cheryl Potts (Alleyside Press, 1995).

"Dear Santa Claus," from page 8 of *It's Christmas* by Jack Prelutsky (Greenwillow Books, 1981).

"Does Santa Have a Reindeer?," a song that can be read as a humorous poem, from http://www.susan mdailey.com/; click on "New Themes," then "Christmas."

"Merry Christmas!" and "Shoes and Stockings," from pages 86 and 87, respectively, of *A School Year of Poems: 180 Favorites from Highlights*, selected by Walter B. Barbe (Boyds Mills Press, 2005).

"My Gingerbread House," from page 127 of *The Best of Holidays and Seasonal Celebrations—Issues 9–13, PreK-K*, edited by Donna Borst (Teaching and Learning Company, 2001).

"My Stockings," from page 141 of *The Best of Holidays and Seasonal Celebrations—Issues 5–8, PreK-K*, edited by Donna Borst (Teaching and Learning Company, 2000).

"Singing Christmas Carols," from page 180 of *Be Glad Your Nose Is on Your Face and Other Poems* by Jack Prelutsky (Greenwillow Books, 2008).

"The Twenty-Fourth of December" and "Merry Christmas," from page 21 of *Month-by-Month Poetry: December, January, and February* by Marian Reiner (Scholastic Professional Books, 1999).

"The Wreath Is Hanging on Our Door," from page 61 of *Marmalade Days Winter: Complete Units for Busy Teachers of Young Children* by Carol Taylor Bond (Partner Press, 1987).

## Books ————————————————————————————————————————

Balian, Lorna. *Bah! Humbug?* Star Bright Books, 2006. ISBN: 978-1595720368.
This is a reissue of a classic title first published in 1977. Margie's older bossy brother believes that Santa Claus is a humbug and he plans to prove it by creating a trap to catch him. But he might be wrong about Santa after all!

Buehner, Caralyn. *Snowmen at Christmas.* Dial, 2005. ISBN: 978-0803729957.
On Christmas Eve, snowmen hold a party in the center of town and celebrate with food, music, dancing, and presents.

Cousins, Lucy. *Maisy's Snowy Christmas Eve.* Candlewick Press, 2003. ISBN: 978-0763621964.
It's Christmas Eve, and snow is falling everywhere—on Maisy's house, on her friends' houses, even on Eddie!

Dewdney, Anna. *Llama, Llama, Holiday Drama.* Viking Juvenile, 2010. ISBN: 978-0670011612.
Little Llama and Mama Llama rush around, shopping for presents, baking cookies, decorating the tree...but how long is it until Christmas? Will it ever come?

Falconer, Ian. *Olivia Helps with Christmas.* Simon and Schuster UK, 2007. ISBN: 978-1847382726.
Christmas is coming, and Olivia is incredibly busy. She has to wait for Santa, make sure Dad sets up the tree, wait for Santa, watch mom make the Christmas dinner, wait for Santa, oversee the care with which the stockings are hung and, of course, open her presents!

Freedman, Claire. *Ten Christmas Wishes.* Little Tiger Press, 2010. ISBN: 978-1848951099.
Count the wishing stars as Little Mouse and his friends wish for sparkling snow, a giant Christmas tree, and lots and lots of presents!

Greene, Rhonda G. *Santa's Stuck.* Dutton Juvenile, 2004. ISBN: 978-0525472926.
When Santa eats so many sweet treats that he can't get back up the chimney, a family cat, dog, and all of the reindeer push and pull, to no avail!

Hale, Nathan. *The Twelve Bots of Christmas.* Walker Books for Young Readers, 2010. ISBN: 978-0802722379.
Take one robotic Santa, nine cyber-reindeer pulling his techno-sleigh, and twelve days of Christmas circuitry and wizardry—and this incredible holiday offering is guaranteed to add up to every gearhead's delight!

Katz, Karen. *Counting Christmas.* Margaret K. McElderry, 2003. ISBN: 978-0689849251.
Three young children make the transition from Christmas Eve to Christmas Day by counting backward from 10 to 1.

Lester, Helen. *Tacky's Christmas.* Houghton Mifflin Books for Children, 2010. ISBN: 978-0547172088.
Tacky, Goodly, Lovely, Angel, Neatly, and Perfect are celebrating the holiday with good cheer, singing, and lots of presents.

London, Johnathan. *Froggy's Best Christmas.* Puffin, 2002. ISBN: 978-0140567359.
Froggy has never celebrated Christmas; usually he's taking his long winter's nap. But not this year! Froggy's best friend, Max the beaver, wakes him up to join in the fun.

McCourt, Lisa. *Merry Christmas, Stinky Face.* Cartwheel Books, 2008. ISBN: 978-0439731232.
"What if Santa's lips get chapped?" Stinky Face asks. "What if the sack of toys starts to rip?" As always, Mama lovingly addresses each and every one of her child's concerns. Of course, Stinky Face leaves Santa lip balm and duct tape...just in case.

Rey, H.A. *Merry Christmas, Curious George!* HMH Books, 2006. ISBN: 978-0618692378.
Curious George goes Christmas tree shopping with the man in the yellow hat, and climbs into a tree that gets delivered to a children's hospital.

---

**Older Gems, or Titles Too Good to Pass Up**

Gackenbach, Dick. *Claude the Dog: A Christmas Story.* Turtleback, 1984. ISBN: 978-0613775281.
  A dog demonstrates the real spirit of giving at Christmas.

Janovitz, Marilyn. *What Could Be Keeping Santa?* North-South Books, 1997. ISBN: 978-1558588202.
  The reindeer are concerned because Santa is late on Christmas Eve.

Kovalski, Maryann. *Jingle Bells.* Joy St. Books, 1998. ISBN: 978-0316502580.
  Grandma takes Jenny and Joanna on a plane ride to New York City where they pile into a horse and carriage and set off through a snowy Central Park.

Numeroff, Laura. *If You Take a Mouse to the Movies.* HarperCollins, 2000. ISBN: 978-0060278670.
  Numeroff's mouse is back! Going from movie theater, to Christmas tree lot, to the neighbor's yard for snowmouse-building, he's a very demanding mouse indeed—in only the best way, of course!

Van Allsburg, Chris. *The Polar Express.* Houghton Mifflin, 1985. ISBN: 978-0395389496.
  A magical train ride on Christmas Eve takes a boy to the North Pole to receive a special gift from Santa Claus. A holiday classic!

---

Rox, John. *I Want a Hippopotamus for Christmas.* HarperCollins, 2005. ISBN: 978-0060529420.
  Christmas is coming, and one little girl wants nothing more than a hippopotamus to play with and enjoy. Based on a 1950s song that was done as a way to raise money for Oklahoma City Zoo's first hippopotamus! (Instead of reading the story, why not sing it instead?)

Sabuda, Robert. *Cookie Count: A Tasty Pop-Up.* Little Simon, 1997. ISBN: 978-0689811913.
  A hands-down classic! Each page is a feast of sweet, sugary treats. Coconut kisses, peanut butter cookies, Linzer hearts, and more are carefully concocted and counted by mouse chefs.

Scotton, Robert. *Merry Christmas, Splat.* HarperCollins, 2009. ISBN: 978-0060831608.
  It's the night before Christmas, and Splat wonders if he's been a good enough cat this year to deserve a really big present.

Shannon, David. *It's Christmas, David!* Blue Skye Press, 2010. ISBN: 978-0545143110.
  From playing with delicate ornaments to standing in an endlessly long line for Santa, here are common Christmas activities—but with David's naughty trimmings!

Thompson, Lauren. *Mouse's First Christmas.* Turtleback, 2003. ISBN: 978-0613910392.
  A tale of a curious young mouse who explores the sensory delights of Christmas Eve.

Wells, Rosemary. *Max's Christmas.* Viking Juvenile, 2010. ISBN: 978-0670887156.
  Hiding by the chimney corner on Christmas Eve, toddler bunny Max hopes to catch of glimpse of Santa Claus, much to the chagrin of his big sister, Ruby, who resists her own curiosity in her effort to get little Max to bed.

Wilson, Karma. *Bear Stays Up for Christmas.* Margaret K. McElderry, 2008. ISBN: 978-1416958963.
  It's the day before Christmas, and Bear's friends have gathered in his lair to wake him to celebrate the holiday.

# Activities —————————————————————————————————————————

**Coloring Pages**

Consult your favorite pattern books or holiday coloring books for pages to use as coloring sheets. Be sure to search online as well. There's lots of great stuff out there!

- Visit http://dulemba.com/index_ColoringPages.html for author and illustrator Elizabeth O. Dulemba's great collection of holiday coloring pages! While there, sign up for her Coloring Page Tuesdays e-mails!

### Cut-and-Tell

**"Rain, Dear?"**    This scissor tale, perfect for a reindeer-themed program, can be found on pages 30–34 of *Scissor Tales for Special Days* by Jan Grubb Philpot (Incentive Publications, 1994).

**"C"**    This cut-and-tell story, which ends up being a candle, is found on pages 15–18 of *Paper Cutting Stories from A to Z* by Valerie Marsh (Alleyside Press, 1992).

**"Santa's House and the Snowy Winter"**    This cut-and-tell story with patterns can be found on pages 64–69 of *Fold-and-Cut Stories and Fingerplays* by Marj Hart (Fearon Teacher Aids, 1987). Perfect for a reindeer-themed program!

**"Morris Mouse and His Christmas Trees"**    This cut-and-tell story that makes five trees, the last one perfect for a mouse's house, is found on pages 11–13 of *Paper Stories* by Jean Stangl (Fearon Teacher Aids, 1984).

### Draw-and-Tell

**"Santa Claus"**    This draw-and-tell story, of which Santa is the end result, can be found on pages 157–161 of *Drawing Stories from Around the World and a Sampling of European Handkerchief Stories* by Anne Pellowski (Libraries Unlimited, 2005).

**"Getting Ready for Christmas"**    This draw-and-tell story that creates Santa's face appears on pages 111–113 of *Chalk in Hand: The Draw and Tell Book* by Phyllis Noe Pflomm (Scarecrow Press, 1986).

### Flannel/Velcro Board

**"A Christmas Wish"**    This flannel/Velcro-board story and accompanying patterns can be found on pages 165–168 of *Storytelling with the Flannel Board, Book Two* by Paul S. Anderson (T.S. Denison and Company, 1970). Put together piece by piece as the story is told, the resulting picture is Santa himself!

**What Am I?**    The text for this simple guessing game can be found on page 127 of *The Big All-Year Book of Holidays and Seasonal Celebrations: Preschool/Kindergarten, Issues 14–18*, edited by Donna Borst (Teaching and Learning Company, 2002). Players must guess six Christmas items: candy cane, present, candle, star, stocking, and bell. Each item has a stanza of clues. To make visuals for the items, I simply looked them up on Google image search, copied them into Microsoft Publisher to enlarge/reduce, then printed and laminated them. Place each item on the board as it is guessed.

**Rudolph, Rudolph**    The text for this activity can be found at http://www.advantagespeech.com/ resources/Rudolph%20Color%20Poem.pdf. With each stanza, Rudolph's nose changes color. To make this for presentation, find a picture of a reindeer that will work as Rudolph. Paste it onto brown construction paper. The particular one that I found (in a coloring/clip art book) had a nice clear nose and a necklace of jingle bells around the neck. I printed the jingle bell necklace on yellow paper and affixed that to the brown reindeer, and then made a nose in each color mentioned in the poem and attached them to the reindeer. Making sure the reindeer's head is brown makes the nose really stand out. I then laminated the pieces for durability. When reading the poem, pause and let participants guess the color of the nose. It will be obvious from the text rhyming what the color will be.

**Decorate the Christmas Tree!**    The patterns for the tree and ornaments for this activity can be found on pages 214–216 of *Felt Board Fun for Everyday and Holidays* by Liz and Dick Wilmes (Building Blocks Publications, 1984). Enlarge the tree to a decent size that will hold a number of ornaments. Either color it green or copy onto 11-by-17-inch dark green paper. Laminate the tree for durability. Place "hook" pieces of Velcro around the inside of the tree area. The ornament patterns that appear are just the right size for the tree. Copy them and color them in. For my version of this, in addition to the decorations that go on the tree, I typed out a piece of paper for each one that told what the decoration was: for example, a snowman, a blue ornament, a trumpet, a star, etc. I paper-clipped these to each decoration. I then passed these out just as I do for my matching game: the participants received an ornament, and I kept the piece of paper describing what the decoration was. Once all were passed out, I began the activity by pulling out of my pocket one of the slips that described the ornament. Whoever had this one could then come up to the tree shape on the flannel/Velcro board and place the decoration wherever they desired. The activity continues until all decorations are placed on the tree.

**"Ellie the Evergreen"; "The Little Blue Dishes"; "Eight Little Candles"**    These three holiday stories can be found on pages 27–35 of *Short-Short Stories: Simple Stories for Young Children Plus Seasonal Activities*, compiled by Jean Warren (Warren Publishing House, 1987). All of them could easily be adapted for flannel/Velcro-board telling.

**"Who's in the Forest?"**    This flannel/Velcro-board story, which ends up being a reindeer, can be found on page 40 of *FlannelGraphs: Flannel Board Fun for Little Ones, Preschool–Grade 3*, by Jean Stangl (Fearon Teacher Aids, 1986). The patterns can be found on page 73.

**"Santa Around the World"**    I came up with this idea to introduce participants to the many names of Santa around the world. I first researched some of the names of Santa in different countries. Then I searched on Google to find decent-sized pictures that I could use. I printed and laminated these. I attached a piece of Velcro to the back of each so that I could affix them to my board. Here is the text that I use:

In the Netherlands, he's Sinterklass.

In England, he's Father Christmas.

In France, he's Pere Noel [or Father Christmas—use this one if you desire].

In Switzerland, he's Samichlaus.

In Germany, he's Weihnachtsmann (Christmas Man).

In Austria and Hungary, he's Niklaus.

In Italy, it's an old lady named Befana who brings gifts.

In Russia, he's Grandfather Frost.

In Scandinavia, he's Jultomten.

In China, he's Dun-che-lao-ren.

But, in the United States, he's Santa Claus, of course!

**Ten Little Christmas Elves**    This rhyme can be done as a flannel/Velcro-board presentation or as stick puppets. The text and patterns can be found on pages 23–28 of *Super Story Telling* by Carol Elaine Catron and Barbara Catron Parks (T.S. Denison and Company, 1986).

**"Eight Little Reindeer"**    The text for this reindeer countdown, which would work well as a flannel/Velcro-board presentation, can be found on page 10 of *The Best of Totline Magazine, Volume 2*, compiled by Gayle Bittinger (McGraw-Hill Children's Publishing, 2003). Consult your favorite pattern books to find a suitable reindeer pattern.

**Santa's Clothes**    This cute flannel/Velcro-board story that dresses Santa comes from Susan M. Dailey, and can be found on her site at http://www.susanmdailey.com/. Click on the "New Stories" link on the left-hand side of the homepage and then click on the story link to be taken to the text of the story. The text page also contains links to PDF files of Santa and his clothes.

## Games

**Christmas Matching Game**    Patterns for a variety of Christmas symbols (candle, tree, elf, gingerbread man, bell, poinsettia, present, reindeer, Santa, sleigh, star, stocking, wreath) appear on pages 31–32 and 39–62 of *Holiday Patterns*, compiled by Jean Warren (Warren Publishing House, 1991). The best patterns to use would be the ones that are already enclosed in a square, as this would make cutting them out very simple. Copy two of each on different colors of construction paper. Pass out one of each pair of patterns to participants, keeping one for yourself, either in an apron pocket or container of some sort (perhaps a Christmas stocking). Begin the game by placing your copies of the pictures, one at a time, on your board and allowing the participants to match them.

This game could also be done with Christmas shapes cut from Ellison dies. Cut two of each color and laminate for durability.

You can also vary this game, depending on the Christmas theme you have chosen for the week. For example, if your theme is bells, simply use that shape or picture in different colors of paper.

**Pass the Stocking**    You could do this game with any type of Christmas object: an ornament (non-breakable), a stuffed Santa, a stuffed reindeer, etc. Pass the object around as you play holiday music. Stop the music. The participant holding the object when the music stops gets a treat, such as a candy cane, etc. Restart the music and play until everyone has received a treat. To include all, if the object ends up with a participant who already has a treat, have them pass the object to their left or right, depending on who hasn't received a treat yet.

**Pin the Nose on Rudolph**    This game is a variation of the tried-and-true Pin the Tail on the Donkey. Find a picture of Rudolph that you can enlarge to a decent size. Laminate for durability. You will also want to make a number of large, red circle noses and laminate these as well. Play this game just as you would Pin the Tail on the Donkey.

**Light Bulb Hunt**    Susan M. Dailey has written a couple of books for Neal-Schuman, but she also has a website (http://www.susanmdailey.com/) with ideas that are not included in either of her books. Click on the "New Fingerplays" link on the left-hand side of the homepage. Then scroll down to about midpage, and you will find the instructions for this cute activity and a light bulb pattern to use!

## Miscellaneous

**Jingle All the Way!**    The Christmas season is a great time to break out your rhythm band instruments, especially your bells! Use any of the Christmas music listed in the Musical Selections section and let your participants play along. Of course, the song "Jingle Bells" just begs to be performed!

**"One More Thing in the Stocking"**    This story, complete with props list, can be found on pages 84–85 of *The Storytelling Handbook: A Young People's Collection of Unusual Tales and Helpful Hints on How to Tell Them* by Anne Pellowski (Simon and Schuster Books for Young Readers, 1995).

**Christmas Stocking Dot-to-Dot**    The pattern for this dot-to-dot can be found on page 166 of *Marmalade Days Winter: Complete Units for Busy Teachers of Young Children* by Carol Taylor Bond (Partner Press, 1987). Copy this pattern onto colored paper and laminate for durability. Have your participants say the alphabet with you, which completes the picture when done. Laminating the pattern allows you to wipe it off after use so that it can be reused.

**"Santa's Christmas Sack"**    This is a pocket story. Santa is enlarged to poster-board size. A plastic baggie is placed over the sack area, so that toys can be put "into" it. The text and patterns appear on pages 150–153 of *Super Story Telling* by Carol Elaine Catron and Barbara Catron Parks (T.S. Denison and Company, 1986).

**Decorate the Tree Magnet Board Activity**    This activity can be found on pages 172–173 and 176–177 (patterns) of *Magnet Board Fun for Everyday, Seasons, and Holidays* by Liz and Dick Wilmes (Building Blocks Publications, 1998). A tree is drawn on the board, and participants sing a song, "Old St. Nicholas," to the tune of "Old McDonald Had a Farm" and decorate the tree with ornaments.

## Fingerplays ─────────────────────────────────────────────

### Bells

**Five Little Bells**

*(This rhyme would also work well as a flannel/Velcro-board presentation.)*

| | |
|---|---|
| Five little bells hanging in a row. | *(Hold up five fingers.)* |
| The first one said, "Ring me slow." | *(Move thumb slowly.)* |

The second one said, "Ring me fast." *(Move index finger quickly.)*
The third one said, "Ring me last." *(Move middle finger.)*
The fourth one said, "I'm like a chime." *(Move ring finger.)*
The fifth one said, "Ring us all at Christmastime." *(Wiggle all fingers.)*

—Author unknown

### Christmas Time

*(This can be sung to the tune of "Row, Row, Row Your Boat.")*

Ring, ring, ring the bells, *(Make motion of bells ringing.)*
Ring them loud and clear,
To tell the children everywhere
That Christmas time is here.

*(You could also use real bells while reading this rhyme.)*

—Author unknown

## Elves

### In Santa's Workshop

*(This rhyme would also work well as a flannel/Velcro-board presentation or with small finger puppets.)*

In Santa's workshop far away,
Ten little elves work night and day. *(Hold up ten fingers.)*
This little elf makes candy canes; *(Point to little finger on one hand.)*
This little elf builds streamlined trains; *(Point to ring finger.)*
This little elf paints dolls for girls; *(Point to middle finger.)*
This little elf puts in their curls; *(Point to pointer finger.)*
This little elf dips chocolate drops; *(Point to thumb.)*
This little elf makes lollipops; *(Point to little finger on other hand.)*
This little elf packs each jack-in-the-box; *(Point to ring finger.)*
This little elf sews dolly socks; *(Point to middle finger.)*
This little elf wraps books for boys; *(Point to pointer finger.)*
This little elf checks off the toys, *(Point to thumb.)*
As Santa packs them in his sleigh,
Ready for you on Christmas Day. *(Point to children.)*

—Author unknown

### Santa's Workshop

Here is Santa's workshop, *(Form peak with both hands.)*
Here is Santa Claus. *(Hold up thumbs.)*
Here are Santa's little elves *(Wiggle fingers.)*
Putting toys upon the shelves.

—Author unknown

### Where Are Santa's Elves?

*(This is sung to the tune of "The Farmer in the Dell." Photocopy enough elf shapes so that each child can have one. You might also wish to use the elf-shaped Ellison die. Laminate for durability. On the last line of the song, have a child bring his or her elf to the flannel or Velcro board. Continue until all have had a chance.)*

Where are Santa's elves? *(Hold out hands in questioning motion.)*
Who help him make the toys
He passes out on Christmas Eve *(Pretend to hand out packages.)*

To all the girls and boys?
They help him sew and saw.                    (*Pretend to sew and saw.*)
They help him paint and pound.                (*Pretend to paint and pound.*)
Where, oh where, are Santa's elves?
Look, one has been found!

—Susan M. Dailey
*A Storytime Year* (Neal-Schuman, 2001, p. 347)

## Reindeer

### Santa's Reindeer

One, two, three, four, five little reindeer.    (*Point to one finger at a time.*)
Stood by the North Pole gate.
"Hurry, Santa," called the reindeer.
"Or we will all be late."
One, two, three, four, five little reindeer.    (*Point to fingers again.*)
Santa said, "Please wait!
Wait for three more reindeer,
Then we will have eight."                        (*Hold up three fingers on the other hand.*)

(*Ask children to name the reindeer: Vixen, Comet, Cupid, Dancer, Dasher, Donner, Blitzen, and Prancer. Ask how many reindeer there are. What if we add Rudolph? Then how many?*)

—Author unknown

## Santa Claus

### Santa Fingerplay

Someone's peeping through my window,    (*Peek through fingers.*)
Tapping at my door,                      (*Make knocking motions.*)
Sliding down my chimney,                 (*Make sliding motions with hands.*)
Landing on the floor.                    (*Stamp feet.*)
He's filling all the stockings,          (*Make filling motions.*)
And looking at the tree.                 (*Turn head and widen eyes.*)
He has lots of presents,                 (*Pretend to count on fingers.*)
Some for you and some for me.            (*Point to others and to self.*)
I'm peeking 'round the doorway,          (*Peek around hand.*)
And oh, what do I see?                    (*Look surprised.*)
The jolly face of Santa                  (*Smile.*)
Peeking back at me!                       (*Peek through fingers.*)

—Author unknown

### Shy Santa

Isn't it the strangest thing
That Santa is so shy?                    (*Hide face with hands.*)
We can never, never catch him,           (*Make catching motion.*)
No matter how we try.                    (*Make running motion with arms.*)
It isn't any use to watch,               (*Hold hand over eyes and look around.*)
Because my mother said,
"Santa Claus will only come
When children are in bed."                (*Lay head on hands.*)

—Author unknown

### Christmas Eve

| | |
|---|---|
| When Santa fills my stocking, | *(Pretend to fill stocking.)* |
| I wish that I could peek. | *(Peek through fingers.)* |
| But Santa never, ever comes | *(Shake head "no.")* |
| Until I am fast asleep. | *(Rest cheek on folded hands.)* |

—Author unknown

### Here Is the Chimney

| | |
|---|---|
| Here is the chimney, | *(Make a fist and tuck in thumb.)* |
| Here is the top. | *(Put other hand over flat top of fist.)* |
| Open the lid, | *(Remove hand.)* |
| Out Santa will pop! | *(Pop up thumb.)* |

—Author unknown

### Santa Is Back

| | |
|---|---|
| Two merry blue eyes, | *(Point to eyes.)* |
| A cute little nose, | *(Point to nose.)* |
| A long snowy beard | *(Make motion as if stroking beard.)* |
| Two cheeks like a rose, | *(Point to cheeks.)* |
| A round, chubby form, | *(Rub tummy.)* |
| A big bulging sack. | *(Bend shoulders to show weight; hands hold sack.)* |
| Hurrah for old Santa! | *(Clap hands.)* |
| We're glad he's back! | |

—Author unknown

### Clap for Santa Claus

| | |
|---|---|
| O, clap, clap the hands, | |
| And sing with glee! | |
| For Christmas is coming | |
| And merry are we. | *(Clap hands on all four lines.)* |
| How swift o'er the snow | |
| The tiny reindeer | |
| Are trotting and bringing | |
| Good Santa Claus near. | *(On all lines, lock thumbs together and make walking motion with other fingers on lap to indicate reindeer and sleigh.)* |
| | |
| Our stockings we'll hang, | |
| And while we're asleep, | *(Point down with four fingers of one hand.)* |
| Then down through the chimney | |
| Will Santa Claus creep. | *(Put one fist on top of the other to represent chimney and put upper thumb inside of upper fist to represent Santa Claus going down the chimney.)* |
| | |
| He'll empty his pack, | |
| Then up he will come | *(Raise thumb from upper fist as Santa comes up the chimney.)* |
| And calling his reindeer | |
| Will haste away home. | *(Lock thumbs and walk fingers on lap again.)* |
| Then clap, clap the hands! | |
| And sing out with glee, | |
| For Christmas is coming, | |
| And merry are we! | *(Clap on all four lines.)* |

—Emilie Poulsson
*Fingerplays for Nursery and Kindergarten* (D. Lothrop Company, 1893)

### Santa and His Sleigh

| | |
|---|---|
| Here is old Santa, | *(Hold up right thumb.)* |
| Here is his sleigh. | *(Hold up left thumb.)* |
| There are the reindeer | |
| Which he drives away. | *(Show eight fingers.)* |
| Dasher, Dancer, Prancer, Vixen, | |
| Comet, Cupid, Donner, Blitzen. | *(Bob a finger at each name.)* |
| Ho, ho, ho, | |
| Away they all go! | *(Lock thumbs and run fingers in front and away.)* |

—Author unknown

### Santa Claus

| | |
|---|---|
| Down the chimney dear Santa crept, | *(Hold up left arm and creep fingers of right hand down it.)* |
| Into the room where the children slept. | *(Close eyes and put head on hands.)* |
| He saw their stockings hung in a row, | *(Suspend three fingers of left hand.)* |
| And he filled them with goodies from top to toe. | *(Make motion of filling stockings.)* |
| Although he counted them, one, two, three, | *(Count on three fingers.)* |
| The baby's stocking he couldn't see. | |
| "Ho, ho," said Santa, "That won't do!" | *(Hold tummy and laugh.)* |
| So he popped her present right into her shoe! | *(Cup left hand and pop in fingers of right hand.)* |

—Author unknown

## Trees

### A Little Christmas Tree

| | |
|---|---|
| A little Christmas tree, | *(Make a small triangle.)* |
| A bigger Christmas tree, | *(Form a larger triangle.)* |
| A great big Christmas tree. | *(Make large triangle with arms pointed.)* |
| Now let's count the trees: | |
| One, two, three. | *(Hold up three fingers.)* |
| Three trees I see. | |

—Author unknown

### Our Christmas Tree

| | |
|---|---|
| We went out looking for a Christmas tree, | *(Cup hand above eye and start walking.)* |
| We went to see what we could see. | *(Look all around.)* |
| The first tree we found was much too small, | *(Lower hand near floor.)* |
| The second tree we found was much too tall. | *(Raise hand up high.)* |
| The third tree we found was much too broad, | *(Spread arms out wide.)* |
| The fourth tree we found was thin as a rod. | *(Hold up one arm.)* |
| The fifth tree we found looked just about right, | *(Form outline of tree with hands.)* |
| So we chopped it down with all our might. | *(Pretend to chop down tree.)* |
| We took our tree home and set it straight, | *(Pretend to set up tree.)* |
| Everyone thought that it looked just great. | *(Clasp hands and smile.)* |
| Then we all joined hands and circled 'round | *(Form circle with others.)* |
| The beautiful tree that we had found. | |

—Author unknown

### Underneath the Christmas Tree

| | |
|---|---|
| Underneath the Christmas tree, | *(Place hands over head with fingertips together.)* |
| There were some presents for my family. | |
| The first one was a bouncing ball, | *(Jump up and down.)* |
| Then came a soldier who stands straight and tall. | *(Stand stiffly, then salute.)* |
| Next came a dancer who twirls on her toes. | *(Twirl on tiptoes.)* |
| Then came a train that chugs when it goes. | *(Move arms in a circular pumping motion; make whistle sound.)* |
| | |
| The last one made a funny sound, | *(Cup hand around ear.)* |
| Then it began to wiggle around. | *(Wiggle.)* |
| I opened it slowly. | *(Crouch down and pretend to open box.)* |
| What could it be? | *(Put hands out in questioning position.)* |
| Out jumped a puppy dog | *(Jump up.)* |
| And he licked me! | *(Lick air and make slurping sound.)* |

—Susan M. Dailey
*A Storytime Year* (Neal-Schuman, 2001, p. 346)

## Miscellaneous

### Five Little Spiders

| | |
|---|---|
| Five little spiders on Christmas Eve | *(Hold up five fingers.)* |
| Wanted to see the pretty Christmas tree. | *(Point to fingers in succession.)* |
| One said, "I'm afraid to go into the room. | |
| Two said, "We're afraid of the mop and the broom." | |
| Three said, "I hope someone won't step on us." | |
| Four said, "I hope we won't cause a fuss." | |
| Five said, "We just love pretty Christmas trees." | |
| All said, "We hope that nobody sees." | |
| So they crept through a hole in the wall that night, | *(Make creeping motion.)* |
| And the next morning, there was a wonderful sight. | *(Point to eyes.)* |
| For on Christmas Day all over the tree | |
| Were the shiniest webs that you ever did see! | *(Wiggle fingers in the air to indicate shininess.)* |

—Author unknown

### Presents

*(This rhyme would also work well as a flannel/Velcro-board presentation.)*

| | |
|---|---|
| See all the presents by the Christmas tree; | |
| Some for you, | *(Point to neighbor.)* |
| And some for me. | *(Point to self.)* |
| Long ones, | *(Show length with two hands spread far apart.)* |
| Tall ones, | *(Measure with hand from floor.)* |
| Short ones, too; | *(Measure shortness.)* |
| And here is a round one | *(Make circle with arms.)* |
| Wrapped in blue. | |
| Isn't it fun to look and see | |
| All of the presents by the Christmas tree? | *(Point hands to shape tree.)* |

—Author unknown

### Make a Plum Pudding

| | |
|---|---|
| Into a big bowl put the plums; | *(Drop imaginary plums in bowl.)* |
| Stir-about, stir-about, stir-about, stir! | *(Stir, as if with a big wooden spoon.)* |
| Next the good white flour comes; | *(Add flour.)* |
| Stir-about, stir-about, stir-about, stir! | *(Stir.)* |
| Add sugar, and peel, eggs, and spice; | *(Add new ingredients as they are mentioned.)* |
| Stir-about, stir-about, stir-about, stir! | *(Stir.)* |
| Mix them, and fix them, and cook them twice. | *(Stir, then place bowl in oven.)* |
| Then eat it up! Eat it up! Eat it up! | *(Pretend to eat.)* |
| YUMMMMMMM! | *(Rub stomach.)* |

—Based on an Old English rhyme

### The Toy Shop

| | |
|---|---|
| Here is the toy shop | *(Make roof overhead with hands for shop.)* |
| And happy are we, | |
| For this is the good toyman's shop that we see. | *(Point to eyes.)* |
| So many, many toys | |
| All in a row | *(Hands show expanse.)* |
| And bright colored tops | |
| That sing as they go. | *(Turn in place.)* |
| And here in a box | |
| Is a doll that can talk, | *(Keeping stiff, rock sideways from foot to foot.)* |
| And here is black wooly dog | |
| That can walk. | *(Stoop down to put hands on floor.)* |
| Just see this funny old | |
| Jack in the box, | *(Jump up.)* |
| Watch him pop out! | |
| Oh my! What a shock! | |
| Here is the counter | *(Extend arms, bend elbows, and put fingertips together to form a counter.)* |
| Piled high with toys, | *(Show height.)* |
| For you, little girls | |
| And you, little boys. | |
| Here is the toyman | *(Hold up one hand.)* |
| And here is his clerk | *(Hold up the other hand.)* |
| To sell all those toys, | |
| How hard they must work. | *(Wipe sweat from forehead.)* |
| Now gently close | |
| The toy shop door | *(Place hands slowly flat together in prayer position.)* |
| And look at the toys | |
| In the window once more. | *(Make window, thumbs touching and index fingers touching.)* |
| We hope, little toys, | |
| That some of you may | |
| Come straight to use | |
| On glad Christmas Day. | *(Shake head "yes.")* |

—Author unknown

### Little Jack Horner

| | |
|---|---|
| Little Jack Horner sat in a corner | |
| Eating his Christmas pie. | *(Make eating motion.)* |
| He stuck in his thumb | *(Pretend to stick thumb into pie.)* |
| And pulled out a plum, | *(Pull thumb out.)* |
| And said, "What a good boy am I!" | *(Point to self.)* |

—Adapted traditional rhyme

### Christmas Is Coming

| | |
|---|---|
| Christmas is coming. | |
| The geese are getting fat. | *(Pat tummy.)* |
| Please put a penny | |
| In the old man's hat. | *(Pretend to put a penny in one palm.)* |
| If you haven't got a penny, | |
| A ha'penny will do; | *(Pat palm.)* |
| If you haven't got a ha'penny, | |
| Then God bless you! | *(Point to a child.)* |

—Traditional rhyme

### I Can Be as Tall as a Christmas Tree

| | |
|---|---|
| I can be as tall as a Christmas tree, | *(Stand up tall on tiptoes, hands stretching high.)* |
| As round as Santa, | *(Extend hands in front, making a big round belly.)* |
| And as tiny as an elf. | *(Crouch down.)* |
| I can bend like a candy cane, | *(Bend sideways at waist, with head and arms tilted over.)* |
| Look like a star, | *(Spread arms and feet wide.)* |
| And prance like a reindeer! | *(Prance in place with front "hooves" in the air.)* |

—Author unknown

### Jack-in-the-Box

| | |
|---|---|
| Jack-in-the-box | |
| Sits so still; | *(Children hide faces in their arms.)* |
| Will you come out? | |
| Yes, I will! | *(Children sit up tall.)* |

—Author unknown

---

#### More Great Fingerplays

Visit TheBestKidsBooksite.com to find additional Christmas-related fingerplays, including "Elves in Santa's Shop," "Eight Little Reindeer," Santa's Little Reindeer," "Five Little Candy Canes," "Five Little Gingerbread Men," and "Gingerbread." Go to http://www.thebestkidsbooksite.com/fingerplay.cfm, click on the "Fingerplays" link, locate the title in the list, and click on the "Show Me" button at the bottom.

"Five Fat Reindeer," from page 12 of *Stories That Stick: Quick and Easy Storyboard Tales* by Valerie Marsh (Upstart, 2002). The reindeer patterns appear on page 59.

"I Heard Santa Say," from page 245 of *1001 Rhymes and Fingerplays for Working with Young Children*, compiled by the Totline Staff (Warren Publishing House, 1994).

"What Do I Hear?," an action rhyme, can be found online at http://www.susanmdailey.com/. Click on the "New Fingerplays" link on the left-hand side of the homepage, and then scroll down to the bottom of the page.

"Gingerbread People" and "Gingerbread," from page 75 of *Preschool Favorites: 35 Storytimes Kids Love* by Diane Briggs (American Library Association, 2007).

**Jack-in-the-Box**

Jack, Jack, down you go,                    *(Crouch down.)*
Down in your box, down so low.
Jack, Jack, there goes the top,
Quickly now, up you pop!                    *(Jump up in the air.)*

—Author unknown

## Musical Selections

*Holiday Magic* CD from Hap Palmer. Hap-Pal Music. ASIN: B00000DTD0. Check out "Jingle Bells/Jingle Song."

*A Holly Jolly Kids Christmas* CD. Hip-O Records. ASIN: B000W7Y1ZQ.

"I Hear Santa Claus," "We're All Going to the North Pole," "Santa's Out Tonight," and "Christmas Parade" from *Songs for All Seasons* by Geof Johnson. Available from http://www.songsforteaching.com/.

"It's the Holiday Time of Year (December)" and "Milton the Dancing Christmas Mouse" from *Rhythms and Rhymes for Special Times* by Jack Hartmann. Available from http://www.songsforteaching.com.

"Jingle Bells," "Jingle Bell Rock," and "SANTA" from *Happy Everything* by Dr. Jean. Melody House. ASIN: B000SM3N0E.

*60 Christmas Carols for Kids* (three-CD set of both classic and new Christmas songs). Madacy Kids. ASIN: B000AA4KMO.

"We Wish You a Merry Christmas" and "What a World We'd Have if Christmas Lasted All Year Long" from *Holiday Songs and Rhythms* by Hap Palmer. Available from http://www.songsforteaching.com/.

## Crafts

**Rudolph, the Shapely Reindeer**   The poem that goes with this craft appears on page 134 of *The Best of Holidays and Seasonal Celebrations—Issues 5–8, PreK–K*, edited by Donna Borst (Teaching and Learning Company, 2000). Basic shapes form Rudolph's head. It would be a great idea to have all of the pieces precut and perhaps placed in a baggie for each participant, along with a copy of the poem. The poem itself gives directions on how Rudolph's head is put together.

**Gingerbread Man**   This pattern is found on page 71 of *December Patterns, Projects, and Plans to Perk Up Early Learning Programs* by Imogene Forte (Incentive Publications, 1989). Reproduce the pattern on brown construction paper. Provide craft items to decorate your gingerbread man with—rickrack, buttons, craft foam shapes. You may wish to brush areas of the gingerbread man with glue and shake some cinnamon or gingerbread spice onto them to create a sweet-smelling craft!

**Santa Pattern**    This cute craft allows participants to color Santa's face and hat and then have fun adding cotton balls for his beard, mustache, and trim on his hat. Pattern appears on page 17 of *December Holidays, Preschool-Kindergarten*, edited by Angie Kutzer et al. (The Education Center, 2000).

**Jingle Bell Bracelets**    This is a super-simple craft that preschoolers will love! All you need are pipe cleaners/chenille sticks in Christmas colors, pony beads, and jingle bells! You can use either regular pipe cleaners/chenille sticks or the bumpy, fuller ones. To make the bracelet, simply thread pony beads and bells onto the pipe cleaner/stick. You may wish to thread on a bead, a bell, and a bead or any combination that is pleasing. When finished, form it into a circle by looping the ends of the pipe cleaner together. Participants may wish to twist two colors of cleaners/sticks together for a cool design.

**Trotting Reindeer**    The instructions and pattern for this simple craft can be found on pages 52–53 of *Arts and Crafts for All Seasons, Grades 1–3* (The Education Center, 1999). Patterns include head, body, and four legs, which are attached with brads so that they move to make the reindeer "trot."

**Elf Paper Craft**    The instructions and patterns for this craft can be found at http://dltk-holidays .com/xmas/mpaperelf.htm. Templates are available in both large and small sizes, but using the larger size would be easier for little hands. This craft makes an elf holding a candy cane.

**Santa's Beard**    This cute craft appears on page 45 of *Lollipops Magazine*, Issue 107 from 2001 (often available through interlibrary loan). Santa is colored, cut out, and the dotted lines on his beard are cut to fringe them. In the past, I have also added cotton balls, glued onto the brim and tassel of his hat.

**Advent/Christmas Chain**    You may wish to do this craft in late November to get the full effect. Have red and green paper strips available for participants. Allow them to glue or staple them together so that they have 25 in the chain. Attach a holiday shape (Ellison dies would work well for this) to the last one. Explain to them that they will take a link from the chain every day beginning December 1st. When they reach the last link, it will be Christmas Day!

**Craft Stick Reindeer**    Instructions for this easy craft appear on page 101 of *Christmas Parties: What Do I Do?* by Wilhelmina Ripple (Oakbrook Publishing House, 2000). Three craft sticks form the head. Add wiggle eyes, pom-pom nose, and pipe cleaner antlers, and you have a great Christmas tree ornament!

**Angel**    This cute angel would make a nice ornament for a Christmas tree or a table decoration. The pattern is found on page 11 of *Christmas Activities for Primary Children* by Rachelle Cracchiolo and Mary Dupuy Smith (Teacher Created Materials, 1985). Using the pattern, cut out the angel and color it. Glue two pieces of the angel's dress in the back to make it stand.

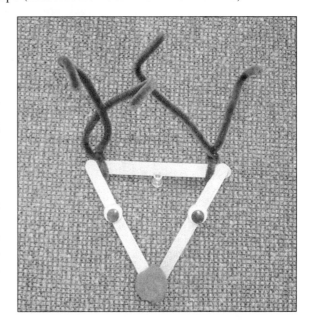

# Cinco de Mayo

*Similar to St. Patrick's Day, a day when you don't have to be Irish to celebrate, Cinco de Mayo is a day when you do not have to be Hispanic to enjoy the sights, sounds, and foods of this delightful holiday!*

## History

Cinco de Mayo is a Mexican holiday that is celebrated on May 5th. On that day in 1862, the Mexican peasants defeated French soldiers in the Battle of Puebla. The French had planned to capture Mexico City and take over the country. However, a ragtag group of Mexican peasants, although outnumbered, managed to defeat the French army with a combination of determination and spirit. (See "Cinco de Mayo Activities for Kids and Teachers" at http://www.kiddyhouse.com/Holidays/Cinco/.)

Many consider this holiday the most important in Mexican history, and as such, it is a national holiday. Today, flags and banners decorate streets, festive parties are held, and piñatas are usually the highlight of the celebrations for children. (See Jasmine Julia's *Multicultural Holidays: Share Our Celebration* [Teacher Created Materials, 1994].)

## Poetry

"Cinco de Mayo," from page 271 of *The Best of Holidays and Seasonal Celebrations—Issues 18–21, Grades 1–3*, edited by Donna Borst (Teaching and Learning Company, 2000).

---

**More Great Poetry**

"Come to the Puebla" and "A Dress for Cinco de Mayo" are available from Classroom Jr. at http://www.classroomjr.com/cinco-de-mayo-kids-poems/. Smaller versions of the poem pages appear at this site. Click on them for larger versions to print!

Check out *Fiesta! A Guide to Latino Celebrations* by Sherry Shahan (August House, 2009). This book has month-by-month rhymes that celebrate Latin traditions, including Cinco de Mayo.

---

## Books

Ada, Alma Flor. *Let Me Help!/Quiero Ayudar!* Children's Book Press, 2010. ISBN: 978-0892392322.
   After escaping from his cage, Perico, a parrot, sees his family preparing for a Cinco de Mayo celebration and wants to be part of the excitement.

Ada, Alma Flor, and F. Isabel Campoy. *Celebrate Cinco de Mayo with the Mexican Hat Dance.* Alfaguara Infantil, 2006. ISBN: 978-1598201307.
   As students prepare to celebrate Cinco de Mayo, they practice a Mexican dance and try their best not to step on the hat. This book includes an informative section about Cinco de Mayo.

Baca, Ana. *Tia's Tamales*. University of New Mexico Press, 2011. ISBN: 978-0826350268.
   Luz's school day is canceled because of snow, and her grandmother decides it's the perfect time to teach her to make tamales.

Cox, Judy. *Cinco de Mouse-O!* Holiday House, 2010. ISBN: 978-0823421947.
Mouse enjoys the sights and smells of Cinco de Mayo despite being trailed by a determined cat.

Doering, Amanda. *Cinco de Mayo: Day of Mexican Pride.* Capstone Press, 2006. ISBN: 978-0736869300.
Provides a brief description of what Cinco de Mayo is, how it started, and the ways people celebrate this cultural holiday.

Garcia, Aurora C. *Cinco de Mayo.* Heinemann Library, 2003. ISBN: 978-1403435014.
Part of the Holiday Histories series, this book discusses the holiday Cinco de Mayo, celebrated by Mexicans and Mexican-Americans in remembrance of the Mexican army's defeat of the French army in Puebla, Mexico, in 1862.

Guy, Ginger F. *Fiesta!* Greenwillow Books, 2003. ISBN: 978-0060092634.
Here's a counting and vocabulary book that, in a refreshing twist, teaches in English and Spanish.

Guy, Ginger F. *Siesta!* Greenwillow Books, 2005. ISBN: 978-0060560614.
Just as *Fiesta* introduces the reader to counting, this companion uses a bilingual approach to reinforce an understanding of colors.

Heiman, Sarah. *Mexico ABCs: A Book about the People and Places of Mexico.* Picture Window Books, 2002. ISBN: 978-1404800236.
An alphabetical explanation of the people, geography, animals, plants, history, and culture of Mexico.

Kelman, Marcy. *Handy Manny: "Sinko" de Mayo.* Disney Press, 2008. ISBN: 978-1423110217.
Today is Cinco de Mayo, and Mrs. Portillo is planning a big fiesta in honor of the special day. But her sink is broken and she can't wash the fruit for her homemade empanadas. It's Handy Manny to the rescue!

Krebs, Laurie. *Off We Go to Mexico.* Barefoot Books, 2008. ISBN: 978-1846861598.
This picture book follows a family as they swim in the ocean, traverse canyons, climb pyramids, and celebrate Independence Day.

Levy, Janice. *Celebrate! It's Cinco de Mayo!* Albert Whitman and Company, 2007. ISBN: 978-0807511770.
A very simple history of the holiday is interspersed with the story of a young boy celebrating Cinco de Mayo with his family.

McKissack, Fredrick. *Cinco de Mayo: Count and Celebrate!* Enslow Elementary, 2009. ISBN: 978-0766031047.
Children count from 1 to 10 as they learn about the history and customs of Cinco de Mayo.

Mora, Pat. *Listen to the Desert.* Turtleback, 2001. ISBN: 978-0613355339.
Onomatopoeia will hold young listeners in this simple bilingual story with lots of sound effects!

Owens, L.L. *Cinco de Mayo.* Magic Wagon, 2009. ISBN: 978-1602706026.
This Cultural Holidays book teaches young readers about the background, traditions, foods, and celebrations of the Mexican holiday. Easy-to-read text combines with colorful illustrations to provide entertainment and facts for even the youngest audience.

Ryan, Pam M. *Mice and Beans.* Scholastic, 2001. ISBN: 978-0439183031.
Rosa Maria is preparing for her granddaughter's birthday party while some mice also get ready for a party.

Sanger, Amy W. *Hola! Jalapeno.* Tricycle Press, 2002. ISBN: 978-1582460727.
From burritos to quesadillas to molé, lively mixed media and cut-paper collages take readers on a tour of their favorite foods of Mexico.

Tafolla, Carmen. *Fiesta Babies.* Tricycle Press, 2010. ISBN: 978-1582463193.
Short lines of bouncy, rhyming text describe how several adorable, chubby babies and toddlers participate in their local Hispanic celebration.

---

### Older Gems, or Titles Too Good to Pass Up

Aardema, Verna. *Borreguita and the Coyote.* Turtleback, 1998. ISBN: 978-0613046251.
  This classic trickster tale from Ayutla, Mexico, pits a gullible coyote against a fetchingly fluffy lamb.

Ehlert, Lois. *Cuckoo: A Mexican Folktale.* Sandpiper, 2000. ISBN: 978-0152024284.
  Beautifully illustrated and with text in both English and Spanish, Ehlert tells the story of the beautiful but lazy cuckoo bird.

Elya, Susan. *Eight Animals on the Town.* Putnam Juvenile, 2000. ISBN: 978-0399234378.
  This bright, clever picture book, in which 8 animals head into town for dinner, stands out because of its seamless instruction in Spanish and English, which is apparent in both the text and the illustrations. Also by this author: *Eight Animals Bake a Cake*, and *Eight Animals Play Ball*.

Hill, Sandi. *Celebrating Cinco de Mayo: Fiesta Time!* Creative Teaching Press, 1999. ISBN: 978-1574715729.
  Part of the Learn to Read, Read to Learn holiday series, this is an introduction to the holiday for young children.

Mora, Pat. *Uno, Dos, Tres: 1 2 3.* Clarion Books, 1996. ISBN: 978-0395672945.
  A rhyming text weaves together numbers from 1 to 10 in English and Spanish as two sisters gather presents from a Mexican market for Mama's birthday.

Schaefer, Lola. *Cinco de Mayo.* Capstone Press, 2000. ISBN: 978-0736806619.
  Simple text and photographs explain the history of Cinco de Mayo and how this commemoration of the victory of the Mexican army over the French army on May 5, 1862, is celebrated.

Soto, Gary. *Big Busy Mustache.* Knopf Books for Young Readers, 1998. ISBN: 978-0679880301.
  For his class's Cinco de Mayo play, Ricky, about six years old, turns down swords, pistols, a cape, a serape, a sombrero, and other accoutrements for a fake mustache so he can play the role of a victorious Mexican soldier.

---

Vamos, Samantha R. *The Cazuela That the Farm Maiden Stirred.* Charlesbridge Publishing, 2011. ISBN: 978-1580892421.

  As a farm girl prepares arroz con leche (rice pudding), all the animals want to help. Key English words change to Spanish as the recipe unfolds and the story reaches a delicious ending.

Worsham, Adria. *Max Celebrates Cinco de Mayo.* Picture Window Books, 2008. ISBN: 978-1404847596.

  Jose invites Max to his house to help celebrate Cinco de Mayo with his family.

## Activities ——————————————————————————————————————————

### Coloring Pages

Consult your favorite pattern books or holiday coloring books for pages to use as coloring sheets. Be sure to search online as well. There's lots of great stuff out there!

- Visit http://dulemba.com/index_ColoringPages.html for author and illustrator Elizabeth O. Dulemba's great collection of holiday coloring pages. While there, sign up for her Coloring Page Tuesdays e-mails.
- A Celebrate Cinco de Mayo coloring page appears on page 253 of *The Big All-Year Book of Holidays and Seasonal Celebrations: Preschool/Kindergarten, Issues 14–18*, edited by Donna Borst (Teaching and Learning Company, 2002).
- A Cinco de Mayo coloring page appears on page 7 of *May Patterns and Projects* (Newbridge Educational, 2000).

### Cut-and-Tell

**"Cinco de Mayo"**   This cut-and-tell story with patterns can be found on pages 30–31 of *Paper-Cutting Stories for Holidays and Special Events* by Valerie Marsh (Alleyside Press, 1994). The end result is two soldiers.

### Flannel/Velcro Board

**La Hormiguita**   The text and patterns for this Hispanic flannel/Velcro-board story can be found on pages 49–56 of *Multicultural Folktales: Stories to Tell Young Children* by Judy Sierra and Robert Kaminski (Oryx Press, 1991). A Spanish translation is also included. A variant can be found on pages 76–82 of *Multicultural Folktales for the Feltboard and Readers' Theatre* by Judy Sierra (Oryx Press, 1996).

**"The Flea"**   The text for this Mexican folktale can be found on pages 5–7 of *Horse Hooves and Chicken Feet: Mexican Folktales*, selected by Neil Philip (Clarion Books, 2003). It could be easily adapted into a flannel/Velcro-board presentation.

**"Little Lizard's Big Race"**   This Mexican folktale about a clever lizard who wins a race with Deer and Rabbit can be found on pages 144–145 of *The Best of Totline Stories* by Jean Warren (Totline Publications, 2000). It would make a great flannel/Velcro-board presentation.

### Games

**Cinco de Mayo Count**   This simple game can be found on page 260 of *The Best of Holidays and Seasonal Celebrations—Issues 9–13, PreK–K*, edited by Donna Borst (Teaching and Learning Company, 2001). Enlarge this page and then laminate for durability. The word "cinco" means five. In each of the outlined areas are flowers. Have participants count the number of flowers in each area. With a dry-erase marker, add in enough flowers to make five in all areas. Lamination allows you to use this activity year after year.

**Cinco de Mayo Match**   Use Ellison die cuts such as the sombrero, chili pepper, maraca, and perhaps a cactus in the large sizes to cut shapes (two of each) from different colors of construction paper. Laminate for durability and place flannel or Velcro to the backs of the pieces. To play the game, hand out shapes/colors to all participants, keeping one for yourself and placing it in a container or apron pocket. Once all participants have a color/shape, begin the game by bringing out, one by one, the colors/shapes that you have. Place them on the board and allow the participant who has the match to bring it up and place it next to its match. Continue until all shapes/colors have been matched.

### Miscellaneous

**Just Where Is Mexico, Anyway?**   Have a large map you can display and locate Mexico on. Show participants its proximity to the United States. Check out *It's a Big Big World Atlas*, edited by Angela Rahaniotis and Jane Brierly (Tormont Publications, 1994). The first pages of this large-format board book show a map of the world, so that participants can see where other continents/countries are in relation to the United States. The third page shows a large-format rendering of North America and Central America, including the United States, Canada, and Mexico. If you want smaller maps to display, check out the maps available on EnchantedLearning.com. Under their Zoom School area, there is a great color map that you can print out and laminate. Also pictured is the flag of Mexico, in color and in a black-and-white printable that participants can color. Enchanted Learning's site has a subscription price of $20.00 per year, but this price is very reasonable considering the access you get to all sorts of wonderful things to print and use in your programming.

**Piñata Fun!**   Have a piñata for participants to break open to end your storyhour session. Check out page 75 of *Read Me a Rhyme in Spanish and English* by Rose Zertuche Trevino (American Library

Association, 2009) for two traditional piñata songs that can be recited. Text is given in both Spanish and English.

**Mexican Hat Dance**   Obtain a large sombrero. These can easily be found online or from companies such as U.S. Toy (http://www.ustoy.com/). Play some music (choose from selections listed in the Musical Selections section) and have participants dance around the hat.

**Cinco de Mayo Parade**   Use the idea for this parade found on page 161 of *The Best of Totline Newsletter*, compiled by Jean Warren (Warren Publishing House, 1995). Use music from the Musical Selections section of this chapter. Get out those rhythm instruments, especially the tambourines and maracas or shakers!

**Latino Play Food**   Use this realia, available from Becker's School Supplies, to introduce Latin foods to your participants who may not be familiar with them. Set includes tamale, enchilada, tacos, quesadilla, empanada, rice, beans, chips, salsa, pepper, and flan. The cost for the set is $14.99. Contact information for Becker's School Supplies can be found in Appendix A at the end of this book.

**Cinco de Mayo Songs**   The piggyback songs (new songs sung to familiar tunes) "Mexican Hat Dance" and "Cinco de Mayo's Here" can be found on pages 142–143 of *The Best of Totline Magazine, Volume 2*, compiled by Gayle Bittinger (McGraw-Hill Children's Publishing, 2003).

**Cactus Ring-Toss Game**   Check out Oriental Trading Company's main catalog under the Fiesta! section to find this great game. The set (inflatable cactus and three rings) costs only $9.99. Contact information for Oriental Trading Company is located in Appendix A at the end of this book.

## Fingerplays ——————————————————————————————————————

### Come Join the Fun

*(This is sung to the tune of "Frere Jacques.")*

Cinco de Mayo, Cinco de Mayo,                *(Hold up five fingers for "cinco.")*
Is lots of fun for everyone.                 *(Spread arms to show expanse.)*
Many celebrations,
Loved ones get together.                     *(Hug self.)*
Come join the fun, with everyone!            *(Make beckoning motion with arm.)*

—Adapted from PreschoolEducation.com

---

**More Great Fingerplays**

"Here Is Our Pinata" is available online at PreschoolEducation.com at http://www.preschooleducation .com/cinco.shtml.

"Cinco de Mayo," from page 277 of *Celebrate the Seasons: The Best of Holidays and Seasonal Celebrations—Issues 9–12, PreK–3*, edited by Donna Borst (Teaching and Learning Company, 1998).

Check out MamaLisa.com. Click on the North American map on the homepage, and then Mexico on the country list on the right. This site has an extensive number of rhymes and songs with the English and Spanish words provided. There are MP3 and midi files for many of the rhymes and songs provided. If the songs are singing games, directions for play are also given.

Also check out *Diez Deditos: Ten Little Fingers and Other Play Rhymes and Action Songs from Latin America* by José-Luis Orozco (Penguin, 2002). This source will provide you with more than 30 bilingual rhymes for use in your program.

## Musical Selections

"Cinco de Mayo" from *All Year* by Intelli-Tunes. Available from http://www.songsforteaching.com/.

"Cinco de Mayo" by Greta Pedersen. Available from www.songsforteaching.com.

"Cinco de Mayo" from *Happy Everything* by Dr. Jean. Melody House. ASIN: B000SM3N0E.

"Cinco de Mayo" from *Holiday Songs and Rhythms* by Hap Palmer. Available from http://www.songsforteaching.com/.

"La Cucaracha" from *I Have a Dream: World Music for Children* by Daria. Dariamusic. ASIN: B000CA6YZS.

"Mexican Bean Bag Dance" from *Me and My Bean Bag*. Kimbo. ASIN: B0001Z8VYQ.

"Mexican Handclapping Song" from *Multicultural Children's Songs* by Ella Jenkins. Smithsonian Folkways. ASIN: B000001DOE.

"Mexican Hat Dance" from *Kidsongs: I Can Dance!* by The Kidsong Kids. ASIN: B00005LDPF.

"Mexico (La Cucaracha)" from *Multicultural Rhythm Stick Fun*. Kimbo. ASIN: B00000DARR.

"The Mexican Hat Dance" from *Mommy and Me: More Playgroup Favorites*. Concord Records. ASIN: B00012QMUE.

## Crafts

**Let's Make Tacos!** The instructions for this neat craft appear on page 268 of *The Best of Holidays and Seasonal Celebrations—Issues 1–4, PreK–K*, edited by Donna Borst and Janet Armbrust (Teaching and Learning Company, 1999). The base is a light brown or tan construction paper circle, cut to about a 6-inch diameter. The "ingredients" of the taco are made from construction paper shapes also listed. Explain to participants that this is a special food for the holiday.

**Mexican Hat** This cute craft makes a mini sombrero! Copy the pattern onto card stock for durability. Color and decorate as desired. Small jewels glued on would really make this hat sparkle! Add a construction-paper strip to the hat pattern and fit to the participant's head! Instructions and pattern appear on pages 26–27 of *May Patterns and Projects* (Newbridge Educational, 2000).

**Maraca Shake-Up**    This craft makes paper maracas to which beans are added. As with the Mexican Hat, I would copy the pattern onto card stock for durability. Each participant receives two patterns to color. A craft stick is glued inside the "handle" to strengthen it and the paper patterns are stapled together to hold the beans. Instructions and patterns for maracas appear on pages 29–30 of *May Patterns and Projects* (Newbridge Educational, 2000). Once your craft is completed, put on some Mexican music and shake away!

**Miniature Sombrero**    This simple mini sombrero is constructed from a paper circle and an individual egg carton section. Instructions appear on page 38 of *Daily Discoveries for May: Thematic Learning Activities for Every Day*, edited by Elizabeth C. Midgley (Teaching and Learning Company, 2006).

**Cinco de Mayo Sombrero**    Instructions and patterns appear on pages 67–68 of *Cut and Create! Holidays: Easy Step-by-Step Projects That Teach Scissor Skills* by Kim Rankin (Teaching and Learning Company, 1997). The patterns, reproduced on colorful paper, make a festive-looking Mexican hat!

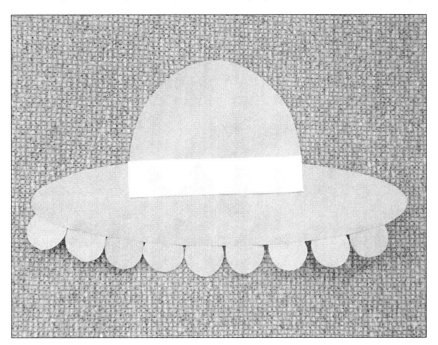

**Easy Donkey Piñata**    This mini piñata has a zip-to-seal sandwich bag as its base. Instructions and patterns appear on pages 42 and 44 of *Holiday and Seasonal Crafts from Recycled Materials* by Deborah Whitacre and Becky Radtke (Teaching and Learning Company, 1995). Filled with candy, this is a great take-home item for your participants.

**Maracas**    This craft turns plastic cups into maracas! If you find that plastic cups are too large for little hands, why not use small Dixie cups? Participants decorate the cups, insert beans, and tape the cups together! Instructions appear on page 17 of *The Mailbox 1998–1999 Yearbook: Kindergarten*, edited by Jan Trautman (The Education Center, 1999).

**Flag of Mexico**    Instructions are available from CraftsKaboose.com at http://crafts.kaboose .com/colors-of-mexico-flag.html. To make this flag, attach a half-sheet of paper to a dowel. Glue green, red, and white crepe paper (the colors of Mexico) to the paper.

**Cinco de Mayo Streamers**    You will need empty toilet paper rolls, glue, red or green craft sand, red, white, and green ribbon (half-inch-wide ribbon works well), and a hole punch. Paint the toilet paper roll with glue and roll in colored sand. Allow to dry. Use the hole punch to punch six equally spaced holes about a half-inch up from the bottom of the roll. Give each participant six lengths of ribbon (two of each color). Show them how to tie knots in one end of the ribbon and thread the other end through the hole. Let them wave their finished streamers around as they dance to Mexican music! (Idea courtesy of TheHolidayZone.com.)

**Jumping Bean Paintings**    You will need assorted dried beans, heavy white paper or card stock, one or more boxes with lid (slightly larger than paper), and assorted bright colors of paint. Give each participant a sheet of paper. Let them take turns putting their sheets of paper in the bottom of a paint box. Have them dip a handful of beans into various colors of paint then drop the beans into the box. Cover the box and shake for at least 30 seconds. Remove the finished painting and allow to dry. (Idea courtesy of TheHolidayZone.com.)

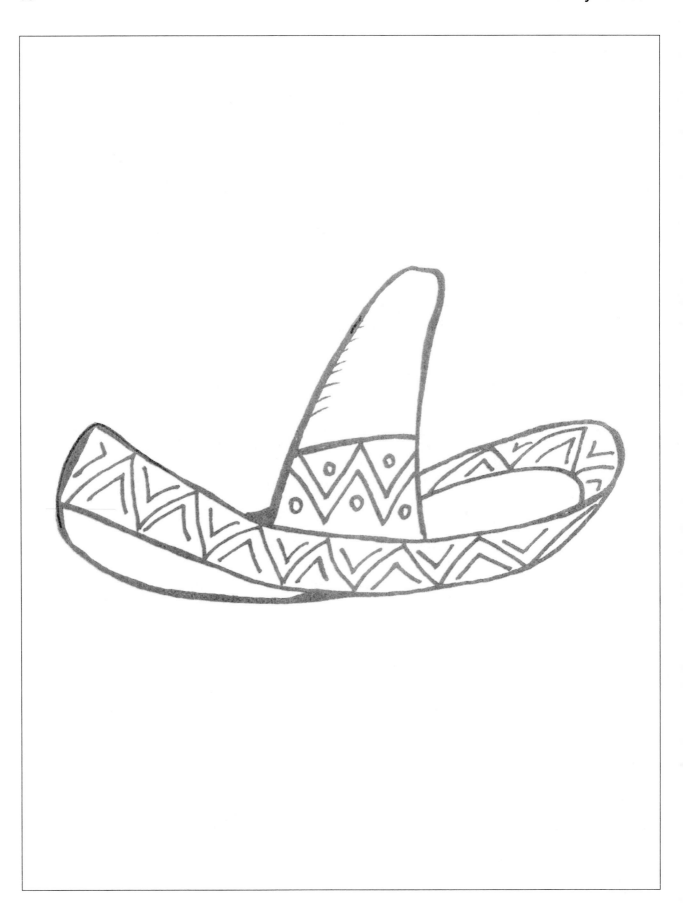

# Columbus Day

*Celebrate the life and history of this great explorer!*

## History

Columbus Day celebrates the arrival of Christopher Columbus in North America in 1492. Columbus left Spain, sailing three ships (the Nina, the Pinta, and the Santa Maria) that had been given to him by the king and queen. He headed West, hoping to reach India. After three weeks, the ship's crews became restless and wanted to return home. On October 10th, Columbus promised the crews that if they did not sight land within three days, they would turn back. After a voyage of 72 days, land was sighted. Columbus landed at the Caribbean islands off the southeastern coast of North America on October 12, 1492. He and his crew landed on an island called Guanahani. Columbus renamed this island San Salvador. Columbus thought he had reached Asia, and called this area the Indies and its native inhabitants Indians. He had not reached India, but instead discovered two new continents: North America and South America. (See "Christopher Columbus: Explorer" at http://www.enchanted learning.com/explorers/page/c/columbus.shtml.)

Columbus Day has been celebrated since the early 1900s, but was proclaimed a national holiday by President Franklin D. Roosevelt in 1937. Originally observed on October 12th, the United States Congress in 1971 made the second Monday in October Columbus Day.

## Poetry

"Columbus Day," from page 81 of *A School Year of Poems: 180 Favorites from Highlights* selected by Walter B. Barbe (Boyds Mills Press, 2005).

"In 1492," from MamaLisa.com at http://www.mamalisa.com/blog/columbus-day-poem-in-1492-columbus-sailed-the-ocean-blue/.

---

### More Great Poetry

Check out the Child Fun website at http://www.childfun.com/index.php/holidays/fall-holidays/columbus-day/627-columbus-day-songs-poems-a-fingerplays-columbus-day-crafts-and-activities.html. It lists several rhymes that could easily be turned into poems to use for your program.

---

## Books

Aloian, Molly. *Columbus Day*. Crabtree Publishing Company, 2010. ISBN: 978-0778747604.
   Part of the Celebrations in My World series, this title introduces the reader to Christopher Columbus and the importance of the Columbus Day holiday.

Bauer, Marion Dane. *Christopher Columbus*. Scholastic, 2010. ISBN: 978-0545142326.
   This book discusses how Christopher Columbus dreamed of adventure and discovery. He sailed across the ocean to an unknown land, and led the way that many others followed.

Kurtz, Jane. *What Columbus Found: It Was Orange, It Was Round*. Aladdin, 2007. ISBN: 978-0689867637.
   Part of Aladdin's Ready-to-Read series, an introduction to the voyage of Christopher Columbus.

---

**Older Gems, or Titles Too Good to Pass Up**

Adler, David A. *A Picture Book of Christopher Columbus*. Holiday House, 1991. ISBN: 978-0823408573.
A brief account of the life and accomplishments of Christopher Columbus.

Carpenter, Eric. *Young Christopher Columbus: Discoverer of New Worlds*. Troll Communications, 1991. ISBN: 978-0816725267.
An easy-to-read biography of the famous explorer who became one of the first people to sail to America.

DeRubertis, Barbara. *Columbus Day: Let's Meet Christopher Columbus*. Kane, 1992. ISBN: 978-0791519035.
Did you know that before embarking on his voyage of discovery to the New World, Christopher Columbus travelled the seas as a pirate? The sea battle from which Columbus was forced to swim to Portugal opens this easy-to-read book.

Gardeski, Christina M. *Columbus Day*. Children's Press, 2000. ISBN: 978-0516263106.
Part of the Rookie Read-About Holidays series, this volume introduces young readers to the explorer and the holiday.

Marzollo, Jean. *In 1492*. Scholastic, 1991. ISBN: 978-0590444132.
The author uses the familiar rhyme "In 1492, Columbus sailed the ocean blue" as an opening for a very simplified rhyming account of the famous voyages.

---

Leavitt, Arnie J. *Christopher Columbus*. Mitchell Lane Publishers, 2007. ISBN: 978-1584155782.
Part of the "What's So Great About…" series, an introduction to the life of Christopher Columbus.

Markle, Sandra. *Animals Christopher Columbus Saw: An Adventure in the New World*. Chronicle Books, 2008. ISBN: 978-0811849166.
While nothing about Christopher Columbus's journey was expected, he couldn't have imagined feasting on roast lizard.

## Activities

---

**Coloring Pages**

Consult your favorite pattern books for pages to use as coloring sheets. Be sure to search online as well. There's lots of great stuff out there!

- A Christopher Columbus coloring page appears on page 101 of *The Best of Holidays and Seasonal Celebrations—Issues 1–4, PreK–K*, edited by Donna Borst and Janet Armhurst (Teaching and Learning Company, 1999).
- Another great coloring page (a ship) appears on page 29 of *October Patterns, Projects, and Plans to Perk Up Early Learning Programs* by Imogene Forte (Incentive Publications, 1989).

---

### Draw-and-Tell

**"Christopher Columbus"**  This draw-and-tell story, which creates the three ships sailed by Columbus, is found on pages 103–104 of *Chalk in Hand: The Draw and Tell Book* by Phyllis Noe Pflomm (Scarecrow Press, 1986).

### Flannel/Velcro Board

**Columbus Day Flannel Board**  The instructions, story and flannel-board figure patterns appear on pages 17–21 of *October Patterns and Projects* (Newbridge Educational, 1999). The story could be adapted for the age of your group.

**Columbus Day Flannel Board/Activity**    Instructions, text, and flannel/Velcro-board patterns can be found on pages 189–192 of *Felt Board Fun for Everyday and Holidays* by Liz and Dick Wilmes (Building Blocks Publications, 1984).

**"Happy Columbus Day"**    This flannel board tells a simplified version of the story of Columbus's voyage. Participants can get into the swing of the story by pretending to row the boat. The story and patterns appear on pages 30–37 of *Felt Board Stories* by Liz and Dick Wilmes (Building Blocks Publications, 2001).

## Games

**Ship Matching Game**    The patterns for this matching game can be found on page 33 of *A Tisket A Tasket: Matching Games for Colors, Shapes, and Patterns* by Marilynn G. Barr (Monday Morning Books, 2006). These ships have different shapes in the centers. Reproduce the ships on different colors of paper so that participants will be matching not only colors but shapes. Laminate for durability and place Velcro on the back. Pass out one of a pair of colors/shapes to each of your participants, keeping the mate and placing it in a pocket or container. Play the game by pulling your colors/shapes out, one by one, and allowing participants to bring up the matches.

## Miscellaneous

**"Columbus Sailed the Sea" Action Song**    Words and motions to this song can be found on pages 257–259 of *Marmalade Days Fall: Complete Units for Busy Teachers of Young Children* by Carol Taylor Bond (Partner Press, 1987).

**Christopher Columbus Paper Dolls**    Dover Publications offered, to commemorate the 500th anniversary of Columbus's voyage, a set of nine paper dolls representing Christopher Columbus, his sons and sailing companions, and the king and queen of Spain. These would be a great addition to purchase, cut out, and then laminate and use for display purposes, as they depict authentic costumes of the era. Dover also offers a set of King Ferdinand and Queen Isabella in a separate book. Tom Tierney is the author of both books and they are available on Amazon.com.

***Columbus Discovers America Coloring Book***    This title, authored by Peter F. Copeland, was published by Dover Publications, and is currently available on Amazon.com. The coloring pages could be used as such, or they could be used for display purposes to explain the voyage of Columbus to participants. This book contains 41 drawings.

**Columbus Day Songs**
- The piggyback songs (new songs sung to old tunes) "Columbus," "Columbus Day," and "Columbus Sailed the Ocean Blue" can be found on pages 8–9 of *Holiday Piggyback Songs*, compiled by Jean Warren (Warren Publishing House, 1998).
- Also, the songs "He Sailed the Ocean Blue," "Columbus Sailed Three Ships," and "Christopher Columbus" can be found on page 314 of *The Best of Totline Newsletter*, compiled by Jean Warren (Warren Publishing House, 1995).

# Fingerplays ——————————————————————————————

### Columbus Sailed the Ocean

*(This rhyme can be sung to the tune of "Pop Goes the Weasel.")*

| | |
|---|---|
| All around the great wide world, | *(Spread arms to show expanse.)* |
| Columbus sailed the ocean. | *(Make arm go up and down in wave motion.)* |
| To prove the world was big and round. | *(Make large circle with arms.)* |
| That's real devotion! | *(Shake head "yes.")* |

—Adapted from PreschoolEducation.com

---

**More Great Fingerplays**

"Three Ships" and "Columbus and the Three Ships," from page 69 of *Rhymes for Learning Times* by Louise B. Scott (T.S. Denison and Company, 1983).

"Christopher Columbus" and "Columbus," from page 285 of *1001 Rhymes and Fingerplays for Working with Young Children*, compiled by the Totline Staff (Warren Publishing House, 1994).

---

## Musical Selections

"A Brand New World," "A Shorter Way to the Indies," "Let's Celebrate Columbus Day," and "The Nina, The Pinta, The Santa Maria" from *Christopher Columbus Rockin' Biography* by Ben Stiefel. Available from http://www.songsforteaching.com/.

"Columbus" from *All Year* by Intelli-Tunes. Available from http://www.songsforteaching.com/.

"Columbus Day" from *Happy Everything* by Dr. Jean. Melody House. ASIN: B000SM3N0E.

"Columbus Revisited" from *Friends* by Two of a Kind. Available from http://www.songsforteaching .com/.

"1492" from *Sun Sun Shine: Songs for Curious Children* by Nancy Schimmel. Available from http://www.songsforteaching.com/.

## Crafts

**Sail On, Columbus**    This cute craft uses the child's hand to form the ship. Instructions appear on page 74 of *Hand-Shaped Art* by Diane Bonica (Good Apple, 1989).

**Columbus Puppet**    The pattern for this great puppet can be found on page 28 of *The Best of Holidays and Seasonal Celebrations: Songs, Action Rhymes, and Fingerplays, PreK–3*, compiled by Ellen

Sussman (Teaching and Learning Company, 2000). Participants can color and cut out the puppet and then attach arms and legs with brads. They can then glue a paint stick or large craft stick to the back.

**Sailor Hat**     This craft makes a sailor hat like Columbus would have worn! A paper headband is stapled to the hat and fitted to the participant's head. I would duplicate the hat and feather patterns on card stock for durability. Instructions and hat pattern appear on pages 28–29, and the feather pattern appears on page 32, of *October Patterns and Projects* (Newbridge Educational, 1999).

**Columbus Day Ship**     Instructions and patterns appear on pages 16–17 of *Cut and Create! Holidays: Easy Step-by-Step Projects That Teach Scissor Skills* by Kim Rankin (Teaching and Learning Company, 1997). Simple shapes form a ship with sails.

**Ship Pockets**     Instructions and patterns for this craft can be found on page 147 of *International Fall Festivals* by Marilynn G. Barr (Good Apple, 1994). This craft makes a cute sailing ship from a paper plate.

# Diwali/Divali

*What a great opportunity to learn the history and customs behind this holiday from India!*

## History

Diwali (sometimes spelled Divali) is celebrated by Hindu people in India and around the world. This holiday takes place in either late October or early November. It is considered the Hindu New Year. It is the most popular festival of the year for Hindus.

The word Diwali (or Divali) means a garland or row of lights and small lamps such as those that line roads and other areas to welcome Lakshmi Mata, the goddess of light, wealth, and good fortune. Some people may even place these lighted lamps in rivers to see if they float to the other side before sinking, which is a sure sign of future good fortune. However, the most well-known history behind the holiday tells of the return of Lord Rama from exile after he has defeated evil demons.

The celebration of Diwali lasts for five days. The first day, Dhanteras, is used to shop and prepare for the celebration. Houses are cleaned to welcome the New Year and windows are opened so that Lakshmi Mata can come in. The second day, Naraka Chaturdashi, marks the beginning of the lighting of the lamps. Tradition says that Lakshmi Mata cannot enter a house that is not lit, so every home burns special clay lamps, called diyas, to light the way for the goddess. Firecrackers are also set off to celebrate the defeat of evil spirits and to ward them off. The third day, Diwali itself, is the center of the celebration. The fourth day, Annakut, is marked by feasts. The fifth and last day, Bhayiduj, is reserved for brothers and sisters. Brothers give their sisters special presents for cooking and caring for them.

During the celebration, children may have days off from school. Gifts are given and holiday foods are prepared and exchanged. New clothing and jewelry is worn. Parties are held and dice and card games are played.

Because India is comprised of many castes and regions of India, the holiday can be celebrated in many ways. (See Reenita Malhotra Hora's "Diwali, India's Festival of Light" at http://www.nationalgeographic .com/kids/stories/peopleplaces/diwali.)

## Poetry

"Diwali by Golly," from page 102 of *Every Day's A Holiday: Amusing Rhymes for Happy Times* by Dean Koontz (HarperCollins, 2003).

"Ganesha, Ganesha," from pages 40–41 of *Eric Carle's Dragons, Dragons and Other Creatures That Never Were* compiled by Laura Whipple (Philomel Books, 1991).

"Happy Diwali," available from http://www.theholidayspot.com/diwali/poems.htm.

## Books

Brown, Marcia. *Once a Mouse: A Fable Cut in Wood*. Aladdin, 1989. ISBN: 978-0689713439.
This Caldecott Award winner is a classic tale from India about a hermit who can use magic to change a small mouse into a cat, a dog, and a majestic tiger!

Cleveland, Rob. *The Drum: A Folktale from India*. August House, 2006. ISBN: 978-0874838022.
A poor boy's dream of having a drum takes him on an unlikely path. He meets several people that guide him along the way. In time, he learns to make his own magic in this world.

Ganeri, Anita. *The Divali Story*. Evans Brothers, 2003. ISBN: 978-0237524715.
This is an illustrated children's guide to the Hindu festival of Divali.

Gardeski, Christina. *Diwali*. Children's Press, 2001. ISBN: 978-0516223728.
This title in the Rookie Read-About Holidays series offers a very basic introduction to the festival of light that marks the Hindu New Year.

Jordan, Denise M. *Diwali*. Heinemann Library, 2002. ISBN: 978-1588107367.
A simple introduction to the holiday.

Kadodwala, Dilip. *Divali*. Evans Brothers, 2011. ISBN: 978-0237541200.
Showing how the festival is marked and its cultural and religious importance to the communities involved, this title explores and celebrates all things Divali with comprehensive text and gorgeous full-color photographs.

Kumar, Manisha. *Diwali: A Festival of Lights and Fun*. MeeraMasi, 2006. ISBN: 978-0977364572.
This joyous book explores the merriment of Diwali, one of India's most special festivals now celebrated worldwide, with a charming family who brings the festival of lights to life.

Makhijani, Pooja. *Mama's Saris*. Little, Brown Books for Young Readers, 2007. ISBN: 978-0316011051.
On her seventh birthday, the narrator helps her mother select a sari to put on for her party, and they recall the various occasions for which she wore each beautiful outfit.

McDermott, Gerald. *Monkey: A Trickster Tale from India*. Harcourt Children's Books, 2011. ISBN: 978-0152165963.
Monkey is hungry for the delicious mangoes on the island in the river, but he can't swim! How will he get there?

Preszler, June. *Diwali: Hindu Festival of Lights*. Capstone Press, 2006. ISBN: 978-0736863957.
This book describes the history and meaning of Diwali and how the holiday is celebrated today.

Sandhu, Rupi K. *Twinkling Lights, Diwali Nights*. Trafford Publishing, 2008. ISBN: 978-1425183332.
This dual-language (English/Punjabi) picture book is about Diwali, one of the most important festivals in India.

Senker, Cath. *Divali*. Franklin Watts, Ltd., 2009. ISBN: 978-0749690601.
This book introduces the reader to the festival of Divali and explores how one child and her family celebrate it.

---

### Older Gems, or Titles Too Good to Pass Up

Demi. *One Grain of Rice*. Scholastic, 1997. ISBN: 978-0590939980.
In this folktale from India, a resourceful village girl outsmarts a greedy raja, turning a reward of one grain of rice into a feast for a hungry nation.

Gilmore, Rachna. *Lights for Gita*. Tilbury House Publishers, 1995. ISBN: 978-0884481508.
In this picture book first published in Canada, an immigrant child from India celebrates the Hindu holiday of Divali for the first time in her new home.

Pandva, Meenal. *Here Comes Diwali: The Festival of Lights*. MeeRa Publications, 2000. ISBN: 978-0963553935.
Through the eyes of a young boy, readers learn about the preparations for and celebrations of this five-day holiday.

Torpie, Kate. *Diwali*. Crabtree Publishing Company, 2008. ISBN: 978-0778742821.

> The "festival of lights" is one of the most popular festivals on the Hindu calendar. Like most Hindu festivals, Diwali celebrates the triumph of good over evil. Part of the Celebrations in My World series.

Trueit, Trudi S. *Diwali*. Children's Press, 2006. ISBN: 978-0531118351.

> Part of the Rookie Read-About Holidays series, this book is a simple introduction to the holiday.

Zucker, Jonny. *Lighting a Lamp: A Diwali Story*. Barron's Education Series, 2004. ISBN: 978-0764126703.

> This book is a simple and delightful introduction to the Hindu festival of Diwali—suitable for the very youngest child.

## Activities

---

### Coloring Pages

Consult your favorite pattern books for pages to use as coloring sheets. Be sure to search online as well. There's lots of great stuff out there!

- The Activity Village website has a number of coloring pages for this holiday; go to http://www.activityvillage.co.uk/diwali_colouring.htm. Included on this site is a link to a number of wonderful rangoli designs, colorful geometric designs made near the entrance of Indian homes to welcome visitors to the house. These designs, drawn during Diwali to welcome the goddess Lakshmi, could also be used as coloring pages.
- Also, a quick scan of your favorite pattern books will uncover suitable patterns for animals such as elephants, tigers, or peacocks that could be used as simple coloring pages.
- Pages 161 and 162 of *Festivals Together: A Guide to Multicultural Celebration* by Sue Fitzjohn et al. (Hawthorn Press, 1993) have some great designs that could be slightly enlarged for great coloring pages.

---

### Flannel/Velcro Board

**"A Drum"**     This story from India, which could be easily adapted for telling on the flannel/Velcro board, can be found on pages 37–40 of *Tales Alive! Ten Multicultural Folktales with Activities*, retold by Susan Milord (Williamson Publishing, 1995).

**"The Rabbit and the Tiger"**     Although this tale is Vietnamese in nature, I think it would work well for Diwali, since tigers and snakes are animals that are also found in the country of India, also part of the Asian continent. In this tale, Tiger is fooled by Rabbit, who uses his brain instead of strength. The text for the story and the patterns are found on pages 24–27 of *Multicultural Folktales for the Feltboard and Readers' Theatre* by Judy Sierra (Oryx Press, 1996).

**"Kanchil and the Crocodile: An Indonesian Folktale"**     Kanchil is the Indonesian name for the mouse deer, a small animal that looks like a deer but is much smaller. In this tale, the Kanchil outwits Crocodile and saves Water Buffalo from being his dinner. The text and patterns for the story are found on pages 30–34 of *Multicultural Folktales for the Feltboard and Readers' Theatre* by Judy Sierra (Oryx Press, 1996).

**"The Bird and Her Babies: A Sri Lankan Folktale"**     This circular or chain tale about a mother bird who needs help getting her babies out of a tree can be found on pages 54–59 of *Multicultural Folktales for the Feltboard and Readers' Theatre* by Judy Sierra (Oryx Press, 1996).

**"Crocodile! Crocodile!"; "Crocodile Hunts for the Monkey"**     These two folktales from India can be found in *Crocodile! Crocodile! Stories Told Around the World* by Barbara Baumgartner (Dorling

Kindersley, 1994) on pages 8–12 and 13–15, respectively. Notes at the back of the book advise readers on how to turn the stories into puppet plays, but I believe that the stories would also work well as flannel/Velcro-board stories.

## Miscellaneous

**Just Where Is India, Anyway?**    Have a map of the area, and locate the country of India on it. Check out *It's a Big Big World Atlas*, edited by Angela Rahaniotis and Jane Brierly (Tormont Publications, 1994). The first pages of this large-format board book show a map of the world, so participants can see where other continents/countries are in relation to the United States. Pages 9–10 show where India is located, along with surrounding countries on the continent of Asia. The site EnchantedLearning.com has some great outline maps, as well as a color printout of the country's flag. There is also a large outlined flag of India that can be printed out and colored. This site does require a subscription, which is $20.00 per year. This fee is pretty nominal, considering the access you gain to all of the available printables.

**"Sparrow and Crow"**    This folktale from India concerns a pearl that Sparrow wants but Crow has taken. Sparrow calls upon 11 different characters to help him get the pearl back. The tale is found on pages 70–78 of *15 Easy Folktale Fingerplays* by Bill Gordh (Scholastic Professional Books, 1997).

**Learn Some Hindi**    In India, people in different areas speak different languages, but there is a national language called Hindi. Check out Akhlesh.com (http://www.akhlesh.com/); on the left-hand side, click on the "Conversation" button and then "Kidspeak" under the drop-down menu to find simple phrases that you might want to introduce to your program participants. Scroll down further and click on the numbers, and you will see how to count in Hindi.

## Fingerplays

### Here Is My Light

| | |
|---|---|
| Here is my light | *(Cup hands, pretending to hold light.)* |
| Let it shine, shine, shine. | |
| Here is my diya | *(Cup hands, pretending to hold light.)* |
| Let it shine, shine, shine. | |
| Let it shine up, up, up in the sky. | *(Hold light up.)* |
| Let it shine down, down, down near the ground. | *(Hold light down.)* |
| Here are my lights, they shine bright, bright, bright | *(Cup hands, holding light in front of body.)* |
| All around the world these nights. | *(Make large circle with arms, representing the Earth.)* |

—Kathy Buchsbaum

### These Are My Clothes

| | |
|---|---|
| This is my shirt, so nice and new. | *(Point to shirt.)* |
| I see you have a new one, too! | *(Point to eyes and shake head "yes.")* |
| These are my pants, so nice and new. | *(Point to pants.)* |
| I see you have new ones, too! | *(Point to eyes and shake head "yes.")* |
| These are my shoes, so nice and new. | *(Point to shoes.)* |
| I see you have new ones, too! | *(Point to eyes and shake head "yes.")* |
| My clothes are new this special day | *(With hands on either side of body, starting at head, move downward to point to clothes.)* |
| It is fun to celebrate this way! | *(Shake head "yes.")* |

—Kathy Buchsbaum

---

**More Great Fingerplays**

"Little Lamps," available from http://www.preschoolexpress.com/holiday_station02/holiday_station_sep02.shtml.

"Tiger, Tiger," from page 90 of *Once Upon a Childhood: Fingerplays, Action Rhymes, and Fun Times for the Very Young* by Dolores C. Chupela (Scarecrow Press, 1998).

Check out the selection of nursery rhymes from India on MamaLisa.com. Click on the map of Asia under the Kid Songs from Around the World heading. Then click on India in the list of countries. The page that follows contains links to rhymes in Hindi, Malayalam, Tamil, and Telugu. These might make a nice addition to your Diwali program!

---

### Diwali

| | |
|---|---|
| Time to clean! | *(Point to wrist, indicating watch.)* |
| Sweep, sweep, sweep! | *(Make motion of using a broom.)* |
| Wear new things! | *(Point to clothes.)* |
| Neat, neat, neat! | *(Pretend to iron.)* |
| Open windows! | *(Make motion of opening windows.)* |
| Up, up, up! | |
| Let Lakshmi Mata in! | *(Make beckoning motion.)* |
| Let the holiday begin! | *(Clap in rhythm to the last line.)* |

—Kathy Buchsbaum

## Musical Selections ——————————————————————

*Songs and Dances of India* CD. Available from Music in Motion. http://www.musicinmotion.com/.

*Traditional Songs and Dances of India: Ragas with Sitar* CD by the India National Sitar Ensemble. Legacy International. ASIN: B000002NSV.

## Crafts ——————————————————————

**Diya Craft**　The instructions for this craft can be found at http://www.activityvillage.co.uk/diya_craft_1.htm. Fast-drying clay is shaped around the bottom of a cup to form a bowl. A very similar craft can be found on page 42 of *Crafts from World Cultures: Easy-to-Make Multicultural Art Activities* by Janice Veith and Anne Weber (Monday Morning Books, 1995). Also, if you live in an area that has an Indian population and there is a store at which you can purchase diyas cheaply, why not go that route? Diyas can be easily decorated with paint, glitter, etc.

**Flower Garland**　In parts of India, it is customary to wear a necklace of fresh flowers as part of the Diwali celebration. This craft requires a length of yarn, colorful drinking straws cut into pieces, Ellison flower dies with a small circle punched in the middle, and large plastic needles (available at craft stores). Make sure that

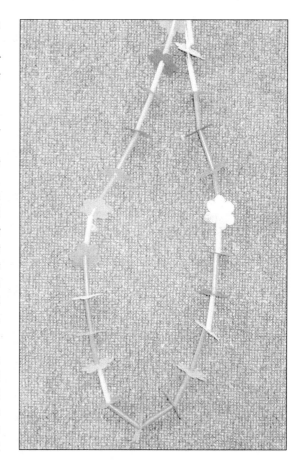

the length of yarn is long enough to make a nice necklace. Take one piece of drinking straw and tie it onto one end of the yarn. Thread the opposite end through the plastic needle. This will prevent the straws and flowers that will be threaded onto the yarn from sliding off. Have flower shapes cut from different colors of construction paper. Alternately thread pieces of drinking straws and flower shapes onto the yarn. Leave enough yarn to tie off to make the necklace.

**Doorstep Decorations**    This idea comes from Jean Warren's Preschool Express website (http://preschoolexpress.com/holiday_station02/holiday_station_sep02.shtml). During Diwali, good-luck doorstep decorations are made with colored powders. Provide participants with large pieces of white construction paper and colored chalk. Allow them to draw free-form designs on paper.

**Mosaic Candles**    Instructions for these candles can be found at http://www.kinderart.com/seasons/mosaiccandles.shtml. While the creators of the site rate this craft for ages 6+, I can certainly see preschoolers doing this with adult help. The base is a toilet paper roll to which small squares (to represent the mosaic) and foam or crepe paper heart shapes (to represent the flames) are added.

**Dipa Lamps**    Patterns for this simple craft appear on page 35 of *International Winter Festivals* by Marilynn G. Barr (Good Apple, 1993). This craft makes a small diya lamp.

**Diwali Flower Garlands**    Patterns and instructions for this craft appear on page 38 of *International Winter Festivals* by Marilynn G. Barr (Good Apple, 1993). Flower patterns are glued onto a crepe paper streamer.

**Diwali Flower Vase Place Mat**    Instructions and patterns for this craft appear on pages 38–39 of *International Winter Festivals* by Marilynn G. Barr (Good Apple, 1993). The flower patterns from the Diwali Flower Garlands craft serve double duty when they are placed in the vase, which is glued onto a grocery bag mat.

**Mehndi Design**    Check out the Mehndi Hand Design under Crafts in this book's "Ramadan" chapter.

**Bengal Tiger Craft**    Instructions for this simple craft can be found on page 34 of *World Holidays: Art and Movement Activities for Hands, Fingers, Feet, and Toes* by Carol Hauswald and Alice Maskowski (Monday Morning Books, 1996). Patterns for the tiger's head and tail can be found on pages 39–40. They are glued to a small brown paper bag, as are traced patterns of the participant's feet. The bag is stuffed lightly and stapled shut.

**Paper Plate Tiger Mask**    Instructions for this craft can be found on page 91 of *Once Upon a Childhood: Fingerplays, Action Rhymes, and Fun Times for the Very Young* by Dolores C. Chupela (Scarecrow Press, 1998). The mask pattern is glued onto a paper plate. A craft stick or paint stick can be added so that the participant can hold the mask in front of his or her face.

**Elephant**    This elephant, created by the participant's handprint, is found on pages 66–67 of *Happy*

*Hands and Feet: Art Projects for Young Children* by Cindy Mitchell (Incentive Publications, 1989). A similar craft can also be found on page 21 of *March Arts and Crafts: A Month of Arts and Crafts at Your Fingertips, Preschool-Kindergarten*, edited by Mackie Rhodes and Jan Trautman (The Education Center, 2000).

**Tiger Clothespin Animal**     This craft, for which the legs of the tiger are clip clothespins, is found on pages 5 (instructions) and 61 (patterns) of *Paper Crafts: Patterns for Cut-and-Paste Projects* by Marilynn G. Barr (Monday Morning Books, 1989).

# Easter

*This holiday offers many options for programming at your library: rabbits, chicks, Easter eggs—even jelly beans!*

## History

Easter always falls on the first Sunday after the first full moon of spring.

Easter is an extremely important holiday for many people around the world. It is the holiest day of the Christian calendar. Christians believe Jesus Christ rose from the dead on this day. Many others celebrate Easter as the beginning of the spring season and the beginning of new life, as the earth brings forth new life after the cold of winter. Many animals and other items are associated with Easter: rabbits, eggs, lilies, chocolate bunnies, jelly beans, Easter bonnets, ducks, chicks, and, of course, the Easter Bunny!

The Easter Bunny may have had its origins in relation to the goddess Eostre, the German goddess of spring. Rabbits were sacred to her, as were eggs. The Easter egg is a traditional symbol in many parts of the world. However, they are not always brought by a rabbit. Doves, cranes, or foxes sometimes deliver the eggs! (See Edna Barth's *Lilies, Rabbits, and Painted Eggs: The Story of the Easter Symbols* [Houghton Mifflin/Clarion Books, 1970].)

## Poetry

"Bunny Riddle," a cute poem for bunny-themed storytimes, from page 106 of *A Child's Seasonal Treasury*, compiled and written by Betty Jones (Tricycle Press, 1996).

"Easter Eggs," a poem that can also be done as an action rhyme, from page 98 in *The Best of Holidays and Seasonal Celebrations: Songs, Action Rhymes, and Fingerplays, PreK–3*, edited by Ellen Sussman (Teaching and Learning Company, 2000).

"Easter Morning" and "Sing a Song of Easter," from page 92 of *A School Year of Poems: 180 Favorites from Highlights*, selected by Walter B. Barbe (Boyds Mills Press, 2005).

"From the Easter Bunny," "Bunny Ears," "Easter Worm," and "Easter Clothes" appear on pages 129–130 of *Fingerplays and Rhymes: For Always and Sometimes* by Terry Lynne Graham (Humanics Ltd. Partners, 1987).

"Hildy," a great poem about a hen who lays Easter eggs, from page 232 in *The Best of Holidays and Seasonal Celebrations—Issues 5–8, PreK–3*, edited by Donna Borst (Teaching and Learning Company, 1997).

"Jelly Beans," a poem perfect for jelly bean-themed storytimes, by Aileen Fisher, from page 78 of *The Poetry Break: An Annotated Anthology with Ideas for Introducing Children to Poetry* by Caroline Feller Bauer (H.W. Wilson, 1995).

## Books

Brett, Jan. *The Easter Egg*. Putnam Juvenile, 2010. ISBN: 978-0399252389.
Hoppi, a small but industrious bunny, takes a tour of the woods and sees how other rabbits are preparing fancily decorated eggs in the hopes of being chosen to assist the official Easter Rabbit.

Carter, David A. *Easter Bugs: A Springtime Pop-Up*. Little Simon, 2001. ISBN: 978-0689818622.
  The author gussies up his tried-and-true format in this pert pop-up, this time concealing his whimsical "bugs" behind Easter egg-shaped flaps.

Chaconas, Dori. *Looking for Easter*. Albert Whitman and Company, 2011. ISBN: 978-0807547502.
  Little Bunny can sense something new in the air, and it smells like sunshine and warm breezes.

deGroat, Diane. *Lola Hides the Eggs*. HarperFestival, 2005. ISBN: 978-0060583903.
  This Easter, Lola (little sister of Gilbert) is putting on her bunny ears to hide eggs for her family. Soon all the eggs are found—except one. Where could it be?

dePaola, Tomie. *My First Easter*. Grosset and Dunlap, 2008. ISBN: 978-0448447902.
  The importance of both family and sharing are emphasized in this board book with simple descriptions about Easter celebrations.

Dunrea, Olivier. *Ollie's Easter Eggs*. Houghton Mifflin Books for Children, 2010. ISBN: 978-0618532438.
  Gossie, Gertie, BooBoo, and Peedie are all dyeing Easter eggs. Ollie wants Easter eggs too, and he has a plan for how he'll get them!

Grambling, Lois G. *Here Comes T. Rex Cottontail*. HarperCollins, 2010. ISBN: 978-0060531348.
  The Easter Bunny is sick and can't deliver his Easter eggs. In comes T. Rex to save the day! He wobbles when he hops and completely ruins the eggs for the town's children. Can Easter be saved?

Hill, Eric. *Spot's Easter Surprise*. Putnam Juvenile, 2007. ISBN: 978-0399247439.
  Spot loves spending time at his grandparents' house. At Easter, he and his friends like to go there to hunt for Easter eggs.

Numeroff, Laura. *Happy Easter, Mouse!* Balzer & Bray, 2010. ISBN: 978-0694014224.
  Join Mouse as he tries to figure out who's leaving Easter eggs all over his house!

O'Conner, Jane. *Fancy Nancy's Elegant Easter*. HarperFestival, 2009. ISBN: 978-0061703799.
  Nancy prepares an elegant Easter affair in this fancy new lift-the-flap book!

Potter, Beatrix. *Happy Easter, Peter!* Frederick Warne and Company, 2011. ISBN: 978-0723266686.
  Peter Rabbit has a huge colorful basket of eggs to hand out to his friends, but he has to find them first!

Rey, H.A. *Happy Easter, Curious George*. Houghton Mifflin, 2010. ISBN: 978-0547048253.
  When the man in the yellow hat takes Curious George to the park on Easter, the mischievous little monkey can't wait to pet the rabbits, dye eggs, and take part in an Easter egg hunt!

Schulman, Janet. *10 Easter Egg Hunters: A Holiday Counting Book*. Knopf Books for Young Readers, 2011. ISBN: 978-0375867873.
  The adorable kids from the bestseller *10 Trick-or-Treaters* are back, and they're counting their way to Easter!

Smath, Jerry. *The Best Easter Eggs Ever!* Cartwheel Books, 2003. ISBN: 978-0439443210.
  Easter Bunny has always painted all the Easter eggs himself, but this year his eyes are tired! So he holds an Easter Egg Painting Contest among his helpers to find the best new design.

Spurr, Elizabeth. *Sparkling Easter Surprise*. Sterling, 2011. ISBN: 978-1402771415.
  Shiny ribbons and foil-wrapped chocolates, a big glittery egg filled with candy and toys, and sparkling springtime flowers—this book offers lots of treats for one and all!

Stalder, Paivi. *Ernest's First Easter*. North-South Books, 2010. ISBN: 978-0735822412.
  As an Easter Bunny in training, Ernest is under a lot of pressure! Can he find his way to Tommy's house? Will he hide the eggs in the perfect spot without breaking any?

Trasler, Janee. *Benny's Chocolate Bunny*. Cartwheel Books, 2011. ISBN: 978-0545261272.
  Everyone in the class gets an Easter treat and Benny gets a big chocolate bunny! The other kids eat their candy, but Benny adopts the bunny as his friend.

---

**Older Gems, or Titles Too Good to Pass Up**

Ashley, Jill. *What Can It Be? Riddles about Easter.* Silver Press, 1991. ISBN: 978-0671727265.
A collection of rhyming riddles describing various aspects of Easter and its celebration.

Auch, Mary Jane. *The Easter Egg Farm.* Holiday House, 1992. ISBN: 978-0823409174.
Mrs. Pennywort's hen, Pauline, claims she's "just different" because she can't lay eggs when she's pressured. When she does produce one, it resembles whatever was in sight at the moment!

Freeman, Don. *Corduroy's Easter Party.* Penguin Putnam, 2000. ISBN: 978-0448421542.
As he and his friends get ready to celebrate Easter with a special party, Corduroy wonders if the Easter Bunny is real.

Kunhardt. Edith. *Danny and the Easter Egg.* Greenwillow Books, 1989. ISBN: 978-0688080367.
Danny colors Easter eggs with his friends then hunts for them after they are hidden by the Easter Bunny, and gives a special one to his grandmother.

Mayer, Mercer. *Happy Easter, Little Critter.* Golden Books, 1988. ISBN: 978-0307617238.
Mercer Mayer's popular Little Critter experiences all the joys of Easter, despite his little sister constantly tugging at his sleeve.

Moncure, Jane B. *Word Bird's Easter Words.* Child's World, 1987. ISBN: 978-0516065750.
Word Bird puts words about Easter in his word house.

Nerlove, Miriam. *Easter.* Albert Whitman and Company, 1989. ISBN: 978-0807518719.
Rhyming text follows two children as they celebrate Easter with their family by decorating eggs, enjoying Easter baskets, going to church, and returning home to an egg hunt and Easter dinner.

Wells, Rosemary. *Max's Chocolate Chicken.* Turtleback, 2000. ISBN: 978-0613285711.
When Max goes on an egg hunt with his sister Ruby, he finds everything but Easter eggs!

Ziefert, Harriet. *I Need an Easter Egg! A Lift-the-Flap Story.* Little Simon, 1999. ISBN: 978-0689819943.
Little Rabbit is looking for the perfect Easter egg for his grandma. But nobody seems to know where to find one.

---

Vainio, Pirkko. *Who Hid the Easter Eggs?* North-South Books, 2011. ISBN: 978-0735823049.
Harry the squirrel must save the annual Easter egg hunt when someone takes a keen interest in the hidden eggs.

Wells, Rosemary. *Max Counts His Chickens.* Viking Juvenile, 2007. ISBN: 978-0670062225.
Max has always liked to do things his own way, and his search for marshmallow chicks is no exception.

Wilhelm, Hans. *I Love Easter!* Cartwheel Books, 2011. ISBN: 978-0545134765.
Noodles the dog goes on an early-morning Easter egg hunt without his best friend, Teddy.

## Activities

---

**Coloring Pages**

Consult your favorite pattern books or holiday coloring books for pages to use as coloring sheets. Be sure to search online as well. There's lots of great stuff out there!

- Visit http://dulemba.com/index_ColoringPages.html for author and illustrator Elizabeth O. Dulemba's great collection of holiday coloring pages! While there, sign up for her Coloring Page Tuesdays e-mails.
- Also, Diane deGroat has a great coloring page of Gilbert and an Easter egg to decorate at www.dianedegroat.com/Diane_deGroat_5.html. This would be a great follow-up activity to reading her book, located in the Books section of this chapter!

### Cut-and-Tell

**"Sarah's Prize Egg: An Easter Egg Scissor-Tale"**    The text, instructions, and patterns for this scissor story can be found on pages 51–53 of *Scissor-Tales for Special Days* by Jan Grubb Philpot (Incentive Publications, 1994).

**"The Chocolate Easter Egg"**    This cut-and-tell story, which ends up being an egg and two rabbits, is found on pages 30–32 of *Paper Stories* by Jean Stangl (Fearon Teacher Aids, 1984).

### Draw-and-Tell

**"The Easter Bunny"**    This draw-and-tell story can be found on pages 15–16 of *Tell and Draw Stories* by Margaret J. Olson (Creative Storytime Press, 1984).

**"Mama's Egg"**    This draw-and-tell story, which creates an Easter Bunny, is found on pages 98–99 of *Chalk in Hand: The Draw and Tell Book* by Phyllis Noe Pflomm (Scarecrow Press, 1986).

### Flannel/Velcro Board

**"The Egg Who Couldn't Decide"**    The text and patterns for this flannel/Velcro-board story can be found on pages 297–303 of *The Everything Book for Teachers of Young Children* by Valerie Indenbaum and Marcia Shapiro (Partner Press, 1983). The egg in the story cannot decide what color to be for Easter.

**"The Egg Hunt"**    The text for this flannel/Velcro-board presentation can be found on page 166 of *The Best of Totline Flannelboards* by Kathleen Cubley (Totline Publications, 2000). You may wish to use the patterns on page 167, or simply cut your eggs using an Ellison die. The directions say to give out the eggs to participants, but unless you have enough for all, simply hold the eggs yourself and place them on the board as they are mentioned in the rhyme. Let participants guess the colors of the eggs. It will be evident with the rhyming of the words as to what color is coming next.

**"The Easter People"**    This flannel/Velcro-board story, in which the candy animals in the Easter basket come alive, is found on page 42 of *FlannelGraphs: Flannel Board Fun for Little Ones, Preschool–Grade 3*, by Jean Stangl (Fearon Teacher Aids, 1986). The patterns are found on page 74.

**"No Eggs for Easter"**    This flannel/Velcro-board story, in which the Easter Bunny gathers all different types of eggs to give away at Easter, is found on pages 43–44 of *FlannelGraphs: Flannel Board Fun for Little Ones, Preschool–Grade 3*, by Jean Stangl (Fearon Teacher Aids, 1986). The patterns are found on pages 75–76.

### Games

**Easter Matching Game**    Patterns for a variety of Easter symbols (basket, chick, Easter Bunny, Easter egg, Easter lily, rabbit) appear on pages 105–116 of *Holiday Patterns*, compiled by Jean Warren (Warren Publishing House, 1991). The best patterns to use are ones that are already enclosed in a square, as this would make cutting them out simple. Copy two of each on different colors of construction paper. Give each participant one of the patterns/colors. Keep one for yourself and place in an apron pocket or container of some sort. Begin the matching game by pulling out your copies, one at a time, placing them on the board, and allowing participants to match them.

**Easter Basket Matching Game**    The patterns for this matching game can be found on pages 20–21 of *A Tisket A Tasket: Matching Games for Colors, Shapes, and Patterns* by Marilynn G. Barr (Monday Morning Books, 2006). These baskets have different shapes in the centers. Reproduce them on different colors of paper so that participants will be matching not only colors but shapes. Follow the instructions for the game listed in the previous activity.

**Pass the Eggs Game**    Directions for this game can be found on page 152 of *Games for All Seasons* by Alexandra Cleveland and Barbara Caton (Building Blocks Publications, 1999).

**Ring Toss Rabbit**    The instructions for this simple game can be found on page 279 of *The Storytime Sourcebook II: A Compendium of 3500+ New Ideas and Resources for Storytellers* by Carolyn N. Cullum (Neal-Schuman, 2007). Adapt this game by having inflatable rabbits and small plastic Frisbees to land over the ears.

## Miscellaneous

**"Rabbit Story"**    This story, in which a handkerchief is folded into a rabbit shape, appears on pages 67–68 of *The Family Storytelling Handbook* by Anne Pellowski (Macmillan, 1987).

**"The Basket the Bunny Brought" (A Cumulative Story)**    This story can be found at Susan M. Dailey's website (http://www.susanmdailey.com/). Click on the "New Stories" link on the left-hand side of the homepage. Then click on the title link to be taken to the story. She does this story with props, all of which would be easy to find!

# Fingerplays

## Easter Baskets

### Easter Basket

| | |
|---|---|
| Fill the Easter basket with grass, | *(Pretend to put grass in basket.)* |
| Sprinkle around jelly beans. | *(Move hand in circle.)* |
| Add some bright-colored eggs, | *(Make oval with hands.)* |
| Prettiest ever seen. | |
| Pop in a chocolate bunny | *(Pretend to place in basket.)* |
| And some eggs made of candy. | *(Make ovals with hands.)* |
| Tie a ribbon on it. | *(Pretend to tie.)* |
| Doesn't it look dandy? | *(Put hands out in questioning manner.)* |

—Susan M. Dailey
*A Storytime Year* (Neal-Schuman, 2001, p. 60)

## Easter Eggs

### Three Little Eggs

| | |
|---|---|
| Three little eggs, white and plain. | *(Hold up three fingers.)* |
| "We're so boring," they complain. | *(Yawn.)* |
| The first little egg dives in some dye. | *(Point to first finger.)* |
| He comes out as blue as the sky. | |
| The second little egg says, "I think | *(Point to second finger.)* |
| I will be a pretty shade of pink." | |
| The third little egg just laughs and laughs | *(Point to third finger.)* |
| When he comes out half and half. | |
| The three colorful eggs shout, "Hooray, | |
| Now we're ready for Easter Day!" | |

—Susan M. Dailey
*A Storytime Year* (Neal-Schuman, 2001, pp. 59–60)

**Five Little Easter Eggs**

*(Begin this rhyme with five fingers up and take away fingers as the rhyme progresses. This rhyme would also work well on the flannel/Velcro board with eggs the colors that are mentioned.)*

Five little Easter eggs lovely colors wore.
Mother ate the green one, then there were four.
Four little Easter eggs, two and two you see.
Daddy ate the red one, then there were three.
Three little Easter eggs, before I knew,
Sister ate the orange one, then there were two.
Two little Easter eggs, oh what fun—
Brother ate the pink one, then there was one.
One little Easter egg, see me run.
I ate the very last one, and then there were none.

—Author unknown

## Rabbits

### Mr. Easter Rabbit

Mr. Easter Rabbit goes hip, hop, hip.

*(Extend index and middle fingers and make hand hop.)*

See how his ears flip, flop, flip.

*(Place hands on head and move them forward and backward.)*

See how his eyes go blink, blink, blink. *(Blink eyes.)*
See how his nose goes twink, twink, twink. *(Wiggle nose with finger.)*
Stroke his warm coat soft and furry. *(Stroke fist.)*
Hip, hop, hip, he's off in a hurry. *(Extend two fingers and hop them away.)*

—Author unknown

### I Saw a Rabbit

I saw a rabbit. *(Wiggle two fingers behind head.)*
I said, "Hello." *(Wave.)*
He didn't stop. *(Shake head "no.")*
He went down a hole. *(Swoop right hand through curved left arm.)*
Now don't you fret—
You might see one, too. *(Wiggle two fingers behind ears.)*
An Easter Rabbit
With some eggs for you! *(Cup hands together and hold out.)*

—Author unknown

### My Rabbit

My rabbit has two big ears, *(Hold up index and middle fingers for ears.)*
And a funny little nose. *(Join other three fingers for nose.)*
He likes to nibble carrots, *(Move thumb away from other two fingers.)*
And he hops wherever he goes. *(Move whole hand jerkily.)*

—Author unknown

### The Rabbit

Can you make a rabbit
With two ears so very long? *(Hold up two fingers of one hand for rabbit.)*
And let him hop and hop about
On legs so small and strong? *(Hop hand up and down.)*

He nibbles, nibbles carrots
For his dinner every day.                                   *(Nibble with thumb and pointer finger.)*
As soon as he has had enough,
He scampers far away.                                      *(Hop hand behind back.)*

—Author unknown

### I Caught a Hare

One, two, three, four, and five,                           *(Count out on fingers.)*
I caught a hare alive.
Six, seven, eight, nine, and ten,                          *(Continue to count out on fingers.)*
I let him go again.

—Traditional Mother Goose rhyme

### Tired Bunnies

"Come my bunnies, it's time for bed."                      *(Make beckoning motion with hand.)*
That's what Mother Bunny said.
"But first I'll count you just to see                       *(Place finger on chin, contemplating.)*
If you have all come back to me.
Bunny one, bunny two, bunny three, oh dear,               *(Hold up each finger as bunnies are counted.)*
Bunny four, bunny five, yes, you're all here.             *(Continue to hold up fingers.)*
You're the sweetest things alive,
My bunnies one, two, three, four, five."                  *(Hug bunnies to chest.)*

—Author unknown

### Five Little Rabbits

*(Use five fingers or five bunny finger puppets for this rhyme.)*

Five little rabbits under a log;                           *(Hold up fingers of one hand.)*
This one said, "Shh! I hear a dog!"                        *(Point to first finger.)*
This one said, "I see a man!"                              *(Point to second finger.)*
This one said, "Run while you can!"                        *(Point to third finger.)*
This one said, "I'm not afraid!"                           *(Point to fourth finger.)*
This one said, "Let's hide in the shade!"                  *(Point to thumb.)*
A man and his dog went hurrying by,                        *(Make thumb and fingers of other hand hurry by.)*
And you should have seen those rabbits fly!                *(Move fingers away quickly.)*

—Author unknown

### I Had a Little (Easter) Bunny

I had a little (Easter) bunny.                             *(Hold up one finger.)*
One day she ran away.                                      *(Make fingers run.)*
I looked for her by moonlight,
I looked for her by day.                                   *(Shade eyes with hand.)*
I found her in the meadow
With her babies 1, 2, 3.                                   *(Count on fingers.)*
So now I have four rabbit pets                             *(Hold up four fingers.)*
To run and jump with me!

—Author unknown

### Little Bunny

*(This rhyme would also work well with a bunny finger or hand puppet.)*

There was a little bunny who lived in the wood.
He wiggled his ears as a good bunny should.               *(Use forefingers on either side of head for ears; wiggle them.)*

| | |
|---|---|
| He hopped by a squirrel, | (Hold up two fingers and close the others on one hand; hop them down other arm.) |
| He hopped by a tree. | (Repeat motion.) |
| He hopped by a duck, | (Repeat motion.) |
| And he hopped by me. | (Hop over the opposite fist.) |
| He stared at the squirrel. | (Stare.) |
| He stared at the tree. | (Stare.) |
| He stared at the duck, | |
| But he made faces at me! | (Wiggle nose in rabbit fashion.) |

—Author unknown

### A Fat Bunny

| | |
|---|---|
| A fat bunny rabbit with ears so tall, | (Place hands on head to form ears.) |
| And two pink eyes about this small, | (Form two circles with thumbs and index fingers.) |
| Went hop, hop, hopping to get some lunch. | (Hop one hand.) |
| He found a fresh carrot, | |
| O yum-yum, crunch-crunch! | (Make munching motion with hand.) |

—Author unknown

### Easter Bunny

| | |
|---|---|
| Easter Bunny's ears are floppy. | (Place hands on each side of head and make them flop.) |
| Easter Bunny's feet are hoppy. | (Hop feet.) |
| His fur is soft, | (Stroke arm.) |
| And his nose is fluffy, | (Touch nose.) |
| Tail is short and powder-puffy. | (Form tail with hands behind body.) |

—Author unknown

### Easter Rabbits

*(This rhyme would also work well on a flannel/Velcro board.)*

| | |
|---|---|
| Five little Easter rabbits | (Hold up five fingers.) |
| Sitting by the door. | |
| One hopped away and then there were four. | (Bend down one finger.) |
| REFRAIN: | |
| Hop, hop, hop, hop; | (Clap on each hop.) |
| See how they run! | |
| Hop, hop, hop, hop! | (Clap on each hop.) |
| They think it great fun! | |
| Four little Easter rabbits | (Hold up four fingers.) |
| Under a tree. | |
| One hopped away and then there were three. | (Bend down one finger.) |
| *(Repeat refrain.)* | |
| Three little Easter rabbits | (Hold up three fingers.) |
| Looking at you. | |
| One hopped away, and then there were two. | (Bend down one finger.) |
| *(Repeat refrain.)* | |
| Two little Easter rabbits | (Hold up two fingers.) |
| Resting in the sun. | |
| One hopped away, and then there was one. | (Bend down one finger.) |
| *(Repeat refrain.)* | |

One little Easter rabbit
Left all alone.
He hopped away, and then there were none.     *(Hand behind back.)*
New Refrain:
Hop, hop, hop, hop!     *(Clap on each hop.)*
All gone away!
Hop, hop, hop, hop!     *(Clap on each hop.)*
They'll come back some day.

—Author unknown

### Rabbits

A family of rabbits lived under a tree;     *(Close right hand and hide it under left arm.)*
A father, a mother, and babies three.     *(Hold up index finger, middle finger, ring finger, pinkie finger, and thumb in succession.)*

Sometimes the bunnies would sleep all day;     *(Make a fist.)*
But when night came, they liked to play.     *(Wiggle fingers.)*
Out of the hole they'd go creep, creep, creep,     *(Move fingers in creeping motion.)*
While the birds in the trees were all asleep.     *(Rest face on hands; place palms together.)*
Then the bunnies would scamper about and run.     *(Wiggle fingers.)*
Uphill, downhill! Oh, what fun!     *(Move fingers vigorously.)*
But when mother said, "It's time to rest."     *(Hold up index finger.)*
Pop! They would hurry     *(Clap hands after "pop.")*
Right back to their nest!     *(Hide hand under arm as before.)*

—Author unknown

### Hop and Stop

*(Begin rhyme with one finger up and add fingers as the rhyme progresses. This rhyme would also work well as a flannel/Velcro-board story.)*

The first little rabbit went hop, hop, hop.
I said to the first rabbit, "Stop, stop, stop!"
The second little rabbit went run, run, run.
I said to the second rabbit, "Fun, fun, fun!"
The third little rabbit went thump, thump, thump.
I said to the third rabbit, "Jump, jump, jump!"
The fourth little rabbit went sniff, sniff, snuff.
I said to the fourth rabbit, "That is enough!"
The fifth little rabbit went creep, creep, creep.
I said to the fifth rabbit, "It's time to sleep!"

—Author unknown

### Bunny in a Hole

A bunny lived in a little hole,     *(Put thumb down in the middle of fist.)*
Lived softly in a little hole.     *(Place other hand over top of fist.)*
When all was quiet as quiet can be . . .
Out popped he!     *(Pop thumb out of fist.)*

—Traditional folk rhyme

### This Is the Bunny

This is the bunny with ears so funny.     *(Make fist with two fingers raised for ears.)*
This is his hole in the ground.     *(Cup other hand.)*

When a noise he hears, he pricks up his ears,    *(Wiggle "ears" back and forth.)*
And jumps into his hole in the ground!    *(Dive fist into cupped hand.)*

—Traditional rhyme

### Little Bunny

Here's the little bunny
With ears so white and long.    *(Hold up two fingers.)*
Watch it hop and hop about
On legs so small and strong.    *(Hop hand around.)*

—Author unknown

### Rabbit, Rabbit, Carrot Eater

Rabbit, rabbit, carrot eater,    *(Hold up index finger and middle finger for rabbit's ears.)*
He says there is nothing sweeter,    *(Rub tummy.)*
Than a carrot every day,
Munch and crunch, and run away.    *(Move fingers together in a "chewing" motion, then run fingers behind back.)*

—Traditional rhyme

### This Little Bunny

*(Hold up five fingers and bend each one down with each verse, or simply point to each finger as the rhyme progresses.)*

This little bunny has two pink eyes.
This little bunny is very wise.
This little bunny is soft as silk,
This little bunny is as white as milk.
This little bunny just nibbles away
At lettuce and carrots all the day.

—Author unknown

### Once I Saw a Bunny

Once I saw a bunny    *(Extend index and middle finger of one hand upward for ears.)*

And a green, green cabbage head.    *(Make a fist of other hand.)*
"I think I'll have some cabbage,"
The little bunny said.
So he nibbled and he nibbled    *(Make bobbing motion with finger and thumb of first hand.)*

And he perked his ears to say,    *(Extend index and middle fingers upward.)*
"Now I think it's time
I should be hopping on my way."    *(Let hand hop away.)*

—Traditional rhyme

### Little Bunny

Here's a little bunny    *(Raise the index and middle fingers to represent rabbit's ears.)*

On a shelf in a shop.    *(Sit the "rabbit hand" on the back of the opposite hand.)*
Wind him up slowly,    *(Make rotating motions beside "rabbit hand" as though winding him up.)*

And away he'll hop    *(Make "rabbit hand" hop away.)*

—Author unknown

---

**More Great Fingerplays**

"Two Easter Baskets," from page 263 of *1001 Rhymes and Fingerplays for Working with Young Children*, compiled by the Totline Staff (Warren Publishing House, 1994).

"In My Easter Basket," from page 144 of *Felt Board Fingerplays* by Liz and Dick Wilmes (Building Blocks Publication, 1997).

"Hunting for Eggs" and "Four Easter Eggs," from page 262 of *1001 Rhymes and Fingerplays for Working with Young Children*, compiled by the Totline Staff (Warren Publishing House, 1994). "Hunting for Eggs" would make a great flannel/Velcro-board presentation as well, or simply cut out large eggs in the colors of those mentioned and hold them up.

"Easter Eggs," from page 261 of *1001 Rhymes and Fingerplays for Working with Young Children*, compiled by the Totline Staff (Warren Publishing House, 1994).

"Easter Time Is Here," an action rhyme, from page 263 of *1001 Rhymes and Fingerplays for Working with Young Children*, compiled by the Totline Staff (Warren Publishing House, 1994).

"Jelly Bean Jiggle Action Verse," an action rhyme, from page 38 of *Holiday Hoopla: Songs and Fingerplays* by Kathy Darling (Monday Morning Books, 1990).

---

## Miscellaneous

### Here Is the Church

| | |
|---|---|
| Here is the church. | *(Place back of hands together and interlock fingers; place palms together.)* |
| Here is the steeple. | *(Point index fingers upward.)* |
| Open the doors and here are the people. | *(Open palms.)* |

—Traditional rhyme

### Some Things That Easter Brings

| | |
|---|---|
| Easter duck and Easter chick, | *(For duck, put both hands behind back and stick hands out with palms up [duck's tail]. For chick, flap both arms at sides as though a chick were flapping its wings.)* |
| Easter eggs with chocolate thick, | *(Touch index finger to thumb on each hand to form two small ovals to represent eggs.)* |
| Easter hats for one and all; | *(Put hands on head with fingers touching, making a little peak to indicate a hat.)* |
| Easter bunny makes a call! | *(With backs of wrists on top of head, raise hands to point upward to represent rabbit's ears.)* |
| Happy Easter always brings Such a lot of pleasant things! | *(Fold hands in lap.)* |

—Author unknown

## Musical Selections ————————————————————————————————————

"Bunny Boogie" from *Rhythms and Rhymes for Special Times* by Jack Hartmann. Available from http://www.songsforteaching.com/.

"Easter Bunny Boogie" and "I Can Do the Bunny Hop, Too!" from *Movement Songs Children Love* CD and book set. Available from http://www.songsforteaching.com/.

*Easter Party Music* CD. DPM. ASIN: B0013TO81E.

"Easter Time Is Here Again" from *Holiday Songs and Rhythms* by Hap Palmer. Available from http://www.songsforteaching.com/.

*Happy Easter Songs* CD. Sony Special Product. ASIN: B000002YZN.

---

### More Great Music

The Songs for Teaching website offers two multiple-holiday CDs that include Easter songs, *Celebrate Holidays* and *Seasons and Celebrations*. Go to http://www.songsforteaching.com/ to access downloads of both music and printable lyrics.

---

## Crks

**Baby Chick Surprise Egg** This cute craft can be found on pages 181–182 of *Multicultural Holidays: Share Our Celebrations* by Julia Jasmine (Teacher Created Materials, 1994). Reproduce the pattern of the chick and egg on construction paper, color, cut out, and put together with a brad. The egg opens up to reveal a cute chick!

**Decorated Eggs** The egg pattern that is the base of this craft is found on page 240 of *The Best of Holidays and Seasonal Celebrations—Issues 5–8, PreK–3*, edited by Donna Borst (Teaching and Learning Company, 1997). Make patterns for participants to trace; cardboard works well for the patterns. Once patterns have been traced onto white paper, allow participants to draw designs on the egg. Cover the designs with glue and use any of the following suggested items to cover the designs: uncooked rice, colored sand, or gravel, any type of dry cereal (the multicolored Fruity Pebbles cereal would look particularly nice here), small seeds, uncooked macaroni, popped popcorn, dried beans.

**Stand-Up Bunny** The base of this pattern is a toilet paper roll. The pattern and instructions for the bunny can be found on page 246 of *The Best of Holidays and Seasonal Celebrations—Issues 1–4, PreK–K*, edited by Donna Borst and Janet Armbrust (Teaching and Learning Company, 1999). The bunny pattern is placed on the fold of a piece of paper. Pipe-cleaner whiskers and Easter grass complete this cute bunny craft.

**Bunny Card** This craft makes a bunny card from a folded piece of blue paper. The pattern is traced, cut out, and whiskers and a cotton tail are added. Instructions and pattern appear on pages 55–56 of *Calendar Crafts: Things to Make and Do for Every Month, PreK–2*, by Carolyn Argyle (Teaching and Learning Company, 2006). This would be a great craft to make for someone special, such as grandparents, at Easter time!

**Easter Mobile** Instructions and patterns appear on pages 240–241 of *The Best of Holidays and Seasonal Celebrations—Issues 9–13, PreK–K*, edited by Donna Borst (Teaching and Learning Company, 2001). Pieces are colored, cut out, and strung together with yarn for a simple mobile.

**Bunny Craft** The pattern and instructions for this simple craft appear on pages 34–35 of *Holiday and Seasonal Patterns* (Edupress, 1988). Facial features are added to a large pattern and a cotton ball is added to the reverse side for a tail. Yarn could be added for hanging.

**Bunny Hop** Instructions for this craft can be found on page 28 of *Hand-Shaped Art* by Diane Bonica (Good Apple, 1989). It turns a child's handprint into an adorable bunny!

**Build a Nest** Instructions for this craft can be found on page 89 of *Arts and Crafts for All Seasons, Preschool/Kindergarten* (The Education Center, 1999). The base is a paper plate that is covered with scrap art supplies (such as string, pipe cleaners, shredded paper, etc.). Chocolate eggs are added when the nest is completed.

# Father's Day and Mother's Day

*Take this opportunity to celebrate moms and dads!*

## History

The history of Mother's Day can be traced back to a holiday celebrated in England called "Mothering Sunday." In the history of the United States, a woman named Anna Jarvis is credited with establishing a national Mother's Day. She began campaigning for a national holiday in 1907, but it was not until 1914 that President Woodrow Wilson made the second Sunday in May officially Mother's Day.

Father's Day was an idea from a woman named Sonora Dodd. Upon hearing a sermon on Mother's Day, Dodd decided that there needed to be a day set aside for fathers as well. Her own father had raised her and five other children after the death of their mother. Dodd circulated a petition in 1910, and on June 19th of that year, the first Father's Day was celebrated. President Richard Nixon declared the celebration a national holiday in 1972. (See Julia Jasmine's *Multicultural Holidays: Share Our Celebrations* [Teacher Created Materials, 1994].)

## Poetry

"All About Mothers," from page 284 of *The Best of Holidays and Seasonal Celebrations—Issues 13–17, Grades 1–3*, edited by Donna Borst and Janet Armbrust (Teaching and Learning Company, 1999).

"Dads," from page 296 of *The Best of Holidays and Seasonal Celebrations—Issues 13–17, Grades 1–3*, edited by Donna Borst and Janet Armbrust (Teaching and Learning Company, 1999).

"Dads" by Mary Tucker, from page 291 of *The Best of Holidays and Seasonal Celebrations—Issues 1–4, PreK–K*, edited by Donna Borst and Janet Armbrust (Teaching and Learning Company, 1999).

"For Father's Day," from page 55 of *Month-by-Month Poetry: March, April, May, and June* by Marian Reiner (Scholastic Professional Books, 1999).

"For Father's Day" and "Papa Is a Bear," from pages 38–39 of *Ring Out, Wild Bells: Poems about Holidays and Seasons*, selected by Lee Bennett Hopkins (Harcourt Brace Jovanovich, 1992).

"I Wish My Father Wouldn't Try to Fix Things Anymore," from page 102 of *Something Big Has Been Here* by Jack Prelutsky (Greenwillow Books, 1990).

"Mother's Day" and "Father's Day," from page 131 of *Fingerplays and Rhymes: For Always and Sometimes* by Terry Lynne Graham (Humanics Ltd. Partners, 1987).

"Mummy Slept Late and Daddy Fixed Breakfast" by John Ciardi and "Daddy Fell into the Pond" by Alfred Noyes, from pages 147 and 156, respectively, of *The Random House Book of Poetry for Children* by Jack Prelutsky (Random House, 1983).

"On Mother's Day," from page 40 of *Month-by-Month Poetry: March, April, May, and June* by Marian Reiner (Scholastic Professional Books, 1999).

## Books

Andreae, Giles. *I Love My Mommy*. Hyperion/Disney, 2011. ISBN: 978-1423143277.
An adorable toddler tells some of the reasons he loves his mother.

Bauer, Marion D. *The Very Best Daddy of All.* Simon and Schuster Children's Publishing, 2004. ISBN: 978-0689841781.

> This heartwarming book shows various animal dads as they provide comfort, safety, companionship, and steady support to their youngsters.

Berenstain, Stan and Jan. *The Berenstain Bears and the Papa's Day Surprise.* Random House, 2003. ISBN: 978-0375811296.

> Papa Bear thinks Father's Day is nothing but a greeting card holiday. So, his family decides they won't celebrate it if that's how he feels.

Butterworth, Nick. *My Dad Is Awesome.* Candlewick Press, 2003. ISBN: 978-0763620561.

> Kids who idolize their dads just may recognize them in this portrait of one terrific father.

deGroat, Diane. *Mother, You're the Best! (But Sister, You're a Pest!).* HarperCollins, 2008. ISBN: 978-0061238996.

> It's Mother's Day and Gilbert wants to show his mother that she's the best. But how can he do that when his sister always manages to be in the way?

Guarino, Deborah. *Is Your Mama a Llama?* Perfection Learning, 2004. ISBN: 978-0756982591.

> A rhyming humorous text invites audience participation in this story about animal mothers. Consider buying this one in a Big Book format.

Krensky, Stephen. *Mother's Day Surprise.* Marshall Cavendish Children's Books, 2010. ISBN: 978-0761456339.

> Violet, a young snake, observes other animal children busily creating Mother's Day gifts, but all the projects seem to require things Violet doesn't have: arms, legs, or teeth.

London, Jonathan. *Froggy's Day with Dad.* Perfection Learning, 2004. ISBN: 978-0756969882.

> It's Father's Day, and Froggy is looking forward to special time with his dad.

Lukas, Catherine. *Hooray for Mother's Day!* Simon Spotlight/Nickelodeon, 2003. ISBN: 978-0689852411.

> Little Bill can hardly contain his excitement. It is Mother's Day and he is determined to make it a wonderful day for his mom.

Mayer, Mercer. *Just Me and My Dad.* Random House, 2001. ISBN: 978-0307118394.

> This story of a father-and-son camping trip is filled with Little Critter's mistakes and good intentions.

Mayer, Mercer. *Just Me and My Mom.* Random House, 2001. ISBN: 978-0307125842.

> Little Critter enjoys a special day in the city with his mother.

Mayer, Mercer. *Little Critter: Happy Father's Day.* HarperFestival, 2007. ISBN: 978-0060539658.

> Father's Day is just around the corner, and Little Critter and Little Sister have decided to plan a big surprise for Dad and Grandpa.

Mayer, Mercer. *Little Critter: Happy Mother's Day.* HarperFestival, 2009. ISBN: 978-0060539702.

> Mother's Day is almost here, and Little Critter has a special surprise in store for Mom.

Perlman, Willa. *Pocket Kisses.* LB Kids, 2011. ISBN: 978-0316077873.

> Each page celebrates the special kisses Mommy leaves behind—all revealed under lift-up flaps.

Piper, Sophie. *I Love My Mom.* Lion UK, 2011. ISBN: 978-0745963167.

> In this picture book, a range of baby animals tell why they love their mothers so much.

Plourde, Lynn. *Dad, Aren't You Glad?* Dutton Juvenile, 2005. ISBN: 978-0525473626.

> On his father's special day, a youngster announces that he is going to do all the "dad" stuff so that the man can rest and relax.

Robbins, Maria Polushkin. *Mother, Mother, I Want Another*. Dragonfly Books, 2007. ISBN: 978-0517559475.

> Trying to get baby mouse to go to sleep, Mrs. Mouse enlists the help of her friends in response to his cries of "Mother, mother, I want another," thinking he wants another mother, until he tells her he wants another kiss. Originally published in 1976, this one is a definite classic!

Van Genechten, Guido. *My Daddy*. Clavis Publishing, 2011. ISBN: 978-1605370989.

> A tender and sweet story about a boy and his dad.

Walker, Anna. *I Love My Dad*. Simon and Schuster Books for Young Readers, 2010. ISBN: 978-1416983194.

> Ollie the zebra and his dog friend celebrate all the things they love about Dad.

Walker, Anna. *I Love My Mom*. Simon and Schuster Books for Young Readers, 2010. ISBN: 978-1416983187.

> Ollie the zebra describes all the things he loves about his mom.

---

### Older Gems, or Titles Too Good to Pass Up

Asch, Frank. *Just Like Daddy*. Simon and Schuster Children's Publishing, 1981. ISBN: 978-0671664565.

> A very young bear describes all the activities he does during the day that are just like his daddy's.

Bunting, Eve. *The Mother's Day Mice*. Turtleback, 1988. ISBN: 978-0833517579.

> Three mouse brothers, clad in bright plaid shirts and lederhosen, leave their snug cottage, intent upon finding the perfect gifts for their mother.

Bunting, Eve. *A Perfect Father's Day*. Turtleback, 1993. ISBN: 978-0785709480.

> It's Father's Day, and four-year-old Susie has planned a perfect outing with all the things she knows her dad will like the best.

Carle, Eric. *Does a Kangaroo Have a Mother, Too?* HarperCollins, 2000. ISBN: 978-0060287689.

> An unseen child asks variations on the same question: Do various types of animals have a mother, too?

Carle, Eric. *Papa, Please Get the Moon for Me*. Simon and Schuster Children's Publishing, 1991. ISBN: 978-0887081774.

> A simple story, briefly told, which revolves around the waxing and waning of the moon. Monica asks Papa to bring her the moon, so that she might play with it. Children are always enthralled by the fold-out pages contained within this tale!

Hines, Anna G. *Daddy Makes the Best Spaghetti*. Clarion Books, 1986. ISBN: 978-0899193885.

> Dad can do lots of cool things, like cook, make bath time fun, and more!

Murphy, Jill. *Five Minutes' Peace*. Turtleback, 1999. ISBN: 978-0613147224.

> Mrs. Large wants just five minutes' peace from her three rambunctious children—that's all.

Pringle, Laurence. *Octopus Hug*. Boyds Mills Press, 1993. ISBN: 978-1563970344.

> Dad invents lots of games to play while Mom is out.

Sharmat, Marjorie W. *Hooray for Father's Day*. Holiday House, 1987. ISBN: 978-0823406371.

> Father Mule's two loving children spend Father's Day showering him with lively presents that leave him exhausted, when the gift he really needs is a dose of peace and quiet.

Sharmat, Marjorie W. *Hooray for Mother's Day*. Holiday House, 1986. ISBN: 978-0823405886.

> Alaric Chicken is one neurotic bird—a real worrier. He goes to a department store to buy a Mother's Day present for his mom, but nothing is right.

## Activities

> ### Coloring Pages
>
> Consult your favorite pattern books or holiday coloring books for pages to use as coloring sheets. Be sure to search online as well. There's lots of great stuff out there!
> - Diane deGroat has a great Mother's Day coloring page featuring Gilbert and his mom on her site, located at www.dianedegroat.com/Diane_deGroat_5.html. This page would be a great follow-up to reading her book, located in the Books section of this chapter.

### Cut-and-Tell

**Mother's Day Is Coming!**    The instructions, text, and patterns for this scissor story can be found on pages 57–59 of *Scissor-Tales for Special Days* by Jan Grubb Philpot (Incentive Publications, 1994). The instructions note that this story can be adapted for use with Father's Day.

**"Not Just Another Tie"**    This cut-and-tell story with patterns can be found on pages 36–38 of *Paper-Cutting Stories for Holidays and Special Events* by Valerie Marsh (Alleyside Press, 1994).

**"L"**    This cut-and-tell story, which ends up being a ladder, is found on pages 39–41 of *Paper Cutting Stories from A to Z* by Valerie Marsh (Alleyside Press, 1992). Although the holiday in the story is the father's birthday, you could easily adapt the text for use for Father's Day.

**"Where Does Your Father Work?"**    This cut-and-tell story and instructions can be found on pages 7–8 of *Fold and Cut Stories* by Jerry J. Mallett and Timothy S. Erwin (Alleyside Press, 1993).

### Draw-and-Tell

**"Dad Makes Me Glad"**    This draw-and-tell story can be found on pages 17–20 of *Draw Me a Story, Volume 1*, by Barbara Freedman (Feathered Nest Productions, 1989).

### Flannel/Velcro Board

**"Monkey Face"**    Perfect for Mother's Day! The text and pictures for this story appear on pages 342–371 of *The Everything Book for Teachers of Young Children* by Valerie Indenbaum and Marcia Shapiro (Partner Press, 1983). It is based on a book published in the 1970s by Frank Asch with the same title. Use the illustrations to do the story as a flannel/Velcro-board presentation.

### Games

**Father's Day/Mother's Day Matching Game**    Consult your favorite clip art sites or books for art to use, such as flowers or hats for Mother's Day and ties and slippers for Father's Day. If needed, enlarge or reduce pictures, copy two of them, and then copy onto different colors of paper. Laminate for durability. To play this game, pass out one of each pair to participants. Keep the other in either an apron pocket or container of some sort. Once all pieces have been passed out, begin the matching game by drawing one of the colors from your pocket and placing it on your flannel/Velcro board and allow the participant holding the match to bring it up and place it. Continue until all pieces have been matched.

**Gift Giving**    This simple matching game is found on page 280 of *Celebrate the Seasons: The Best of Holidays and Seasonal Celebrations—Issues 9–12, PreK–3*, edited by Donna Borst (Teaching and Learning Company, 1998). A description of a gift is given, and participants are to match that description with pictures that appear by drawing a line from the description to the gift. I would adapt the game this way: Enlarge the illustrations of the gifts to a decent size. Laminate them for durability and place flannel or Velcro on the back so that they can be attached to your board. Place all of them on the board to begin the game. Read off the description of the gifts, one at a time, and let participants tell you what gift fits the description.

## Miscellaneous

### Father's and Mother's Day Songs

- The following piggyback songs (new songs sung to familiar tunes) can be found on pages 71–76 of *Holiday Piggyback Songs*, compiled by Jean Warren (Warren Publishing House, 1988): "It's Your Special Day," "Mommy Takes Good Care of Me," "Happy Mother's Day to You," "You Are My Mother," "Mommy Is My Special Friend," "Mom Says," "Three Kisses for Mother," "Thank You, Mom!," and "I Love You, Mom."
- The following piggyback songs can be found on pages 78–82 of *Holiday Piggyback Songs*, compiled by Jean Warren (Warren Publishing House, 1988): "D-A-D," "Gifts for Dad," "I Love Daddy," "The Daddy Song," "He Is Very Special," and "Hugs for Daddy."
- In addition to these songs, *Piggyback Songs to Sign* by Jean Warren and Susan Shroyer (Warren Publishing House, 1992) has the following songs with American Sign Language motions: "Happy Day," "May All Your Dreams Come True," "Very Much," and "We Honor Them Today." The songs will work for either Mother's Day or Father's Day.
- More piggyback songs appear on page 12 of *Simply Super Storytimes: Programming Ideas for Ages 3–6* by Marie Castellano (Upstart, 2003): "Mommy's Special," "Daddy, Daddy, I Love You," "I Love Mommy," and "I Love My Mommy."

# Fingerplays ————————————————————————————————————————

### Happy Father's Day

*(This can be used for Mother's Day as well; just change the title and the last line to "Happy Mother's Day.")*

It's the day that we show,  (*Shake head "yes."*)
And take the time to say,  (*Point to wrist as if pointing to a watch.*)
Just how much we love you so!  (*Place hands over heart, then clap.*)
Happy Father's Day!

—Barbara Scott

---

**More Great Fingerplays**

"Daddy," "Daddy, Daddy," and "Best Daddy" (action rhymes), from pages 280–281 of *1001 Rhymes and Fingerplays for Working with Young Children*, compiled by the Totline Staff (Warren Publishing House, 1994).

"Mommy's Hands," "On Mother's Day," and "In Mommy's Lap" (action rhyme), from pages 277–278 of *1001 Rhymes and Fingerplays for Working with Young Children*, compiled by the Totline Staff (Warren Publishing House, 1994).

"I Love Mommy" (fingerplay), from TheBestKidsBooksite.com at http://www.thebestkidsbooksite.com/fingerplay.cfm. Click on the "Fingerplays" link, locate the title in the list, and click on the "Show Me" button at the bottom.

"My Mom" and "My Dad" (fingerplays), from pages 292–293 of *Celebrate the Seasons: The Best of Holidays and Seasonal Celebrations—Issues 9–12, PreK–3*, edited by Donna Borst (Teaching and Learning Company, 1998).

---

**More Great Fingerplays**

"My Mommy" and "Mommy and Me" (clapping rhymes), from page 80 of *Seasonal Storytime Crafts* by Kathryn Totten (Upstart, 2002). "Daddy's Shoes," "Playing Catch with Dad," and "Piggyback Ride" (fingerplays) can be found on page 88 of the same book.

"My Dad" (fingerplay), from page 48 of *Storytime Crafts* by Kathryn Totten (Alleyside Press, 1998).

"My Mom" and "Here Is a Little Girl" (fingerplays), from page 27 of *52 Programs for Preschoolers: The Librarian's Year-Round Planner* by Diane Briggs (American Library Association, 1997). These rhymes can easily be changed for Father's Day.

---

## Musical Selections

"A Box for Mommy" and "He's My Dad" from *Happy Everything* by Dr. Jean. Melody House. ASIN: B000SM3N0E.

"As You Sleep So Peacefully (A Father's Day Nightmare)" from *Juggling Babies* by Barry Polisar. Rainbow Morning Music. ISBN: 978-0938663461.

"Daddy Do Ya Wanna?" by Susan Harrison. Available from http://www.songsforteaching.com/.

"Daddy's Special Stew" and "This Mother's Day" from *Movin' 2 Math* by Jack Hartmann. Available from http://www.songsforteaching.com/.

"Moms (Mother's Day Song)" by Ron Brown. Available from http://www.songsforteaching.com/.

"Moms" and "Dear Old Dad" from *All Year* by Intelli-Tunes. Available from http://www.songsforteaching.com/.

"Mother's Day Song" by The Uncle Brothers. Available from http://www.songsforteaching.com/.

Mother's Day and Father's Day songs from *Seasons and Celebrations*. Available from http://www.songsforteaching.com/.

## Crafts

**Handprint Craft**   The base of this craft is a piece of white construction paper. Provide tempera paint in different colors for participants to dip their hands into. With help, have them place their hands onto the paper and press the handprints onto it, one handprint on either side of the paper. The poem that will be pasted between them appears on page 283 of *Celebrate the Seasons: The Best of Holidays and Seasonal Celebrations—Issues 9–12, PreK–3*, edited by Donna Borst (Teaching and Learning Company, 1998). This poem appears also at http://www.dltk-holidays.com/dad/ mhandprint.html. Reproduce enough copies of the poem for each participant. Have them glue the poem in the middle of the paper between the handprints. What a great reminder for Mom or Dad of little hands! There is also a poem just for dads that can be done with footprints. This poem appears at http://www.dltk-holidays.com/dad/mfootprints.html.

S&S Worldwide offers kits with this poem and everything you will need to produce a wonderful item for participants to take home. The kits run $19.99 per package of 30. The price drops to $18.49 if three or more sets are ordered. Contact information for S&S appears in Appendix A at the end of this book.

**Photo Flower**   The pattern for this craft appears on page 256 of *The Best of Holidays and Seasonal Celebrations—Issues 1–4, PreK–K*, edited by Donna Borst and Janet Armbrust (Teaching and Learning Company, 1999). Have participants bring a picture of themselves to glue in the center of the flower.

**Flower Wreath**   Use the flower patterns found on page 48 of *May Patterns and Projects* (Newbridge Educational, 2000). Reproduce on construction paper. Let participants color these flower shapes.

Take a large paper plate and remove the center. Glue the flower shapes around the circle. I found that, in constructing this craft, you will want to provide two pages of the flower patterns in order to have enough to go around the plate.

**Lazy Daisy Bookmark**    The base of this bookmark is denim material from blue jeans. The flowers are constructed of felt and yarn. You may wish to have the felt pieces cut out ahead of time. Otherwise, participants will need adult help for the tracing and cutting. Detailed instructions and patterns can be found on pages 45–46 of *Holiday and Seasonal Crafts from Recycled Materials* by Deborah Whitacre and Becky Radtke (Teaching and Learning Company, 1995). This would make a great gift for Mom!

**Tribute Tie to Dad**    This cute craft makes a tie for Dad from a large brown grocery bag. You should be able to cut several patterns from the opened-up bag. Yarn and a poem and other decorations are added to the tie. Instructions and patterns can be found on pages 69–71 of *Holiday and Seasonal Crafts from Recycled Materials* by Deborah Whitacre and Becky Radtke (Teaching and Learning Company, 1995). With the yarn added, Dad can actually wear this tie!

**Mother's Day Banner**    Instructions for this craft are found on page 56 of *Month-by-Month Arts and Crafts: March, April, May* compiled by Marcia Schonzeit (Scholastic Professional Books, 1991). The base of this craft is cloth or colored construction paper. Ellison die letters could be used to spell out "M-O-M." Smaller die cuts could also provide additional decorations. This craft could also be used for Father's Day. Decorations and letters could be cut from construction paper, foam, or decorative scrapbooking papers!

**Flowers for Mom**    This craft makes a gift and a card for Mom, all in one! Instructions appear on page 63 and pattern appears on page 106 of *The Best of The Mailbox Magazine Arts and Crafts, Grades 1–3*, edited by Karen A. Brunak (The Education Center, 1999).

**Mother's Day Drawer Sachets**    This simple craft makes a fragrant sachet that participants can give Mom as a gift! Instructions appear on page 60 of *Calendar Crafts: Things to Make and Do for Every Month, PreK–2*, by Carolyn Argyle (Teaching and Learning Company, 2006).

**Dad's Bookmark**    Instructions appear on page 73 of *Calendar Crafts: Things to Make and Do for Every Month, PreK–2*, by Carolyn Argyle (Teaching and Learning Company, 2006).

**Mother's Day Bookmark**    Instructions and pattern for this bookmark appear on page 81 of *Seasonal Storytime Crafts* by Kathryn Totten (Upstart, 2002). The end result is a bookmark with a rose and verse.

**Baseball Photo Frame**    Instructions and pattern for this craft can be found on page 89 of *Seasonal Storytime Crafts* by Kathryn Totten (Upstart, 2002). This makes a decorative paper frame. Add a piece of magnet strip to the back to hang on the refrigerator.

**Mother's Day Kisses Craft**    Instructions and patterns can be found on page 79 of *Storytime Crafts* by Kathryn Totten (Alleyside Press, 1998). The verse given is pasted in the middle of a piece of construction paper and participants can add pink "kisses" to place around it.

**Notes for Dad**    Instructions for this craft can be found on page 104 of *Arts and Crafts for All Seasons, Preschool/Kindergarten* (The Education Center, 1999). Car or truck shapes are added to clip clothespins. Add a magnetic strip to the back of the clothespin so that Dad can hang this on the refrigerator to hold notes.

# Fourth of July/Independence Day
## and Flag Day

*Since these two holidays have flags in common, I have placed them together as a theme. Many of the ideas included in this chapter could be used for either holiday!*

## History

It is widely thought that Betsy Ross was designated to create the first American flag. George Washington, as the General of the First Continental Army, flew the first Union flag on Prospect Hill in Somerville, Massachusetts, on January 1, 1776.

Flag Day is celebrated yearly on June 14th. On this day in 1777, the Continental Congress decided what the flag of our country would look like: "13 stripes, alternate red and white, that the 'Union' be 13 stars, within a blue field." The thirteen stripes and stars represented the original 13 colonies. This original idea, however, did not set out the arrangement of the stars, or allow for the addition of new states to the union. With the addition of the states of Kentucky and Vermont, a new draft was made of the original resolution: the flag would have 15 stars and 15 stripes.

Seeing that the addition or a stripe for each new state would give the flag a very strange shape indeed, Naval officer Captain Samuel C. Reid urged the Congress to pass a law keeping the number of stripes at 13 (for the original colonies) and simply adding a star for each new state. This law was passed by the U.S. Congress in 1818.

On July 4th, we celebrate the birthday of our country, the United States of America. It was on this day in 1776 that representatives from a majority of the 13 original colonies adopted the Declaration of Independence. This important document paved the way for the independence of the colonies from the rule of England and its king. It also began the Revolutionary War.

The Declaration of Independence had its first public reading in Philadelphia, Pennsylvania. This celebration included ringing of bells, which is still part of the celebration today, along with parades, concerts, picnics, and fireworks. (See Julia Jasmine's *Multicultural Holidays: Share Our Celebrations* [Teacher Created Materials, 2010].)

## Poetry

"Boom Bang!" and "Birthday Fireworks," listed as fingerplays but great short opening poems, from page 186 of *Yearful of Circle Times* by Liz and Dick Wilmes (Building Blocks Publications, 1989).

"Firecracker-Loud," from page 73 of *Circle-Time Poetry Around the Year* by Jodi Simpson (Scholastic, 2005).

"Fourth of July" and "Flag Day," from pages 131 and 132 of *Fingerplays and Rhymes: For Always and Sometimes* by Terry Lynne Graham (Humanics Ltd. Partners, 1987).

"June Fourteenth," a poem for Flag Day, from page 54 of *Month-by-Month Poetry: March, April, May, and June* by Marian Reiner (Scholastic Professional Books, 1999).

"Our Flag," "To July," and "Fourth of July Parade," from pages 37, 40, and 41, respectively, of *Ring Out, Wild Bells: Poems about Holidays and Seasons*, selected by Lee Bennett Hopkins (Harcourt Brace Jovanovich, 1992).

"Parade," from pages 16–17 of *A Rumpus of Rhymes: A Book of Noisy Poems* by Bobbi Katz (Dutton Children's Books, 2001).

"Summer Celebration," from page 279 of *The Big All-Year Book of Holidays and Seasonal Celebrations: Preschool/Kindergarten, Issues 14–18*, edited by Donna Borst (Teaching and Learning Company, 2002).

"Whose Birthday Is It?," from http://www.childfun.com/index.php/holidays/summer-holidays/ independence-day/623-4th-of-july-songs-poems-a-fingerplays-independence-day-crafts-and-activities.html.

## Books

Capucilli, Alyssa. *Biscuit's Fourth of July*. HarperFestival, 2005. ISBN: 978-0060094645.
> Biscuit celebrates America's birthday. There's a parade and fireworks to watch and lots of treats to share with family and friends.

Holub, Joan. *Fourth of July, Sparkly Sky*. Little Simon, 2003. ISBN: 978-0689857188.
> Fireworks burst and flags fly. It's our country's birthday—the fourth of July!

Kimmelman, Leslie. *Happy 4th of July, Jenny Sweeney!* Albert Whitman and Company, 2003. ISBN: 978-0807531525.
> It's the Fourth of July and all over town, people are getting ready.

Lewison, Wendy. *F Is for Flag*. Turtleback, 2002. ISBN: 978-0613452632.
> June 14th is Flag Day, but with so many American flags proudly displayed, every day seems like Flag Day.

McCue, Lisa. *Corduroy's Fourth of July*. Viking Juvenile, 2007. ISBN: 978-0670061594.
> Today is the Fourth of July, and Corduroy and his friends are having a fun-filled picnic.

---

### Older Gems, or Titles Too Good to Pass Up

Chall, Marsha W. *Happy Birthday, America!* HarperCollins, 2000. ISBN: 978-0688130510.
A family celebrates the Fourth of July, complete with flags flying, a neighborhood parade, a picnic feast, swimming in the lake, games on the lawn, and, of course, fireworks at night.

Herman, John. *Red, White, and Blue*. Grosset and Dunlap, 1998. ISBN: 978-0448412702.
Describes how the American flag came into being, how it has changed over the years, and its importance as the symbol of our country.

Joosse, Barbara. *Fourth of July*. Knopf Books for Young Readers, 1985. ISBN: 978-0394851952.
Everyone thinks Ross is too little to participate, but when he can walk the length of the parade carrying a banner, he proves he is old enough for sparklers.

Keller, Holly. *Henry's Fourth of July*. Greenwillow Books, 1985. ISBN: 978-0688040130.
Henry has a fun-filled day celebrating the Fourth of July with his family and friends.

Lasky, Kathryn. *Fourth of July Bear*. William Morrow and Company, 1991. ISBN: 978-0688082871.
Becca, a city girl, is apprehensive about spending the summer by the sea.

Seymour, Tres. *Jake Johnson: The Story of a Mule*. DK Children, 1999. ISBN: 978-0789425638.
Farmer Puckett plans to use the "hu-mon-gous" Jake Johnson to "haul fireworks to the fairgrounds for the Independence Day Social." Jake has other ideas. The mule plants his prodigious behind on the lawn, refuses to do a lick of work, and stomps a hole in a water pipe when he gets thirsty.

Watson, Wendy. *Hooray for the Fourth of July*. Sandpiper, 2000. ISBN: 978-0618040360.
Celebrate Independence Day in America with this cheerful book for preschoolers and early readers.

Osborne, Mary P. *Happy Birthday, America.* Square Fish, 2008. ISBN: 978-0312380502.
This sparkling tribute to the Fourth of July depicts how a family of eight living in a small town celebrates this favorite holiday.

Roberts, Bethany. *Fourth of July Mice.* Clarion Books, 2004. ISBN: 978-0618313662.
It's the most patriotic of all holidays—Independence Day! The Holiday Mice take part in all the activities that make the Fourth of July fun.

Weber, Jill. *Yankee Doodle.* Sixth Avenue Books, 2004. ISBN: 978-1931722193.
This is a board book presentation of the classic song.

Wells, Rosemary. *McDuff Saves the Day.* Hyperion Books for Children, 2005. ISBN: 978-0786856756.
When a pack of ants invades owners Fred and Lucy's Fourth of July picnic, McDuff the dog finds the perfect solution.

Wong, Janet S. *Apple Pie Fourth of July.* Harcourt Children's Books, 2002. ISBN: 978-0152025434.
This simply told story explores a child's fears about cultural differences and fitting in with understanding and affection.

Ziefert, Harriet. *Hats Off for the Fourth of July!* Puffin, 2002. ISBN: 978-0140567090.
Ziefert shows how the townspeople of Chatham, Massachusetts, celebrate our nation's birthday while striking illustrations richly enhance the small-town ambience.

## Activities ———————————————————————————————————————

---

### Coloring Pages

Consult your favorite pattern books or holiday coloring books for pages to use as coloring sheets. Be sure to search online as well. There's lots of great stuff out there!

- Visit http://dulemba.com/index_ColoringPages.html for author and illustrator Elizabeth O. Dulemba's great collection of holiday coloring pages. While there, sign up for her Coloring Page Tuesdays e-mails.
- *CopyCat Magazine's* May/June 2002 issue (now out of print but often available through interlibrary loan) has a great full-page flag pattern that would make a great coloring page.

---

### Cut-and-Tell

**"The Liberty Bell"**    This cut-and-tell story and patterns can be found on pages 39–41 of *Paper-Cutting Stories for Holidays and Special Events* by Valerie Marsh (Alleyside Press, 1994).

### Draw-and-Tell

**"Happy Birthday, USA"**    This draw-and-tell story can be found on pages 100–102 of *Chalk in Hand: The Draw and Tell Book* by Phyllis Noe Pflomm (Scarecrow Press, 1986).

### Flannel/Velcro Board

**Flag and Bell Matching Game**    Use the Ellison dies for American flag and Liberty Bell to cut out flag and bell shapes from different-colored construction paper. If you do not have the Liberty Bell shape, the simple bell shape will do. Laminate for durability. Pass out one of the shapes to each participant and keep one for yourself. Once every child has a shape, begin to match the shapes by placing one of the ones you are holding on your flannel/Velcro board. Continue until all shapes/colors handed out are matched. As a variation on this matching game, you could use Ellison star and stripe shapes for the "Stars and Stripes."

**America Matching Game**    Patterns for a variety of symbols (American flag, Liberty Bell, outline map of United States) appear on pages 117–122 of *Holiday Patterns*, compiled by Jean Warren (Warren Publishing House, 1991). The best patterns to use are the ones that are already enclosed in a square, as this makes cutting them out simple. Follow the instructions of the matching game listed previously in this section.

## Games

*(See also the previous section.)*

**Pin the Stars on the Flag Game**    Construct a background of the flag with stars and stripes and leave the field of blue empty. Laminate for durability. This game is played just like Pin the Tail on the Donkey. Give each participant a star to try to place in the field of blue once they are blindfolded. The smaller inside star of Ellison die Star #1A would work well, as would the Tiny Stars die, depending on what size you wish your stars to be. Laminate these stars for durability. Continue until all participants have had the chance to place stars on the flag.

**Patriotic Beanbag Toss**    Find a good-sized box. Cut out several star shapes on the top of the box. Paint the box using patriotic colors. When the box is dry, let participants throw beanbags through the star-shaped holes.

**Capture the Flag (American Flag, That Is!)**    Use the small American flags that you would top cupcakes with for this game. Hide them around your room/area. Before the game starts, show participants what one of the flags looks like. Then let them hunt! When all of the flags have been found, gather and count out how many flags each player has found. A great closing activity for this game would be to serve cupcakes with more of these flags on top!

## Miscellaneous

**It's a Parade!**    Provide small American flags for each participant. Use some of the music mentioned later in this chapter and march around your storyhour area! If you can broadcast the music over a PA or phone system, take your patriotic parade around the library! This would also be a great opportunity to use your rhythm band instruments.

**Symbols of America**    Find pictures of symbols of America, such as the America flag, the eagle, the Liberty Bell, the Statue of Liberty, etc., and talk briefly about each.

**Patriotic Color Day**    Send home a flyer a week to two weeks before your program encouraging participants to wear red, white, and blue. You might want to color only with red, white, and blue crayons, or even have red, white, and blue snacks!

### Fourth of July/Flag Day Songs
- The following piggyback songs (new songs sung to familiar tunes) can be found on pages 83–87 of *Holiday Piggyback Songs*, compiled by Jean Warren (Warren Publishing House, 1988): "Stars and Stripes," "Wave Your Flag," "See Our Flag," "I'm Proud of Our Flag," "Yankee Doodle Flag," "Here's My Flag," "Oh, When the Flags," "Old Glory," "Down at the Flagpole," and "Way Up in the Sky."
- The following piggyback songs can be found on pages 88–92 of *Holiday Piggyback Songs*, compiled by Jean Warren (Warren Publishing House, 1988): "Designs in the Sky," "On the Fourth of July," "See the Parade," "Hurrah for July Fourth!," "At the Fireworks Show," and "Fireworks Light the Sky." The song "Happy Birthday to America" can be found on page 37 of *More Piggyback Songs*, compiled by the Totline Newsletter Staff (Warren Publishing House, 1984).
- The following piggyback songs and American Sign Language motions would work well for either Flag Day or the Fourth of July: "The Red, White, and Blue," "Down at the Flagpole," and "A Flag

for Me and You." They are found on pages 86–87 of *Piggyback Songs to Sign* by Jean Warren and Susan Shroyer (Warren Publishing House, 1992).

- The songs "Pop! Go the Fireworks," "Wiggle Your Fingers," and "Fireworks Pop!" can be found on page 86 of *The Best of Totline Magazine, Volume 2*, compiled by Gayle Bittinger (McGraw-Hill Children's Publishing, 2003).
- "The Flag Is Flying," "Wave Your Flags," and "Our Special Flag" can be found on page 116 of *The Best of Totline Magazine, Volume 4*, compiled by Gayle Bittinger (McGraw-Hill Children's Publishing, 2004). The songs "America's Birthday," "Today We Celebrate," and "Red, White, and Blue" can be found on page 117 of the same book.
- The songs "This Is July," "Beat a Drum," "Colors of Our Flag," "Wave a Flag," and "Statue of Liberty" can be found on pages 218–219 of *The Best of Totline Newsletter*, compiled by Jean Warren (Warren Publishing House, 1995).
- "Betsy Ross Song" can be found on page 40 of *Yankee Doodle Birthday Celebrations* by Elizabeth McKinnon (Warren Publishing House, 1990).

## Fingerplays

### Our Flag

| | |
|---|---|
| As red as a fire, | *(Wiggle fingers to represent fire.)* |
| As blue as the sky, | *(Point to sky.)* |
| As white as the snow— | *(Flutter fingers down.)* |
| See our flag fly! | *(Point to eyes.)* |
| Three pretty colors | *(Hold up three fingers.)* |
| Wave at the sky. | *(Wave.)* |
| Red, white, and blue | |
| On the Fourth of July! | *(Hold up four fingers.)* |
| Red, white, and blue | *(Count out on fingers.)* |
| Those colors are, | |
| And every state has | |
| Its very own star. | *(Draw star shape in the air.)* |
| Hold up the flag, | *(Hold pretend flag on pole.)* |
| Hold it up high, | *(Hold pretend flag up higher.)* |
| And then say, "Hurrah, | |
| For the Fourth of July!" | *(Pump fist in the air.)* |

—Author unknown

### The Fourth of July Parade

| | |
|---|---|
| We are having a Fourth of July parade, | *(March in place.)* |
| A parade on the Fourth of July! | |
| Sammy proudly carries the flag, | *(Pretend to carry flag.)* |
| Straight, and tall, and high. | |
| Sally plays a triangle, ding! | *(Pretend to play triangle.)* |
| Billy tootles a flute. | *(Pretend to play flute.)* |
| Beth bangs two lids with a clang! | *(Pretend to hold lids and clang.)* |
| And Jack wears a sailor suit. | *(Point to clothes.)* |
| Elizabeth loudly blows a horn. | *(Pretend to blow horn.)* |
| Jimmy whistles a tune. | *(Whistle.)* |
| Mary hits a frying pan, | |
| With a big, long iron spoon. | |
| Hooray, hooray for the Fourth of July! | *(Pretend to hit pan with spoon.)* |
| | *(Pump fist in the air.)* |

For the Fourth of July, hooray!
We will march along,                                     *(March.)*
And sing a song,
For the good old USA.                            *(Place hands over heart.)*

—Author unknown

### Look Way Up High

Look way up high                                   *(Put hand above eyes; look upward.)*
In the dark night sky.
See pretty fireworks                            *(Open and close hands quickly while moving them around.)*

On the Fourth of July.
"Ooh" and "aah"                                  *(Say "ooh" and "aah.")*
The crowd will say
Until the last burst                            *(Open and close hands slowly and move them in a downward motion to lap.)*

Fades away.

—Susan M. Dailey
*A Storytime Year* (Neal-Schuman, 2001, p. 152)

### The Fourth of July

The Fourth of July is the day for boys!
'Tis the day for girls! 'Tis the day for noise!
Here is a slow match,                          *(Hold out index finger.)*
The end is hot.
I will fire these crackers all in one lot!     *(Clap hands to represent firecrackers going off.)*
Here's a big pinwheel,
Just see it go!                                   *(Circle arm in the air.)*
Slowly at first, very swiftly, then slow!     *(Move arm as motions suggest.)*
Here are torpedoes!                         *(Make small circles with thumbs and index fingers.)*
Now let us see,
What kind of noise they will make!
One! Two! Three!                             *(Make three loud claps.)*
Here's a toy pistol!                         *(Hold out index finger to form gun.)*
I'll put in a cap,
And pull the trigger!                       *(Pull thumb up.)*

---

### More Great Fingerplays

"Firecrackers," from page 264 of *1001 Rhymes and Fingerplays for Working with Young Children*, compiled by the Totline Staff (Warren Publishing House, 1994).

"Fireworks, Fireworks in the Sky," from page 48 of *Fabulous Holiday and Seasonal Fingerplays!* by Jane Kitson (Delmar Thomson Learning, 1999).

"Independence Day," from page 104 of *Little Hands Fingerplays and Action Songs: Seasonal Activities and Creative Play for 2- to 6-Year-Olds* by Emily Stetson and Vicky Congdon (Williamson Publishing, 2001).

"Watching the Fireworks," an action rhyme, from page 96 of *Seasonal Storytime Crafts* by Kathryn Totten (Upstart, 2002).

"Our Country's Flag," "Our Flag," and "Stars and Stripes," from page 279 of *1001 Rhymes and Fingerplays for Working with Young Children*, compiled by the Totline Staff (Warren Publishing House, 1994).

My, didn't it snap!
See the sky rocket
Gosh...way up high.                          *(Point up into the air.)*
Spreading its fingers in the sky!            *(Put hand in the air; wiggle fingers.)*
Some grown people grumble and wonder why
We little folks like the Fourth of July!     *(Point to self.)*

—Maude Burnham
*Rhymes for Little Hands* (Milton Bradley Company, 1910, pp. 87–90)

## Musical Selections

"America," "It's the Flag Along the Way," and "Dancing in the USA" from *America: An Album for All Ages* by Bobby Susser. New Hope Records. ASIN: B002K576WS.

"America to Me" from *I've Got the Music in Me* by Jack Hartmann. Available from http://www.jackhartmann.com/.

"Happy Birthday America" from *Seasons and Celebrations*. Available from www.songsforteaching.com/.

"On the Fourth of July" by Ben and Elizabeth Stiefel. Available from http://www.songsforteaching.com/.

"Red, White, and Blue" from *Friends* by Two of a Kind. Available from http://www.songsforteaching.com/.

"Red, White, Blue" from *Debbie's Ditties 4: Come Dance S'More!* by Debbie Clements. Available from http://www.rainbowswithinreach.com/.

"Rockin' the USA" and "This Land Is Your Land" from *Rockin' Down the Road* by Greg and Steve. Youngheart. ASIN: B00000DGMU.

*Songs of America* CD by Cedarmont Kids. ASIN: B000068C7C.

"Star Spangled Banner" from *Holiday Songs and Rhythms* by Hap Palmer. Available from http://www.songsforteaching.com/.

*Strike Up the Band* by U.S. Military Bands. Available from http://www.songsforteaching.com/.

"United We Stand" from *Ready, Set, Move* by Greg and Steve. Greg and Steve Productions. ASIN: B000153K1U.

"We Love Our Flag" and "The Fourth of July" from *Happy Everything* by Dr. Jean. Melody House. ASIN: B000SM3N0E.

"Yankee Doodle" from *57 Greatest Kids Songs* by The Hit Crew. TUTM/Drew's Famous. ASIN: B002JECS8W.

*Yankee Doodle Mickey* CD. Walt Disney Records. ASIN: B00004TC2Y.

"You're A Grand Old Flag" and "God Bless America" from *Musical Scarves and Activities* by Georgiana Stewart. Kimbo. ASIN: B0001AC3KO.

## Crafts

**Happy Birthday USA Crown**    Cut out a simple crown shape from white construction paper. Allow participants to color the crown shape or leave white. Use red and blue gummed star stickers to decorate the crown!

**Fireworks**    Provide participants with black construction paper. Also have available red, silver, and blue glitter. Let participants swirl glue all around the black paper, then sprinkle glitter over the design. Shake off excess glitter. To make the firework bursts look more realistic, place a spot of glue onto the construction paper and use a Q-tip to move the glue out and away from the spot! A variation of this craft uses sea sponges that participants dip in red, white, and blue paint and apply to black construction paper.

**Toilet Paper Roll Firecrackers**    Cover toilet paper rolls with white construction paper cut to fit the roll. Use gummed red and blue star stickers to decorate the outside of the roll. Locate glitter chenille stems at your local craft store or online and cut them in half. Glue them inside the toilet paper roll and bend them to resemble firecracker sparks!

**Flag Craft**    The pattern for this flag is found at http://www.first-school.ws/t/ap/us_flag_color_by_word.htm. Print the pattern in color, as the pattern is color-coded. The site suggests adding 13 white star stickers or white fingerprints to the blue area for the 13 original colonies.

If you are just looking for a simple flag pattern, one appears on page 292 of *The Best of Holidays and Seasonal Celebrations—Issues 18–21, Grades 1–3*, edited by Donna Borst (Teaching and Learning Company, 2000).

Also, Childcraft School Specialty offers mini flag kits to decorate. Each kit includes 12 6-by-8-inch canvas flags and dowels. The cost is $18.99 per kit. Contact information for Childcraft can be found in Appendix A, located at the end of this book.

**Star Wreath**    This great craft idea comes from EnchantedLearning.com. You could use either the Ellison regular star or puffy star dies to provide the star shapes for this craft. The base is a paper plate. Directions can be found at http://www.enchantedlearning.com/crafts/memorialday/starwreath/.

**Star Rubbings**    Cut star shapes from paper doilies or sandpaper. An Ellison star die would be very useful for this. Tape these stars to tables. Have children place a piece of white construction paper over the stars and rub crayons over the stars. Use other shapes as well, such as Ellison dies of firecracker, Statue of Liberty, Liberty Bell (or bell). To make these even more patriotic-looking, use only red and blue crayons on the white paper!

**Fourth of July Firecracker**    Instructions and patterns appear on pages 79–80 of *Cut and Create! Holidays: Easy Step-by-Step Projects That Teach Scissor Skills* by Kim Rankin (Teaching and Learning Company, 1997). Simple shapes create a neat-looking firecracker.

**Red, White, and Blue Windsock**    Instructions for this windsock, which is made from blue (base) and white construction paper (stars), and red crepe paper appear on page 77 of *The Best of The*

*Mailbox Magazine Arts and Crafts, Grades 1–3*, edited by Karen A. Brunak (The Education Center, 1999). This would look great hanging outside on a porch to celebrate the holiday!

**USA Bear**     Patterns and instructions for this craft can be found on page 97 of *Seasonal Storytime Crafts* by Kathryn Totten (Upstart, 2002). This bear holds a banner and has stars glued to his belly! Enlarge the patterns provided to make it easier for little hands.

**Star Necklaces**     Supply participants with star-shaped beads and yarn or lanyard. You can also cut star shapes from construction paper, then use a hole punch to make a hole in the center of the star so that they can be threaded onto a piece of yarn.

**Patriotic Parade Sticks**     Make these for your patriotic parade through the library! Each participant will need a paper towel roll, red, white, and blue construction paper, pencil, scissors, glue, crepe paper streamers, and a star pattern. Cover the paper towel roll with colored paper and glue in place. Cut out stars and glue them to the roll. Cut 12-inch crepe paper streamers in red, white, and blue and staple them together at one end. Attach the streamers to the end of the roll.

**Patriotic Door Hanger**     Use the Ellison door hanger die-cut as the base for this craft. You may wish to cut it from red, white, or blue poster board. Have patriotic cut-outs available in red, white, and blue for your participants. Ellison dies such as USA, the Statue of Liberty, firecrackers, the Liberty Bell, or stars would work perfectly. Instead of construction paper, these pieces could also be cut from craft foam.

**Lincoln Penny Pendant**     The templates and instructions for this craft can be found at http://www .enchantedlearning.com/crafts/pennypendant/. Red, white, and blue stars of different sizes are glued atop one another and a shiny penny is added to the middle.

**Fourth of July Star Man**     Instructions for this cute craft can be found at http://www.allkidsnetwork .com/crafts/4th-of-july/4th-of-july-star-man.asp. A large star shape is the body. Accordion-folded paper strip arms and legs are added and smaller stars are glued on for hands and feet! The extra-large Puffy Star Ellison die is perfect for the body.

# Grandparents Day

*Use this day to celebrate the rich heritage that our grandparents give us!*

## History

This holiday is celebrated annually on the second Sunday in September. The day was first celebrated as a state holiday in West Virginia. Marian McQuade wrote to her state's governor in 1973, asking him to declare a special day for grandparents. In 1978, Senator Jennings Randolph of West Virginia introduced a bill to Congress asking that the second Sunday in September be officially made Grandparents Day. President Jimmy Carter signed an official proclamation making the day a holiday on September 6, 1979. (See "A Brief History of National Grandparents Day" at http://www.grandparents-day .com/2009/history_new/html/history/short_ver-nv2.html.)

## Poetry

"Grandma's Kisses," from page 19 of *A Bad Case of the Giggles: Kids' Favorite Funny Poems* selected by Bruce Lansky (Meadowbrook Press, 1994).

"Grandmother," from page 50 of *The Best of Holidays and Seasonal Celebrations—Issues 18–21, Grades 1–3*, edited by Donna Borst (Teaching and Learning Company, 2000).

"Grandpa's Farm," "Fun at Grandma's," and "Grandma's Story Box," from pages 96–97 of *A School Year of Poems: 180 Favorites from Highlights* selected by Walter B. Barbe (Boyds Mills Press, 2005).

## Books

Blackstone, Stella. *My Granny Went to the Market*. Barefoot Books, 2005. ISBN: 978-1841487922.
This international counting rhyme combines elements of the "Twelve Days of Christmas" and cumulative folktales as Granny buys a flying carpet from a man in Istanbul and travels around the world, purchasing items indigenous to each country she visits.

Brunsvold, Eric. *Gardening with Grandma*. Specialized Printing, LLC, 2010. ISBN: 978-0615389448.
A charming story about a young boy who starts a vegetable garden in his grandma's yard and the wonderful time they both have taking care of it.

Butterworth, Nick. *My Grandpa Is Amazing*. Candlewick Press, 2003. ISBN: 978-0763620578.
A child describes his amazing grandpa, in this brief story with cartoon illustrations. Also by this author: *My Grandma Is Wonderful*.

Hallinan, P. K. *Grandma Loves You*. Candy Cane Press, 2008. ISBN: 978-0824967284.
In this book the author expresses the unique bond between grandmother and grandchild.

Hill, Eric. *Spot Visits His Grandparents*. Turtleback, 2005. ISBN: 978-0606028370.
Lift the flaps to bake a cake and spend time with Spot and his grandparents!

Hillard, Shirley. *One Big Hug*. Mamoo House, 2005. ISBN: 978-1933014203.
A grandmother and her grandson have a contest to describe how big the love is between them.

Horrocks, Anita. *Silas' Seven Grandparents*. Orca, 2010. ISBN: 978-551435619.
> Silas usually likes all the love and attention he gets from his seven grandparents, although sometimes it gets to be a bit overwhelming.

Katz, Karen. *Grandma and Me*. Little Simon, 2002. ISBN: 978-0689849053.
> Someone special is at the door. Who could it be?

Katz, Karen. *Grandpa and Me*. Little Simon, 2004. ISBN: 978-0689866449.
> Let's make a pizza with Grandpa! You can help. Lift the large, sturdy flaps to find everything you need.

Lester, J.D. *Grandma Calls Me Gigglepie*. Robin Corey Books, 2011. ISBN: 978-0375859045.
> This board book captures the affection and playfulness of grandmother and grandchild with funny text and illustrations.

Lord, Janet. *Here Comes Grandma!* Henry Holt and Company, 2005. ISBN: 978-0805076660.
> Grandma sends a letter to her grandchild announcing that she is coming for a visit.

Mayer, Mercer. *Grandma, Grandpa and Me*. HarperFestival, 2007. ISBN: 978-0060539511.
> Little Critter is having a sleepover at Grandma and Grandpa's farm! He's excited—there is so much to see and do.

---

### Older Gems, or Titles Too Good to Pass Up

Buckley, Helen E. *Grandmother and I*. HarperCollins, 1994. ISBN: 978-0688125325.
> This tender, full-color book reminds children of all ages that grandmothers are special people. This author also published a companion book, *Grandfather and I*.

Douglass, Barbara. *Good as New*. William Morrow and Company, 1982. ISBN: 978-0688519834.
> Can Grandpa fix Grady's teddy bear, so it is as "good as new"?

Lum, Kate. *"What!" Cried Granny: An Almost Bedtime Story*. Dial, 1999. ISBN: 978-0803723825.
> This chuckler of a bedtime romp pits the wiles of a young procrastinator against his no-nonsense grandmother.

Numeroff, Laura. *What Grandmas Do Best, What Grandpas Do Best*. Simon and Schuster Books for Young Readers, 2000. ISBN: 978-0689805523.
> This two-for-one picture book is split in half to tell the same simple story twice.

Paul, Ann W. *Everything to Spend the Night from A to Z*. DK Children, 1999. ISBN: 978-0789425119.
> You never know what you're going to need to pack when you're spending the night at Grandpa's house. The little red-haired girl in this exuberant, rhyming story needs quite a bit of this and that, from apples to the zipper on her overnight bag, and everything in between.

Van Leewen, Jean. *Oliver, Amanda, and Grandmother Pig*. Dial, 1987. ISBN: 978-0803703612.
> When Grandmother Pig comes for a visit, Oliver and Amanda learn just how much fun it is to have a grandmother in the house.

Wells, Rosemary. *Bunny Cakes*. Perfection Learning, 2000. ISBN: 978-0756940898.
> Max bakes an earthworm cake for his grandmother.

Wood, Audrey. *The Napping House*. Harcourt Children's Books, 1984. ISBN: 978-0152014179.
> The snoring granny is an important part of this wonderful, cumulative story!

Ziefert, Harriet. *Grandmas Are for Giving Tickles*. Puffin, 2000. ISBN: 978-0140567182.
> Spending time with Grandma is so much fun! She knows all about butterflies, snails, and computers. And she has great ideas for new adventures.

Ziefert, Harriet. *Grandpas Are for Finding Worms*. Puffin, 2000. ISBN: 978-0140567199.
> When you need worms for fishing, Grandpa knows just where to look.

Mayer, Mercer. *Just Grandma and Me*. Random House, 2001. ISBN: 978-0307118936.
    Little Critter and his grandmother spend the day at the beach in this funny-and-true picture book about Mercer Mayer's popular character.

Mayer, Mercer. *Just Grandpa and Me*. Random House, 2001. ISBN: 978-0307119360.
    Little Critter and his grandfather have fun on a trip to the department store.

Parr, Todd. *The Grandma Book*. Little, Brown Books for Young Readers, 2006. ISBN: 978-0316058025.
    This book celebrates all of the different types of grandmas.

Parr, Todd. *The Grandpa Book*. Little, Brown Books for Young Readers, 2006. ISBN: 978-0316058018.
    There are all types of grandpas in the world. This book shows us just some of them.

Uslander, Arlene. *That's What Grandparents Are For*. Peel Productions, 2001. ISBN: 978-0939217601.
    Illustrations and rhyming text describe the special bond between grandparents and their grandchildren.

## Activities ————————————————————————————————————————————

---

### Coloring Pages

Consult your favorite pattern book or holiday coloring books for pages to use as coloring sheets. Be sure to search online as well. There's lots of great stuff out there! For example, coloring pages can be found at http://www.dltk-kids.com/crafts/grandparents/mgrandpa poster.htm.

---

### Cut-and-Tell

**"Granny's Treasure"**    This scissor-tale can be found on pages 65–68 of *Scissor-Tales for Any Day* by Jan Grub Philpot (Incentive Publications, 1994).

**"Two Packages"**    This cut-and-tell story plus patterns can be found on pages 44–46 of *Paper-Cutting Stories for Holidays and Special Events* by Valerie Marsh (Alleyside Press, 1994). The results are fishing poles and sewing needles.

### Draw-and-Tell

**"What Are You Making, Grandpa?"**    This draw-and-tell story can be found on pages 50–52 of *Stories to Draw* by Jerry J. Mallett and Marian R. Bartch (Freline, 1982).

**"Another Story, Grandpa, Please"**    This draw-and-tell story can be found on pages 31–32 of *More Stories to Draw* by Jerry J. Mallett and Timothy S. Ervin (Alleyside Press, 1990).

**"Grandma's Flower Garden"**    This draw-and-tell story can be found on pages 29–31 of *Terrific Tales to Tell from the Storyknifing Tradition* by Valerie Marsh (Alleyside Press, 1997).

### Flannel/Velcro Board

**Grandma's Happy Hat**    Text, patterns, and telling instructions for this flannel/Velcro-board story are found on pages 94–100 of *Once Upon a Felt Board* by Roxane Chadwick (Good Apple, 1986).

**String Beans**    This story, a variation of the Jack and the Beanstalk fairy tale, is found on pages 65–67 of *Celebrations: Read-Aloud Holiday and Theme Book Programs* by Caroline Feller Bauer (H.W. Wilson, 1985). With some searching in your favorite pattern books, you should be able to find all of the characters needed to turn this into a flannel/Velcro-board story.

**"Grandpa's Magic Seed"**    This flannel/Velcro-board story appears on pages 20–21 of *FlannelGraphs: Flannel Board Fun for Little Ones, Preschool–Grade 3*, by Jean Stangl (Fearon Teacher Aids, 1986). You can either use props (listed) or use the patterns on page 60.

## Games

**Grandpa's Hat Matching Game**    The patterns for this matching game can be found on pages 61–62 of *A Tisket A Tasket: Matching Games for Colors, Shapes, and Patterns* by Marilynn G. Barr (Monday Morning Books, 2006). These hats either have different shapes in the centers, or the hat has a recognizable pattern on it. Reproduce the hats (two of each) on different colors of paper so that participants will be matching not only colors but shapes. Laminate for durability and place Velcro on the back. Play the game by passing out to participants one of pair of colors/shapes or colors/patterns of the hats, keeping one in either a pocket or some sort of container. (A hat would be great for this activity!) Pull out your colors/shapes or colors/patterns cards one by one, place on the board, and allow participants to match them!

**Grandparents Day Matchup**    This simple matching game (matching items such as a broom with dustpan, hammer with nails, etc.) can be found on page 40 of *The Best of Holidays and Seasonal Celebrations—Issues 9–13, PreK–K*, edited by Donna Borst (Teaching and Learning Company, 2001). The page can be enlarged and laminated for durability. Lamination also allows you to use dry-erase markers, letting you reuse this item.

## Miscellaneous

**"The Squeaky Door"**    This audience participation story can be found on pages 45–49 of *Crazy Gibberish and Other Story Hour Stretches* by Naomi Baltuck (Linnet Books, 1993). Your participants will love making the sound effects!

**Grandparents Day Songs**
- The piggyback song (new song sung to a familiar tune) "Grandma's Coming Soon to Visit" can be found on page 13 of *Special Day Celebrations* by Elizabeth McKinnon (Warren Publishing House, 1989). This song can also be adapted for Grandpa!
- The song "Grandma and Grandpa" can be found on page 13 of *Simply Super Storytimes: Programming Ideas for Ages 3–6* by Marie Castellano (Upstart, 2003).

# Fingerplays ———————————————————————————————

**Here Are Grandma's Glasses**

| | |
|---|---|
| Here are Grandma's glasses, | *(Circle fingers around eyes to make glasses.)* |
| Here is Grandma's cap. | *(Make big circle with fingers and thumbs and hold on head for cap.)* |
| This is the way she folds her hands, | *(Fold hands and put in lap.)* |
| And lays them in her lap. | *(Repeat this verse, substituting Grandpa for Grandma.)* |

—Traditional rhyme

**Grandfather, Grandmother Tat**

*(Do actions as directed in the rhyme.)*

Grandfather, Grandmother Tat,
Wave one hand like that.
Grandfather, Grandmother Tat,
Clap two hands like that.

Grandfather, Grandmother Tat,
Stamp two feet like that.
Grandfather, Grandmother Tat,
Nod their heads like that.
Funny old Grandfather,
Funny old Grandmother,
Sit back down like that.

—Author unknown

---

### More Great Fingerplays

"Clap for Grandma" (fingerplay) at http://www.thebestkidsbooksite.com/fingerplay.cfm. Click on the "Fingerplays" link, locate the title in the list, and click on the "Show Me" button at the bottom. Note: The word "Grandpa" could be substituted into this rhyme.

---

## Musical Selections

"Grandma Slid Down the Mountain" from *Grandma Slid Down the Mountain* by Cathy Fink. Rounder. ASIN: B0000003F4.

"Grandmas and Grandpas" from *Deep in the Jungle* by Joe Scruggs. Shadow Play. ASIN: B0000058A9.

"Grandma's Feather Bed" from *Skinnamarink TV* by Sharon, Lois, and Bram. Kids Motion. ASIN: B0007DGBK8.

"Grandma's Sleeping in My Bed Tonight" from *Late Last Night* by Joe Scruggs. Big Kid Productions. ASIN: B0002B9B66.

"Grandpa Knows So Many Things" from *All Roads Lead to Home* by Bobby Susser. New Hope Records. ASIN: B0018068BQ.

"Grandparents' Day" from *Happy Everything* by Dr. Jean. Melody House. ASIN: B000DSM3N0E.

"Grandpa's Farm" from *Great Big Hits* by Sharon, Lois, and Bram. Available at http://www.songsforteaching.com/.

"Let's Sing with Our Grandmas and Grandpas" from *Songs for a Great Day!* by Maryann Harman. Available from http://www.songsforteaching.com/.

"My Grandma and Me" from *Sing and Dance* by Jack Grunsky. Casablanca Kids. ASIN: B0000DZ6RT.

"Where My Grandma Lives" from *Toddlin' Tunes* by Cathy Bollinger. Available from http://www.songsforteaching.com/.

## Crafts

**Paper Plate Handprints**    This great craft appears on page 45 of *Celebrate the Seasons: The Best of Holidays and Seasonal Celebrations—Issues 9–12, PreK–3*, edited by Donna Borst (Teaching and Learning Company, 1998). The base is a large paper plate. The child dips his or her hand in washable finger paint and presses it in the middle of the plate. A hole is punched in the top for hanging. The child should write his or her name and the date on the plate. They could also write a message of "I love you" to their grandma or grandpa!

---

### More Great Crafts

Take a second look at the crafts offered in the "Father's Day and Mother's Day" chapter. Many of them could be easily adapted for Grandma and Grandpa.

---

**Grandparents Day Bookmark**    Instructions and patterns are found on pages 9–10 of *Cut and Create! Holidays: Easy Step-by-Step Projects That Teach Scissor Skills* by Kim Rankin (Teaching and Learning Company, 1997). The pattern is a three-scoop ice cream cone made of simple shapes to which a message is added. You may wish to laminate these bookmarks for durability.

**Grandparents Day Basket**    This craft allows participants to fill a basket with pictures of what they would like to give their grandparents for Grandparents Day. The original instructions ask participants to draw items, but you could also provide pictures from old magazines that could be pasted into the basket. The basket pattern appears on page 16 of *September Patterns, Projects, and Plans to Perk Up Early Learning Programs* by Imogene Forte (Incentive Publications, 1989).

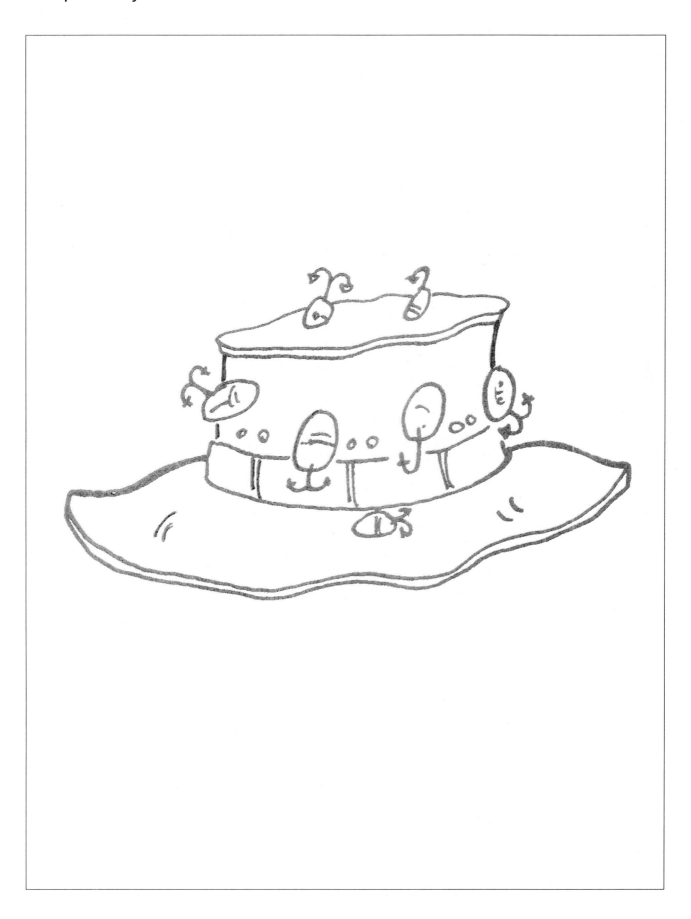

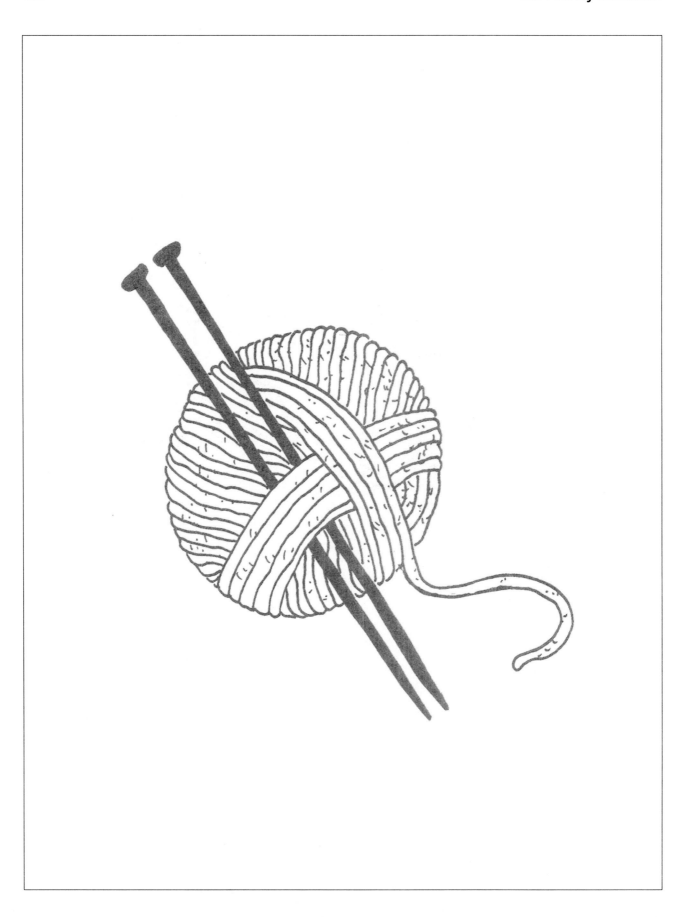

# Groundhog Day

*This holiday provides a great opportunity not only to learn about our furry little friend but to introduce the concept of shadows!*

## History

This holiday is celebrated on February 2nd in the United States and Canada. Many years ago, people who lived in England, Scotland, and Germany believed that the hedgehog (or badger, depending on location) would wake up during the middle of the winter, check the weather, and then decide whether or not to go back to sleep. When German immigrants came to the United States in the 1800s, they brought this custom with them, and they began watching the groundhog or woodchuck. Many of these people settled in the state of Pennsylvania, home of the most famous groundhog of all, Punxsutawney Phil! Phil is the "official" groundhog and his forecast is reported by radio, television, and print journalists. (See The Punxsutawney Groundhog Club's "Groundhog Day History" at http://www.groundhog.org/groundhog-day/history/.)

If the groundhog comes out of his burrow on this day and the sun is shining, a shadow is present. This means six more weeks of winter. If there is no shadow, spring is just around the corner!

Today, Punxsutawney Phil lives in a climate-controlled habitat adjoining the Punxsutawney Library. (See Infoplease's "Groundhog Day" at http://www.infoplease.com/spot/groundhogday1.html.)

## Poetry

"The Groundhog," from page 65 of *Circle Time Book for Holidays and Seasons* by Liz and Dick Wilmes (Building Blocks Publications, 1982).

"Groundhog Day," from page 188 of *Classroom Celebrations: The Best of Holidays and Seasonal Celebrations*, edited by Donna Borst (Teaching and Learning Company, 1996).

"Groundhog Day," from page 51 of *Quick Tricks for Holidays* by Annalisa McMorrow (Monday Morning Books, 2001).

"Groundhog Day," from page 178 of *The Preschool Calendar* by Sherrill B. Flora (T.S. Denison and Company, 1987).

"Groundhog Day," "The Second of February," and "The Groundhog," from http://www.canteach.ca/elementary/songspoems12.html.

"Here's A Little Groundhog," a fingerplay that can be used as a poem, from page 274 of *1001 Rhymes and Fingerplays for Working with Young Children*, compiled by the Totline Staff (Warren Publishing House, 1995).

"The Second of February," a rhyme from page 101 of *Totally Winter* by Sherrill B. Flora (T. S. Denison and Company, 1988), would work great as a poem.

"Wake Up, Ground Hog!," from page 27 of *CopyCat Magazine*, January/February 1992 (now out of print but often available through interlibrary loan).

## Books

Becker, Michelle A. *Groundhog Day*. Children's Press, 2003. ISBN: 978-0516279244.
Part of the Rookie Read-About Holidays series, a great introduction to Groundhog Day.

Cox, Judy. *Go to Sleep, Groundhog!* Holiday House, 2004. ISBN: 978-0823418749.
Groundhog goes to sleep on Columbus Day as usual, setting his alarm clock for February 2nd, but he keeps tossing and turning.

Freeman, Don. *Gregory's Shadow*. Puffin, 2002. ISBN: 978-0142301968.
Gregory Groundhog always feels braver when his best pal, his shadow, accompanies him.

Helig, Kathryn. *Ten Grouchy Groundhogs*. Cartwheel Books, 2009. ISBN: 978-0545134149.
A hilarious countdown story about a den of grouchy, grubby, gobbling, gabby, giggly, groovy, graceful, glitzy, gleeful, groggy groundhogs getting ready for their great big day.

Holub, Joan. *Groundhog Weather School*. Putnam Juvenile, 2009. ISBN: 978-0399246593.
When the annual Groundhog Day forecast proves inaccurate in Rabbit's locale, he encourages Professor Groundhog to open a weather school with students from around the continent.

McMullan, Kate. *Fluffy Meets the Groundhog*. Cartwheel Books, 2002. ISBN: 978-0439206723.
When Fluffy stumbles upon a strange den, he finds himself face to face with one very shy groundhog.

Miller, Pat. *Substitute Groundhog*. Albert Whitman and Company, 2006. ISBN: 978-0807576434.
Groundhog comes down with the flu just before his big day, so he has to hold auditions for substitute weather tellers.

Roberts, Bethany. *Double Trouble Groundhog Day*. Henry Holt and Company, 2008. ISBN: 978-0805082807.
Grampie Groundhog decides to turn over the family job of forecasting the weather to one of his grandchildren, but which one? Gregory wants to do it, but so does his twin, Greta.

Vojta, Pat S. *Mr. Groundhog Wants the Day Off*. Raven Tree Press, 2010. ISBN: 978-1934960783.
Mr. Groundhog tries to give his Groundhog Day duties away. He does not want to be blamed for six more weeks of winter anymore!

---

### Older Gems, or Titles Too Good to Pass Up

Asch, Frank. *Bear Shadow*. Silver Burdett, 1996. ISBN: 978-0382336560,
Bear tries everything he can think of to get rid of his shadow.

Cohen, Carol. *Wake Up, Groundhog!* Crown Publishers, 1988. ISBN: 978-0517516935.
Miss Pigeon tries all sorts of ways to wake up the sleeping Groundhog.

Delton, Judy. *Groundhog's Day at the Doctor*. Dutton Children's Books, 1981. ISBN: 978-0819310415.
Groundhog visits the doctor and dispenses his own medical advice while there.

Glass, Marvin. *What Happened Today, Freddy Groundhog?* Crown Publishers, 1989. ISBN: 978-0517571408.
Freddy the groundhog hears about the tradition of February 2nd from his father, and learns that it will be his turn this year to make the official early check on the approaching spring season.

Hamberger, John. *This Is the Day*. Price Stern Sloan, 1971. ISBN: 978-0448261942.
One special February day all the forest animals go to the groundhog's burrow to see if he will come out.

Koscielniak, Bruce. *Geoffrey Groundhog Predicts the Weather*. Turtleback, 1988. ISBN: 978-0613069687.
Predicting the weather seems easy to Geoffrey Groundhog, who recalls his mother's advice regarding the sighting of his shadow on February 2nd.

Kroll, Steven. *It's Groundhog Day!* Holiday House, 1987. ISBN: 978-0823406432.
Worried that an early spring will ruin his ski lodge business, Roland Raccoon takes drastic steps to prevent Godfrey Groundhog from looking for his shadow on Groundhog Day.

Levine, Abby. *Gretchen Groundhog, It's Your Day!* Albert Whitman and Company, 1998. ISBN: 978-0807530597.
Gretchen has been newly appointed to look for her shadow on Groundhog Day so the townspeople will know if spring is just around the corner.

Worsham, Adria F. *Max Celebrates Groundhog Day*. Picture Window Books, 2008. ISBN: 978-1404847606.

    The class is going on a field trip for Groundhog Day. Will Max and Zoe get to see a real groundhog?

## Activities

> ### Coloring Pages
>
> Consult your favorite pattern books or holiday coloring books for pages to use as coloring sheets. Be sure to search online as well. There's lots of great stuff out there! For example, a great page that can be printed and enlarged is found at http://www.groundhog.org/fileadmin/sitecontent/Teachers/colormephil.jpg.

### Cut-and-Tell

**Little Georgie Groundhog Cut-and-Tell Story**    The text for this story is actually the same as the fingerplay "A Little Groundhog" by Jean Warren. The text, plus cutting instructions, can be found on pages 62–65 of *Cut and Tell: Scissor Stories for Winter* by Jean Warren (Warren Publishing House, 1984).

**Shadows**    This paper-cutting rhyme and patterns can be found on pages 37–38 of *Scissor-Tales for Special Days* by Jan Grubb Philpot (Incentive Publications, 1994).

### Flannel/Velcro Board

**Gregory Groundhog Looks for His Shadow**    The script for this presentation can be found on pages 92–99 of *Felt Board Stories* by Liz and Dick Wilmes (Building Blocks Publication, 2001). Gregory sees all sorts of animal shadows that are not his, among them a deer, a frog, and several others. This story and patterns also appear on page 65 (text of story) and pages 186–191 (animal patterns) of *Table and Floor Games* by Liz and Dick Wilmes (Building Blocks Publications, 1994). I copied two of the animal patterns, one that can be colored in, and one on black construction paper. I then taped the two together, so that one side shows the complete black color (the shadow); when flipped, it becomes the colored-in animal pattern.

**Animal Shadows**    My original patterns for this game came from a book whose title is long since lost, since the book was parted out for patterns for different activities. However, the concept is easy to replicate. Consult your favorite clip art books for good-sized patterns of familiar animals. My original game has the following: rhinoceros, camel, penguin, lion, bear, rabbit, fish, rooster, elephant, and seal. An easy way to make the shadows is to copy them onto black construction paper and then cut out around them. Laminate for durability, placing your flannel or Velcro pieces on the side where you can see the pattern copied. That way, only the plain black side will be visible to participants. Put up each shadow, one at a time, after saying the following rhyme: "Will you look, and will you see, whose shadow could this be?" Allow participants to guess the animal.

    *Note:* Even doing a Google search of each type of animal paired with the word "silhouette" finds some great-looking shadows!

**Groundhogs**    This rhyme, found on page 220 of *The Biggest Holiday Book Ever!* by Patti Carson and Janet Dellosa (Carson-Dellosa Publishing, 1987), is shown as a fingerplay, but can easily be adapted into a flannel/Velcro-board presentation. I do mine with five groundhog figures that I found, enlarged, copied, and laminated. You could add the items that three of them are holding as well: feather duster, flowers, and a brush. My patterns came from the February/March 2005 issue of *The Mailbox Magazine* (often available through interlibrary loan), Preschool Edition.

## Games

**Groundhog Bowling**     Use 2-liter bottles as the base for this craft. It would even be fun to use the actual small plastic bowling sets. Find a clip art picture of a groundhog (preferably in color) that you can enlarge. Laminate for durability. Tape to the front of 2-liter bottles or plastic pins. Use the ball provided with the set or a small ball as your "bowling" ball to knock down the groundhogs!

**Groundhog Matching Game**     Use the Ellison groundhog die to cut out groundhogs, two of each color, using either construction paper or colored paper. Laminate for durability. Place Velcro on the backs. To play the game, hand out one of each of the pair to participants. You keep one of the pair either in an apron pocket or container. Once everyone has a groundhog, begin by pulling the ones you have out, one at a time, placing them on your board, and allowing participants to match. Continue until all colors have been matched.

## Miscellaneous

**Huff and Puff on Groundhog Day**     This story and pattern, told with puppets cut from paper plates, can be found on pages 48 (story) and 69 (patterns) of *The Best of Totline Newsletter*, compiled by Jean Warren (Warren Publishing House, 1995).

**"The Groundhog Family"**     This story can be found on pages 91–92 of *The Storytelling Handbook: A Young People's Collection of Unusual Tales and Helpful Hints on How to Tell Them* by Anne Pellowski (Simon and Schuster Books for Young Readers, 1995).

**Groundhog Day Printable Poster**     Use this color poster, found at http://www.activityvillage .co.uk/groundhog_day_poster_printable.htm, as a way to explain to participants what happens when the groundhog sees/doesn't see his shadow. Print out and laminate for durability.

### Groundhog Songs
- The piggyback song "Groundhog Song" can be found on page 43 of *Holiday Piggyback Songs*, compiled by Jean Warren (Warren Publishing House, 1988).
- The songs "On Groundhog Day" and "Little Groundhog" can be found on page 22 of *More Piggyback Songs*, compiled by the Totline Newsletter Staff (Warren Publishing House, 1984).
- Also, the songs "Little Groundhog" and "Can You Play?," along with American Sign Language motions, can be found on pages 46–47 of *Piggyback Songs to Sign* by Jean Warren and Susan Shroyer (Warren Publishing House, 1992).
- The song "Mr. Groundhog" can be found on page 72 of *The Best of Totline Magazine, Volume 3*, compiled by Gayle Bittinger (McGraw-Hill Children's Publishing, 2003).

# Fingerplays ——————————————————————————————————————————

### Groundhog Day

| | |
|---|---|
| February second | *(Hold up two fingers.)* |
| Is Groundhog Day. | |
| Will he see his shadow? | *(Shade eyes with hands.)* |
| And what will he say? | |
| If he says, "More cold," | *(Hug body.)* |
| If he says, "More snow," | *(Raise arms and let fingers wiggle as they fall.)* |
| Then into his hole | |
| He will surely go. | *(Place fist behind back.)* |

—Author unknown

---

**More Great Fingerplays**

"Little Groundhog," an action rhyme, from page 274 of *1001 Rhymes and Fingerplays for Working with Young Children*, compiled by the Totline Staff (Warren Publishing House, 1994).

"Groundhog Day," an action rhyme, from page 74 of *A Child's Seasonal Treasury*, compiled and written by Betty Jones (Tricycle Press, 1996).

"The Groundhog," from page 212 of *Celebrate the Seasons: The Best of Holidays and Seasonal Celebrations—Issues 9–12, PreK–3*, edited by Donna Borst (Teaching and Learning Company, 1998).

"Groundhogs," from page 97 of *The Big All-Year Book of Holidays and Seasonal Celebrations: Preschool–Kindergarten, Issues 14–18*, edited by Donna Borst (Teaching and Learning Company, 2002).

"Groundhogs," from page 157 of *The Big All-Year Book of Holidays and Seasonal Celebrations: Preschool–Kindergarten, Issues 14–18*, edited by Donna Borst (Teaching and Learning Company, 2002). (This fingerplay is different from the one listed previously with the same title.)

"Shadow, Shadow," an action rhyme, from page 48 of *The Best of Totline Magazine, Volume 2*, compiled by Gayle Bittinger (McGraw-Hill Children's Publishing, 2003).

"Little Shadow" and "Groundhog Day," action rhymes, from page 31 of *Four Seasons Movement* by Jean Warren (Warren Publishing House, 1996).

"Groundhog Day," from page 1 of *Let's Learn . . . : Holiday Finger Plays, Worksheets and Art Projects* by Katherine Oana, Patti Carson, and Janet Dellosa (Carson-Dellosa Publishing, 1983).

"Pop Up, Little Groundhog," an action rhyme, from page 247 of *Storytime Magic: 400 Fingerplays, Flannelboards, and Other Activities* by Kathy MacMillan and Christine Kirker (American Library Association, 2009).

"Groundhog in His Hole," "The Groundhog," and "Five Little Groundhogs," from page 18 of *52 Programs for Preschoolers: The Librarian's Year-Round Planner* by Diane Briggs (American Library Association, 1997).

"Five Groundhogs," from page 105 of *Rhymes for Learning Times* by Louise B. Scott (T.S. Denison and Company, 1983).

## Musical Selections

"Groundhog" from *Sing about Martin and Other Miss Jackie Favorites* by Miss Jackie Silberg. Miss Jackie Music. ASIN: B0009Y9COC.

"Groundhog Day" from *Happy Everything* by Dr. Jean. Melody House. ASIN: B000SDM3N0E.

"Groundhog's Day Song" by Daria. Available from http://www.songsforteaching.com/.

"Groundhog's Day Song/Punxatawney Phil" by Marla Lewis and Les Julian. Available from http://www.songsforteaching.com/.

## Crafts

**Groundhog Lunch Bag Puppet**    The pattern for the groundhog used for this puppet is found on page 174 of *The Best of Holidays and Seasonal Celebrations—Issues 5–8, PreK–3*, edited by Donna Borst (Teaching and Learning Company, 1997). Cut the pattern into two pieces as shown and glue to the lunch bag. Show participants how to place their hand inside the paper bag to manipulate the puppet.

**Groundhog Shadow Puppet**    The pattern for this groundhog puppet is found on page 83 of *The Best of Holidays and Seasonal Celebrations: Songs, Action Rhymes, and Fingerplays, PreK–3*, compiled by Ellen Sussman (Teaching and Learning Company, 2000). This craft also uses an 8-ounce Styrofoam cup and a craft stick. The craft stick is used to poke a hole in the bottom of the cup that allows it

to slide up and down freely. The groundhog pattern is glued to the craft stick once it is colored. The craft stick allows the groundhog to "pop up" out of the cup!

**Groundhog Paper Bag Puppet**    This super-simple craft has all of the groundhog's body parts (head, legs, hands, and tail) attached to a regular brown paper bag! Instructions and patterns appear on pages 12–15 of *February Patterns and Projects* (Newbridge Educational, 2000).

**Groundhog Shadow Puppet**    This simple craft makes a groundhog and his shadow. The pattern will have to be duplicated twice for each participant, so that each receives one brown groundhog and one black groundhog. I would duplicate onto card stock for durability and so that they stand easily. They are then glued to a craft stick that enables them to stand! Instructions appear on page 24 and pattern appears on page 30 of *February Arts and Crafts, Grades 1–3*, edited by Susan Walker (The Education Center, 2000).

**Groundhog**    Instructions and patterns are found on pages 47–48 of *Cut and Create! Holidays: Easy Step-by-Step Projects That Teach Scissor Skills* by Kim Rankin (Teaching and Learning Company, 1997). Simple shapes make a cute groundhog's head decoration.

**Groundhog Puppet**    The base of this craft is a large paper plate onto which a pattern with verse is glued. A groundhog figure is then attached to a straw which is put through the center of the plate.

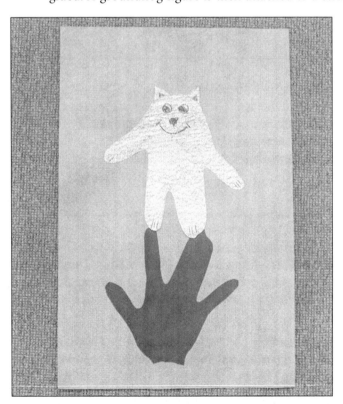

Directions and patterns for this puppet can be found on pages 19 and 21 of *CopyCat Magazine*, January/February 2004 (now out of print but often available through interlibrary loan).

**Furry Weatherman**    Instructions for this cute craft are on page 8 of *Hand-Shaped Art* by Diane Bonica (Good Apple, 1989). The base is the participant's hand, which makes the groundhog and his shadow.

**Sleeping Groundhog**    The original name for this pattern is Hibernating Chipmunk, but I think if the stripes are left off the back, it looks just like a sleeping groundhog, all curled up and snug in his den! Patterns and instructions can be found on pages 22–24 of *Cut and Create! For All Seasons: Easy Step-by-Step Projects That Teach Scissor Skills*, by Nancee McClure (Teaching and Learning Company, 1995). In addition, there are also groundhog instructions and patterns on pages 46–48, for a groundhog peeking out of his hole!

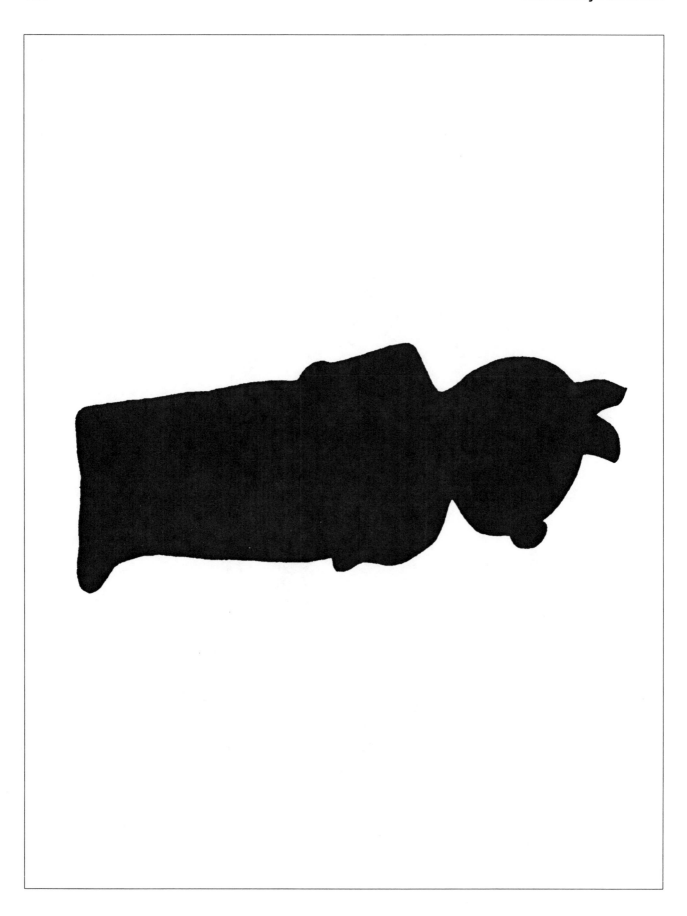

# Halloween

*You can go so many ways with programming for this holiday— ghosts, skeletons, pumpkins, and more! You even can provide an opportunity for your storyhour participants to show off that Halloween costume one more time!*

## History

Centuries ago, people who lived in what is now England, France, and Ireland were known as Celts. The Celts believed in both good and evil spirits. These people spent much time in the spring and summer growing food that would last them throughout the winter. When harvest time came, they held a festival called Samhain, which thanked the good spirits for their help. As part of this celebration, people wore costumes, ate lots of food, and made sacrifices to keep the evil spirits away.

Back in 853 AD, the Roman Catholic Church made November 1st a church holiday honoring all of the saints. This day was called by several names: All Saint's Day, Hallowmas, or Allhallows. People celebrated October 31st as All Hallows' Eve. Over time, the name was shortened to Halloween. Because November 1st was a day for good spirits and souls, the night before (October 31st) was thought to be a time when evil spirits roamed freely on the earth. People began to put lanterns in their windows and in front of their doors to scare away these evil spirits. These lanterns were made from carved turnips and other vegetables. November 2nd was a holy day on the Roman Catholic calendar called All Souls' Day, when all dead people were honored. (See Edna Barth's *Witches, Pumpkins, and Grinning Ghosts: The Story of the Halloween Symbols* [Clarion Books/Ticknor and Fields, 1972].)

Of course, today, Halloween is celebrated in most communities by trick or treat or Beggars' Night, with children (and some adults, too) dressing in costume and going door-to-door collecting candy and goodies! This custom can be traced back to the practice of "souling," during which the poor would go door-to-door on November 1st, receiving food in return for prayers for the dead on November 2nd. Other activities that might be held on Halloween are bonfires and visiting "haunted" houses. (See "History of Halloween" at http://www.halloweenhistory.org/.)

The custom of dressing up is something we can trace back to early history, when people dressed in costumes to scare away the spirits of the dead that they believed roamed the earth on All Hallows' Eve. We have also adopted the custom of placing a hollowed-out vegetable (a pumpkin) in windows and on porches.

Trick or treat really seems to have become established in American culture during the early 1950s. It was featured in a Walt Disney cartoon titled "Trick or Treat." The popular television show *Ozzie and Harriet* featured a Halloween episode and UNICEF conducted its first national campaign during these years.

## Poetry

"Bats," from page 89 of *Something Big Has Been Here* by Jack Prelutsky (Greenwillow Books, 1990).

"Ghosts" and "Skeletons," from page 28 of *Poetry Fun by the Ton with Jack Prelutsky* by Cheryl Potts (Alleyside Press, 1995).

"Halloween" by Nike J. Lewis, from page 58 of *The Best of Holidays and Seasonal Celebrations— Issues 1–4, PreK–K*, edited by Donna Borst and Janet Armbrust (Teaching and Learning Company, 1999).

"A Halloween Pumpkin," "Little Jack Pumpkin Face," "Spooks," and "Bats," from pages 42, 43, 47, and 48, respectively, of *Month-by-Month Poetry: September, October, and November* by Marian Reiner (Scholastic Professional Books, 1999).

"Haunted House" and "Jack-O'-Lanterns," from pages 16 and 30, respectively, of *Who Said Boo? Halloween Poems for the Very Young* by Nancy White Carlstrom (Simon and Schuster Books for Young Readers, 1995).

"I Don't Believe in Bigfoot" by Eileen Spinelli from page 24 of *Cobwebs, Chatters, and Chills: A Collection of Scary Poems* compiled by Patricia M. Stockland (Compass Point Books, 2004).

"Mr. Pumpkin," from page 54 of *Move Over Mother Goose! Finger Plays, Action Verses and Funny Rhymes*, edited by Kathleen Charner (Gryphon House, 1987).

"One Halloween Night" by Patricia O'Brien, from page 75 of *Celebrate the Seasons: The Best of Holidays and Seasonal Celebrations—Issues 9–12, PreK–3*, edited by Donna Borst (Teaching and Learning Company, 1998).

"...or Treat," from page 36 of *It's Halloween* by Jack Prelutsky (Greenwillow Books, 1977).

"Plump Pumpkin" and "Pumpkins Grin" from pages 30–31 of *Autumnblings* by Douglas Florian (Greenwillow Books, 2003).

"Pumpkin Face" and "Halloween Cat," from page 82 of *A School Year of Poems: 180 Favorites from Highlights*, selected by Walter B. Barbe (Boyds Mills Press, 2005).

"Pumpkin Nights," from page 17 of *Circle-Time Poetry Around the Year* by Jodi Simpson (Scholastic, 2005).

"Skeleton Parade" and "The Time Has Come," from pages 82 and 107, respectively, of *Be Glad Your Nose Is on Your Face and Other Poems* by Jack Prelutsky (Greenwillow Books, 2008).

"What Should I Be?" and "Jack O'Lantern," from pages 3 and 31, respectively, of *Skeleton Bones and Goblin Groans: Poems for Halloween* by Amy E. Sklansky (Henry Holt and Company, 2004).

"The Witch's Invitation," from page 20 of *A Rumpus of Rhymes: A Book of Noisy Poems* by Bobbi Katz (Dutton Children's Books, 2001).

## Books

Alexander, Elizabeth. *Little Pumpkin's Big Surprise!* Golden Books, 2008. ISBN: 978-0375841484.
Little Pumpkin's dream is to become a Halloween jack-o'-lantern, so he is upset when a squirrel tells him that he cannot achieve his ambition because he is still green. This book has an extra attraction: it lights up!

Balian, Lorna. *Humbug Witch.* Star Bright Books, 2004. ISBN: 978-1595720092.
This book is probably my *absolute* favorite! The story profiles a little witch who looks the part, but who cannot get her magic to work. The ending will surprise you. This book was originally written in 1965, but has been reissued in paperback.

Behn, Harry. *Halloween.* North-South Books, 2003. ISBN: 978-0735817661.
A skeleton, a witch, and a devil go out for trick or treat, but are frightened by every sound they hear and everything they see.

Cimirusti, Marie. *Peek-A-Boooo!* Dutton Juvenile, 2005. ISBN: 978-0525474357.
Toddlers will enjoy playing peek-a-boo with familiar, friendly, not-at-all frightening Halloween figures!

Crimi, Carolyn. *Where's My Mummy?* Candlewick Press, 2008. ISBN: 978-0763631963.
One deep, dark night, as all of the monsters are preparing for bed, Little Baby Mummy bravely searches for his mother until he sees a truly terrifying creature.

Cushman, Doug. *Halloween Good Night.* Henry Holt and Company, 2010. ISBN: 978-0805089288.
On Halloween night, monsters, from hairy werewolves on the moors to scaly swamp creatures in a black lagoon, say goodnight to their mommies and daddies.

Cuyler, Margery. *Skeleton Hiccups*. Margaret K. McElderry, 2010. ISBN: 978-0689847707.
  Ghost tries to help Skeleton get rid of the hiccups.

Depken, Kristen L. *One, Two—Boo!* Golden Books, 2009. ISBN: 978-0375844188.
  This book invites young readers inside a haunted house to lift the flaps and discover increasing numbers of spooky creatures getting ready to celebrate Halloween.

Kneen, Maggie. *The Halloween Kittens*. Chronicle Books, 2004. ISBN: 978-0811842280.
  Lift the flaps and discover all sorts of sneaky fun with the mischievous kitten brothers Trick and Treat as they prepare for Halloween.

Leuck, Laura. *One Witch*. Walker Books for Young Readers, 2004. ISBN: 978-0802788603.
  One witch has an empty pot to fill in this spooky tale that's also a counting exercise.

Mantle, Ben. *Five Little Pumpkins*. Tiger Tales, 2010. ISBN: 978-1589258563.
  An illustrated counting book with five little pumpkins who experience the fun of Halloween night.

McDermott, Tom. *The Ghouls Come Haunting One by One*. Pelican Publishing Company, 2010. ISBN: 978-1589807860.
  This counting book for young readers offers a rhyming Halloween twist on the old camp song "The Ants Go Marching One by One."

Mead, David. *Who's at the Door?* Smart Kids Publishing, 2010. ISBN: 978-0824914318.
  Who could be ringing the doorbell tonight? Is it a monster? A goblin? Or maybe even a ghost? Open the lift-the-flap doors on each page to find out who's lurking on the doorstep on Halloween night!

Montijo, Rhode. *The Halloween Kid*. Simon and Schuster Children's Publishing, 2010. ISBN: 978-1416935759.
  "YEE-HA-LLOWEEN!" is the battle cry of the Halloween Kid, who rides his stick horse into suburban anytown USA and rids the place of all manner of Halloween-hatin' varmints.

Neubacker, Robert. *Too Many Monsters! A Halloween Counting Book*. Little Simon, 2010. ISBN: 978-1442401723.
  Children will love counting kooky monsters from 1 to 10.

Nikola-Lisa, W. *Shake Dem Halloween Bones*. Turtleback, 2000. ISBN: 978-0613301237.
  It's Halloween night. The city is quiet. The city is still. But as the lights go down, the music comes up—and the guests start to arrive at the hip-hop Halloween ball! And oh, what a party it is! Pair this book with the song "Dem Bones"!

---

### Older Gems, or Titles Too Good to Pass Up

Asch, Frank. *Popcorn: A Frank Asch Bear Story*. Parents Magazine Press, 1979. ISBN: 978-0819310018.
  Another of my very favorite Halloween tales! Sam the Bear invites his friends to an impromptu Halloween party and asks them to bring a treat.

Marshall, James. *Space Case*. Puffin, 1992. ISBN: 978-0140547047.
  When the thing from outer space visits Earth, it is taken first for a trick-or-treater and then for a robot!

Roberts, Bethany. *Halloween Mice!* Sandpiper, 1997. ISBN: 978-0395866191.
  Costumed mice frisk, whisk, whirl, and twirl through the moonlight to party in the pumpkin patch.

Silverman, Erica. *Big Pumpkin*. Simon and Schuster Children's Publishing, 1992. ISBN: 978-0027826838.
  A witch decides to mark the holiday by baking a pumpkin pie. But there is one problem: the pumpkin she has planted is stuck on the vine. This story is based on the Russian folktale "The Turnip."

Williams, Linda. *The Little Old Lady Who Was Not Afraid of Anything*. HarperCollins, 1986. ISBN: 978-0690045840.
  A clever reworking of the classic story of a ghostly body that appears bit by bit.

Root, Phyllis. *Who Said Boo?* Little Simon, 2005. ISBN: 978-0689854088.
> Someone said boo. But who? Lift the flaps to solve this spooky mystery!

Schulman, Janet. *10 Trick-or-Treaters: A Halloween Counting Book.* Knopf Books for Young Readers, 2005. ISBN: 978-0375832253.
> Ten trick-or-treaters start out on Halloween night, but they disappear one by one as they encounter a spider, a vampire, a ghost, and other scary creatures.

Steer, Dugald. *Snappy Little Halloween.* Silver Dolphin Books, 2003. ISBN: 978-1571459183.
> Perfect for kids who are just getting excited about Halloween, this title features a colorful collection of creepy pop-up characters, including a skeleton, mummy, ghosts, vampires, cats, and bats.

Stoeke, Janet Morgan. *Minerva Louise on Halloween.* Dutton Children's Books, 2009. ISBN: 978-0525421498.
> On her first Halloween, Minerva Louise the hen puzzles over costumes but enjoys her first taste of candy corn.

Tripani, Iza. *Haunted Party.* Charlesbridge Publishing, 2009. ISBN: 978-1580892469.
> In this counting book that introduces numbers from 1 to 10, a ghost and his supernatural friends give a party on Halloween night.

Vaughn, Marcia. *Five Pesky Pumpkins.* Little Simon, 2008. ISBN: 978-1416939054.
> As the text counts down from 5, the pumpkins cause mischief on a spooky and scary night while readers practice counting.

## Activities

---

### Coloring Pages

Consult your favorite pattern books or holiday coloring books for pages to use as coloring sheets. Be sure to search online as well. There's lots of great stuff out there!

- Visit http://dulemba.com/index_ColoringPages.html for author and illustrator Elizabeth O. Dulemba's great collection of holiday coloring pages. While there, sign up for her Coloring Page Tuesdays e-mails.

---

### Cut-and-Tell

**"The Little Orange House"**    This great story can be found on pages 4–6 of *Paper Stories* by Jean Stangl (David S. Lake Publishers, 1984). It ends up being a pumpkin, complete with face! This story and pattern are also found online at http://www.toddlervillage.net/THE%20LITTLE%20ORANGE%20HOUSE 102005.pdf. A very similar story, titled "Perky Pumpkin's Open House Surprise," can be found on pages 41–43 of *Storytelling with the Flannelboard, Book Two* by Paul S. Anderson (T.S. Denison and Company, 1970). *The Everything Book for Teachers of Young Children* by Valerie Indenbaum and Marcia Shapiro (Partner Press, 1983) also contains a similar story, titled "Perky Pumpkin," on pages 76–77.

**"Little Black Cat"; "Two Friendly Ghosts"; "Three Brave Hunters"**    All three of these cut-and-tell stories involve using paper plates. They can be found on pages 37–59 of *Cut and Tell: Scissor Stories for Fall* by Jean Warren (Warren Publishing House, 1984).

**"G"**    This cut-and-tell story, which ends up being a ghost, is found on pages 26–27 of *Paper Cutting Stories from A to Z* by Valerie Marsh (Alleyside Press, 1992).

### Draw-and-Tell

**"The Tale of a Black Cat"**    This can be found on pages 155–158 of *When the Lights Go Out: 20 Scary Tales to Tell* by Margaret Read MacDonald (H.W. Wilson, 1988).

**"Halloween"**     This story can be found on pages 78–80 of *Top Dot Tales* by Valerie Marsh (Alleyside Press, 2001).

**"Trick-or-Treat"**     This draw-and-tell story can be found on pages 36–37 of *Stories to Draw* by Jerry J. Mallett and Marian R. Bartch (Freline, 1982).

**"The Halloween Witch"**     This draw-and-tell story can be found on pages 60–87 of *Chalk Talk Stories* by Arden Druce (Scarecrow Press, 1993).

**"Trick or Treat"**     This draw-and-tell story that creates a jack-o'-lantern is found on pages 105–106 of *Chalk in Hand: The Draw and Tell Book* by Phyllis Noe Pflomm (Scarecrow Press, 1986).

## Flannel/Velcro Board

**"Scat-the-Cat"**     This story is found on pages 88–89 of *The Everything Book for Teachers of Young Children* by Valerie Indenbaum and Marcia Shapiro (Partner Press, 1983). Scat changes his color over and over again!

**"Halloween Countdown"**     This flannel/Velcro-board activity is found on pages 190 and 224–229 of *Low-Cost, High-Interest Programming: Seasonal Events for Preschoolers* by Gail Benton and Trish Waichulaitis (Neal-Schuman, 2004). Patterns are included in the text. Another great story from this source is "Halloween at the Zoo." Patterns for this story are also included in the text.

**"The Chocolate Chip Ghost"**     In doing a Google search (using simply the title), I came across several variations of the story that would be perfect to use. The story is about a family of ghosts who eat things that they shouldn't and end up turning different colors. It's fun for kids to guess what color the ghosts will turn once they have eaten a particular food! A simple ghost pattern will suffice for the characters. Color them or cut them out of colored paper depending on what they have eaten! A great pattern for a ghost appears on page 59 of *October Patterns and Projects* (Newbridge Educational, 1999), or you can use the one included at the end of this chapter.

**"Halloween Night"**     Text and patterns for this flannel/Velcro-board activity can be found on pages 193–195 of *Felt Board Fun for Everyday and Holidays* by Liz and Dick Wilmes (Building Blocks Publications, 1984).

**"The Giant Pumpkin"; "Better Silly Than Sorry"**     These stories, both of which could be easily adapted for flannel/Velcro-board telling, can be found on pages 10–15 of *Short-Short Stories: Simple Stories for Young Children Plus Seasonal Activities*, compiled by Jean Warren (Warren Publishing House, 1987).

**"A Terrible Sight"**     This song, sung to the tune of "Three Blind Mice," would work well as a flannel/Velcro-board presentation. The text can be found on page 272 of *Marmalade Days Fall: Complete Units for Busy Teachers of Young Children* by Carol Taylor Bond (Partner Press, 1987). A quick search of your favorite pattern books would yield all of the characters you need. Copy off the appropriate number for each verse of the song. Instead of putting them out individually for each verse, group them in pleasing arrangements for your numbers 2–10. That way, the characters can all be put on the board at one time for the verse in which they are mentioned.

**"Halloween Night"**     Rob Reid has taken this story by Elizabeth Hatch and adapted it into a story for the flannel/Velcro board. Use the actual book, *Halloween Night* by Elizabeth Hatch (Random House, 2005), for the text. Patterns for the story appear on pages 25–28 of Reid's book *Shake and Shout: 16 Noisy, Lively Story Programs* (Upstart, 2008).

**"Five Orange Pumpkins"**     This flannel/Velcro-board story about five pumpkins who all find uses for Halloween is found on page 12 of *FlannelGraphs: Flannel Board Fun for Little Ones, Preschool–Grade 3*, by Jean Stangl (Fearon Teacher Aids, 1986). Patterns appear on page 54.

**"A Ghost Called Matt"**    This story about a little ghost who changes colors can be found on pages 34–35 of *FlannelGraphs: Flannel Board Fun for Little Ones, Preschool–Grade 3*, by Jean Stangl (Fearon Teacher Aids, 1986). Patterns appear on page 70.

**"The Witch Who Couldn't Fly"**    This story about a little witch who learns to fly is found on pages 36–37 of *FlannelGraphs: Flannel Board Fun for Little Ones, Preschool–Grade 3*, by Jean Stangl (Fearon Teacher Aids, 1986). Patterns appear on page 71.

**"Eight Giggling Ghosts"**    This cute rhyme can be done as a flannel/Velcro-board presentation or as stick puppets. The rhyme and patterns are found on pages 21–22 of *Super Story Telling* by Carol Elaine Catron and Barbara Catron Parks (T.S. Denison and Company, 1986). (*Note:* The text of this rhyme can also be found in the Fingerplays section of this chapter under "Ghosts and Goblins.")

**"Mouse's Halloween House"**    This cute story, about a little mouse who makes a jack-o'-lantern by nibbling away parts of a pumpkin to make a house for herself and her children, can be found on pages 43–44 of *Mother Goose's Playhouse* by Judy Sierra (Bob Kaminski Media Arts, 1994). Patterns are included.

## Games

**Pumpkin Matching Game**    Use a favorite pattern or an Ellison die-cut pattern to make pumpkins of different-colored paper. Laminate for durability. Pass out one pumpkin to each participant, and keep the match in an apron pocket or perhaps a pumpkin basket or plastic trick-or-treat pumpkin. Once everyone has a pumpkin, pull out pumpkins, one by one, and place on your flannel/Velcro board, matching colors as you go. A fun variation on this game is to have pumpkins with different faces, two of each, and match the faces. The patterns that I used came from page 19 of *Bulletin Boards Through the Year* by Pat Spencer (Teacher Created Materials, 1988). You could easily draw your own shapes for eyes, noses, and mouths! Another source for pumpkins with different faces that you could reproduce on different-colored paper comes from the October/November 2005 issue of *The Mailbox Magazine*, Preschool Edition, in an article titled "Plentiful Pumpkins!"

**Halloween Matching Game**    Patterns for a variety of Halloween symbols (bat, cat, cornstalk, ghost, pumpkin, scarecrow) appear on pages 7–17 of *Holiday Patterns*, compiled by Jean Warren (Warren Publishing House, 1991). The best patterns to use are the ones that are already enclosed in a square, as this would make cutting them out simple. Copy two of each on different colors of construction paper. For instructions, see the Pumpkin Matching Game in this section.

**Pin the Nose (Hat, Mouth, Eyes, etc.) on the Jack-O'-Lantern**    Instructions for this simple game can be found on page 51 of *A Child's Seasonal Treasury*, compiled and written by Betty Jones (Tricycle Press, 1996).

**Pumpkin Toss**    This great game comes from *Celebrate the Seasons: The Best of Holidays and Seasonal Celebrations—Issues 9–12, PreK–3*, edited by Donna Borst (Teaching and Learning Company, 1998). This game can be played independently or by dividing participants into teams. Use large plastic pumpkins and several beanbags. Have participants take turns tossing the beanbags into the pumpkin from an established starting line.

## Miscellaneous

**Halloween Costume Parade**    If your participants wear costumes to your Halloween storyhour session, why not have a parade through the library? Use one of the Halloween CDs listed in the Musical Selections section. If you can broadcast the music over a PA or phone system, allow participants to march throughout the library with music!

**"Let's Go on a Ghost Hunt!"**    The text and motions for this audience participation story, a variant of "Let's Go on a Bear Hunt," can be found on pages 148–154 of *When the Lights Go Out: 20 Scary Tales to Tell* by Margaret Read MacDonald (H.W. Wilson, 1988).

**"The Ghost and the Pumpkin"**    The text, motions, and pattern for this activity can be found on pages 62–63 of *Fold-and-Cut Stories and Fingerplays* by Marj Hart (Fearon Teacher Aids, 1987). A white paper bag is perfect for the ghost character!

**"If You're a Ghost and You Know It"**    Rob Reid created this great song by adapting the traditional "If You're Happy and You Know It." The lyrics appear on pages 20–21 of his book *Shake and Shout: 16 Noisy, Lively Story Programs* (Upstart, 2008).

**"Gotcha!"**    This paper-folding story, which creates a pocket of air that makes a loud pop when moved, is found on pages 20–23 of *Holiday Folding Stories: Storytelling and Origami Together for Holiday Fun* by Kristine Kallevig (Storytime Ink International, 1992).

**"Halloween Hilda"**    This is a pocket story. The character (Hilda) is enlarged to poster-board size. Her apron area is covered with a plastic baggie so that items may be dropped into it as she "eats" them. The text and patterns can be found on pages 145–147 of *Super Story Telling* by Carol Elaine Catron and Barbara Catron Parks (T.S. Denison and Company, 1986).

## Fingerplays ————————————————————————————————————————

### Cats

#### I Am the Witch's Cat

| | |
|---|---|
| I am the witch's cat. | *(Point to self.)* |
| Meow, meow, meow. | |
| My fur is black as darkest night. | *(Stroke right hand with left.)* |
| My eyes are glaring, green and bright. | *(Point to eyes.)* |
| I am the witch's cat, | *(Point to self again.)* |
| Meow, meow, meow. | |

—Author unknown

### Ghosts and Goblins

#### BOO!

| | |
|---|---|
| See my great big scary eyes. | *(Hold fingers around eyes.)* |
| Look out now for a big surprise. | |
| Oo-oo-ooo. | *(Walk like ghost.)* |
| I'm looking right at you. | |
| BOO! | *(Jump and shout.)* |

—Author unknown

#### Halloween Ghost

| | |
|---|---|
| There once was a ghost, | *(Extend hand and wiggle fingers.)* |
| Who lived in a cave. | *(Form hollow with palm for "cave.")* |
| She scared all the people | *(Point to children.)* |
| And the animals away. | |
| She said "Boo" to a fox, | *(Point.)* |
| She said "Boo" to a bee, | *(Point.)* |
| She said "Boo" to a bear, | *(Point.)* |
| She said "Boo" to me! | *(Point to self.)* |

Well, she scared that fox,                     (*Nod head "yes."*)
And she scared that bee.                        (*Nod head "yes."*)
She scared that bear,                           (*Nod head "yes."*)
But she didn't scare me!                         (*Shake head "no."*)

—Author unknown

### Eight Giggling Ghosts

(*Use your fingers to represent the ghosts; point to fingers in succession. This would be a great rhyme to do as a flannel/Velcro-board presentation.*)

Eight giggling ghosts
Like to give you a fright,
When they come out to play
On Hallowe'en night.
One ghost laughs,
And one ghost giggles.
One ghost ha-has,
And one ghost wiggles.

One ghost cackles,
And one ghost roars.
One ghost howls,
And one rolls on the floor.
Eight giggling ghosts
Aren't much of a fright,
When they come out to play
On Hallowe'en night.

—Author unknown

### Little Ghosts

(*Begin rhyme with five fingers up. Starting with thumb, point to each in succession.*)

The first little ghost floated by the store.
The second little ghost stood outside the door.
The third little ghost tried her best to hide.
The fourth little ghost stood by my side.

The fifth little ghost near the window sill,
Gave everybody a great big thrill.
The five little ghosts were all my friends,
And that is the way that this story ends.

—Author unknown

### Five Little Goblins

(*Begin this rhyme with five fingers up and bend them down one at a time. Or, hold up five fingers and point to each in succession. This rhyme would also work well as a flannel/Velcro-board presentation.*)

Five little goblins on Halloween night,
Made a very, very spooky sight.
The first one danced on his tippy-tip-toes.
The next one tumbled and bumped his nose.

The next one jumped high up in the air.
The next one walked like a fuzzy bear.
The next one sang a Halloween song.
Five little goblins played the whole night long!

—Author unknown

### Two Little Ghosts

A very old witch was stirring a pot.             (*Make a stirring motion.*)
Ooo-ooo! Ooo-ooo!
Two little ghosts said,
"What has she got?"                               (*Put hands on hips; bend over as if looking into pot.*)
Ooo-ooo! Ooo-ooo!
Tiptoe. Tiptoe. Tiptoe.                           (*Make fingers creep forward in the air.*)
BOO!                                              (*Raise hands high above head and jump.*)

—Traditional rhyme

### Five Little Ghosts

Five little ghosts dressed all in white
Were scaring each other on Halloween night.

"Boo!" said the first one. "I'll catch you!" *(Hold up pointer finger.)*
"Whoo," said the second, "I don't care if you do!?" *(Hold up middle finger.)*
The third ghost said, "You can't run away from me!" *(Hold up ring finger.)*
And the fourth one said, "I'll scare everyone I see!" *(Hold up little finger.)*
Then the last one said, "It's time to disappear!" *(Hold up thumb.)*
See you at Halloween time next year.

—Traditional rhyme

### Halloween Goblins

One little goblin standing at the door, *(Hold up one finger.)*
Two little goblins dancing 'cross the floor. *(Wiggle two fingers.)*
Three little goblins peeking through the latch, *(Bring two fingers and thumb together and peek through.)*

Four little goblins, what a happy batch! *(Hold up four fingers, then clap hands once.)*
Five little goblins, and more that can't be seen, *(Hold up five fingers, then look all around.)*
We're all getting ready for Halloween!

—Author unknown

### The Friendly Ghost

I'm a friendly ghost—almost! *(Point to self.)*
And I can chase you, too! *(Point to child.)*
I'll just cover me with a sheet *(Pretend to cover self; end with hands covering face.)*

And then call "scat" to you. *(Uncover face quickly and call out "scat.")*

—Author unknown

## Halloween

### Halloween Characters

Here's a witch with a tall, tall hat; *(Form peak over head with hands.)*
Two green eyes on a black, black cat. *(Encircle eyes with fingers and thumbs.)*
Jack-o'-lanterns in a row, *(Form balls with hands and move them toward right.)*

Funny clowns are laughing, "Ho, ho, ho!" *(Put palms on tummy and laugh.)*
Bunny's ears flopping up and down; *(Put thumbs at temples, fingers wiggling.)*
Fairy queen wears a fairy crown. *(Use thumbs and index fingers to make circle.)*
Gypsy plays a tambourine; *(Hit open left palm with right fist.)*
Cowboy twirls a rope. It's Halloween! *(Twirl right hand in a horizontal circle. Clap on each syllable of Halloween.)*

—Author unknown

### Hallowe'en

It was the finest pumpkin that you have ever seen. *(Make circle with arms.)*
It grew in Tommy's garden on the night of
  Hallowe'en.
He took his knife to cut the top, *(Make cutting action.)*
He scooped it with a spoon. *(Make scooping action.)*
He made two eyes, *(Make round circles with fingers at eyes.)*
A nose so long, *(Point to nose.)*
A mouth just like a moon. *(Draw half moon in air.)*
He put a candle in it, *(Hold up one finger.)*

Then still as any mouse,
He crept up very slowly to a window in his house.    (*Move fingers in creeping motion.*)
He held the jack o'lantern                           (*Pretend to hold.*)
Till his mother cried, "Look here!
It seems to me some brownies
Are hiding very near!"

—Maude Burnham
*Rhymes for Little Hands* (Milton Bradley Company, 1910, pp. 63–66)

### Halloween Is Here

When goblins prowl,                          (*Make fingers walk.*)
And hoot owls howl,                          (*Make goggles with hands and place around face.*)
"Whoooo! Whoooo!"                            (*Cup hands around mouth.*)
When witches fly,                            (*Flutter hands in air.*)
And pale ghosts sigh,                        (*Raise and lower hands slowly.*)
"OOOO! OOOO!"
Boys and girls, don't shake with fear,       (*Shake head "no."*)
It just means Halloween is here!

—Author unknown

## Pumpkins

### A Funny Fellow

See my pumpkin round and fat.                (*Make circle with fingers.*)
See my pumpkin yellow.
Watch him grin on Halloween.                 (*Point to smiling mouth.*)
He's a very funny fellow.

—Author unknown

### Orange Pumpkin

(*This rhyme can be sung to the tune of "I'm a Little Teapot."*)

I'm an orange pumpkin,
Fat and round,                               (*Hold arms out to indicate roundness.*)
Sitting in the cornfield
On the ground.
I'll be a jack-o'-lantern,
With two big eyes,                           (*Circle eyes with fingers.*)
Or made into a big fat pie.                  (*Make pie shape with arms.*)

—Author unknown

### Five Little Pumpkins

(*Begin this rhyme with five fingers up and point to each in succession. This rhyme also makes a great flannel/Velcro-board presentation.*)

Five little pumpkins sitting on a gate;
The first one said, "My, it's getting late."
The second one said, "There are witches in the air."
The third one said, "But we don't care."
The fourth one said, "Let's run, let's run."
The fifth one said, "It's Halloween fun."
WOOOOOOO went the wind,                      (*Sway hand through air.*)
And out went the lights.                     (*Make loud clap.*)

These five little pumpkins
Ran fast out of sight.                                    (*Place hands behind back.*)
—Author unknown

## My Jack-O-Lantern

I laugh at my jack-o-lantern.                             (*Hold stomach and smile.*)
I think he is funny to see.                               (*Point to eyes.*)
He must be thinking the same thing,                       (*Point to head.*)
'Cause he's laughing at me.                               (*Make same laughing motion as above.*)
—Author unknown

## Four Big Jack-O-Lanterns

(*This rhyme would also work well as a flannel/Velcro-board presentation.*)

Four big jack-o-lanterns made a funny sight,             (*Hold up four fingers.*)
Sitting on a gate post Halloween night.                  (*Begin with index finger and point to fingers in succession.*)

Number one said, "I see a witch's hat."
Number two said, "I see a big, black cat."
Number three said, "I see a scary ghost."
Number four said, "By that other post."
Four big jack-o-lanterns weren't a bit afraid.           (*Shake head "no."*)
They marched right along in the Halloween parade.        (*March in place.*)
—Author unknown

## Ten Little Pumpkins

(*Begin this rhyme with ten fingers up and take away fingers as the rhyme progresses. This rhyme would also work well as a flannel/Velcro-board presentation.*)

Ten little pumpkins all in a line;
One became a jack-o'-lantern, then there were nine.
Nine little pumpkins peeking through the gate;
An old witch took one, then there were eight.
Eight little pumpkins (there never were eleven);
A green goblin took one, then there were seven.
Seven little pumpkins full of jolly tricks;
A white ghost took one, then there were six.
Six little pumpkins glad to be alive;
A black cat took one, then there were five.
Five little pumpkins by the barn door;
A hoot owl took one, then there were four.
Four little pumpkins, as you can plainly see;
One became a pumpkin pie, then there were three.
Three little pumpkins feeling very blue;
One rolled far, far away, then there were two.
Two little pumpkins alone in the sun,
One said, "So long," and then there was one.
One little pumpkin left all alone;
A little boy chose him, then there were none.
Ten little pumpkins in a patch so green
Made everyone happy on Hallowe'en!
—Author unknown

## Jack-O'-Lantern

I am a pumpkin, big and round.                           (*Use arms to show size of pumpkin.*)
Once upon a time I grew on the ground.                   (*Point to ground.*)
Now I have a mouth, two eyes, a nose.                    (*Point to each feature on own face.*)
What are they for, do you suppose?                       (*Put right forefinger to forehead—thinking gesture.*)

When I have a candle inside shining bright,              (*Hold up right forefinger.*)
I'll be a jack-o'-lantern on Halloween night.            (*Put thumbs in armpits—bragging gesture.*)
—Author unknown

### What Am I?

| | |
|---|---|
| A face so round, | *(Hands in circle.)* |
| And eyes so bright. | *(Touch eyes.)* |
| A nose that glows. | *(Touch nose.)* |
| My, what a sight! | |
| A fiery mouth, | *(Touch mouth.)* |
| With jolly grin. | *(Grin.)* |
| No arms, no legs, | *(Shake arms, legs.)* |
| Just head to chin. | *(Put one hand on top of head and other on chin.)* |
| Answer:  Jack-o-lantern. | |

—Author unknown

### I've a Jack-O-Lantern

| | |
|---|---|
| I've a jack-o-lantern | *(Make a ball with open fist, thumb at top, sticking up for stem.)* |
| With a great big grin. | *(Grin.)* |
| I've got a jack-o-lantern | |
| With a candle in. | *(Insert other index finger up through bottom of fist.)* |

—Author unknown

### Three Little Pumpkins

| | |
|---|---|
| Three little pumpkins, laying very still | *(Hold up three fingers.)* |
| In a pumpkin patch on a hill. | |
| This one said, "I'm very green, | *(Point to index finger.)* |
| But I'll be orange by Halloween." | |
| This one said, "I'm on my way | *(Point to middle finger.)* |
| To be a jack-o-lantern some day." | |
| This one said, "Oh my, oh my, | *(Point to ring finger.)* |
| Today I'll be a pumpkin pie." | |

—Author unknown

### This Is Jack-O-Happy

| | |
|---|---|
| This is Jack-O-Happy. | *(Make happy face.)* |
| This is Jack-O-Sad. | *(Make sad face.)* |
| This is Jack-O-Sleepy. | *(Make sleepy face.)* |
| This is Jack-O-Mad. | *(Make mad face.)* |
| This is Jack-O-Broken | *(Hold hands out to serve pumpkin pie.)* |
| Into pieces small, | |
| Baked in a pumpkin pie | |
| That's the best of all. | *(Rub tummy.)* |
| YUM! YUM! | |

—Author unknown

## Witches

### Here Is the Witch's Tall Black Hat

| | |
|---|---|
| Here is the witch's tall black hat. | *(Hold arms together over head.)* |
| Here are the whiskers on her cat. | *(Put index fingers and thumbs together and pull back and forth under nose.)* |
| Here is an owl sitting in a tree. | *(Circle eyes with fingers.)* |
| Here is a goblin! Hee, hee, hee! | *(Hold hand on stomach.)* |

—Author unknown

### Three Little Witches

One little, two little, three little witches,     (Hold up fingers one by one.)
Ride through the sky on a broom.     (Move hand quickly "through the sky.")
One little, two little, three little witches,     (Hold up fingers again.)
Wink their eyes at the moon.     (Wink one eye while making circle with arms.)

—Author unknown

### A Little Witch

A little witch in a pointed cap,     (Make pointed cap with fingertips touching.)
On my door went rap, rap, rap.     (Rap at door.)
When I went to open it,
She was not there;
She was riding on a broomstick,     (Sweep arm through the air.)
High in the air.

—Author unknown

### Halloween Witches

One little, two little, three little witches,     (Hold up one hand; nod fingers at each count.)
Fly over the haystacks     (Fly hand in up-and-down motion.)
Fly over ditches.
Slide down moonbeams without any hitches.     (Glide hand downward.)
Heigh-ho! Halloween's here.

—Author unknown

### A Witch

If I were a witch,
I'd ride on a broom     (One fist rides on top of other, waving through air.)
And scatter the ghosts
With a zoom, zoom, zoom!     (Make sweeping motion.)

—Author unknown

### Halloween

A witch once went for a ride on her broom,     (Raise thumb of right hand. Zoom and dip.)
Up through the frosted sky.
She zoomed and zoomed, and she dipped and
    zipped,
And she winked at the moon as she passed by.     (Wink.)
At the moon in the frosty sky.
She wore a hat that was pointed tall,     (Make a pointed hat with two fingers.)
And a cape that was flowing wide,     (Make rippling motion with fingers.)
And a fierce black cat with a stand-up tail     (Point index finger up.)
Rode merrily by her side,
Rode merrily be her side.     (Make dipping motion with hand.)

—Author unknown

## Miscellaneous

### Scary Eyes

See my big and scary eyes.     (Circle thumb and index fingers around eyes.)
Look out now
A big surprise-Boo!     (Pull hands away; shout "Boo!")

—Author unknown

---

### More Great Fingerplays

"Halloween Time" and "Pumpkin Head" can be found on page 31 of *Rhymes for Circle Time* by Louise B. Scott (Instructional Fair/T.S. Denison, 1999).

"Hookey Spooky," an action rhyme, from page 26 of *Channels to Children: Early Childhood Activity Guide for Holidays and Seasons* by Carol Beckman (Channels to Children, 1982).

*1001 Rhymes and Fingerplays for Working with Young Children*, compiled by the Totline Staff (Warren Publishing House, 1994), includes the following fingerplays:

- "Black Cat" (action rhyme, page 226)
- "Dancing Ghost" (action rhyme, page 227)
- "Little Ghost" (page 227)
- "Little Pumpkin" (page 231)
- "Don't Be Afraid on Halloween" (page 233)

---

## Criss Cross Applesauce

*(Have children sit in front of another child or parent; the parent or other child should do the actions as indicated to the child sitting in front of them. An alternative is to have children sit in a train line so that they can draw on one another's backs.)*

| | |
|---|---|
| Criss, cross, applesauce | *(Draw an "X" on your partner's back, then pat their shoulders with both hands.)* |
| Spiders crawling up your back. | *(Walk fingers up partner's back.)* |
| Tight squeeze, | *(Give a big hug from behind.)* |
| Cool breeze, | *(Blow gently on partner's neck.)* |
| Now you've got the shivers! | *(Tickle partner all over the back.)* |

—Author unknown

## Musical Selections

"The Bats Go Flying" from *Sesame Street Kids' Favorite Songs 2*. Koch Records. ASIN: B0013D8J6K.

"Boogie Man Boogie" from *Monster Teaching Time: Songs and Learning Fun* by Kathleen Patrick, Camille Gift, and Libby Beardon; Pat Patrick Productions. Kimbo. ASIN: B000BYCV16.

"Dem Bones" from *Wee Sing for Halloween* by Pamela Conn Beall and Susan Hagen Nipp. Price Stern Sloan. ASIN: B002N2XI4I.

"Five Little Pumpkins" from *Singable Songs for the Very Young* by Raffi. Rounder. ASIN: B0000003H4.

"Fly Little Bats" from *Wee Sing for Halloween* by Pamela Conn Beall and Susan Hagen Nipp. Price Stern Sloan. ASIN: B001BHULQO.

"Ghost Says Boo," "Halloween Wind," "Howl at the Moon," "Walkin' Home on Halloween," "Trick or Treat," "Monster Band," and "Halloween Dance" from *Songs for All Seasons* by Geof Johnson. Available from http://www.songsforteaching.com/.

"Halloween on Parade" from *Holidays and Special Times* by Greg and Steve. Youngheart. ASIN: B00000DGN5.

"The Haunted House," "The Pumpkin Man," and "The Boogie Woogie Ghost" from *Holly Daze* by Mary Miche. Available from http://www.songsforteaching.com/.

"Have a Good Time on Halloween Night" from *Holiday Songs and Rhythms* by Hap Palmer. Available from http://www.songsforteaching.com/.

"It's Halloween" from *All Year* by Intelli-Tunes. Available from http://www.songsforteaching.com/.

"Monster Boogie" from *Buzz Buzz* by Laurie Berkner. Two Tomatoes. ASIN: B00004S36S.

"Monster Mash" from *A Child's Celebration of Rock and Roll* (performed by the original artists). Music for Little People. ASIN: B000002M7T.

"Say Boo" and "The Boogie Woogie Pumpkin Man" from *Holiday Songs* by Wendy Rollin. Available from http://www.songsforteaching.com/.

"The Skeleton Song" from *Spin Your Web* by Mary Kaye. Mary Kaye Music. ASIN: B000FEBV2M.

*Spooky Favorites* CD. Music for Little People. ASIN: B00000JNJF.

"Stirring Our Brew and Three Little Witches," "Halloween Medley," and "Five Days of Halloween" from *Happy Everything* by Dr. Jean. Melody House. ASIN: B000SM3N0E.

"The Transylvania Polka" from *Silly Songs Sesame Street*. Sony Wonder. ASIN: B000002BEZ.

"Twenty Pumpkins" from *Get Ready, Get Set, Sing!* by Sarah Barchas. Available from http://www.cduniverse.com/.

*Walt Disney Halloween Songs and Sounds* CD. Walt Disney Records. ASIN: B0009DVNF4.

"Witches' Brew" from *Witches' Brew* by Hap Palmer and Martha Cheney. Available from http://www.songsforteaching.com/.

## Crafts

**Easy Skeletons**    The September/October 2001 issue of *Totline Magazine* (often available through interlibrary loan) has a cute skeleton craft that requires cutting out a simple skull shape (pattern included in the magazine) and adding ten Q-tips. Some of the Q-tips will be cut in half. Glue the skull shape onto black construction paper. You may wish to draw a face on it, or add stickers to make a face. One full Q-tip is glued directly below the skull to form the spine. Next, take four Q-tips and cut them in half. Glue them on either side of the spine to form the ribs. For the legs, glue on two full Q-tips. The feet are formed by cutting one Q-tip in half and gluing each half at the bottom of the legs. The arms are two full Q-tips glued on either side of the ribs.

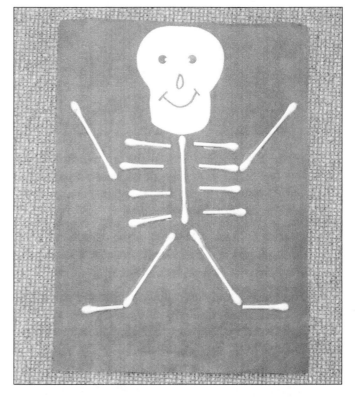

**Halloween Rubbing Plates**    These fun plates are available from KwikCrafts.com. The set includes 17 designs on 6 plates for $9.99. Place plates under white construction paper and allow participants to use crayons to transfer designs.

**Halloween Wreath**    The base of this craft is a paper plate with the center circle cut out. Use tempera paint to paint the plate a desired color. Use Ellison die Halloween shapes (pumpkins, ghosts, bats, cats, etc.) and glue around the circle. Add glitter, yarn, or ribbon if you choose.

**Lollipop Ghosts**    This is an easy and fun traditional craft. Provide each participant with a Tootsie Pop or similar lollipop. Each participant should also have either a white tissue (Kleenex) or a piece of white tissue paper and a piece of white yarn or twine. Place the tissue or tissue paper over the lollipop. Use the yarn or twine to secure the tissue/tissue paper. Use a black marker to draw on eyes and a mouth.

**Spooky Jack-O'-Lantern**    Another simple pumpkin craft can be found on pages 58–59 of *The Best of Holidays and Seasonal Celebrations—Issues 9–13, PreK–K*, edited by Donna Borst (Teaching and

Learning Company, 2001). Color the pumpkin. Color, cut out, and glue on facial features. A simple story with pumpkin facts can be cut out and pasted below the pumpkin.

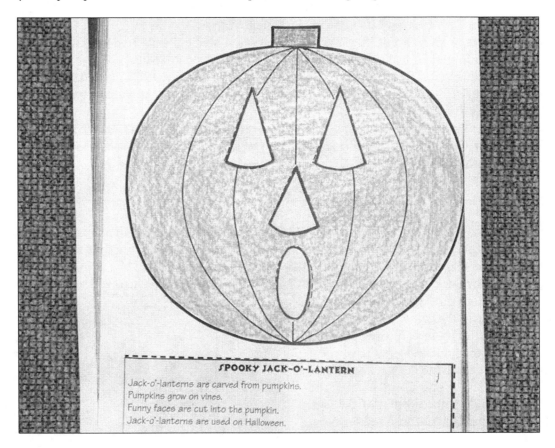

**Stand-Up Witch**    This witch's large dress allows her to stand freely when pasted together. Pattern and instructions for this craft appear on page 63 of *October Patterns, Projects, and Plans to Perk Up Early Learning Programs* by Imogene Forte (Incentive Publications, 1989). This would make a great table decoration for the holiday.

**Spooky Spiders**    Take egg carton cups, black paint, pipe cleaners and googly eyes, and you have the makings of a spider! Instructions appear on page 117 of *Calendar Crafts: Things to Make and Do for Every Month, PreK–2,* by Carolyn Argyle (Teaching and Learning Company, 2006).

**Halloween Pumpkin**    Instructions and patterns for this cute craft can be found on pages 23–24 of *Cut and Create! Holidays: Easy Step-by-Step Projects That Teach Scissor Skills* by Kim Rankin (Teaching and Learning Company, 1997). Simple shapes form a pumpkin. Options for features for the pumpkin are provided.

**Ghost Lacing Card**    The pattern for this craft can be found on page 26 of *Seasonal Cut-Ups* by Marilynn G. Barr (Monday Morning Books, 2005). Copy the pattern onto construction paper or card stock. Provide participants with crayons, yarn, large plastic needles, and a hole punch. Have them color their ghost (or leave him white) and background, if desired. Allow them to either straight-lace or loop-lace their yarn around the picture. These two types of lacing are explained on page 7. They may wish to leave enough yarn at the top of the picture so that it can be hung on a doorknob.

**Pumpkin Lacing Card**    The pattern for this craft is found on page 44 of *Seasonal Cut-Ups* by Marilynn G. Barr (Monday Morning Books, 2005). Follow the instructions for the Ghost Lacing Card. Ellison also offers a pumpkin lacing die in the XL size, which could be used for this craft.

# Hanukkah

*Use this holiday celebration to learn about this important time in Jewish history!*

## History

Hanukkah (also known as Chanukah) is the Jewish Festival of Lights. It lasts for 8 days and usually falls in late November or December. This holiday is traditionally considered a minor Jewish holiday, like Tu B'Shevat. But in America, the celebrations, presents, and parties are more extravagant because of its proximity to Christmas.

Hanukkah commemorates the Miracle of the Oil. The temple of Jews had been overtaken by invading Syrians, and many of the holy items in the temple were either broken or destroyed. The invading troops put up idols of their own in the temple. Judah Maccabee and a group of Jewish farmers and shepherds fought for the temple and reclaimed it from the Syrians. When the men went to find oil to relight the holy lamp, they found only one container of oil. The oil in this lamp, which should have stayed lit for only one night, lasted eight days! Jewish people remember this miracle by placing eight candles in a menorah (a special candleholder) and lighting one candle for each evening of the celebration. Every night of Hanukkah, families gather around the menorah, and say blessings. Then they light the shamash, or helper candle, and then light one for each night of the holiday. Also during Hanukkah, people exchange gifts and give to the poor and needy. (See Alecia Dixon's "All About Chanukah" at http://holidays.kaboose.com/chanukah/history/chanukah-about.html.)

Hanukkah also is celebrated by playing a game with a special top called a dreidel and eating special holiday foods, such as potato pancakes called latkes or other fried foods such as doughnuts. The oil used to fry these foods reminds them of the oil in the temple. Children may receive a gift on each night of the Hanukkah celebration in addition to gelt (money). Gelt is often chocolate wrapped in gold foil to resemble money. (See Julia Jasmine's *Multicultural Holidays: Share Our Celebration* [Teacher Created Materials, 1994].)

As with other Jewish holidays, each day of celebration starts at sunset.

## Poetry

"Dreidl," from page 12 of *Poems for Jewish Holidays*, selected by Myra Cohn Livingston (Holiday House, 1986).

"Hanukkah Candles," from page 66 of *The Best of Holidays and Seasonal Celebrations: Songs, Action Rhymes, and Fingerplays, PreK–3*, compiled by Ellen Sussman (Teaching and Learning Company, 2000).

*Hanukkah Lights: Holiday Poetry*, a collection of poems that celebrate the activities and experiences of Hanukkah, selected by Lee Bennett Hopkins (HarperCollins, 2004).

"Happy Hanukkah!," from page 64 of *The Bill Martin Jr. Big Book of Poetry*, edited by Bill Martin Jr. (Simon and Schuster Books for Young Readers, 2008).

"Menorah," "Hanukkah," "Hanukkah: Feast of Lights," "Menorah, Your Candles We Light," from pages 145–147 of *Big Learning for Little Learners: Easy Guide for Teaching Early Childhood Activities* by Sally Stavros and Lois Peters (Partner Press, 1987).

*My First Hanukkah Book*, including poems relating to Hanukkah, the fun it involves, and the memory of its origin, by Aileen Fisher (Children's Press, 1985).

"Small Miracles," from pages 15–16 of *Winter Lights: A Season in Poems and Quilts* by Anne Grossnickle Hines (Greenwillow Books, 2005).

"Song of Hanukkah" and "Hanukkah Rainbow," from page 20 of *Month-by-Month Poetry: December, January, and February* by Marian Reiner (Scholastic Professional Books, 1999).

## Books

Adler, David A. *The Story of Hanukkah*. Holiday House, 2011. ISBN: 978-0823422951.
  In simple text, the story of the Maccabees and the miracle in the temple is retold.

Balsley, Tilda. *Maccabee! The Story of Hanukkah*. Kar-Ben Publishing, 2010. ISBN: 978-0761345084.
  Presents the story of Hanukkah for young readers.

Baum, Maxie. *I Have a Little Dreidel*. Cartwheel Books, 2006. ISBN: 978-0439649971.
  A favorite Hanukkah song is given new life in this charmingly illustrated variation.

Berlin, Bill. *The Kvetch Who Stole Hanukkah*. Pelican Publishing Company, 2010. ISBN: 978-1589807983.
  In the town of Oyville, the children were preparing for Hanukkah. But the kvetch who lived high on the hill said what he said every year: "The latkes smell bad, the dreidels make me dizzy, and to hear children laugh puts me in a tizzy."

Capucilli, Alyssa S. *Biscuit's Hanukkah*. HarperCollins, 2005. ISBN: 978-0060094699.
  Biscuit tries to participate as a girl makes a menorah for Hanukkah. The dialogue emphasizes the number of candles needed and the tradition of telling stories.

Carter, David A. *Chanukah Bugs*. Little Simon, 2002. ISBN: 978-0689818608.
  Each spread features a flap designed to resemble a gift box, one for each of the eight nights.

Cartwright, Amy. *Dreidel, Dreidel, Dreidel*. Price Stern Sloan, 2010. ISBN: 978-0843198997.
  Every kid knows the dreidel song, but now they can play along!

Cooper, Alexandra. *Spin the Dreidel!* Little Simon, 2004. ISBN: 978-0689864308.
  In this board book, a family plays dreidel while a simple rhyming text explains the meaning of each letter in turn. Includes a removable dreidel.

dePaola, Tomie. *My First Chanukah*. Grosset and Dunlap, 2008. ISBN: 978-0448448596.
  With simple text and clear cheerful illustrations, dePaola has created a board-book introduction to Chanukah.

Edwards, Michelle. *The Hanukkah Trike*. Albert Whitman and Company, 2010. ISBN: 978-0807531266.
  When Gabi falls from her new Hanukkah trike, she gets the courage to try again by remembering the brave Maccabees.

Freeman, Don. *Happy Hanukkah, Corduroy*. Viking Juvenile, 2009. ISBN: 978-0670011278.
  Corduroy's having a Hanukkah party for all of his friends.

Glaser, Linda. *Hoppy Hanukkah*. Albert Whitman and Company, 2009. ISBN: 978-0807533789.
  A family of happy floppy rabbits enjoys Hanukkah by lighting candles, eating latkes, and playing dreidel.

Glaser, Linda. *Mrs. Greenberg's Messy Hanukkah*. Albert Whitman and Company, 2004. ISBN: 978-0807552988.
  What's the first night of Hanukkah without latkes? But Rachel's parents are too busy to think about cooking, so Rachel pays a visit to elderly Mrs. Greenberg, whose sparkling kitchen begs to be invaded by an energetic little girl with potato pancakes on her mind.

Goodman, L.J. *Oh, Chanukah*. Price Stern Sloan, 2003. ISBN: 978-0843105087.
    Children are encouraged to lift flaps and discover the many joys of Chanukah—-treats, presents, family, and more!

Holub, Joan. *Light the Candles: A Hanukkah Lift-the-Flap Book*. Puffin, 2000. ISBN: 978-0140567571.
    Hanukkah is here! There are so many fun things to do—light candles on the menorah, open presents, eat latkes and chocolate coins, play the dreidel game, and more!

Howland, Naomi. *Latkes, Latkes Good to Eat*. Sandpiper, 2004. ISBN: 978-0618492954.
    A girl does a kind deed for an old woman, who gives her a magic pan that will fry up latkes. Her brothers overhear the secret words that will start the pan cooking, but not those that will stop it.

Ivanov, Olga and Aleksey. *Hanukkah, Oh Hanukkah!* Marshall Cavendish Children, 2011. ISBN: 978-0761458456.
    A family gathers joyfully to celebrate Hanukkah by lighting the menorah, enjoying tasty latkes and other holiday dishes, dancing the hora, and spinning dreidels. This book is based on a popular Yiddish folk song (lyrics included).

Katz, Karen. *Where Is Baby's Dreidel?* Little Simon, 2007. ISBN: 978-1416936237.
    It's Chanukah, and Baby wants to spin the dreidel—but where is it?

Kimmel, Eric A. *The Golem's Latkes*. Marshall Cavendish Children, 2011. ISBN: 978-0761459040.
    When Rabbi Judah's housemaid enlists the help of the golem to make the latkes for the Hanukkah celebration, and then leaves him alone while she visits with a friend, latkes soon overrun the entire town!

Levine, Abby. *This Is the Dreidel*. Albert Whitman and Company, 2003. ISBN: 978-0807578841.
    A simple introduction to the Festival of Lights, told in rhymed couplets.

Lissy, Jessica. *A Blue's Clue's Chanukah*. Simon Spotlight, 2003. ISBN: 978-0689858406.
    Blue and her friends have been invited to a party at Orange Kitten's house.

Newman, Leslea. *Runaway Dreidel!* Square Fish, 2007. ISBN: 978-0312371425.
    This humorous picture book introduces children to aspects of the holiday by using terms such as latkes, menorah, and the letters on the dreidel.

Randall, Ronnie. *The Hanukkah Mice*. Chronicle Books, 2002. ISBN: 978-0811836234.
    With flaps hiding shiny foil surprises, readers will find a different Hanukkah tradition on each page!

Rauschwerger, Diane L. *Dinosaur on Hanukkah*. Kar-Ben Publishing, 2005. ISBN: 978-1580131438.
    When a loveable, mayhem-causing dinosaur arrives to help a small boy celebrate Hanukkah, he brings chaos in his wake!

Regan, Dian Curtis. *Eight Nights of Chanukah Lights*. Little Simon, 2002. ISBN: 978-0689845685.
    The candles glow for all eight nights. Gather around the Chanukah lights!

Rosen, Michael J. *Chanukah Lights*. Candlewick Press, 2011. ISBN: 978-0763655334.
    Pop-up master Robert Sabuda has illustrated this celebration of the holiday!

Roth, Susan L. *Hanukkah, Oh Hanukkah*. Dial, 2004. ISBN: 978-0803728431.
    In this illustrated version of the song, a family of mice and their assorted relatives eat latkes, read stories, dance the hora, light the menorah, and spin dreidels.

Scholastic. *A Chanukah Present for: Me!* Cartwheel Books, 2009. ISBN: 978-0545148740.
    With glitter flocking and an embossed "bow," this simple story highlights the most popular Chanukah icons and traditions.

Silverman, Erica. *The Hanukkah Hop*. Simon and Schuster, 2011. ISBN: 978-1442406049.
　　The whole family gets together to celebrate the holiday in this lively picture book!

Stone, Tanya Lee. *D Is for Dreidel: A Hanukkah Alphabet Book*. Price Stern Sloan, 2002. ISBN: 978-0843145762.
　　Children will love learning about Hanukkah with this dreidel-shaped alphabet book!

Yoon, Salina. *My First Menorah*. Little Simon, 2005. ISBN: 978-0689877469.
　　Turn the candle-shaped pages one by one to learn about the eight days of this Jewish holiday and celebrate with blessings, gifts, and family fun.

---

### Older Gems, or Titles Too Good to Pass Up

Aleichem, Sholem. *Hanukah Money*. Mulberry Books 1991. ISBN: 978-0688109936.
Two young brothers wonder how much money they will receive from their relatives for Hanukkah.

Drucker, Malka. *Grandma's Latkes*. Houghton Mifflin, 1992. ISBN: 978-0152004682.
As Grandma and Molly prepare latkes for the family's traditional Hanukkah meal, Grandma explains the custom of eating latkes and discusses the historical background and traditions of Hanukkah.

Glaser, Linda. *The Borrowed Hanukkah Latkes*. Albert Whitman and Company, 1997. ISBN: 978-0807508411.
Rachel and her mother are busy preparing for their Hanukkah celebration. When eight more people are suddenly added to the guest list and there are no more potatoes in the cellar, Rachel goes next door to borrow some from Mrs. Greenberg.

Hirsh, Marilyn. *Potato Pancakes All Around*. Jewish Publication Society, 1982. ISBN: 978-0827602175.
A wandering peddler teaches the villagers how to make potato pancakes from a crust of bread.

Kimmel, Eric A. *The Magic Dreidels*. Holiday House, 1996. ISBN: 978-0823412563.
While everyone else in the house prepares for Hanukkah, Jacob wants to do nothing but play with his new brass dreidel. What happens when he accidentally drops it down the well while fetching water?

Kimmelman, Leslie. *The Runaway Latkes*. Albert Whitman and Company, 2000. ISBN: 978-0807571767.
In a joyful Hanukkah version of "The Gingerbread Man," Kimmelman tells of three big, round latkes, crisp and brown, that jump out of the pan and roll off to see the town.

Kuskin, Karla. *A Great Miracle Happened There: A Chanukah Story*. HarperCollins, 1995. ISBN: 978-0064434263.
On the first night of Chanukah, a young boy invites a friend to his family's annual celebration.

Poskanzer, Susan Cornell. *What Can It Be? Riddles about Hanukkah*. Silver Press, 1990. ISBN: 978-0671705539.
A collection of rhyming riddles describing various aspects of Hanukkah and its celebration.

Rouss, Sylvia A. *Sammy Spider's First Hanukkah*. Kar-Ben Publishing, 1993. ISBN: 978-0929371467.
Sammy watches longingly as Josh Shapiro lights another candle and receives a brightly colored dreidel each night of Hanukkah.

Tanner, Suzy J. *The Great Hanukkah Story*. HarperFestival, 1998. ISBN: 978-0694011215.
It's the first night of Hanukkah—time to light the menorah and celebrate. But where are the candles? Join in the search for the missing candles and discover all sorts of Hanukkah surprises in this lift-the-flap adventure!

Zalben, Jane B. *Beni's First Chanukah*. Henry Holt and Company, 1988. ISBN: 978-0805004793.
On the first night of Hanukkah, a young bear helps his mother prepare latkes, plays "spin the dreidel," and recites a prayer with his father.

## Activities

---

### Cut-and-Tell

**"The Singing Dreidl"**    This story, with patterns, appears on pages 13–19 of *Cut and Tell: Scissor Stories for Winter* by Jean Warren (Totline Publications, 1984). It makes a dreidel and a menorah.

**"Cookie Cutters"**    This story, complete with patterns, appears on pages 56–58 of *Paper-Cutting Stories for Holidays and Special Events* by Valerie Marsh (Alleyside Press, 1994).

### Draw-and-Tell

**"Something from Nothing"**    This draw-and-tell Jewish folktale can be found on pages 52–55 of *Terrific Tales to Tell from the Storyknifing Tradition* by Valerie Marsh (Alleyside Press, 1997).

**"My Dreidel"**    This story can be found on pages 109–110 of *Chalk in Hand: The Draw and Tell Book* by Phyllis Pflomm (Scarecrow Press, 1986).

### Flannel/Velcro Board

**"The Singing Dreidl"**    This story, which can be adapted for the flannel/Velcro board, can be found on pages 52–53 of *The Best of Totline Stories* by Jean Warren (Totline Publications, 2000).

**Chanukah Felt Playtime**    This kit is available from OyToys. It includes board and laminated figures and objects that adhere to felt board to make countless Chanukah pictures.

### Games

**Dreidel Game**    At the end of your storyhour session, allow time for participants to actually play the dreidel game! There is a dreidel craft referenced in the Crafts section of this chapter, or you can buy actual dreidels online. A great pattern that can be printed on thin cardboard appears at http://www.enchantedlearning.com/crafts/hanukkah/dreidel/. The rules also appear at this site. Divide your participants into groups of four to play!

**Pass the Dreidel Game**    Have participants sit on the floor in a circle. With music playing, start passing a toy dreidel around the circle. When the music stops, the child holding it gets a chance to spin it. Continue playing until all participants have had the chance to spin.

**Hanukkah Matching Game**    Patterns for a variety of Hanukkah symbols (candle, dreidel, menorah, star of David) appear on pages 31–38 of *Holiday Patterns*, compiled by Jean Warren (Warren Publishing House, 1991). The best patterns to use are the ones that are already enclosed in a square, as this would make cutting them out simple. Copy two of each on different colors of construction paper. Give each participant one of the patterns/colors. Keep one for yourself and place in an apron pocket or container of some sort. Begin the matching game by pulling out your copies, one at a time, placing them on the board, and allowing participants to match them. You could also use any Ellison die shapes of Jewish symbols, located in the Religious Studies section of their catalog. Choices include a dreidel, a Star of David, and a Torah scroll, among others.

**Pin the Sword on Judah**    This idea is detailed on page 104 of *The Jewish Kids' Catalog* by Chaya M. Burstein (Jewish Publication Society, 1993). It is played just like Pin the Tail on the Donkey. A line drawing of Judah Maccabee is included on the page. With an overhead projector, it could easily be made the perfect size!

## Miscellaneous

**Hanukkah Gelt**    Gelt, a treat that Jewish children often get during the holiday, can be money or chocolate coins. Once your participants have sat down to a coloring sheet or craft, give each several chocolate coins to enjoy! Another idea would be to hide chocolate coins around your room for participants to find!

**"Why the Menorah Has Its Distinctive Shape"**    This story can be found on pages 81–83 of *The Storytelling Handbook: A Young People's Collection of Unusual Tales and Helpful Hints on How to Tell Them* by Anne Pellowski (Simon and Schuster Books for Young Readers, 1995).

**Jewish Holiday Foods**    Use this realia, available from Becker's School Supplies. Plastic foods that are representative of a Jewish holiday meal come in a carrying bag for $39.99. Included are roast chicken, gefilte fish, kugel, matzo balls, and more. The contact information for Becker's School Supplies can be found in Appendix A at the end of this book.

**Light the Candles Magnet Board Activity**    This activity includes a song ("Hanukkah's a Happy Time," sung to the tune of "Mary Had a Little Lamb"). The patterns include a menorah, candles, and flames for the candles. As the song is sung, the candles are placed and lit. It can be found on pages 170–171 of *Magnet Board Fun for Everyday, Seasons, and Holidays* by Liz and Dick Wilmes (Building Blocks Publications, 1998).

**Hanukkah Songs**
- The following piggyback songs (new songs sung to familiar tunes) can be found on pages 24–28 of *Holiday Piggyback Songs*, compiled by Jean Warren (Warren Publishing House, 1988): "Hanukkah, Hanukkah," "Hanukkah Is Here," "Happy Hanukkah," and "The Latkes Are Frying in the Pan."
- *Piggyback Songs to Sign*, by Jean Warren and Susan Shroyer (Warren Publishing House, 1992), contains the following songs, on pages 32–35, with American Sign Language motions: "Win or Lose," "Round and Round," "It Is Hanukkah," "Little Dreidel," "We're Going to Light the Candles," "Standing in a Row," "Light the Candles," and "One by One."
- The song "A Festival of Lights" can be found on page 75 of *The Best of Totline Magazine, Volume 2*, compiled by Gayle Bittinger (McGraw-Hill Children's Publishing, 2003).
- The song "Hanukkah Begins Tonight" can be found on page 68 of *The Best of Totline Magazine, Volume 3*, compiled by Gayle Bittinger (McGraw-Hill Children's Publishing, 2003).
- The song "Happy Hanukkah" can be found on page 379 of *The Best of Totline Newsletter*, compiled by Jean Warren (Warren Publishing House, 1995).

# Fingerplays

## Candles

### Hanukkah Candles

*(Hold up eight fingers to begin the rhyme and wiggle them to make them "flicker." Bend them slightly as each color is mentioned. This rhyme could also be adapted to a flannel/Velcro-board presentation.)*

Eight little candles
Are standing in a row.
See their pretty colors.
See their bright flames glow.
Violet, orange,

Green, red, and blue,
Yellow and pink,
And a purple one, too.
See our menorah all shiny and bright
Holding so many candles tonight!

—Author unknown

## Hanukkah Lights

I want to be the one who lights
The candles that will brightly glow.
I'll light them all because we know
There is one candle for each night.
Each night of Hanukkah they'll shine,
1, 2, 3, 4, 5, 6, 7, 8 in a line.

*(Point to self.)*
*(Wiggle fingers in the air for candles flickering.)*
*(Put index finger and thumb together; pretend to light candles.)*
*(Hold up one finger.)*

*(Count out eight fingers.)*

—Author unknown

## Come Light the Menorah

*(Explain to participants what "levivot" is: latkes, or potato pancakes. If you wish, substitute the word "latkes" for "levivot" in the rhyme.)*

O Hanukkah, o Hanukkah,
Come light the menorah!
Let's have a party,
We'll all dance the hora.
Gather 'round the table,
We'll give you a treat,
Dreidels small to play with,
Levivot to eat.
And while we are playing,
The candles are burning low.
One for each night,
They shed a sweet light,
To remind us of days long ago.

*(Pretend to light candles.)*

*(Dance in a circle.)*
*(Make circle in front of body with hands.)*

*(Fingers indicate small size.)*
*(Rub tummy.)*

*(Wiggle fingers slowly.)*

*(Put index finger to temple.)*

—Author unknown

## Happy, Happy Hanukkah
## (A Chant-and-Clap Dance)

*(Chant several times, once clapping, another time holding hands and going around in a circle.)*

Happy, happy, Hanukkah,
Candles burning bright.
Happy, happy, Hanukkah,
Festival of Light.
Spin the dreidel,

Light the lights.
Presents are such fun.
Dance and sing,
Eight happy nights—
Are the latkes done?

—Jan Irving and Robin Currie
*Mudlicious* (Libraries Unlimited, 1986, p. 176)

## Eight Little Candles

*(This rhyme can be sung to the tune of "Ten Little Indians." Hold up correct number of fingers as the rhyme is sung.)*

One little, two little, three little candles,
Four little, five little, six little candles.

Seven little, eight little, nine little candles,
And a shamash, too!

—Betsy Diamant-Cohen

## Dreidel

### I'm a Little Dreidel

*(This song can be sung to the tune of "I'm a Little Teapot.")*

I'm a little dreidel made of clay,
Spin me around when you want to play.          *(Pretend to spin dreidel.)*
When I fall down, if you don't win,
Just pick me up and spin again.          *(Pretend to spin dreidel again.)*

—Adapted traditional rhyme

### My Dreidel

I have a little dreidel.          *(Cup hands to form a square.)*
I made it out of clay.          *(Move fingers in a molding motion.)*
And when it's dry and ready          *(Flatten hands as if to hold in hand—palm up, pinkies together.)*

Then with it I will play.          *(Pretend to spin dreidel on the floor.)*

—Author unknown

### Dredel

*(Begin this rhyme with five fingers up and take away as the rhyme progresses. With the colors mentioned, this would make a great flannel/Velcro-board presentation.)*

Dredel, dredel, dredel—see the spinning top.
I will set five spinning, and one will stop.
The green top is going 'round and 'round,
But it's the first top to hit the ground.
The red top is wobbling and wobbling now.
It is stopping to take a bow.

The yellow top is slowing a bit.
It stops when another top hits it.
The white and blue are turning still.
Which do you think can win at will?
The only one spinning is the top that's blue.
It's the one I give to you.

—Lynda Roberts
*Mitt Magic* (Gryphon House, 1985, p. 68)

## Miscellaneous

### Making Latkes

Scrub the potatoes.          *(Pretend to scrub.)*
Grate them thin.          *(Run fist across other palm.)*
Beat some eggs.          *(Pretend to beat eggs.)*
Stir other stuff in.          *(Make circular motion with hand.)*
Fry the latkes
'Til both sides are brown.          *(Flip hand over.)*
At Hanukkah time,
We gobble them down.          *(Pretend to eat.)*

—Susan M. Dailey
*A Storytime Year* (Neal-Schuman, 2001, p. 326)

### I'm a Little Latke

*(This rhyme can be sung to the tune of "I'm a Little Teapot.")*

I'm a little latke, round and fat.          *(Make circle in front of body with hands.)*
You eat me on Chanukah, how about that?          *(Put index finger to side of head, thinking motion.)*
I taste good with applesauce, sour cream too.          *(Rub tummy.)*
Everyone loves latkes, how about you?          *(Point to participants.)*

—Betsy Diamant-Cohen

---

### More Great Fingerplays

"Nine Little Candles," from page 3 of *Marmalade Days Winter: Complete Units for Busy Teachers of Young Children* by Carol Taylor Bond (Partner Press, 1987).

"The Candle," from page 65 of *Finger Frolics: Fingerplays for Young Children*, Revised Edition, by Liz Cromwell, Dixie Hibner, and John R. Faitel (Gryphon House, 1983).

"Hanukkah Lights," from page 65 of *Young Minds at Play* by Elizabeth Kelley and Joanne McConville (Instructional Fair/T.S. Denison and Company, 1997).

"Light the Lights," an action rhyme, from page 76 of *Great Big Holiday Celebrations* compiled by Elizabeth McKinnon (Warren Publishing House, 1991).

"The Menorah Candle" and "Hanukkah Lights," from page 301 of *Creative Resources for the Early Childhood Classroom* by Judy Herr and Yvonne Libby (Delmar, 1990).

"The Spinning Dreidel," an action rhyme, from page 210 of *Celebrate the Seasons: The Best of Holidays and Seasonal Celebrations—Issues 9–12, PreK–3*, edited by Donna Borst (Teaching and Learning Company, 1998).

"My Dreidel," from page 148 of *The Big All-Year Book of Holidays and Celebrations: Preschool/Kindergarten, Issues 14–18*, edited by Donna Borst (Teaching and Learning Company, 2002).

"Hanukkah Spin Action Verse," an action rhyme, from page 26 of *Holiday Hoopla: Songs and Fingerplays* by Kathy Darling (Monday Morning Books, 1990).

"Five Little Dreidels," from page 112 of *101 Fingerplays, Stories, and Songs to Use with Finger Puppets* by Diane Briggs (American Library Association, 1997).

"Hanukkah Gelt," from page 30 of *Clap and Count: Action Rhymes for the Jewish Year* by Jacqueline Jules, (Kar-Ben Copies, 2001), a great year-round resource.

"Five Pieces of Gelt," from page 54 of *Toddle on Over: Developing Infant and Toddler Literature Programs* by Robin W. Davis (Alleyside Press, 1999).

## Musical Selections ————————————————————————————

*Chanukah: A Singing Celebration* CD by Cindy Paley. Cindy Paley. ASIN: B000QQ7RNQ.

*Chanukah Pajamikah!* CD by Doda Mollie. CD Baby. ASIN: B001B8PH5I.

"Dradel, Dradel, Dradel" from *Seasonal Songs in Motion* by The Learning Station. Hug-A-Chug Records. ASIN: B00005TPUN.

"Dreidle Rules" and "Lots of Latkes" from *Shanah Tovah, Shanah M'tukah* by Joanie Calem. Available from http://www.songsforteaching.com/.

"Dreidel Song," "Hava Nagila," "The Latkes," and others from *Hanukkah and Chinese New Year*. Kimbo. ASIN: B00065L6Z2.

"The Dreidel Song" and "Light the Menorah" from *Shanah Tovah: A Good Year—Songs for Jewish Holidays* by Debbie Friedman. Available as a download from http://www.amazon.com/.

"Dreydel" from *Sing Along with Bob #1* by Bob McGrath. Bob's Kids Music. ASIN: B000QZYE6K.

"Hanukkah" from *Holiday Songs and Rhythms* by Hap Palmer. Available from http://www.songsforteaching.com/.

"Hanukkah, Hanukkah" from *Rhythms and Rhymes for Special Times* by Jack Hartmann. Available from http://www.songsforteaching.com/.

"Hanukkah, Oh Hanukkah" by Two of a Kind. Available from http://www.songsforteaching.com/.

*Hanukkah with Fran Avni* CD. Available from http://www.songsforteaching.com/.

*Hap Palmer's So Big* CD. Hap-Pal Music. ASIN: B0000690AD. (Use the "Teddy Bear Playtime" song [music only], and substitute the word "latke" for "teddy bear." Fashion latkes from heavy paper or felt!)

*Happy Chanukah!* by Fran Avni. Available from http://www.songsforteaching.com/.

"Heyvenu Shalom Alechim/Hava Nagilah" from *I Have a Dream: World Music for Children* by Daria. DariaMusic. ASIN: B000CA6YZS.

"If I Had a Dreidle" and "Latka" from *Songs for All Seasons* by Geof Johnson. Available from http://www.songsforteaching.com/.

"Judah Maccabee, the Hammer" from *Sing Shalom! Songs for the Jewish Holidays* by Peter and Ellen Allard. Craig 'n Co. ASIN: B000056JQ4.

"Many Lights" from *Holiday Songs from Wendy Rollin*. Available from http://www.songsforteaching .com/.

"My Dreidel" from *Happy Everything* by Dr. Jean. Melody House. ASIN: B000SM3NOE.

"My Dreydel" from *Singable Songs for the Very Young* by Raffi. Rounder. ASIN: B0000003H4.

"Oh, Chanukah" from *Seasons and Celebrations*. Available from http://www.songsforteaching.com/.

*Shine Little Candles: Chanukah Songs for Children* CD by Rachel Buchman. Rounder. ASIN: B00004Z3US.

*Sing Shalom: Songs for Jewish Holidays* CD by Peter and Ellen Allard. Craig 'n Co. ASIN: B000056JQ4.

## Crafts

**Star of David**   The Star of David is known around the world as the symbol of Judaism. Make a simple Star of David with Popsicle or craft sticks. Make two triangles by gluing the sticks together.

Once dry, glue one triangle on top of the other, with points going in opposite directions, creating a star. I used a hot glue gun at this point in the construction. You may wish to add glitter or foam pieces (or other decorative materials) as I did. String a piece of yarn through the top of the star to hang.

**Dancing Dreidels**   This craft makes a simple dreidel that participants can play with once complete. Craft pattern and instructions appear on page 31 of *December Patterns, Projects, and Plans to Perk Up Early Learning Programs* by Imogene Forte (Incentive Publications, 1989). The book also provides instructions on how to play the dreidel game.

**Hanukkah Menorah**   For this craft, individual patterns for menorah, candles, and flames can all be colored, cut out, and glued together. Patterns appear on pages 32–33 of *December Patterns, Projects, and Plans to Perk Up Early Learning Programs* by Imogene Forte (Incentive Publications, 1989).

**Hanukkah Menorah**   Instructions and patterns can be found on pages 31–32 of *Cut and Create! Holidays: Easy Step-by-Step Projects That Teach Scissor Skills* by Kim Rankin (Teaching and Learning Company, 1997). Easy shapes make a simple menorah that can be glued to a larger piece of construction paper. I like the idea of adding glitter to the candles to give them a sparkling effect.

**Simple Hanukkah Hanging**   The base of this craft is a brown grocery bag. Two hangings can be made from one bag. A menorah pattern (provided) is colored and glued on. Then craft sticks are halved and colored with markers to represent candles and added to the menorah. Instructions and patterns can be found on pages 24–26 of *Holiday and Seasonal Crafts from Recycled Materials* by Deborah Whitacre and Becky Radtke (Teaching and Learning Company, 1995). This makes a great door hanging.

**Decorative Dreidel**     The base of this craft is a simple dreidel shape decorated with construction paper confetti! Instructions appear on page 26 of *The Best of The Mailbox Magazine Arts and Crafts, Grades 1–3*, edited by Karen A. Brunak (The Education Center, 1999).

**Hanukkah Menorah**     Instructions and patterns for this craft appear on pages 47–48 of *International Winter Festivals* by Marilynn G. Barr (Good Apple, 1993). Fancy candle patterns are colored and glued onto a menorah pattern.

**Egg Carton Dreidels**     Instructions and patterns for this craft appear on page 49 of *International Winter Festivals* by Marilynn G. Barr (Good Apple, 1993). Foam egg cartons and straws or toothpicks are used to make this simple dreidel.

**Paper Weave Hanukkah Menorah**     This craft weaves blue paper strips in and out of the candle-holders on the menorah pattern. When finished, construction paper flames are added on each candle branch! Instructions can be found on pages 5–6 of *Marmalade Days Winter: Complete Units for Busy Teachers of Young Children* by Carol Taylor Bond (Partner Press, 1987). The menorah pattern is found on page 13.

**Star of David Hat**     This craft makes a Star of David from two triangle shapes. The shapes are then attached to a headband pattern. The instructions and patterns can be found on page 22 of *Hats, Hats, and More Hats* by Jean Stangl (Fearon Teacher Aids, 1989).

**Dreidel**     This craft is found on page 265 of *The Festive Teacher: Multicultural Activities for Your Curriculum* by Steve Springer et al. (McGraw-Hill, 2008) and offers yet another dreidel pattern. This pattern has the symbols already printed on it. It could be photocopied onto card stock for durability.

**Hanukkah Handprint Menorah**     This cute menorah, made from the participant's handprints, is found on pages 21 (instructions) and 24 (patterns) of *From the Hands of a Child: Special Seasonal Art Activities for Primary Children* by Anthony Flores (Fearon Teacher Aids, 1987).

**Menorah Magic**     Instructions for this craft appear on page 92 of *Hand-Shaped Art* by Diane Bonica (Good Apple, 1989). This craft also uses the participant's hand-prints to make the menorah candles.

**Latke Craft**     This idea is courtesy of Vicky Dworkin of Kaimuki Public Library in Honolulu, Hawaii. It also makes a neat game that participants can play once the craft is finished. Tape a large paint-stirring stick to a paper plate. This will be the "frying pan." Cut latkes from large used manila envelopes. Glue a latke to the pan. Cut more latkes from heavier, stiffer card-board, so that there is one per participant.

Punch a hole in the edge of the paper plate (on the side opposite the handle) and also in the stiffer cardboard latke. Tie the latke to the frying pan with a piece of yarn. Challenge participants to "flip the latke" or "catch the runaway latke" by trying to catch the stiff cardboard latke on the plate. The longer the yarn, the harder this is to do! For younger children, make the yarn length shorter, perhaps 8 inches.

**Hanukkah Craft Kits**     A great source of craft kits for Hanukkah is S&S Worldwide. The kits they offer include the following:

- Star of David Tissue Paper Inlay—Package of 12 is $11.49.
- Judaic Symbols Bead Assortment—Package of 49 is $22.49.
- Leather Star of David Necklace—Package of 12 is $22.49.
- Wooden Menorah—$4.99 each. Price drops to $3.99 each if 3 or more are ordered. (You might wish to purchase this and decorate simply for display purposes.)
- Paint-A-Dreidel—Price is $20.99 per package of 24. The price drops to $19.29 if three or more packages are ordered.

**Paper Cup Menorah**     This easy craft idea uses nut cups, sand, glue, and candles. One nut cup is the base, and the second holds the sand and the candle. It is detailed on page 118 of *The Jewish Kids' Catalog* by Chaya M. Burstein (Jewish Publication Society, 1993).

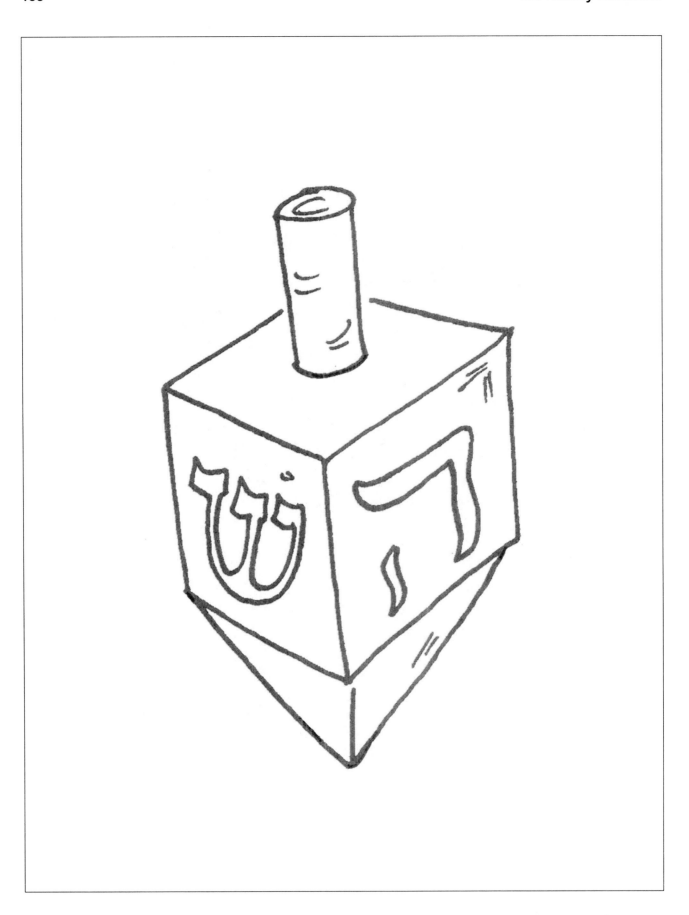

# Kwanzaa

*Kwanzaa is a great time to immerse your program participants in the culture of Africa and African Americans!*

## History

Kwanzaa is a weeklong nonreligious celebration held in the United States honoring universal African heritage and culture. Dr. Maulana Karenga, an African American teacher, first celebrated and founded the holiday in 1966. Dr. Karenga wanted African Americans to have a holiday that made them feel proud of their heritage. It is marked by participants lighting a kinara (candleholder) that holds seven candles. One candle is lit each night of the celebration. Seven symbols are used during the Kwanzaa celebration, and each symbol stands for a different idea or principle: unity (*umoja*, pronounced oo-MOH-jah), self-determination (*kujichagulia*, pronounced koo-jee-chah-goo-LEE-uh), collective work and responsibility (*ujima*, pronounced oo-JEE-mah), cooperative economics (*ujamaa*, pronounced oo-jah-MAH), purpose (*nia*, pronounced NEE-ah), creativity (*kuumba*, pronounced koo-OOM-bah), and faith (*imani*, pronounced ee-MAN-nee). These principles are called Nguzo Saba. The number seven has significant meaning in the African culture—it is associated with the good of life. Many individual cultural festivals of the African people either last seven days or have the number 7 inherent in them.

Kwanzaa is observed December 26th through January 1st every year. During this time, people learn more about the customs and history of Africa. The word "Kwanzaa" is Swahili in origin and means "first fruits of the harvest." (See Julia Jasmine's *Multicultural Holidays: Sharing Our Celebrations* [Teacher Created Materials, 1994].)

Kwanzaa is also a time for families. Families spend time together dressed in traditional African clothing, eating traditional foods, and listening to African music. The traditional feast, called the Kwanzaa Karumu, is held on the night of December 31st. The table is usually decorated with symbolic items, including fruits and vegetables, a place mat, ears of corn, gifts, a unity cup, seven candles (one black, three red, three green), the seven principles of Kwanzaa printed out, and a black, red, and green flag. (See Carol Barkin and Elizabeth James's *The Holiday Handbook* [Clarion Books, 1994].)

The colors black, red, and green also have special significance to the holiday. The color red stands for struggle; the color black stands for the African American people; the color green stands for three things: the hills of Africa, the future, and hope. The candles used in the kinara are these colors. The first three candles are red, the middle one is black, and the last three are green.

## Poetry

"Kwanzaa," from page 154 of *The Best of Holidays and Seasonal Celebrations—Issues 18–21, Grades 1–3*, edited by Donna Borst (Teaching and Learning Company, 2000).

"Kwanzaa," from page 22 of *Winter Lights: A Season in Poems and Quilts* by Anna Grossnickle Hines (Greenwillow Books, 2005).

"Kwanzaa Time Is Here," from page 22 of *Month-by-Month Poetry: December, January, and February* by Marian Reiner (Scholastic Professional Books, 1999).

## Books

Cooper, Melrose. *Seven Days of Kwanzaa*. Cartwheel Books, 2007. ISBN: 978-0439567466.
Sing in celebration of Kwanzaa with this cheerful holiday rhyme. This creative spin on a familiar Christmas song features rhyming text and lively artwork.

Ford, Juwanda. *K Is for Kwanzaa*. Cartwheel Books, 2003. ISBN: 978-0439560719.
Bright colors and blocky, thickly outlined objects and characters join with a simple overview of the African American harvest holiday.

Greene, Stephanie. *The Rugrats' First Kwanzaa*. Simon Spotlight, 2001. ISBN: 978-0689841910.
It's a special time of year and Susie's family is celebrating Kwanzaa for the first time.

Grier, Ella. *Seven Days of Kwanzaa*. Sterling, 2005. ISBN: 978-1402719394.
Stiff pages in progressively gradated widths, each trimmed with an African design, are used to describe the African American harvest festival.

Holub, Joan. *Kwanzaa Kids*. Puffin, 2002. ISBN: 978-0142301999.
A perfect way to begin teaching young children about the meaning and traditions of this joyous holiday.

James, Synthia Saint. *It's Kwanzaa Time!* Little Simon, 2001. ISBN: 978-0689841637.
One or two sentences per page describe the seven days and seven principles of Kwanzaa.

Katz, Karen. *My First Kwanzaa*. Henry Holt and Company, 2003. ISBN: 978-0805070774.
This small picture book introduces the Kwanzaa holiday. A double-page spread for each of the seven days of the holiday shows and tells the seven principles.

McKissack, Fredrick. *Kwanzaa—Count and Celebrate!* Enslow Publishers, 2009. ISBN: 978-0766031029.
Count and learn the principles of Kwanzaa.

Washington, Donna L. *Li'l Rabbit's Kwanzaa*. Katherine Tegen Books, 2010. ISBN: 978-0060728168.
Li'l Rabbit is not having a very good Kwanzaa. Granna Rabbit is sick, and so his family won't celebrate his favorite part of Kwanzaa this year: a big feast called Karamu.

Williams, Nancy. *A Kwanzaa Celebration Pop-Up Book*. Little Simon, 1995. ISBN: 978-0689802669.
This festive book is a true celebration of a joyous African American holiday. Robert Sabuda, paper engineer extraordinaire, provided the illustrations.

---

### Older Gems, or Titles Too Good to Pass Up

Chocolate, Deborah M. Newton. *Kente Colors*. Walker Books for Young Readers, 1997. ISBN: 978-0802775283.
A richly illustrated book that celebrates the tradition and use of the African kente cloth.

Chocolate, Deborah M. Newton. *My First Kwanzaa Book*. Scholastic, 1999. ISBN: 978-0439129268.
During the last week of December, Kwanzaa is a time to dress up in African clothes and gather together with relatives from all over the country. Grandma brings special things to eat, Grandpa lights the candles, and everyone in the family celebrates their heritage.

Kroll, Virginia. *Wood-hoopoe Willie*. Perfection Learning, 1995. ISBN: 978-0780787407.
Willie dreams of playing the African instruments that his Grandpa describes. When the drummer at the African American Center can't make it for the fifth night of Kwanzaa, he gets his chance.

Saint James, Synthia. *The Gifts of Kwanzaa*. Albert Whitman and Company, 1994. ISBN: 978-0807529089.
Following a brief history of the seven-day holiday, a child narrator explains the seven symbols and the seven principles of Kwanzaa, defining each with its African name (and supplying a phonetic pronunciation).

Schaefer, Lola M. *Kwanzaa*. Capstone Press, 2000. ISBN: 978-0736849012.
Simple text and photographs describe and illustrate Kwanzaa, the holiday that was created in 1966 to honor African American culture.

Winne, Joanne. *Let's Get Ready for Kwanzaa*. Children's Press, 2001. ISBN: 978-0516231754.
This book offers a basic overview of the Kwanzaa holiday, with two or three short sentences per page.

## Activities

---

### Coloring Pages

Consult your favorite pattern books or holiday coloring books for pages to use as coloring sheets. Be sure to search online as well. There's lots of great stuff out there!

- A color-coded coloring page of the Kwanzaa kinara can be found at http://www .firstschool.ws/t/ap/cbl_kwanzaac.htm. The color-coding instructs participants to color the candles and candleholder in the correct colors.
- A coloring page with children in traditional African costumes can be found at http:// www.activityvillage.co.uk/pdfs/children-around-the-world-africa.pdf.
- A corn coloring page can be found at http://www.activityvillage.co.uk/corn_coloring_ page.pdf.

---

### Cut-and-Tell

**"Kwanzaa"**     This cut-and-tell story with patterns appears on pages 62–64 of *Paper-Cutting Stories for Holidays and Special Events* by Valerie Marsh (Alleyside Press, 1994). The finished product is a candleholder with candles.

### Draw-and-Tell

**"What Can Happen If You Fall into a Hole"**     This draw-and-tell story from South Africa turns a stick man into a bear. It can be found on pages 203–205 of *Drawing Stories from Around the World and a Sampling of European Handkerchief Stories* by Anne Pellowski (Libraries Unlimited, 2003).

### Flannel/Velcro Board

**"Anansi and the Rock"**     The text and patterns for this flannel/Velcro-board folktale from West Africa can be found on pages 46–48 of *Multicultural Folktales: Stories to Tell Young Children* by Judy Sierra and Robert Kaminski (Oryx Press, 1991).

**"The Great Tug-O-War"**     The text and patterns for this African American flannel/Velcro-board folktale can be found on pages 73–77 of *Multicultural Folktales: Stories to Tell Young Children* by Judy Sierra and Robert Kaminski (Oryx Press, 1991).

**"Seven Candles on the Kinara"**     Use the patterns for the kinara and candles provided at the end of this chapter to make your flannel/Velcro-board pieces. The text for this presentation can be found on page 83 of *Storytime Magic: 400 Fingerplays, Flannelboards, and Other Activities* by Kathy MacMillan and Christine Kirker (American Library Association, 2009). Point to each candle as the principle of Kwanzaa is named.

**The Seven Principles of Kwanzaa**     The seven principles of Kwanzaa are nicely illustrated in color posters that can be found at http://www.first-school.ws/theme/cp_h_kwanzaa.htm. Print each of these color posters out, laminate for durability, and use them for a flannel/Velcro-board presentation to explain the underlying ideas of the Kwanzaa holiday! These principles also appear in a form that can be printed as coloring pages.

**Meaning of Kwanzaa Poster**     A color poster, great for display and to use along with the seven principles posters listed previously, can be found at http://www.dltk-holidays.com/kwanzaa/posters .htm. The poster explains the meaning of the Swahili word *Kwanzaa*. Laminate it for durability.

## Games

**Candle Match**    Since candles are an integral part of this holiday, why not do a matching game with them? Find a favorite pattern or use an Ellison candle die (they offer several different sizes and types) to reproduce or cut out of different colors of paper. Cut two of each color and laminate for durability. Pass out one of each pair of colors to participants and keep one for yourself, placing them in an apron pocket or container, such as a basket. One by one, pull out the candle shapes and place them on your flannel/Velcro board, allowing participants to match them. Make sure that you have cut candles in the following colors: red, black, and green. Reinforce their importance for the holiday.

**Kwanzaa Item Match**    Find Kwanzaa-themed clip art, such as an outline map of Africa, an ear of corn, the kinara, a present, etc. Reproduce two of each on red, green, and black papers. Laminate for durability. Follow the instructions for the Candle Match.

**Kwanzaa Fruit Count**    This simple game appears on page 143 of *The Best of Holiday and Seasonal Celebrations—Issues 9–13, PreK–K*, edited by Donna Borst (Teaching and Learning Company, 2001). A fruit symbolic of the holiday is pictured along with a selection of numbers, one of which corresponds to the number of fruits pictured. This page can be enlarged and laminated. Have participants count the fruits along with you, and use a dry-erase marker to circle the correct number. Laminating the page allows it to be reused.

**The Colors of Kwanzaa**    This idea comes from *The Big All-Year Book of Holidays and Seasonal Celebrations: Preschool/Kindergarten, Issues 14–18*, edited by Donna Borst (Teaching and Learning Company, 2002). I have modified the idea slightly. Tape red, green, and black construction paper around three containers, such as coffee cans or oatmeal containers. Provide participants with a variety of objects in those three colors. Call upon participants, one by one, to come up and drop their object into the correct container.

## Miscellaneous

**Just Where Is Africa, Anyway?**    Have a map handy to show participants exactly where Africa is. Check out *It's a Big Big World Atlas*, edited by Angela Rahaniotis and Jane Brierly (Tormont Publications, 1994). The first pages of this large-format board book show a map of the world, so that participants can see where other continents/countries are in relationship to the United States. A map of Africa is located on the next-to-last page of the book. It also might be fun to check out the areas of Africa where some of the listed games and stories hail from, as the map has the continent divided out into countries! EnchantedLearning.com also has some great color and black-and-white printable maps in smaller format that can be used. For a $20.00 yearly fee, your access to all sorts of items to print is unlimited.

**Swahili Language**    Teach your participants some Swahili! Use the book *Jambo Means Hello: Swahili Alphabet Book* by Muriel Feelings (Dial, 1974) as a jumping-off point. Choose some of the simple words included in the text, such as *baba* (father), *karibu* (welcome), and *tembo* (elephant).

**Counting for Kwanzaa**    This idea comes from Jean Warren's Preschool Express website. Since Kwanzaa lasts for seven days, use the holiday to reinforce the understanding of the number 7. With participants, count out seven things (Kwanzaa candles, fruits and/or vegetables). Or clap hands and stomp feet seven times.

**"The Mosquito"**    This string story from Africa, complete with step-by-step instructions, appears on pages 5–8 of *The Story Vine: A Source Book of Unusual and Easy-to-Tell Stories from Around the World* by Anne Pellowski (Macmillan, 1984). The children particularly love it when the mosquito (made from weaving the string around fingers) "buzzes" them as it flies around. And when you clap your hands and make it "disappear" at the end, they are always amazed!

**"The Lion on the Path"**    This story, using an African thumb piano, can be found on pages 104–106 of *The Story Vine: A Source Book of Unusual and Easy-to-Tell Stories from Around the World* by Anne Pellowski (Macmillan, 1984). A quick Google search will provide sources where thumb pianos can be purchased.

**"Anansi's Good Day"**    The text and telling instructions for this African folktale with the popular Anansi the Spider character can be found on pages 39–42 of *Easy-to-Tell Stories for Young Children* by Annette Harrison (National Storytelling Press, 1992).

**"The Mighty Caterpillar"**    This Masai tale from South Africa can be found on pages 74–78 of *Silly and Sillier: Read-Aloud Tales from Around the World* by Judy Sierra (Alfred A. Knopf, 2002). You could simply read this story to participants, or you could find patterns of the characters and turn it into a flannel/Velcro-board presentation. The caterpillar tricks a number of animals into thinking he is bigger and stronger than he really is!

**Kwanzaa Dot-to-Dots**    I sometimes use simple dot-to-dot puzzles (counting to complete a picture) as an opening for my programs. Four simple dot-to-dot puzzles can be found at ABCTeach.com. On the homepage, click on Holidays and Seasonal on the left-hand side of the page, then Holidays under the subcategories. Then click on Kwanzaa in the alphabetized holiday list. While some items are available only to members, the $39.99 yearly fee seems reasonable since it provides access to more than 40,000 printables.

**Kwanzaa "Friends"**    The website MakingFriends.com has some great paper dolls that you could print out and laminate and use for an opening display for Kwanzaa to illustrate the types of clothing (Kente cloth) worn to celebrate the holiday. The link http://www.makingfriends.com/friends/f+kwanzaa.htm will give you additional links to color clothing, "friend" bodies, and hairstyles. I have personally used these paper dolls for programs on different countries and they really work well!

**Count to 10 in Kiswahili!**    Learn to count from 1 to 10 in Swahili! Visit http://www.kwanzaaland.com/children/counting.html to find the words that correspond to the numbers. Make this a presentation that you can do on a flannel/Velcro board. Use Ellison dies to cut out the numbers, and then use any word-processing program to print out slips with the words on them. To help with your presentation and to prevent mix-up, write the numeral that the word represents on the back of the slip. Laminate all items for durability and put Velcro or flannel on the back so you can use them for presentation on your board. You also may want to consult an online pronunciation guide for the Swahili words.

**African Play Food Set**    Use this realia, available from Becker's School Supplies, as part of your program! For $16.99, you receive a set that includes fish, okra, meat kabob, rice pancake with jam, peanut round, foo foo, and baked plantain. Contact information for Becker's School Supplies can be found in Appendix A at the end of this book.

**Kwanzaa Colors Magnet Board Activity**    In this case, the magnet board is a metal mailbox. This activity is detailed on page 178 of *Magnet Board Fun for Everyday, Seasons, and Holidays* by Liz and Dick Wilmes (Building Blocks Publications, 1998). You will have red, green, and black buttons (with magnetic tape on the backs of each) that will be placed on the mailbox in various patterns.

### Kwanzaa Songs

- The piggyback song (new song sung to a familiar tune) "Kwanzaa Unity" can be found on page 75 of *The Best of Totline Magazine, Volume 2*, compiled by Gayle Bittinger (McGraw-Hill Children's Publishing, 2003).
- The song "Kwanzaa's Here" can be found on page 69 of *The Best of Totline Magazine, Volume 3*, compiled by Gayle Bittinger (McGraw-Hill Children's Publishing, 2003).
- The song "Celebrate" can be found on page 381 of *The Best of Totline Newsletter*, compiled by Jean Warren (Warren Publishing House, 1995).

- Six simple Kwanzaa "piggyback" songs can be found on Jean Warren's Preschool Express website (http://www.preschoolexpress.com/). Click on the Music Rhyme Station on the left-hand side of the homepage, then scroll down to "Winter Songs." Then click on the Kwanzaa link.

## Fingerplays

### Light a Candle on the Kinara

*(Explain to children what a kinara is: it is the candleholder that holds the Kwanzaa candles. This rhyme could also be adapted for the flannel/Velcro board, using the patterns at the end of this chapter.)*

| | |
|---|---|
| Light a candle on the kinara, | *(Hold up one finger and touch it.)* |
| See how it glows. | |
| Now there are six left to light, | *(Hold up six fingers.)* |
| All sitting in a row. | *(Repeat with five, four, three, two, and one.)* |
| The candles are lit on the kinara. | *(Hold up seven fingers.)* |
| See how they glow. | |
| The seven days of Kwanzaa, | |
| All sitting in a row. | |

—Author unknown

### Anansi the Spider

*(Since Anansi is such a popular character in African stories, why not use this adapted version of "The Itsy Bitsy Spider" fingerplay? Use the same motions as you would the original!)*

| | |
|---|---|
| Anansi the Spider | Out came the sun |
| Went up the water spout. | And dried up all the rain, |
| Down came the rain, | And Anansi the Spider |
| And washed Anansi out! | Went up the spout again! |

—Barbara Scott
Adapted traditional rhyme

## Musical Selections

"Celebrate Kwanzaa" from *Rhythms and Rhymes for Special Times* by Jack Hartmann. Available from http://www.songsforteaching.com/.

"Chant and Sing for Kwanzaa" by Caroline and Danny. Available from http://www.songsforteaching.com/.

*Happy Happy Kwanzaa* CD and activity book by Bunny Hull. Available from http://www.songsforteaching.com/.

"Kwanzaa" by Rachel Rambach. Available from http://www.songsforteaching.com/.

"Kwanzaa" from *Happy Everything* by Dr. Jean. Melody House. ASIN: B000DSM3NOE.

"Kwanzaa" from *Seasonal Songs in Motion* by The Learning Station. Hug-A-Chug Records. ASIN: B00005TPUN.

"Kwanzaa Is Here" by Greta Pedersen. Available from http://www.songsforteaching.com/.

"A Swahili Alphabet Book (Kwanzaa Song)" from *Literacy in Motion with The Learning Station.* Available from http://www.songsforteaching.com/.

## Crafts

**Kwanzaa Vest** The base of this craft is a brown grocery bag. Open the bag up completely. If there is an imprint (for example, of a grocery store), make sure that imprint is inside the vest. Cut out a round section for the neck. Have participants put the bag on so that armholes can be lined up. Cut

---

**More Great Fingerplays**

"Kwanzaa Is Here!," from page 54 of *Little Hands Fingerplays and Action Songs: Seasonal Rhymes and Creative Play for 2-to-6-Year-Olds* by Emily Stetson and Vicky Congdon (Williamson Publishing, 2001).

"The Seven Days of Kwanzaa," available from http://stepbystepcc.com/holidays/kwanzaa.html.

"Light The Kwanzaa Candles" and "Going to Africa," available from http://adlil.com/childrensportfolio/kwanzaa.htm.

"Kwanzaa Candles" and "Kwanzaa," available from http://preschool.colonial.net/Teachers/Brown/songs PDFs/holidaysongs2010.pdf.

"Kwanzaa Today" and "Holiday Candles All in a Row," from page 55 of *Toddle on Over: Developing Infant and Toddler Literature Programs* by Robin W. Davis (Alleyside Press, 1998).

"Kwanzaa Candles," from page 267 of *1001 Rhymes and Fingerplays for Working with Young Children*, compiled by the Totline Staff (Warren Publishing House, 1994).

Since Kwanzaa is an African holiday, why not add rhymes about African animals (lions, camels, elephants, monkeys, etc.) to your fingerplay repertoire? You might introduce these rhymes by saying, "The holiday of Kwanzaa has its beginnings in the country of Africa. Here are some rhymes about some animals that live in that country." A quick search of your favorite fingerplay books or online resources will yield lots of results! For example, the fingerplay "Five Little Camels" appears on page 25 of *Storytime Magic: 400 Fingerplays, Flannelboards, and Other Activities* by Kathy MacMillan and Christine Kirker (American Library Association, 2009). The pattern for the camel appears online at http://www.ala.org/ala/aboutala/offices/publishing/editions/webextras/macmillan09775/macmillan09775.cfm. It is number 72 on the PDF list that appears at that site. Simply click on that link and you will be taken to the PDF of the pattern.

---

two armholes. Provide black, red, and green paint and paintbrushes. Allow participants to decorate their vests as they wish.

**Kwanzaa Place Mat**    This great idea comes from page 95 of *The Best of Totline Magazine, Volume 2*, compiled by Gayle Bittinger (McGraw-Hill Children's Publishing, 2003). The base of the craft is a piece of red construction paper. Have participants cut green and black construction paper into small pieces. Glue the green and black pieces onto the red. Once glue has dried, laminate for durability. In my example, I have mixed the colors up, using black as the base. Any combination would work!

**Kwanzaa Flag**    The base of this craft is a piece of black construction paper to which red and green strips are added. The paper is then attached to a wooden skewer that has had the sharp point removed. Instructions appear on page 7 of *December Arts and Crafts, Grades 1–3*, edited by Susan Walker (The Education Center, 2000).

**Shape Kinara**    This craft uses simple shapes (triangle, rectangles, and ovals) to make a Kwanzaa kinara. Instructions appear on page 8 of *December Arts and Crafts, Grades 1–3*, edited by Susan Walker (The Education Center, 2000).

**Kwanzaa Plate**   Instructions and patterns can be found on pates 42–43 of *Cut and Create! Holidays: Easy Step-by-Step Projects That Teach Scissor Skills* by Kim Rankin (Teaching and Learning Company, 1997). A circle shape, representing the plate, has different fruits glued to it.

**African Trading Beads**   This craft uses penne pasta that has been dyed red and green by using food coloring and rubbing alcohol. Use black yarn or black lanyard lengths to hold the pasta. You may also wish to use large plastic needles if you choose to use the yarn. Instructions appear on page 14 of *December Holidays, Preschool-Kindergarten*, edited by Angie Kutzer et al. (The Education Center, 2000).

**Kwanzaa Corn Craft**   The base of this craft is a large letter K that is reproduced on a piece of construction paper. An ear of corn is broken into thirds and then dipped into red, green, and black tempera paint and pressed inside the K shape. Instructions appear on page 31 of *December Holidays, Preschool–Kindergarten*, edited by Angie Kutzer et al. (The Education Center, 2000).

**First Fruits of Kwanzaa Bowl**   Instructions and patterns appear on page 151 of *The Best of Holidays and Seasonal Celebrations—Issues 13–17, Grades 1–3*, edited by Donna Borst and Janet Armbrust (Teaching and Learning Company, 1999).

**Kwanzaa Candle**   Instructions and patterns are found at http://www.dltk-holidays.com/kwanzaa/mcandle.html. The base of this craft is a toilet paper tube to which a striped piece of paper (in Kwanzaa colors) is glued. A flame and ears of corn are then added. Templates may be printed either in color or black and white.

**Beaded Bracelet**   Instructions appear on page 15 of *Storytime Crafts* by Kathryn Totten (Alleyside Press, 1998). This craft uses colorful ring cereal for the "beads."

**Kwanzaa Candle**   This easy craft can be found at http://www.first-school.ws/t/craft/xmas_candle kwanzaab.html. It would make a great refrigerator decoration! When the online pattern is printed, it is only one-half of the page. For preschoolers, I would definitely enlarge the pattern so that it would fit onto an $8\frac{1}{2}$-by-11-inch piece of construction paper or even card stock. When I constructed the craft, I eliminated the tassels on the corn, cutting them off completely. Younger participants would find this cutting too challenging. There is even a short nursery rhyme adaptation of a Kwanzaa verse that participants could learn; it appears on the same page as the candle pattern.

**Unity Cup**   S&S Worldwide offers Unity Cup kits. The unity cup is a communal cup that is used as part of the Kwanzaa celebration. These cups come complete with everything needed to create them, including the crayons. The cups are plastic with a paper wrap around the piece that is decorated. These are then inserted into a plastic cover that protects the decorated paper. The cost is $28.99 per package of 12. If three or more packages are ordered, the price drops to $26.69 per package. Contact information for S&S is located in Appendix A at the end of this book.

# *Martin Luther King Day*

*Use this holiday to celebrate the birth and life of this great civil rights leader!*

## History

Martin Luther King Day is a federal United States holiday that celebrates the birth of the Reverend Dr. Martin Luther King. It is celebrated on the third Monday of January of each year, which is around the time of Dr. King's birthday, January 15th. Dr. King was a prominent spokesperson for the civil rights movement.

King was born in Atlanta, Georgia, in 1929. An intelligent man, he earned his doctorate degree, and he also became a minister in a Montgomery, Alabama, Baptist church.

King believed in nonviolence. Growing up, he had read a book by Mohandas Gandhi, which reflected on how Gandhi had used nonviolent methods to help free the Indian people from the rule of the British. King was also influenced by Henry David Thoreau's essay, "On Civil Disobedience." King helped to found the Southern Christian Leadership Conference. He organized many civil rights marches, including the famous March on Washington in 1963. It was at this march that he gave his famous "I Have a Dream" speech at the Lincoln Memorial. Because of his efforts in the civil rights movement, he was awarded the Nobel Peace Prize in 1964. He was the youngest man ever to have received this award.

Dr. King was assassinated on April 4, 1968, in Memphis, Tennessee. (See Julia Jasmine's *Multicultural Holidays: Share Our Celebrations* [Teacher Created Materials, 1994].)

## Poetry

"Martin Luther King" and "He Had a Dream," from pages 38–39 of *Month-by-Month Poetry: December, January, and February* by Marian Reiner (Scholastic Professional Books, 1999).

"Martin Luther King Day," from page 26 of *Lives: Poems about Famous Americans*, selected by Lee Bennett Hopkins (HarperCollins, 1999).

"Martin Luther King, Jr. Day," from page 13 of *Every Day's a Holiday: Amusing Rhymes for Happy Times* by Dean Koontz (HarperCollins, 2003).

"Martin's Colors" by Marie E. Cecchini, from page 162 of *The Best of Holidays and Seasonal Celebrations—Issues 1–4, PreK–K*, edited by Donna Borst and Janet Armbrust (Teaching and Learning Company, 1999).

## Books

Bauer, Marion D. *Martin Luther King, Jr.* Turtleback, 2009. ISBN: 978-0606105910.
With simple, lyrical text and bold, kid-friendly illustrations, this book introduces the youngest readers to Dr. King.

Cheltenham Elementary School Kindergarten. *We Are All Alike... We Are All Different.* Scholastic, 2002. ISBN: 978-0439417808.
With original drawings and their own lyrical words, a class of kindergartners share the ways they look and feel, the games they play, the foods they like, the homes they live in, and the families they live with, concluding that "We are all alike. We are all different. We are a family."

Katz, Karen. *The Colors of Us.* Turtleback, 2002. ISBN: 978-0613692380.
Lena's mother is an artist, so she knows whereof she speaks when she insists that there are many different shades of brown.

Marzollo, Jean. *Happy Birthday, Martin Luther King, Jr.* Turtleback, 2006. ISBN: 978-0606347747.
An eloquent and powerful introduction to the life and death of Martin Luther King Jr.

McNamara, Margaret. *Martin Luther King Jr. Day.* Aladdin, 2007. ISBN: 978-1416934943.
When Mrs. Conner's class learns about a great man, they discover their own dreams and hopes for a better world.

Medearis, Angela. *Just for You! Singing for Dr. King.* Teaching Resources, 2004. ISBN: 978-0439568555.
In 1965, a young girl helped change America by singing and marching for civil rights with Dr. Martin Luther King. This is her story.

Miller, J. Philip and Sheppard M. Greene. *We All Sing with the Same Voice.* HarperCollins, 2005. ISBN: 978-0060739003.
A classic Sesame Street song becomes a cheerful picture book about children's universal thoughts and feelings.

Moore, Johnny R. *The Story of Martin Luther King, Jr.* Ideals Publications, 2002. ISBN: 978-0824941444.
This little board book uses only approximately 200 words to tell about the life of Martin Luther King Jr. and to explain, in simple terms, how he ended segregation in America.

Rappaport, Doreen. *Martin's Big Words: The Life of Dr. Martin Luther King, Jr.* Hyperion Books for Children, 2001. ISBN: 978-0786807147.
This picture-book biography provides an ideal introduction to this leader and his works.

Reid, Robin. *Thank You, Dr. King.* Topeka Bindery, 2003. ISBN: 978-0613633536.
Part of Bill Cosby's Little Bill series, this volume deals with the celebration of Martin Luther King Day.

Rissman, Rebecca. *Martin Luther King Jr. Day.* Heinemann Raintree, 2010. ISBN: 978-1432940553.
This book introduces readers to what it means to celebrate Martin Luther King Day, and shows them why this holiday is special.

---

### Older Gems, or Titles Too Good to Pass Up

Adler, David A. *A Picture Book of Martin Luther King, Jr.* Holiday House, 1989. ISBN: 978-0823407705.
This beautifully illustrated, easy-to-read biography takes a look at the life, leadership, and ideals of Dr. Martin Luther King Jr.

Davol, Marguerite W. *Black, White, Just Right!* Albert Whitman and Company, 1993. ISBN: 978-0807507858.
A mixed-race child celebrates the rich inclusiveness of her life in a joyful picture book.

Fox, Mem. *Whoever You Are.* Harcourt Children's Books, 1997. ISBN: 978-0152007874.
A one-world, "we-are-all-the-same-under-the-skin" message for the very young.

Kates, Bobbi. *We're Different, We're the Same.* Random House Books for Young Readers, 1992. ISBN: 978-0679832270.
Jim Henson's Sesame Street Muppets cavort cheerfully with people of all sizes, shapes, and ethnicities in this effort to show the ways in which all people are the same, despite obvious physical differences.

McKissack, Pat. *Our Martin Luther King Book.* Child's World, 1987. ISBN: 978-0895653420.
This book describes what a kindergarten class learned about Martin Luther King Jr. on his birthday.

Raschka, Chris. *Yo! Yes?* Scholastic, 1993. ISBN: 978-0531054697.
After the briefest of exchanges, two boys—one black, one white, one shy, one outgoing, one nerdy, one street-smart—decide to take a chance on friendship.

Trueit, Trudi S. *Martin Luther King, Jr. Day*. Children's Press, 2006. ISBN: 978-0531124598.
> This book is part of the Rookie Read-About Holidays series, and focuses on the life of Dr. King.

Walker, Pam. *Martin Luther King, Jr.* Children's Press, 2001. ISBN: 978-0516234366.
> An easy-to-read introduction to the life of Martin Luther King Jr.

Worsham, Adria. *Max Celebrates Martin Luther King Jr. Day*. Picture Window Books, 2008. ISBN: 978-1404847613.
> There is a special school assembly for Martin Luther King Day. What will Max learn about Martin Luther King Jr.?

## Activities

---

### Coloring Pages

Consult your favorite pattern books or holiday coloring books for pages to use as coloring sheets. Be sure to search online as well. There's lots of great stuff out there!

- "Martin Luther King" and "I Have a Dream," from pages 30–31 of *January Patterns and Projects* (Newbridge Educational, 2000). These would make great coloring pages.
- A great coloring page appears at http://www.activityvillage.co.uk/martin_luther_king_coloring_page.htm.

---

### Flannel/Velcro Board

**Martin Luther King Jr. and Family Paper Dolls**    Dover Publications offers this great set, available on Amazon.com. It features Dr. King, his wife, and their four children. Nineteen costumes are offered, including the clothing Dr. King wore for his Selma-to-Montgomery march and his "I Have a Dream" speech. These would be great to cut out, laminate, and use for a flannel/Velcro-board presentation on the life of Dr. King. If you choose to do so, be sure to make enough color copies of the figures for the number of outfits available. You might want to find current pictures of the four children and include them as well!

### Games

**Martin Luther King Day Matching Game**    Patterns for symbols (hand and globe) appear on pages 73–76 of *Holiday Patterns*, compiled by Jean Warren (Warren Publishing House, 1991). The best patterns to use are the ones that are already enclosed in a square, as this would make cutting them out simple. Copy two of each on different colors of construction paper. Give each participant one of the patterns/colors. Keep one for yourself and place in an apron pocket or container of some sort. Begin the matching game by pulling out your copies, one at a time, placing them on the board, and allowing participants to match them. For this game, you could also use the Ellison silhouette die of Dr. King, located in the Social Studies section of their catalog.

### Miscellaneous

**Friendship Stew**    This great idea is courtesy of Kathleen Poznick of Weatherford Public Library in Weatherford, Texas. Her idea puts the emphasis on the concept of friendship, and how we can have many different types of friends. To make "Friendship Stew," pass out small cups of various snacks, such as Cheerios, mini marshmallows, pretzels, M&Ms, raisins, etc., to participants. You should have a large empty bowl and spoon for yourself. Sing the following song:

Friendship Stew, Friendship Stew,      Some for me and some for you,
I'm gonna make some Friendship Stew.      Yummy in my tummy, Friendship Stew.

Kathleen says she uses no particular tune, just one she made up, but I think the song works well to the tune of "Shortnin' Bread." As you are singing the song, ask the participants with a particular snack (Cheerios, for example) to come up and pour their small cups into the large bowl. Continue with each of the snacks you have passed out. Stir the ingredients together and talk about how people can be different and still be friends. When all of the ingredients are mixed, pour some of the mix into each of the small cups for participants to snack on! This would be a great activity to do right before a second story, or before your participants sit down to do a coloring page or simple craft.

**"We Are All the Waves of One Sea"** The words and melody line to this song are found on page 103 of *Crazy Gibberish and Other Story Hour Stretches* by Naomi Baltuck (Linnet Books, 1993). Although no motions are given, it would certainly be easy enough to come up with some.

**Friendship Walk** Instructions for this activity can be found on page 9 of *More Everyday Circle Times for Large and Small Groups of Children* by Liz and Dick Wilmes (Building Blocks Publications, 1992). After you do a Friendship Walk, why not enjoy some Friendship Stew as a treat?

**Martin Luther King Day Songs**
- The piggyback songs (new songs sung to old tunes) "Hand-in-Hand" and "Dr. King Marched" can be found on pages 40–41 of *Piggyback Songs to Sign* by Jean Warren and Susan Shroyer (Warren Publishing House, 1992). ASL (American Sign Language) motion is included.
- The songs "Martin Luther King Had a Dream" and "He Dreamed of World Peace" can be found on page 42 of *Holiday Piggyback Songs*, compiled by Jean Warren (Warren Publishing House, 1988).
- The songs "Martin Was His Name," "A Man with a Dream," and "A Special Man" can be found on page 78 of *The Best of Totline Magazine, Volume 2*, compiled by Gayle Bittinger (McGraw-Hill Children's Publishing, 2003).

# Fingerplays ──────────────────────────────────────────────

### Dr. King Had a Dream

*(This rhyme can be sung to the tune of "Pop Goes the Weasel.")*

| | |
|---|---|
| Dr. King had a dream, | *(Point index finger at temple.)* |
| Friendship we would give. | *(Extend hands out in front of body.)* |
| Today, his dream has come true, | *(Shake head "yes.")* |
| As hand in hand we live. | *(Clasp hands together in front of body.)* |

—Barbara Scott

---

### More Great Fingerplays

"Martin Luther King," an action rhyme, from page 282 of *1001 Rhymes of Fingerplays for Working with Young Children*, compiled by the Totline Staff (Warren Publishing House, 1995).

"Dr. King, He Had a Dream," from page 57 of *Little Hands Fingerplays and Action Songs: Seasonal Rhymes and Creative Play for 2-to-6-Year-Olds* by Emily Stetson and Vicky Congdon (Williamson Publishing, 2001).

"Brotherhood," an action rhyme, from page 146 of *The Big All-Year Book of Holidays and Seasonal Celebrations: Preschool/Kindergarten, Issues 14–18*, edited by Donna Borst (Teaching and Learning Company, 2002).

"The World Is Like a Rainbow: A Rhyme to Sign," action rhyme, from page 83 of *Storytime Magic: 400 Fingerplays, Flannelboards, and Other Activities* by Kathy MacMillan and Christine Kirker (American Library Association, 2009). The rhyme includes ASL motions to use as the rhyme is recited.

## Musical Selections

"Dr. King" from *All Year* by Intelli-Tunes. Available from http://www.songsforteaching.com/.

"Dr. Martin Luther King" from *U.S.A. Hooray!* Available from http://www.songsforteaching.com/.

"The Dream of Martin Luther King, Jr." and "A Tribute to Martin Luther King, Jr" from *Holly Daze* by Mary Miche. Available from http://www.songsforteaching.com/.

"I Have a Dream" from *I Have a Dream: World Music for Children* by Daria. DariaMusic. ASIN: B000CA6YZS.

"I Just Want to Sing Your Name (The Martin Luther King Song)" from *So Many Ways to Be Smart* by Two of a Kind. Magillacutty Music. ASIN: B0006ZP41Y.

"A Man Named King" from *Holidays and Special Times* by Greg and Steve. Youngheart. ASIN: B00000DGH5.

"Martin Luther King" from *When the Rain Comes Down* by Cathy Fink. Rounder. ASIN: B0000003FA.

"Rise Up—Martin Luther King Day" from *Rhythms and Rhymes for Special Times* by Jack Hartmann. Available from http://www.songsforteaching.com/.

"Sing about Martin" from *Sing about Martin and Other Miss Jackie Favorites* by Miss Jackie Silberg. Available at http://www.songsforteaching.com/.

"Stand Up for Martin Luther King" from *Happy Everything* by Dr. Jean. Melody House. ASIN: B000SM3NOE.

## Crafts

**Shake Hands!**    Instructions for this craft appear on page 79 of *Arts and Crafts for All Seasons, Grades 1–3* (The Education Center, 1999). Participants' hands are traced in contrasting skin tones, overlapped, and then secured with a brad fastener. Paper in multicultural colors/skin tones would be perfect for this craft!

**Peace Dove**    Simple shapes create a dove. Instructions and pattern can be found on pages 44–46 of *Cut and Create! Holidays: Easy Step-by-Step Projects That Teach Scissor Skills* by Kim Rankin (Teaching and Learning Company, 1997). Copy onto construction paper. Since there is writing on the pattern pieces and it corresponds to the instructions, simply turn them over to make the craft.

Also, the feathers of the wings require that more than one of the pattern be made. It is a good idea to have these feather patterns copied out ahead of time in the numbers that are needed.

**Great Harmony Place Mat**    The base of this craft is a brown paper grocery bag. One bag will yield two place mats. The bag is colored, a saying is added, and then pictures of people of different races (cut from magazines) are added. Detailed instructions and pattern can be found on pages 18–20 of *Holiday and Seasonal Crafts from Recycled Materials* by Deborah Whitacre and Becky Radtke (Teaching and Learning Company, 1995).

**Martin Luther King Jr. Craft**    This is a simple craft that allows participants to color and cut out Dr. King in two pattern pieces and then glue them together! Patterns appear on page 78 of *February Patterns and Projects* (Newbridge Educational, 2000).

**Handshake Craft**    The pattern and instructions for this craft, which makes a flag when attached to a paper towel tube, can be found on pages 154–155 of *The Big All-Year Book of Holidays and Seasonal Celebrations: Preschool/Kindergarten, Issues 14–18*, edited by Donna Borst (Teaching and Learning Company, 2002).

**Multicultural Mask**    Search craft catalogs such as S&S Worldwide and Becker's School Supplies (see Appendix A) for multicultural paper (paper in varying shades of browns) that you can use to make a basic mask shape. Allow participants to decorate this mask by adding facial features and hair. You may also find this type of paper under "skin tone construction paper." Another variation: If you wish to use white construction paper, use multicultural crayons (crayons in varying skin tones).

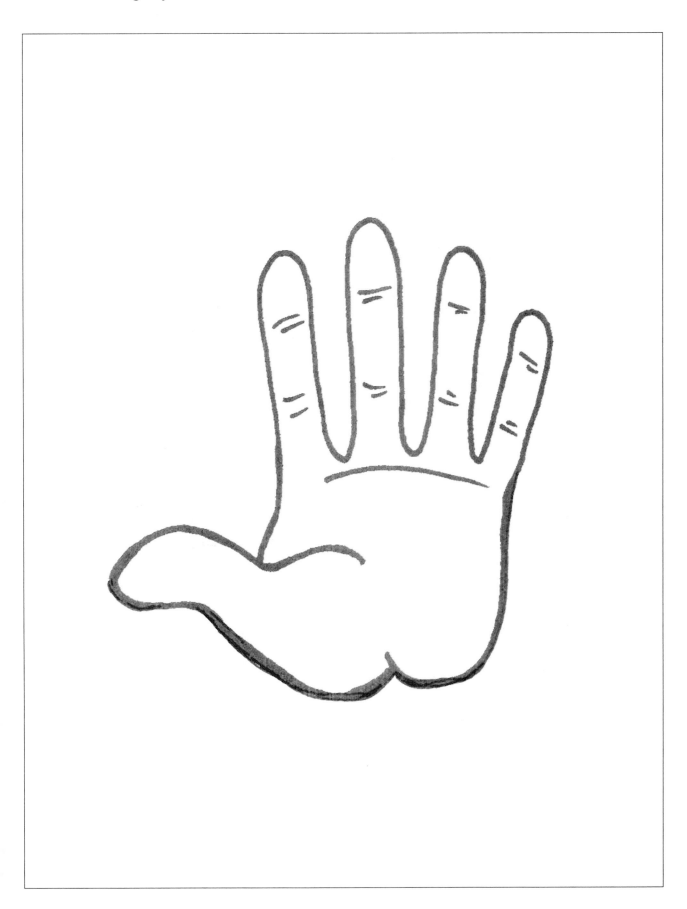

# May Day

*Beautiful baskets of flowers, dancing around the Maypole...Who could ask for more?*

## History

May Day is traditionally celebrated on May 1st. It marks the coming of spring. The holiday has its roots in ancient Roman culture. The Romans worshipped Flora, who was the goddess of fruits and flowers. In early English history, the day was celebrated by dancing around a "Maypole," a large pole that usually was erected in a town square. The pole was decorated with long ribbons that the dancers wove into patterns as they danced. A May Queen was usually chosen to rule over this celebration.

Another practice of the day was to gather fresh flowers and tree branches. This was known as "bringing in the May." The flowers were used in baskets that decorated homes. This tradition has been translated today into making baskets filled with flowers and presenting them to family, friends, and neighbors. Usually the giver of the basket rings the doorbell or knocks on the door, leaves the basket at the receiver's door, and then runs off before he or she can be seen! (See Julia Jasmine's *Multicultural Holidays: Share Our Celebrations* [Teacher Created Materials, 1994].)

## Poetry

"May Basket," from page 251 of *The Best of Holidays and Seasonal Celebrations—Issues 9–13, PreK–K*, edited by Donna Borst (Teaching and Learning Company, 2001).

"May Basket Counting Rhyme" by Jennifer Joseph, from page 262 of *The Best of Holidays and Seasonal Celebrations—Issues 5–8, PreK-K*, edited by Donna Borst (Teaching and Learning Company, 2000).

"May Day," from page 94 of *A Child's Seasonal Treasury*, compiled and written by Betty Jones (Tricycle Press, 1996).

"May Day," from page 32 of *Ring Out, Wild Bells: Poems about Holidays and Seasons*, selected by Lee Bennett Hopkins (Harcourt Brace Jovanovich, 1992).

"May-Time," from page 38 of *Month-by-Month Poetry: March, April, May, and June* by Marian Reiner (Scholastic Professional Books, 1999).

## Books

Since there are not a lot of May Day books out there, I have listed some of my favorite flower-themed books.

Gillingham, Sara. *In My Flower*. Chronicle Books, 2009. ISBN: 978-0811873390.
Turn the colorful die-cut pages of this irresistible book to discover just what makes little butterfly's flower so cozy.

Henkes, Kevin. *My Garden*. Greenwillow Books, 2010. ISBN: 978-0061715174.
A young girl's garden grows as big as her imagination.

Kent, Jeffrey. *May Day/Lei Day*. Bess Press, 2008. ISBN: 978-1573062886.
This book describes how this special holiday is celebrated in England, where it originated more than 700 years ago, and describes how Hawaii came to embrace it as Lei Day.

### Older Gems, or Titles Too Good to Pass Up

Alexander, Lisa. *There's More . . . Much More*. Gulliver Books, 1987. ISBN: 978-0152006051.
  On a lovely, sunny day, Sherri meets Squirrel, who says he is going to fill his May basket with spring.

Bruce, Lisa. *Fran's Flower*. HarperCollins, 2000. ISBN: 978-0060286217.
  Fran is determined to get her flower bud to grow. But what do you feed a fussy flower?

Bunting, Eve. *Flower Garden*. Turtleback, 2000. ISBN: 978-0613284905.
  A girl and her father create a window box as a birthday present for her mother.

Ehlert, Lois. *Planting a Rainbow*. Harcourt Children's Books, 1988. ISBN: 978-0152626099.
  A young child relates in ten simple sentences the yearly cycle and process of planning, planting, and picking flowers in a garden. If you can find this in the Big Book version, it works extremely well with a storytime group. The Big Book version is my go-to choice!

Kroll, Steven. *Queen of the May*. Holiday House, 1993. ISBN: 978-0823410040.
  A lovely variation of Cinderella with a unique twist. Sylvie, who lives with her nasty step-mother and stepsister, wants to pick the prettiest bouquet of flowers. She overcomes many hurdles and, with help from some animal friends, is crowned queen.

Mariana. *Miss Flora McFlimsey's May Day*. Lothrop, Lee, and Shepard Books, 1987. ISBN: 978-0688045463.
  Although Miss McFlimsey knows she isn't beautiful, she discovers she has the potential for another queenly attribute.

McMillan, Bruce. *Counting Wildflowers*. William Morrow and Company, 1986. ISBN: 978-0688028596.
  Number concepts 1 through 20 are presented in full-color, high-quality photographs of common field and woodland wildflowers.

Rockwell, Anne. *Bumblebee, Bumblebee, Do You Know Me? A Garden Guessing Game*. HarperCollins, 1999. ISBN: 978-0060282127.
  On each double-page spread, a riddle about a flower is addressed to an insect.

Silverman, Erica. *On the Morn of Mayfest*. Simon and Schuster Children's Publishing, 1998. ISBN: 978-0689806742.
  A playful cumulative rhyme ends up as a spontaneous Mayfest parade.

Uttley, Alison. *Little Grey Rabbit's May Day*. HarperCollins, 2000. ISBN: 978-0001983946.
  Late one night, just before May Day, Hare steals into the village and dances around the Maypole. He excitedly tells little Grey Rabbit and Squirrel all about it the next morning.

Mora, Pat. The *Rainbow Tulip*. Turtleback, 2003. ISBN: 978-0613616539.
  A Mexican-American first-grader experiences the difficulties and pleasures of being different when she wears a tulip costume with all the colors of the rainbow for the school May Day parade.

Park, Linda S. *What Does Bunny See? A Book of Colors and Flowers*. Clarion Books, 2005. ISBN: 978-0618234851.
  Bunny hops through a garden and is introduced to different colors and flowers along the way.

Wellington, Monica. *Zinnia's Flower Garden*. Dutton Juvenile, 2005. ISBN: 978-0525473688.
  Red-haired Zinnia, with the help of her cat and dog pals, demonstrates the skills that bring forth a brilliant wealth of blossoms.

## Activities

---

| |
|---|
| **Coloring Pages** |
| Consult your favorite pattern books or holiday coloring books for pages to use as coloring sheets. Be sure to search online as well. There's lots of great stuff out there! |
| • May Day Coloring Page, from page 6 of *May Patterns and Projects* (Newbridge Educational, 2000). |

### Games

**Flower Matching Game**   Use any of the numerous Ellison die cuts in the large size to cut flower shapes (two each) from different colors of construction paper. Laminate for durability and attach flannel or Velcro to the backs. To play the game, hand out one of each pair to participants and place the second of the pair into a container (perhaps a pretty basket) or apron pocket. Once all participants have a flower shape/color, begin the game by pulling out flower shapes/colors one by one from your pocket or basket and placing them on the board. Have the participant who has the match bring his or hers up and place it next to yours. Continue until all have been matched.

**May Basket Game**   This idea can be found on page 95 of *Special Day Celebrations* by Elizabeth McKinnon (Warren Publishing House, 1989). It involves using an ordinary basket that you could decorate with ribbons or streamers. Use an Ellison die-cut to cut flower shapes from different colors of construction paper. Place them in a box. Before playing the game, pass the box around and allow each participant to take one flower from the box. Help participants name the color if needed. Then, use the piggyback song (new song sung to a familiar tune) provided, which allows each participant to bring up their flower and place it in the decorated basket as his or her name and color of flower is called.

### Miscellaneous

**May Song and Simple Maypole**   The "May Song" to use for this activity can be found on page 100 of *A Child's Seasonal Treasury*, compiled and written by Betty Jones (Tricycle Press, 1996). The Simple Maypole instructions can be found on page 110 of the same book. Another song that can be sung while dancing around the Maypole is "Now We Go 'Round the Maypole High." It is sung to the tune of "Here We Go 'Round the Mulberry Bush." The text of the song can be found on page 28 of *Festivals, Family, and Food* by Diana Carey and Judy Large (Hawthorn Press, 1982).

**Maypole Dancing**   This activity, which uses a hat rack or other freestanding pole as the base for the Maypole, can be found on page 41 of *More Simply Super Storytimes: Programming Ideas for Ages 3–6* by Marie Castellano Boyum (Upstart, 2006). A simple song to sing is included. You may choose to have children dance around the Maypole with or without using ribbons.

**May Day Songs**
- "May Is Here," a piggyback song (new song sung to a familiar tune), can be found on page 70 of *Holiday Piggyback Songs*, compiled by Jean Warren (Warren Publishing House, 1988).
- The song "A Basket, A Basket," along with American Sign Language motions, can be found on pages 70–71 of *Piggyback Songs to Sign* by Jean Warren and Susan Shroyer (Warren Publishing House, 1992).
- Also, the song "Around the May Pole" can be found on page 141 of *The Best of Totline Magazine, Volume 4*, compiled by Gayle Bittinger (McGraw-Hill Children's Publishing, 2004).

## Fingerplays

**Five May Baskets**

*(Begin this rhyme with five fingers up and take away fingers as the rhyme progresses. This would also work well as a flannel/Velcro-board presentation.)*

Five May baskets waiting by the door—
One will go to _____.
Then there will be four.
Four May baskets, pretty as can be—
One will go to _____.
Then there will be three.
Three May baskets—one is pink and blue.
One will go to _____.
Then there will be two.
Two May baskets waiting in the sun—
One will go to _____.
Then there will be one.
One May basket—I want it to go
To my own dear mother.
She's the nicest one I know.

*(Insert a child's name for each blank.)*

—Lynda Roberts
*Mitt Magic* (Gryphon House, 1985, p. 59)

**May Day**

When May Day comes,
A basket I'll make, *(Make small circle in front of body with hands.)*
And fill it with flowers sweet; *(Pretend to pick flowers.)*
Then for surprise, beneath, I'll put
Some candies sweet to eat. *(Rub tummy.)*
When it is dusk, I'll quickly go *(Run in place.)*
And ring my playmate's bell; *(Pretend to ring doorbell.)*
Then run away and let her guess *(Put index finger to temple, questioning.)*
Whose love the flowers tell. *(Place hands over heart.)*

—Maude Burnham
*Rhymes for Little Hands* (Milton Bradley Company, 1910, p. 85)

**May Day**

Itisket! Itasket! It is the first of May! *(Hold up one finger.)*
I'll leave you this basket, *(Make small circle in front of body with hands.)*
And quickly run away! *(Run in place.)*

—Maude Burnham
*Rhymes for Little Hands* (Milton Bradley Company, 1910, p. 86)

## Musical Selections

From my reading, I have found that there is no specific traditional music for Maypole dancing. Each village had its own dances, usually with regional variations. Celtic or Irish folk music works well. Jigs are good for fast walking or skipping steps, and marches and reels work well for walking steps.

"The Beautiful Month of May" from *Rhythms and Rhymes for Special Times* by Jack Hartmann. Available from http://www.songsforteaching.com/.

*Celtic Songs for Children: Kids at Heart* CD by Golden Bough. ARC Music. ASIN: B00005JXQ3. Many of these lively tunes would be great for Maypole dancing, especially "Frog in the Wall" and "Crabs in the Skillet."

"Greensleeves." Any instrumental recording of this song would work well for dancing.

## Crafts

**My Maypole**    Let each participant decorate a paper towel tube however they choose. They could use crayons, markers, tissue paper, or any other type of craft item. Staple crepe paper or ribbon streamers to one end of the tube. Allow children time to dance and move with their Maypoles! Use any of the music listed in the Musical Selections section.

**May Doorknob Decoration**    This craft allows participants to color and cut out a basket of flowers that can be hung on a doorknob. You may wish to enlarge the pattern. Instructions and pattern are found on page 22 of *May Patterns, Projects, and Plans to Perk Up Early Learning Programs* by Imogene Forte (Incentive Publications, 1990).

**Miniature Maypoles**    This craft constructs a small Maypole from a straw. It is anchored in a paper plate by a piece of clay. Colorful ribbons are attached as well. Instructions can be found on page 80 of *Quick Tricks for Holidays* by Annalisa McMorrow (Monday Morning Books, 2001).

**Doily Nosegays**    This easy craft makes nosegays from small doilies, pipe cleaners, glue, and ribbon. Instructions for this craft can be found on page 82 of *Quick Tricks for Holidays* by Annalisa McMorrow (Monday Morning Books, 2001). Each participant might want to make several to make a "bouquet"!

**May Day Bouquet**    This craft, a cone made from a paper plate into which flowers can be placed, is found on page 24 of *Crafts from World Cultures: Easy-to-Make Multicultural Art Activities* by Janice Veith and Anne Weber (Monday Morning Books, 1995).

**May Basket**    This craft, in which the participant's hands make the side of the basket, is found on pages 51 (instructions) and 54 (patterns) of *From the Hands of a Child: Special Seasonal Art Activities for Primary Children* by Anthony Flores (Fearon Teacher Aids, 1987).

**May Flower Lacing**    Ellison offers a lacing flower die-cut in the XL size. Cut these from heavy paper. I would recommend card stock. Use large plastic craft needles for your yarn. As you lace, you may wish to leave excess yarn so that the finished produced can be hung on a doorknob!

# New Year's Day

*Celebrate the coming of a new year!*

## History

Typically, New Year's celebrations begin on December 31st, New Year's Eve. At midnight, bells will ring and sirens will sound, signaling the end of the old year and the beginning of a brand new one. It is a time for family and friends to celebrate together, exchanging hugs and kisses at midnight. Others may attend church services.

Many of the customs that we enjoy every year come from other countries. The Danish people make noise. The Scottish bang pots and pans together and sing "Auld Lang Syne." The early Anglo-Saxons drank toasts, and Germans were known for making New Year's resolutions.

The custom of New Year's resolutions dates all the way back to ancient Rome. The month of January is named for the Roman god named Janus. Janus had two faces. He was the god of beginnings and endings and of doorways. He had two faces so that he could look both ways at once. Ancient Romans honored him by making promises, or resolutions, to him when they began the New Year. Nowadays, we make resolutions, but they are usually to ourselves. (See "History of New Years Day" at http://new-years-day.com/new-years-history.htm.)

Staying up until midnight may be hard, but most people do try. Many will watch the ball drop in New York City's Times Square to mark the occasion. The first big gala in Times Square was held in 1904, and the first ball drop occurred in 1907. (See "New Year's Traditions" at http://www.infoplease.com/spot/newyearcelebrations.html.)

January 1st is the first day of the year, according to the Gregorian calendar. On this day, some people eat special foods that are considered to be lucky. In the United States, it is a day usually delegated to televised parades and sports contests. (See Julia Jasmine's *Multicultural Holidays: Share Our Celebrations* [Teacher Created Materials, 1994].)

## Poetry

"Happy New Year to You" and "My New Year's Resolution," from http://www.123newyear.com/newyear-poems/.

"Hooray! Hooray! It's New Year's Day," from http://www.poetry4kids.com/poem-190.html.

"My New Year," from page 76 of *The Best of Holidays and Seasonal Celebrations: Songs, Action Rhymes, and Fingerplays, PreK–3*, compiled by Ellen Sussman (Teaching and Learning Company, 2000).

"New Year's Day," from page 35 of *Circle-Time Poetry Around the Year* by Jodi Simpson (Scholastic, 2005).

"New Year's Day," "Promises," and "Welcome to the New Year," from pages 10, 11, and 12, respectively, of *Ring Out, Wild Bells: Poems about Holidays and Seasons*, selected by Lee Bennett Hopkins (Harcourt Brace Jovanovich, 1992).

"Staying Up Till Midnight," a rhyme that could be used as a poem, from page 84 of *Storytime Magic: 400 Fingerplays, Flannelboards, and Other Activities* by Kathy MacMillan and Christine Kirker (American Library Association, 2009).

## Books ————————————————————————————————————————————

Freeman, Don. *Happy New Year, Corduroy*. Viking Juvenile, 2008. ISBN: 978-0670063437.
   Corduroy and his friends are ringing in the New Year with a party.

Holabird, Katharine. *Angelina Ice Skates*. Viking Juvenile, 2007. ISBN: 978-0670062379.
   Angelina and some other mice are preparing for a New Year's Eve ice skating show, but the hockey
   players keep getting in the way—until Angelina gets them involved.

Lewis, Paul O. *P. Bear's New Year's Party: A Counting Book*. Tricycle Press, 2006. ISBN: 978-1582461915.
   On New Year's Eve, P. Bear awaits the arrival of his friends. At one o'clock, whale arrives; at two
   o'clock, two horses arrive, etc. At the end it's time to ring in the New Year and for readers to count
   how many guests came to the party.

Miller, Pat. *Squirrel's New Year's Resolution*. Albert Whitman and Company, 2010. ISBN: 978-0807575918.
   Squirrel knows that New Year's Day is a great day for making resolutions! But what does it mean
   to make a resolution, anyway?

Peppas, Lynn. *New Year's Day*. Crabtree Publishing Company, 2010. ISBN: 978-0778747628.
   From New Year's Eve to New Year's Day, people around the world have different customs to welcome
   in the New Year.

Piernas-Davenport, Gail. *Shante Keys and the New Year's Peas*. Albert Whitman and Company, 2007.
ISBN: 978-0807573303.
   In this multicultural New Year's story, Shanté Keys learns about Chinese New Year and Diwali, as
   well as how January 1st is celebrated in other countries. The author includes additional pages of
   information about diverse New Year's traditions and special foods.

---

### Older Gems, or Titles Too Good to Pass Up

Berger, Lou. *Sesame Street Stays Up Late*. BT Bound, 1999. ISBN: 978-0613023979.
   Big Bird's bash will ring in the New Year with a bang when Sesame Street stays up late for the Monster
   News Network's global TV party.

Clifton, Lucille. *Three Wishes*. Doubleday Books for Young Readers, 1992. ISBN: 978-0385304979.
   On a New Year's Day walk with her friend Victor, Nobie finds a penny with her birth year on it—a sure
   sign that she'll have three wishes granted.

Janice. *Little Bear's New Year's Party*. Lothrop, Lee, and Shepard Books, 1973. ISBN: 978-0688500023.
   Little Bear hosts a New Year's party and welcomes more guests than he invited.

Mariana. *Miss Flora McFlimsey and the Baby New Year*. Lothrop, Lee, and Shepard Books, 1988. ISBN: 978-
0688045333.
   Miss Flora McFlimsey has a surprise late-night visitor on New Year's Eve.

Marx, David F. *New Year's Day*. Children's Press, 2000. ISBN: 978-0516271569.
   Part of the Rookie Read-About Holidays series, this is a great introduction to the customs of New Year's.

Modell, Frank. *Goodbye Old Year, Hello New Year*. Greenwillow Books, 1984. ISBN: 978-0688039387.
   Marvin and Milton want to celebrate the coming of the New Year but fall asleep before midnight.

Stevenson, James. *Un-Happy New Year, Emma!* Greenwillow Books, 1989. ISBN: 978-0688083427.
   Emma struggles with her New Year's resolution to be nicer to the other witches Dolores and Lavinia, as they
   persist in being dreadful to her, until their relationship climaxes in a dreadful revenge on New Year's Day.

Ziefert, Harriet. *First Night*. Putnam Juvenile, 1999. ISBN: 978-0399231209.
   First Night is a fast-growing holiday celebrated in towns and cities all over America. What could be more
   fun than dressing up, marching in a parade, and heralding in the New Year with music and fireworks?

Ruelle, Karen. *Just in Time for New Years! A Harry and Emily Adventure*. Holiday House, 2004. ISBN: 978-0823418411.

> Yippee! It's almost New Year's Eve. Harry and Emily are going to stay up until midnight on the big night. But how will they stay awake?

Wing, Natasha. *The Night Before New Years*. Grosset and Dunlap, 2009. ISBN: 978-0448452128.

> It's the night before New Year's, and the whole family is determined to stay up until midnight!

# Activities

---

### Coloring Pages

Consult your favorite pattern books or holiday coloring books for pages to use as coloring sheets. Be sure to search online as well. There's lots of great stuff out there!

- Visit http://dulemba.com/index_ColoringPages.html for author and illustrator Elizabeth O. Dulemba's great collection of holiday coloring pages. While there, sign up for her Coloring Page Tuesdays e-mails.
- Check out http://www.activityvillage.co.uk/new_year_coloring_AV.htm for a variety of great New Year coloring pages that can be enlarged as PDFs and printed out.
- Happy New Year card patterns can be found on pages 22–23 of *January Patterns and Projects* (Newbridge Educational, 2000). These would make great coloring pages.
- A cute coloring page of Baby New Year can be found at http://www.makingfriends .com/color/color_newyears.htm. Enlarge as desired.

---

## Flannel/Velcro Board

**"The New Year's Affair"**     This story, about a bear who has nothing to wear for a New Year's party, is found on pages 64–65 of *The Best of Totline Stories* by Jean Warren (Totline Publications, 2000).

## Games

**New Year's Matching Game**     Patterns for a variety of New Year's symbols (Baby New Year, party hat, party horn) appear on pages 63–68 of *Holiday Patterns*, compiled by Jean Warren (Warren Publishing House, 1991). The best patterns to use are the ones that are already enclosed in a square, as this would make cutting them out simple. Copy two of each on different colors of construction paper. Give each participant one of the patterns/colors. Keep one for yourself and place in an apron pocket or container of some sort. Begin the matching game by pulling out your copies, one at a time, placing them on the board, and allowing participants to match them.

## Miscellaneous

**Welcome in the New Year Activity**     Instructions and patterns for this activity can be found on pages 160–161 of *Felt Board Fun for Everyday and Holidays* by Liz and Dick Wilmes (Building Blocks Publications, 1984).

**New Year's Songs**
- The following piggyback songs (new songs sung to familiar tunes) can be found on pages 38–40 of *Holiday Piggyback Songs*, compiled by Jean Warren (Warren Publishing House, 1988): "A Brand New Year," "It's a New Year," "A New Year on Our Calendar," "Let's Celebrate," "Happy New Year," and "Celebrate."

- Also, the book *Piggyback Songs to Sign* by Jean Warren and Susan Shroyer (Warren Publishing House, 1992) contains the following songs/American Sign Language motions on pages 38–39: "It's Almost Time," "Hurray!," "Everybody Give a Cheer," and "Happy New Year."

**Welcome the New Year with Instruments!**    This idea using your rhythm band instruments comes from *Special Days Celebrations* by Elizabeth McKinnon (Warren Publishing House, 1989). The piggyback song "Happy New Year," sung to the tune of "Frere Jacques," allows your participants to play the different types of instruments, one kind at a time. The text for the song is found on page 53. You could add a final verse, such as "hear the instruments," and have a real symphony of sound!

## Fingerplays

**New Year's Day**

On New Year's Day the fingers go            *(Walk fingers on lap.)*
To call on little friends they know,
To all they meet along the way            *(Wave to others on either side.)*
"A Happy New Year to you!"
They say.

—Maude Burnham
*Rhymes for Little Hands* (Milton Bradley Company, 1910, p. 76)

**Three Ways to Grow**

For every little finger,            *(Wiggle ten fingers in the air.)*
A New Year has begun.
They'll all be taller, stronger, kinder            *(Sit up straight; show muscles; put hands over heart.)*
When the year is done.

—Maude Burnham
*Rhymes for Little Hands* (Milton Bradley Company, 1910, p. 76)

---

**More Great Fingerplays**

"New Year's Eve," "It's a New Year," "The New Year's Here," and "Cheer the Year," from page 272 of *1001 Rhymes and Fingerplays for Working with Young Children*, compiled by the Totline Staff (Warren Publishing House, 1994).

"New Year's Kickoff Action Verse," action rhyme, from page 28 of *Holiday Hoopla: Songs and Fingerplays* by Kathy Darling (Monday Morning Books, 1990).

"Happy New Year," from page 35 of *Rhymes for Circle Time* by Louise B. Scott (Instructional Fair/T.S. Denison, 1999).

---

## Musical Selections

"Farewell to the Old Year" from *Holly Daze* by Mary Miche. Available from http://www.songsforteaching.com/.

"The First Month of the Year (January)" from *Rhythms and Rhymes for Special Times* by Jack Hartmann. Available from http://www.songsforteaching.com/.

"Happy New Year" from *Seasons and Celebrations*. Available from http://www.songsforteaching.com/.

"It's a New Year!" by Greda Pedersen and Pam Donkin. Available from http://www.songsforteaching.com/.

"Ring in the New Year" from *Happy Everything* by Dr. Jean. Melody House. ASIN: B000SM3N0E.

## Crafts

**New Year's Pot Bangers**    The base of this craft is a wooden spoon! Instructions for this craft can be found at http://www.makingfriends.com/winter/newyears_ spoon.htm. For the preschool age, I would recommend that the spoons be painted ahead of time (or you could skip that step). A great source for inexpensive wooden spoons is your local dollar store!

**Tambourines**    What's New Year's without some noise? The instructions for these simple tambourines made from plastic or paper plates can be found at http://www.makingfriends.com/ music/tambourine .htm.

**New Year Noisemakers**    Instructions for this craft that uses two paper cups, dried beans, and colorful paper strips can be found on page 67 of *Arts and Crafts for All Seasons, Preschool/Kindergarten* (The Education Center, 1999).

**New Year's Noisemaker**    This craft, for which the participant's hands represent the noise coming out of the horn, is found on pages 26 (instructions) and 28 (patterns) of *From the Hands of a Child: Special Seasonal Art Activities for Primary Children* by Anthony Flores (Fearon Teacher Aids, 1987).

# Passover

*Passover is a holiday that has special meaning to people of the Jewish faith.*

## History

Passover is a Jewish holiday that celebrates the exodus, or the exiting, of the Jewish or Hebrew people from the country of Egypt. The holiday marks their deliverance from slavery and from their Egyptian taskmasters. The holiday itself is eight days long, and begins with a special meal, called the Seder. The story of the exodus is read from a book called the Haggadah. During the eight days, many families eat only matzo and kosher foods and do not eat any leavened products, such as pasta and bread. These may be eaten once the holiday is over.

The Seder meal contains special foods, all of which are representative of aspects of the Passover. A roasted lamb bone represents the sacrificial lambs; the hard-boiled egg represents new life; parsley or celery represents springtime; a bitter herb (such as horseradish) represents slavery; charoset (a dish made from apples, nuts, wine, sugar, and vinegar) symbolizes the mortar that was used by the Hebrews to build the cities for the Egyptians during their enslavement. Also on the dinner table at the Seder meal are saltwater, wine, and matzo. Saltwater is symbolic of the tears shed by the Jews; wine is a symbol of the sweetness in life; matzo, or unleavened bread, reminds the Jews of the swiftness of their departure from Egypt—so swift that they did not even have time for their bread to rise!

An extra place is always set at the Seder table. This extra place is for the prophet Elijah, who represents hope and faith.

The youngest child at the Seder table has a special role. He or she is responsible for asking the Four Questions about the holiday. These questions and answers can be found in the Haggadah. (See Julia Jasmine's *Multicultural Holidays: Share Our Celebrations* [Teacher Created Materials, 1994].)

## Poetry

My research turned up very little in the way of Passover poems, but here are a couple of websites to check out:

- Go to http://www.hillel.org/NR/rdonlyres/BD15A450-4766-40F8-B6AC-B04BBA7CABAB/0/passover_guide_b_lerner.pdf. This PDF file, from Foundation for Family Education, is authored by Barry Dov Lerner. Under the "Passover Songs" section, there are piggyback songs (new songs sung to old tunes) that could be used as poetry readings: "Take Us Out of Egypt," "Elijah," and "Our Passover Things."

- Go to http://www.happypassover.net/poems/children-passover-poems.html to find the text for three poems: "The Telling," "How Could the Lord for Our Sake Part the Sea," and "Here We Have a Story for the World."

## Books

Black, Joe. *Afikomen Mambo*. Lerner/Kar-Ben, 2011. ISBN: 978-0761356387.
In this book-and-CD combo, a Latin beat is used to add to the fun of this Passover custom.

dePaola, Tomie. *My First Passover*. Grosset and Dunlap, 2008. ISBN: 978-0448447919.
  The author's straightforward text and simple illustrations provide simple insight into the holiday's background for young readers.

DK Publishing. *My First Passover Board Book*. DK Preschool, 2006. ISBN: 978-0756609818.
  This is an introduction to the holiday of Passover for the youngest child.

Glaser, Linda. *Hoppy Passover!* Albert Whitman and Company, 2011. ISBN: 978-0807533802.
  Bunnies Violet and Simon celebrate Passover with their parents and grandparents.

Howland, Naomi. *The Matzah Man: A Passover Story*. Scholastic, 2004. ISBN: 978-0439636285.
  The Passover Matzah Man escapes from Mr. Cohen's bakery and leads a chase through the town. Includes a glossary of Passover terms in the back of the book.

Jules, Jacqueline. *Going on a Hametz Hunt*. Kar-Ben Publishing, 2010. ISBN: 978-0761351245.
  Little readers will have fun counting and rhyming with a brother and sister on a hametz hunt, looking for breadcrumbs before the start of the Passover holiday.

Linvey, Varda. *What I Like about Passover*. Little Simon, 2002. ISBN: 978-0689844911.
  A little girl lists her favorite elements of the Passover holiday.

Marx, David F. *Passover*. Children's Press, 2001. ISBN: 978-0516271781.
  This book is part of the Rookie Read-About Holidays series and provides a simple introduction to the Passover holiday.

Pearlman, Bobby. *Passover Is Here!* Little Simon, 2005. ISBN: 978-0689865879.
  Lift the flaps to discover why certain foods are eaten and why certain questions are asked in this celebration of freedom for the Hebrew people.

Rauchwerger, Diane L. *Dinosaur on Passover*. Kar-Ben Publishing, 2006. ISBN: 978-1580131568.
  Dinosaur celebrates Passover with a boy and his family, helping perform all of the holiday rituals.

---

### Older Gems, or Titles Too Good to Pass Up

Groner, Judyth. *Where Is the Afikomen?* Kar-Ben Publishing, 1990. ISBN: 978-0929371062.
  This is a great story for introducing children to the traditions of Pesach.

Hildebrandt, Ziporah. *This Is Our Seder*. Holiday House, 1999. ISBN: 978-1422394984.
  In one- to two-line phrases, the author describes the different elements that make up the Passover Seder.

Kahn, Katherine. *My First Seder*. Kar-Ben Publishing, 1986. ISBN: 978-0930494612.
  This book shows a simple progression of events during the Passover meal.

Katz, Bobbi. *The Story of Passover*. Random House Books for Young Readers, 1996. ISBN: 978-0679870388.
  This book presents an easy-to-understand retelling of the story of the Jews' fight for freedom and exodus from Egypt.

Kropf, Latifa B. *It's Seder Time!* Kar-Ben Publishing, 2004. ISBN: 978-1580130929.
  This book follows a preschool class through the preparation of a traditional meal to the reenactment of the story of Passover to the songs that conclude the classroom's festivities.

Nerlove, Miriam. *Passover*. Albert Whitman and Company, 1989. ISBN: 978-0807563601.
  This book, told in rhyming verses, is an introduction to the traditional Jewish holiday.

Ziefert, Harriet. *What Is Passover?* HarperCollins, 1994. ISBN: 978-0694004829.
  Help Jake and his family prepare for a special family Seder in this lift-the-flap book about Passover.

Zolkower, Edie. *Too Many Cooks: A Passover Parable*. Kar-Ben Publishing, 2000. ISBN: 978-1580130639.
  Each time Bubbie gets diverted from making charoses for the Passover Seder, family members add their own secret ingredient until the charoses is atrocious!

Rouss, Sylvia A. *Sammy Spider's First Haggadah*. Kar-Ben Publishing, 2006. ISBN: 978-1580132305.

　　Sammy Spider leads readers through the Passover Seder.

Shulman, Lisa. *The Matzo Ball Boy*. Dutton Juvenile, 2005. ISBN: 978-0525471691.

　　A grandma, preparing a Passover Seder, makes a matzo ball boy who jumps out of the chicken soup and runs off to see the world.

Sollish, Ari. *A Touch of Passover*. Merkos L'Inyonei Chinuch, 2005. ISBN: 978-0826600219.

　　This touch-and-feel book is a mini-guide to the Passover holiday.

Sper, Emily. *The Passover Seder*. Cartwheel Books, 2003. ISBN: 978-0439443128.

　　Along with a simple retelling of the Passover story, this book takes the reader through a hands-on Seder experience.

Stone, Tanya Lee. *P Is for Passover*. Price Stern Sloan, 2003. ISBN: 978-0843102383.

　　Learn about Passover while learning the alphabet as well! The complete story of Passover is found at the back of this book.

Wikler, Madeline. *Let's Ask Four Questions*. Kar-Ben Publishing, 2002. ISBN: 978-1580130714.

　　This board book presents the traditional four questions asked by the youngest child at the Passover Seder.

Zucker, Jonny. *Four Special Questions: A Passover Story*. Barron's Education Series, 2003. ISBN: 978-0764122675.

　　This simple introduction to the Jewish holiday of Passover describes a family as they celebrate their festival of freedom.

## Activities ————————————————————————————————————————————————

---

### Coloring Pages

Consult your favorite pattern books or holiday coloring books for pages to use as coloring sheets. Be sure to search online as well. There's lots of great stuff out there!

- Visit http://dulemba.com/index_ColoringPages.html for author and illustrator Elizabeth O. Dulemba's great collection of holiday coloring pages. While there, sign up for her Coloring Page Tuesdays e-mails.
- A great coloring page can be found on page 174 of *Felt Board Fun for Everyday and Holidays* by Liz and Dick Wilmes (Building Blocks Publications, 1984). It is a plate with the Seder meal foods on it.
- The website OyToys.com sells a kit that has 10 place mats and a 24-page coloring book. They also have a Passover Coloring and Activity Book available that would yield pages for use.

---

### Flannel/Velcro Board

**Pesach Bulletin Board Set**　　This set of seven heavy paper cutouts could be laminated and used as a flannel/Velcro-board presentation of the Seder meal elements. They are available at TheCraftShop Online.com for $14.49.

**"A Rabbi, a Genius"**　　The text of this folktale can be found on pages 168–169 of *The Jewish Kids' Catalog* by Chaya M. Burstein (Jewish Publication Society, 1993). It is about a tailor whose wife thinks their house is too small for Passover, and goes to the rabbi for help. A quick check of pattern books should yield patterns for use with this story!

## Games

**Find the Afikoman**    This game can be done on the flannel/Velcro board. The instructions and patterns can be found on pages 171–173 of *Felt Board Fun for Everyday and Holidays* by Liz and Dick Wilmes (Building Blocks Publications, 1984). Please note that the word afikoman is misspelled as "afrikoman" in this volume. The patterns are of pieces of furniture, and a small afikoman (piece of matzo). You may wish to enlarge the pattern pieces before using them. Hide the afikoman under one of the furniture pieces and let participants guess where it is hidden. Once found, place it under another furniture piece and play again. Continue as long as there is interest. This game is similar to one played at the actual Seder meals, during which the afikoman/matzo is hidden for children to find. Usually they are rewarded with money or candy. Have some candy to pass out to participants afterward!

**Hot Afikoman**    This game is detailed on page 106 of *The Jewish Kids' Catalog* by Chaya M. Burstein (Jewish Publication Society, 1993), and it is played like Hot Potato. Burstein suggests using a piece of real matzo, wrapped securely. You could use some of the plush matzos available from the Jewish product suppliers listed in Appendix A. Instead of singing a song, you also could play music, and stop it at different intervals. Whoever is holding the afikoman is out.

## Miscellaneous

**Plush Matzos**    Check out the three-pack of plush matzos, available from JudaicaforKids.com for just $9.98. Plush Seder plate is sold separately. This would be a great piece of realia to use for your program!

**Passover Play Set**    Also available from JudaicaforKids.com is this play set that includes all elements that would be included on a Seder table. Cost is $39.95.

**Plastic Seder Plate**    This soft plastic Seder plate would be a great tool to introduce Seder foods to your participants! Cost is $3.99. Available from OyToys.com.

**Passover Frog Hand Puppet**    Check out this hand puppet, available from OyToys.com. Cost is $6.95. Also available is a Passover Ten Plagues Finger Puppet set for $17.99.

**Magnetic Seder Plate**    This item is available from OyToys.com and would be great for a magnet-board presentation. Cost is just $7.99.

**Inflatable Matzah Ball**    What fun! Available from OyToys.com, these cost just $7.99 apiece! Imagine the fun you could have bouncing them around on a parachute with your participants!

**Passover Bag of Plagues**    Includes ten toys symbolizing each of the ten plagues as told in the Book of Exodus. Available from OyToys.com for $14.99.

**Soft Seder Set**    This is a great piece of realia for introducing the foods/symbols of the Passover Seder. It is available from OyToys.com for $14.99. Two other Seder sets are available: a plush set for $19.99 and a plush deluxe set for $24.99.

# Fingerplays ——————————————————————————————————————

### I Like Matzah

*(This action rhyme is sung to the tune of "Frere Jacques.")*

| | |
|---|---|
| I like matzah, I like matzah. | *(Point to self with one hand, then the other.)* |
| Yes I do, yes I do. | *(Shake head "yes.")* |
| Yummy, yummy matzah, | *(Rub tummy.)* |
| Yummy, yummy matzah. | |
| For me and you, | *(Point to self, then others.)* |

Me and you.                                 *(Point to self, then others.)*
Afikomen, afikomen,
Where are you, where are you?               *(Put one hand out to the side, questioning, then second hand out, questioning.)*
                                            *(Put hand over eyes, searching.)*
When I find you, when I find you,
The Seder's through, the Seder's through.

—Kathy Buschbaum

### The Matzah Dance

*(Use the illustration of the matzah found at the end of this chapter. Attach to a Popsicle stick or small craft stick. Do the motions as outlined in the rhyme. This is sung to the tune of "The Hokey Pokey.")*

You put your matzah up,
You put your matzah down.
You put your matzah up
And you shake it all around.
You do the matzah dance
And you turn yourself around,
That's the matzah dance!
          *(SHOUT)* Matzah dance!

You put your matzah in front,
You put your matzah in back.
You put your matzah in front,
And you give your head a tap!
You do the matzah dance
And you turn yourself around,
That's the matzah dance!
          *(SHOUT)* Matzah dance!

You put your matzah on your head,
You put your matzah on your toe.
You put your matzah on your head,
And you move it to and fro!
You do the matzah dance
And you turn yourself around,
That's the matzah dance!
          *(SHOUT)* Matzah dance!

You put your matzah on your elbow,
You put your matzah on your nose.
You put your matzah on your elbow,
And you shimmy really low.
You do the matzah dance
And you turn yourself around,
That's the matzah dance!
          *(SHOUT)* Matzah dance!

You put your matzah on your tummy,
You put your matzah on your mouth
You put your matzah on your tummy,
And you eat it up, so yummy!
You do the matzah dance
And you turn yourself around,
That's the matzah dance!
          *(SHOUT)* Matzah dance!

You put your matzah up,
You put your matzah down.
You put your matzah up,
And you shake it all around.
You do the matzah dance
And you turn yourself around,
That's the matzah dance!
          *(SHOUT)* Matzah dance!

—Kathy Buchsbaum

---

### More Great Fingerplays

The fingerplays "The Hungry Passover Mouse," "My Charoset," "Chametz Hunt," "Messy Matzah," "Make a Matzah," and "Five Little Frogs" can be found in *Clap and Count! Action Rhymes for the Jewish Year* by Jacqueline Jules (Kar-Ben Copies, 2001).

---

## Musical Selections

*Mostly Matzah: Passover Songs* CD by Fran Avni. Sisu Home Entertainment. ASIN: B0014DFCN2. Also available for download from http://www.songsforteaching.com/.

*Music from the Mountain: A Jewish Holiday Jam* CD by The Soul Time Singers. Available for download from http://www.songsforteaching.com/.

"Nig Nishtanah/The 4 Questions" from *Shalom Yeladim/Hello Children* by Judy Caplan Ginsburgh. Orchard. ASIN: B00000G31R.

*Passover Sing-a-Long* CD by Paul Zim. Available from http://www.oytoys.com/.

*Seder Nights* CD by Paul Zim. Available from http://www.oytoys.com/.

"Seder Table" and "I Am the Afikoman" from *Shanah Tovah: A Good Year—Songs for Jewish Holidays* by Debbie Friedman. Available as a download from http://www.amazon.com/.

*Shirlala Pesach* CD by Shira Kline. Available from http://www.oytoys.com/.

*So Big* CD by Hap Palmer. Hap-Pal Music. ASIN: B0000690AD. (Use the "Teddy Bear Playtime" song [music only] for Passover by substituting the word "matzah" for "teddy bear." This song also could be used for Hanukkah, by substituting the word "latke" for "teddy bear." Have a "matzah" made from either heavy paper or fabric that the participants can throw into the air and catch. Or use beanbags!)

## Crafts

**Seder Plate**    This craft, which makes a Seder plate with the foods pictured, can be found on page 185 of *Multicultural Holidays: Share Our Celebrations* by Julia Jasmine (Teacher Created Materials, 1994). I would adapt this craft for young participants by slightly enlarging the picture so that it would fit nicely onto a paper plate. I would also refer to the text on page 184 that tells what the foods on the plate symbolize and have a one-word description typed out in a Word document in larger print so that they could be photocopied, cut apart, and pasted underneath the pictures. The instructions say to attach the Seder plate pictures to another piece of paper, but I really think that a paper plate is a nice base for it.

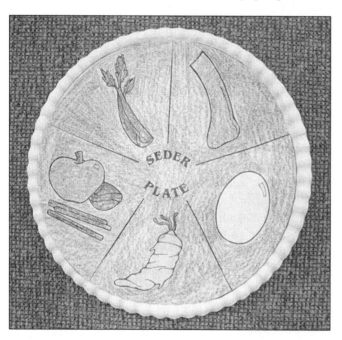

**Craft Kits**    The website JewishCrafts.com offers a variety of simple crafts for Passover. Please note that kits are sold in dozen quantities only. Check out the following:

- "Search for the Chometz" kit—$.99 each.
- "Big n' Tall Elijah's Cup" kit—$1.99 each.
- Foam Passover Characters (fit around drinking cups)—$1.29 each.
- Giant Frog Karpas Cup—$1.39 each.
- Pharaoh's Frog Saltwater Dish—$1.49 each.
- You-Weave-It Matzoh Covers—$2.49 each.
- Variety of Afikoman Bags—Prices range from $.59 each to $2.29 each.
- Variety of Seder Plates—Prices range from $1.89 to 2.89 each. There is also a section called "Spectacular Seder Plates" with big foam pieces for little hands! These cost $2.99 each.

**Kiddush Cup Wooden Cut-Out**    This cutout would be a great base for adding either craft foam shapes or jewels, and is reasonably priced at $.60 apiece! Available from OyToys.com.

**No Chometz Door Hanger**    These kits are priced at just $1.49 each and have everything needed to assemble a neat little craft! Available at TheCraftShopOnline.com.

**Frog Crafts**    Since one of the ten plagues mentioned in the Passover story is that of frogs, why not pull out some of your best frog crafts?

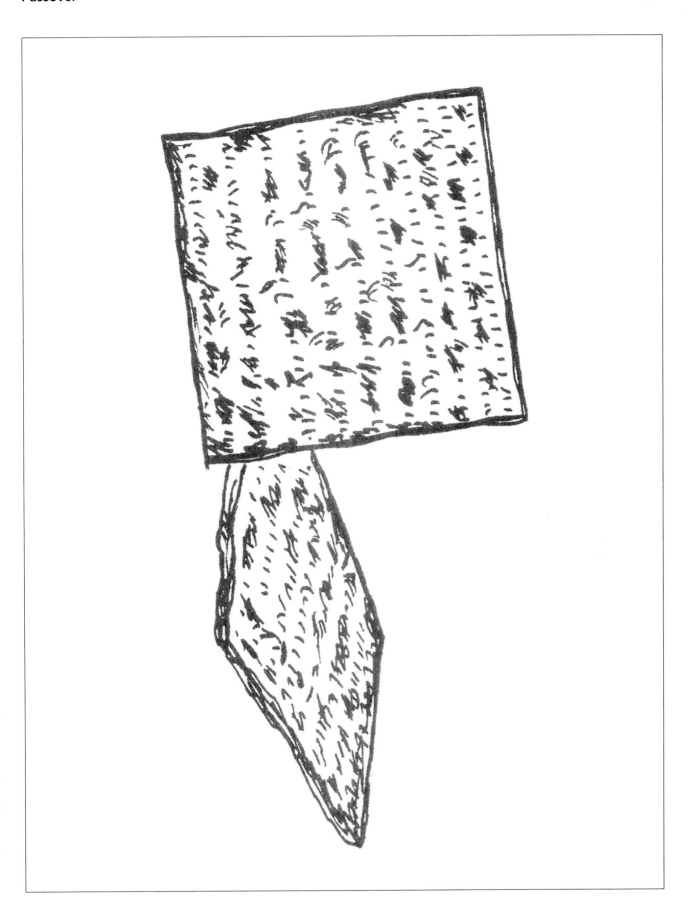

# Presidents' Day

*This programming pays tribute to George Washington and Abraham Lincoln.*

## History

Presidents' Day takes place during the month of February and honors two of our country's greatest presidents, George Washington and Abraham Lincoln. The holiday falls between the actual birthdays of the two men, Lincoln's on February 12th and Washington's on February 22nd.

Abraham Lincoln was born February 12, 1809, and was the sixteenth President of the United States. He is known for freeing the slaves and keeping the United States together as a nation during the Civil War. He is also well-known for the Gettysburg Address and signing the Emancipation Proclamation, which freed the slaves. Lincoln was born in a log cabin in Kentucky. Although he was poor, he was a hard worker and read every book he could find. He would walk miles to borrow books and read them by the light of a candle after his long work day was done. When he was grown, Lincoln became a lawyer and had a law practice in Illinois. He decided to go into politics as well, and was elected President in 1860. While Lincoln worked hard to keep the United States one country during the war, there were those who opposed what he was trying to do. He was assassinated on April 14, 1865.

George Washington was born February 22, 1732, and was our country's first president, helping it through its formative years. Washington was born in Virginia and grew up on the family's plantation at Mount Vernon. His early life was spent farming and working as a surveyor. He fought in the French and Indian War and, after the war was over, was elected to the Continental Congress. Washington was also a great war hero during the Revolutionary War, leading the army of the colonies to victory over the British. After the War, Washington wanted nothing more than to return to Mount Vernon, but he was elected President of the United States in 1781 and served two terms in office. After serving as President, Washington returned to his home at Mt. Vernon, where he died in 1799. Washington is the only U.S. president whose birthday was publically celebrated while he was alive. (See Julia Jasmine's *Multicultural Holidays: Share Our Celebrations* [Teacher Created Materials, 1994].)

## Poetry

"George Washington" and "Lincoln," from pages 56 and 57 of *Month-by-Month Poetry: December, January, and February* by Marian Reiner (Scholastic Professional Books, 1999).

"George Washington's Birthday: Wondering," from page 19 of *Ring Out, Wild Bells: Poems about Holidays and Seasons*, selected by Lee Bennett Hopkins (Harcourt Brace Jovanovich, 1992).

"Like Washington" by Helen M. Richardson, from http://www.apples4theteacher.com/holidays/presidents-day/poems-rhymes/like-washington.html.

"Lincoln" and "Washington," from pages 40–41 of *Projects, Patterns, and Poems for Early Education* by Marion Ruppert (Humanics Learning, 1989).

## Books

deGroat, Diane. *Liar, Liar, Pants on Fire*. Topeka Bindery, 2003. ISBN: 978-0613879262.
    When Gilbert takes on the part of George Washington in a play about the cherry tree, he is determined to do a good job.

Hopkinson, Deborah. *Abe Lincoln Crosses a Creek: A Tall, Thin Tale*. Schwartz and Wade, 2008. ISBN: 978-037583768X.

> In 1816, seven-year-old Abe and his friend Austin Gollaher go down to see Knob Creek, swollen and turbulent after heavy rains, and decide to use a log to cross it.

Jackson, Ellen. *Abe Lincoln Loved Animals*. Albert Whitman and Company, 2008. ISBN: 978-0807501238.

> Using clearly defined sources to provide an accurate account, Jackson offers a warm portrait of Lincoln's love of animals.

Marx, David F. *Presidents' Day*. Children's Press, 2002. ISBN: 978-0516273760.

> Part of the popular Rookie Read-About Holidays series, this volume focuses on Presidents' Day.

McNamara, Margaret. *Presidents' Day*. Simon Spotlight, 2010. ISBN: 978-1416991700.

> It's the week of Presidents' Day and the kids in Mrs. Conner's class learn fun facts about presidents past and present in honor of the holiday. They also learn that someday they can lead the country too.

Peppas, Lynn. *Presidents' Day*. Crabtree Publishing Company, 2008. ISBN: 978-0778747567.

> What began as a day to celebrate the birthday of George Washington, the first President of the United States of America, has grown to include every other president to serve as leader of the country. Learn all about Presidents' Day, from its earliest beginnings to how Americans celebrate this occasion today.

Pingry, Patricia. *The Story of Abraham Lincoln*. Candy Cane Press, 2001. ISBN: 978-0824941079.

> Through simple words and illustrations, a young child can meet Abraham Lincoln, the sixteenth president of the United States.

Rissman, Rebecca. *Presidents' Day*. Heinemann Library, 2010. ISBN: 978-1432940751.

> This book introduces readers to what it means to celebrate Presidents' Day and shows them why this holiday is special.

Rockwell, Anne. *Presidents' Day*. HarperCollins, 2008. ISBN: 978-0060501945.

> Mrs. Madoff's class learns about Presidents' Day and puts on a play about the men who inspired that holiday.

---

### Older Gems, or Titles Too Good to Pass Up

Fisher, Aileen. *My First President's Day Book*. Children's Press, 1987. ISBN: 978-0516429106.

> Recounts in verse some of the highlights from the lives of George Washington and Abraham Lincoln.

Jordan, Kimberly. *Celebrating President's Day: What Is a President?* Turtleback, 1999. ISBN: 978-0613341240.

> Explains the meaning behind Presidents' Day and describes the role of a president.

Muntean, Micheala. *I Want to Be President*. Random House Books for Young Readers, 2000. ISBN: 978-0375805509.

> As Betty Lou of Sesame Street imagines herself giving speeches, signing laws, and meeting with world leaders, kids are treated to a fascinating glimpse of this important job.

Pingry, Patricia. *The Story of George Washington*. Candy Cane Press, 2000. ISBN: 978-0824941888.

> This little board book briefly and simply tells the story of George Washington, the first President of the United States.

Small, David. *George Washington's Cows*. Farrar, Straus, and Giroux, 1997. ISBN: 978-0374425340.

> In this tall tale, Washington is forced to cope with very fussy cows, dandified pigs, and smart sheep. He decides he is not cut out for country life and goes into politics.

Winters, Kay. *Abe Lincoln: The Boy Who Loved Books*. Aladdin, 2006. ISBN: 978-1416912682.
The author recounts events from Lincoln's childhood in Kentucky and Indiana and his young adulthood in New Salem, Illinois.

## Activities ——————————————————————————————————

| **Coloring Pages** |
| --- |
| Consult your favorite pattern books or holiday coloring books for pages to use as coloring sheets. Be sure to search online as well. There's lots of great stuff out there! |

### Flannel/Velcro Board

**Mr. Washington's Sad Song**     This song, sung to the tune of "Yankee Doodle," could easily be adapted into a flannel/Velcro-board presentation. You may wish to sing the story or simply read it through. The text can be found on pages 457–458 of *Marmalade Days Winter: Complete Units for Busy Teachers of Young Children* by Carol Taylor Bond (Partner Press, 1987). Patterns can be found on page 489. The song is about George Washington cutting down the cherry tree.

### Games

**Presidents' Day Matching Game**     Patterns for a variety of Presidents' Day symbols (Lincoln silhouette, log cabin, stovepipe hat, cherries, three-corner hat, Washington silhouette) appear on pages 77–82 and 91–96 of *Holiday Patterns*, compiled by Jean Warren (Warren Publishing House, 1991). The best patterns to use are the ones that are already enclosed in a square, as this would make cutting them out simple. Copy two of each on different colors of construction paper. Give each participant one of the patterns/colors. Keep one for yourself and place in an apron pocket or container of some sort. Begin the matching game by pulling out your copies, one at a time, placing them on the board, and allowing participants to match them. If you don't have access to Warren's book, use Ellison dies of Lincoln and Washington (silhouettes), found in the Social Studies section of their catalog.

**Pass Lincoln's Hat Game**     Directions for this game can be found on page 135 of *Games for All Seasons* by Alexandra Cleveland and Barbara Caton (Building Blocks Publications, 1999).

**Pitching Pennies into Lincoln's Hat**     This game is detailed on pages 44–45 of *Kids Celebrate! Activities for Special Days Throughout the Year* by Maria Bonfanti Esche and Clare Bonfanti Braham (Chicago Review Press, 1998). The hat is made from a 2- or 3-liter plastic pop bottle. The top is cut off. The bottle is then wrapped in black construction paper large enough to cover the bottle's height. A circle of black poster board is then cut and the covered bottle is place in the middle. The circle becomes the hat's brim. The authors recommend hot-gluing the bottle to the poster board. When you are finished, you have a stovepipe hat. Participants are then given five pennies each to try to toss into the hat!

**The Cherry Tree Game**     This game comes from page 203 of *Celebrate the Seasons: The Best of Holidays and Seasonal Celebrations—Issues 9–12, PreK–3*, edited by Donna Borst (Teaching and Learning Company, 1998). Have all participants sit in a circle, with one chosen one standing in the middle. He or she is the "cherry tree." The "cherry tree" closes his or her eyes or is blindfolded. The leader chooses a participant, and this person comes up and touches the "cherry tree." I have modified the game a bit at this point. All participants should shout, "Chop, chop!" when the "tree" is touched. This person then sits back down quickly and quietly. All participants then ask, "Who chopped down the cherry tree?" The "cherry tree" can now open his or her eyes and try to guess who it was who touched him or her. When the correct person is guessed, that person becomes the "cherry tree."

## Miscellaneous

**Coin Rubbings**    Provide a table with paper, crayons, and pennies and quarters. Let participants know that Lincoln's face is on the penny and Washington's is on the quarter. Let them place the coins under the paper and do rubbings with the crayons.

**Dot-to-Dot Lincoln's Hat**    Use this activity as an opener! The pattern for this dot-to-dot can be found on page 394 of *Marmalade Days Winter: Complete Units for Busy Teachers of Young Children* by Carol Taylor Bond (Partner Press, 1987). Duplicate the page and laminate for durability. Encourage your participants to count with you from 1 to 29, which completes the picture—Lincoln's tall hat! Laminating the picture allows you to use dry-erase marker for this activity, and to reuse it.

**Abraham Lincoln Sticker/George Washington Paper Dolls**    Available on Amazon.com, Dover Publications offers this set of 1 paper doll and 23 reusable stickers. This might make a great item for an opening introduction to the life of Lincoln, as the stickers range from a woodcutter's outfit to a tuxedo and stovepipe hat. You could also reproduce the paper doll on a color copier for as many outfits as are needed, and then laminate them for durability. Also available is a set of Abraham Lincoln and His Family paper dolls. This set has 5 dolls and 32 authentic costumes. Again, this set would be great to cut out, dress, and then laminate for durability. In addition, there is a set of George Washington and His Family, which consists of 6 dolls and 32 costumes.

**Presidents' Day Songs**    The following piggyback songs (new songs sung to familiar tunes) can be found on pages 53–56 of *Holiday Piggyback Songs*, compiled by Jean Warren (Warren Publishing House, 1988): "Lincoln," "Lincoln Was Our President," "Thank You, Mr. Lincoln," and "Our First President."

## Fingerplays

### My Hat It Has Three Corners

*(Explain to children that the three-corned, or tricorn hat, was worn in George Washington's time.)*

| | |
|---|---|
| My hat | *(Touch head on the word "hat.")* |
| It has three corners. | *(Touch each elbow on the word "corners.")* |
| Three corners | *(Touch each elbow on the word "corners.")* |
| Has my hat. | *(Touch head on the word "hat.")* |
| And if it hadn't three corners | *(Touch each elbow on the word "corners.")* |
| It wouldn't be my hat. | *(Touch head on the word "hat.")* |

—Traditional rhyme

### George Washington's Birthday

| | |
|---|---|
| Another holiday has come! | |
| Let's wave the flag, | *(Bend arm bent at elbow; wave hand back and forth.)* |
| And beat the drum! | *(Pat thighs as if playing drums.)* |
| From ev'ry steeple | *(Put index fingers together; form steeple.)* |
| Ring the bell! | |
| Come blow the horn! | *(Put hand to mouth; pretend to blow horn.)* |
| Now quickly tell, | |
| What holiday is just begun! | *(Put index finger to cheek; tilt head wondering.)* |
| The birthday of George Washington! | *(Hold index finger in the air.)* |

—Maude Burnham
*Rhymes for Little Hands* (Milton Bradley Company, 1910, pp. 81–82)

---

**More Great Fingerplays**

"Abe Lincoln," "Honest Abe," "Abraham Lincoln," "A Great Man," "Little George," "Little George Washington," "George and the Cherry Tree," and "George Washington," from pages 283–284 of *1001 Rhymes and Fingerplays for Working with Young Children*, compiled by the Totline Staff (Warren Publishing House, 1994).

"Abraham Lincoln," from page 64 of *Little Hands Fingerplays and Action Songs: Seasonal Rhymes and Creative Play for 2-to-6-Year-Olds* by Emily Stetson and Vicky Congdon (Williamson Publishing Company, 2001).

"George Washington," from page 7 of *Let's Learn . . . : Holiday Finger Plays, Worksheets, and Art Projects* by Katherine Oana, Patti Carson, and Janet Dellosa (Carson-Dellosa Publishing, 1983).

---

## Musical Selections

"Abraham Lincoln" and "Presidents' Day" from *Happy Everything* by Dr. Jean. Melody House. ASIN: B000SM3N0E.

"George Washington" from *It's Your Day* by Andy Glockenspiel. Available from http://www.songsfor teaching.com/.

"Hooray for Mr. Lincoln" from *Touched by a Song* by Miss Jackie Silberg. Miss Jackie Music. ASIN: B002K74FCK.

## Crafts

**Cherry Tree Fingerprint Fun**    The pattern to use for this craft is found on page 188 of *The Best of Holidays and Seasonal Celebrations—Issues 5–8, PreK–K*, edited by Donna Borst (Teaching and Learning Company, 2000). Reproduce the cherry tree pattern and cut it out. Use red tempera paint or water-based red stamp pad to make fingerprint "cherries" on the tree.

**Abe and George Wreath**    The base of this craft is a large paper plate with the middle cut out. Cut out star shapes using an Ellison star die. The puffy star die would work exceptionally well for this. Use red, white, and blue construction paper for these stars. Glue them around the plate. Ellison also offers dies that are silhouettes of Washington and Lincoln. If you have these or can borrow them, cut out the silhouette shapes on black paper. Place the silhouette shapes on opposite sides of the plate, gluing them on top of the stars. If you don't have access to these dies, many holiday craft books may have silhouettes that you could cut out ahead of time.

**Abraham Lincoln Figure**    This simple craft allows participants to color and cut out a figure of Abraham Lincoln and then glue him together at the tabs provided.

Patterns appear on pages 27–29 of *Big and Easy Art for Patriotic Holidays* by Dianna Sullivan (Teacher Created Materials, 1986).

**George Washington Figure**  This craft is just like the Abraham Lincoln Figure, but with a figure of Washington. It appears on pages 30–32 of *Big and Easy Art for Patriotic Holidays* by Dianna Sullivan (Teacher Created Materials, 1986).

**Lincoln Penny Pendant**  Red, white, and blue star shapes in graduated sizes are glued together. A penny is then glued to the center and yarn is added for a necklace. The template and instruc-

tions for this craft are available from EnchantedLearning.com at http://www .enchantedlearning.com/crafts/penny pendant/.

**Lincoln's Log Cabin**  This simple craft is comprised of craft sticks to make the cabin wall. Simple shapes are added for roof, door, and window. A penny, with Lincoln's face looking out, should be glued to the window. Instructions for this simple craft are available from Enchanted Learning.com at http://www.enchantedlearning.com/ crafts/lincolnlogcabin/.

**Long Abe Lincoln**  Instructions for this craft can be found on page 12 of *Hand-Shaped Art* by Diane Bonica (Good Apple, 1989). When traced, the participant's hand and arm become Lincoln's hat, face, and beard.

**Truthful Tree**  The participant's hand, dipped in green paint and pressed onto white paper, becomes the top of the tree. Add a trunk and use red paint with a fingertip to add cherries. Instructions for this craft can be found on page 14 of *Hand-Shaped Art* by Diane Bonica (Good Apple, 1989).

**George Washington's General Hat**  This craft makes a general's hat just like one that George Washington would have worn. The base is a 12-by-18-inch piece of black construction paper. Ribbon and a medallion shape (pattern included) are added to the hat. Instructions and patterns can be found on pages 31–32 of *Hats, Hats, and More Hats* by Jean Stangl (Fearon Teacher Aids, 1989).

**Abraham Lincoln Hat**  This craft makes a stovepipe hat from an oatmeal box (with lid) and a paper plate. The entire hat is painted black, so you will need to allow time for this craft to dry. Instructions can be found on page 33 of *Hats, Hats, and More Hats* by Jean Stangl (Fearon Teacher Aids, 1989).

**George Washington's Cherry Tree**  This craft appears on pages 38–39 of *Happy Hands and Feet: Projects for Young Children* by Cindy Mitchell (Incentive Publications, 1989). The hand becomes the trunk of the tree and fingerprints are the cherries.

**Mr. Lincoln**  This craft is found on pages 32 (instructions) and 35 (patterns) of *From the Hands of a Child: Special Seasonal Art Activities for Primary Children* by Anthony Flores (Fearon Teacher Aids, 1987). The participant's handprint makes Mr. Lincoln's beard.

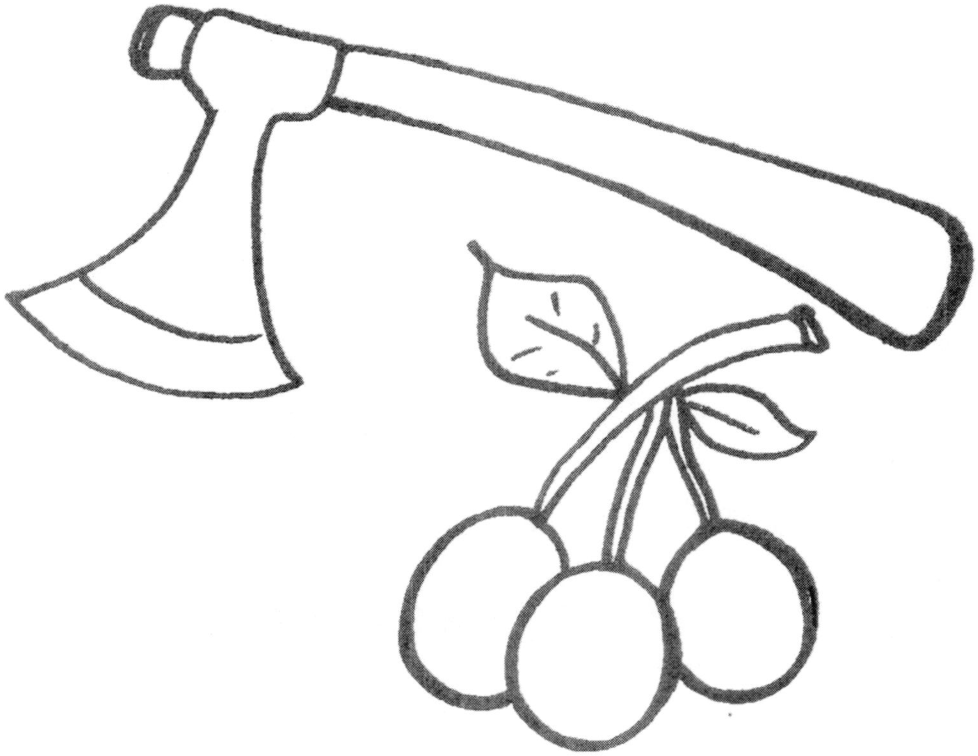

# Purim

*Purim is another important Jewish observance, falling one month before the celebration of Passover. It celebrates the courage of Esther, who saved the Jewish people in Persia from being killed. In the Bible, it is told in the Book of Esther.*

## History

Esther, a beautiful Jewish woman, lived with her cousin Mordecai. She caught the eye of Ahasuerus, who was the King of Persia. The king loved Esther and made her his queen, not knowing that she was Jewish. Her cousin had told her not to reveal her identity to the king.

Mordecai had a mortal enemy in Haman, who was one of the king's advisors. He hated Mordecai because he would not treat him as a superior. Because of this hate, Haman developed a plot to kill all of the Jewish people because they would not observe the king's laws. He convinced the king that this was the right thing to do, and the king allowed Haman to proceed with his plan. Haman also planned to hang Mordecai.

Upon finding out about Haman's plan, Mordecai urged Esther to speak to the king on behalf of the Jews, her people. Esther took a big risk, as she went into the king's presence without being summoned by him. After fasting for three days, Esther visited the king and was welcomed by him. She told him of Haman's plot and the king agreed to save the Jewish people. Haman got his just desserts, as he and his sons were hanged on gallows that he had prepared for his enemy, Mordecai. The word "Purim" means "lots" and it refers to the lottery that Haman used to select the date for the Jews to be killed. (See Tracey R. Rich's "Purim" at http://www.jewfaq.org/holiday9.htm.)

## Poetry

"Purim Song" and "Purim Day," songs that can easily be adapted into simple poems, from http://www.perpetualpreschool.com/holiday_themes/jewish/purimsongs.htm.

"Queen Esther," from http://www.chabad.org/kids/article_cdo/aid/1368/jewish/Queen-Esther.htm.

## Books

Adelson, Leone. *The Mystery Bear: A Purim Story*. Clarion Books, 2004. ISBN: 978-0618337255.
    When Little Bear wakes up from hibernation, he is hungry. His nose takes him to a family who is celebrating Purim with a parade outside of their home. He is invited to join them, as they think he is someone in costume.

Bredeson, Carmen. *Purim*. Children's Press, 2003. ISBN: 978-0516279282.
    Part of the Rookie Read-About Holidays series, this is a simple introduction to the Purim holiday.

Goldin, Barbara D. *Cakes and Miracles: A Purim Tale*. Marshall Cavendish Children's Books, 2010. ISBN: 978-0761457015.
    An angel inspires blind Hershel to make the loveliest Purim cakes in the village.

---

**Older Gems, or Titles Too Good to Pass Up**

Geller, Beverly. *The Mitzvah Girl*. Gefen Publishing House, 2000. ISBN: 978-9652292032.
This title captures the excitement of the Purim holiday as the reader shares in the Megilla reading, preparation of the shalach manot, and Shira's love of her special Queen Esther costume and crown.

Gelman, Rita G. *Queen Esther Saves Her People*. Scholastic, 1998. ISBN: 978-0590470254.
The author retells the stirring story of a young woman who risks her own life to save her people.

Rouss, Sylvia A. *Sammy Spider's First Purim*. Kar-Ben Publishing, 2000. ISBN: 978-1580130622.
The Shapiro family is getting reading for Purim. Sammy wants to participate, but Mrs. Shapiro reminds him that "spiders don't celebrate holidays; spiders spin webs."

Silverman, Maida. *Festival of Esther: The Story of Purim*. Simon and Schuster, 1989. ISBN: 978-0671676636.
A simple, clear telling of the story of Esther and the history and meaning of Purim. Includes a holiday song and recipe!

Topek, Susan R. *A Costume for Noah: A Purim Story*. Kar-Ben Publishing, 1995. ISBN: 978-0929371900.
Noah's classmates are busy making costumes for the Purim parade, but Noah is preoccupied with the imminent arrival of a new baby.

---

Kimmel, Eric A. *The Story of Esther: A Purim Tale*. Holiday House, 2011. ISBN: 978-0823422234.
This book tells the story of Esther and her bravery in saving the Jewish people from being killed.

Kropf, Latifa B. *It's Purim Time!* Kar-Ben Publishing, 2004. ISBN: 978-1580131537.
Large, color photographs show students in a Jewish preschool participating in a variety of activities as they prepare for the Purim holiday.

Zolkower, Edie S. *When It's Purim*. Kar-Ben Publishing, 2009. ISBN: 978-0822589471.
Poetic text describes for the youngest reader how a family of woodland creatures show the ways Purim is celebrated.

Zucker, Jonny. *It's Party Time! A Purim Story*. Frances Lincoln Children's Books, 2004. ISBN: 978-0711220195.
This book is a simple introduction to the Jewish festival of Purim.

## Activities ————————————————————————————————

---

**Coloring Pages**

Consult your favorite pattern books or holiday coloring books for pages to use as coloring sheets. Be sure to search online as well. There's lots of great stuff out there!

- Check out the coloring pages available at http://www.aish.com/h/pur/f/52872417 .html. Download the Coloring Book Easy Print Version, which provides you full-page PDFs of the individual sheets (13 pages)!
- Find Purim coloring pages at http://www.torahtots.com/holidays/purim/purcolr.htm.

---

### Flannel/Velcro Board

**Purim Characters**   TheCraftShopOnline.com offers a set of Purim characters that could be laminated for durability and used in an explanation of the story of the holiday. Cost is $9.99.

## Games

**Knock Down Haman's Sons**    This idea was suggested on the Perpetual Preschool website (http://www.perpetualpreschool.com/holiday_themes/jewish/purim_games.htm). Haman had ten sons—so make faces on ten bowling pins and have fun knocking them down!

**Pin the Crown on Esther**    This idea was also suggested on the Perpetual Preschool website (http://www.perpetualpreschool.com/holiday_themes/jewish/purim_games.htm). Find or draw a suitable picture of Esther's head (or use a princess or queen). Have crowns that participants can try to place in the correct area while blindfolded! They also suggest a variation using a picture of Haman and pinning a hamentashen to his head.

**Esther, Esther, Mordecai**    This game is played just like Duck, Duck, Goose. It is detailed on page 105 of *The Jewish Kids' Catalog* by Chaya M Burstein (Jewish Publication Society, 1993).

## Miscellaneous

**Just Where Is Israel, Anyway?**    Have a map of the area, and locate the country of Israel on it. Check out *It's a Big Big World Atlas*, edited by Angela Rahaniotis and Jane Brierly (Tormont Publications, 1984). The first pages of this large-format board book show a map of the world, so that participants can see where other continents/countries are in relation to the United States. Pages 9–10 show where the country of Israel is located, along with surrounding countries.

**Face Painting**    If you don't want to go all out with costumes, why not do face painting? If you are talented in this area, or have parent volunteers that can help out, utilize them. If you are like me and are not artistically talented, here's a simple idea: use stamp pads and stamps with simple designs (flowers, animals, etc.). Stamp the design onto the participant's hand, arm, or even face, and then color in the design with washable markers! An Internet search may even uncover sources for Jewish-themed stamps to use!

**Purim Finger Puppets**    Check out this great set of finger puppets, available from OyToys.com for $11.99! This would be a wonderful way to teach the story of Purim to young participants!

**Purim Grogger/Drum Noisemakers**    These are plastic clappers, and are available at OyToys.com for $1.79 each. You might use these noisemakers during the telling of the Purim story or the reading of one of the books. It is tradition to sound the noisemakers when the name of the evil Haman is mentioned (because no one wants to hear his name).

**Royal Purim Masks**    OyToys.com offers a pack of three masks (king, queen, and a crown) for $3.95.

**Dress-Up Masks**    Also from OyToys.com, this set of three colorful foam masks will add to young participants' learning of the holiday. Set costs $4.00.

**Purim Parade**    With the masks or crowns that your participants have made from the Crafts section, why not use one (or more) songs (from the Musical Selections section) and have a parade through your library? If you have the capability of broadcasting the music via a public address or phone system, all the better! Add some party horns or groggers as part of your parade to make it more festive (and loud)!

**Let's Learn Some Hebrew**    Teach your participants simple phrases in Hebrew, such as "hello," "please," and "thank you." Pages 83–85 of *The Jewish Kids' Catalog* by Chaya M. Burstein (Jewish Publication Society, 1993) has some simple phrases and pronunciations, as well as a mini-dictionary of some common words. The text also gives some pronunciation tips. You might also share with participants that the Hebrew language is written from right to left, not left to right as English is!

## Fingerplays

### It Is Purim

*(This action rhyme is sung to the tune of "Frere Jacques.")*

| | |
|---|---|
| It is Purim, it is Purim. | |
| Yes it is, yes it is! | *(Shake head "yes.")* |
| Shake the grogger, shake the grogger! | *(Pretend to shake the grogger.)* |
| Celebrate, celebrate! | |
| | |
| Hamentaschen, Hamentaschen | |
| Has three sides, has three sides | *(Make a triangle shape with hands.)* |
| Yummy in my tummy, yummy in my tummy! | *(Rub tummy.)* |
| Celebrate, celebrate! | |
| | |
| It is Purim, it is Purim. | |
| Yes it is, yes it is. | *(Shake head "yes.")* |
| Shake the grogger, | *(Pretend to shake grogger.)* |
| Eat Hamentaschen | *(Rub tummy.)* |
| Celebrate, celebrate! | |

—Kathy Buchsbaum

### Purim

*(This action song is sung to the tune of "Mary Had a Little Lamb.")*

| | |
|---|---|
| King of Persia loved Esther, | *(Hold hands over heart.)* |
| Loved Esther, loved Esther. | |
| King of Persia loved Esther, | |
| And so he made her Queen. | *(Put hands over top of head; make circle to represent a crown.)* |
| | |
| Haman was a bad, bad man | *(Shake finger admonishingly.)* |
| Bad bad man, bad bad man, | |
| Haman was a bad, bad man | |
| And said to kill the Jews. | *(Bring right hand down on left palm in a "chopping" motion.)* |
| | |
| Queen Esther was so brave, | *(Stand or sit up straight, hands on hips.)* |
| Was so brave, was so brave. | |
| Queen Esther was so brave. | |
| She asked to save the Jews. | *(Clasp hands in front, pleading.)* |
| | |
| Now it's time to celebrate, | *(Raise one hand in the air; pump fist.)* |
| Celebrate, celebrate! | *(Raise the other hand in the air; pump fist.)* |
| And now it's time to celebrate. | |
| It's Purim once again! | |
| Hey! | *(Clap hands on last line.)* |

—Kathy Buchsbaum

### Hamentaschen Dance

*(This action song is sung to the tune of "The Hokey Pokey." Make a hamentaschen for each participant to dance with by using the artwork found at the end of this chapter and taping it to a Popsicle or small craft stick. Hamentaschen is a mouthful to say, but it is still fun! Do the motions as described in the song.)*

You put your hamentaschen up,
You put your hamentaschen down,
You put your hamentaschen up
And you shake it all around.
You do the Purim dance,
And you turn yourself around.
That's the Purim Dance!

    *(SHOUT)* Purim dance!

You put your hamentaschen in front,
You put your hamentaschen in back,
You put your hamentaschen in front,
And you give your head a tap!
You do the Purim dance,
And you turn yourself around.
That's the Purim Dance!

    *(SHOUT)* Purim dance!

You put your hamentaschen on your head,
You put your hamentaschen on your toe,
You put your hamentaschen on your head,
And you move it to and fro!
You do the Purim dance,
And you turn yourself around.
That's the Purim Dance!

    *(SHOUT)* Purim dance!

You put your hamentaschen on your elbow,
You put your hamentaschen on your nose,
You put your hamentaschen on your elbow
And you shimmy really low!
You do the Purim dance,
And you turn yourself around.
That's the Purim Dance!

    *(SHOUT)* Purim dance!

You put your hamentaschen on your tummy,
You put your hamentaschen on your mouth,
You put your hamentaschen on your tummy,
And you eat it up, so yummy!
You do the Purim dance,
And you turn yourself around.
That's the Purim Dance!

    *(SHOUT)* Purim dance!

You put your hamentaschen up,
You put your hamentaschen down,
You put your hamentaschen up,
And you shake it all around.
You do the Purim dance,
And you turn yourself around.
That's the Purim Dance!

    *(SHOUT)* Purim dance!

—Kathy Buchsbaum

---

### More Great Fingerplays

The fingerplays "Baking A Hamantasch," "Shalach Manot," "What Shape Is a Hamantasch?," and "Five Little Groggers" can be found on pages 35–38 of *Clap and Count! Action Rhymes for the Jewish Year* by Jacqueline Jules (Kar-Ben Copies, 2001).

---

## Musical Selections

"Ani Purim" and "Chag Purim" from *Shalom Yeladim/Hello Children* by Judy Caplan Ginsburgh. Orchard. ASIN: B00000G31R.

*Latkes and Hamentashen—Purim Time!* CD by Fran Avni and Jackie Cytrynbaum. Available from http://www.songsforteaching.com/.

"Mischak Purim" and "Purim Time Is Here" from *Shanah Tovah, Shanah M'tukah* by Joanie Calem. CD Baby. ASIN: B0034PWOXY.

*Music from the Mountain: A Jewish Holiday Jam* CD by The Soul Time Singers. Available from http://www.songsforteaching.com/.

"Purim Game" from *Shanah Tovah: A Good Year—Songs for Jewish Holidays* by Debbie Friedman. Available from http://www.amazon.com/.

"Purim Parade" from *Sing Shalom! Songs for the Jewish Holidays* by Peter and Ellen Allard. Craig 'n Co. ASIN: B000056JQ4.

*Purim Sing-a-Long* CD by Paul Zim. Available at http://www.oytoys.com/.

## Crafts

**Purim Masks**    Dressing up in masks and costumes is one of the most entertaining parts of the Purim holiday. Check out the masks available at http://www.holidays.net/purim/costumes.html. There is a mask for King Ahashverosh, Queen Esther, and the evil Haman. You may wish to enlarge these patterns slightly before duplicating. Attaching a craft stick or paint stick would add the finishing touch! Oriental Trading Company also offers a great scratch art mask. The kits of 24 masks come complete with scratching tools and elastic strings to hold the mask on! Cost is $5.99!

**Let's Make a Crown!**    Since this holiday concerns a king and his queen, crowns are the perfect craft. *Paper Hat Tricks I* by Patt Newbold and Anne Diebel (Paper Hat Tricks, 1994) has patterns you can use (see King/Queen/Prince/Princess in the table of contents). You can also check online for companies that sell crown kits, complete with decorating supplies.

**Purim Craft Kits**    Check out the kits listed below from the website JewishCrafts.com. Kits are sold in lots of dozens only. Here are just some of the kits available:

- Purim Character Gragers (Noisemakers) printed on peel-and-stick foam so that they adhere right to the plastic clappers provided. Cost is $1.79 each.
- All-in-One Purim Crown/Foam crowns with peel-and-stick foam characters. Cost is $1.29 each.
- Happy Purim Fish Craft for is $.59 each.
- Perfect Petite Purim Crowns kits are $.49 each.
- Who Am I Purim Masks/assorted mask styles cost $.99 each.

- Purim Door Plaque made from precut foam. Kits cost $1.29 each.
- Make N' Shake Gragers kits with one side featuring King Ashashverosh and the other side featuring Queen Esther cost $.99 each.

**More Purim Crafts**   TheCraftShopOnline.com offers a variety of Purim-themed crafts:
- Folding Fun Masks—Pack of 40 for $7.99
- Masks, including 4 styles, cord, feathers, glitter, glue, and sequins—Pack of 24 for $9.99.
- Weaving Crowns, including 28 crowns and 280 weaving strips—Pack of 28 for $18.99.
- Princess Foam Kit at $.99 each.

**Mishloach Manot Bags**   On Purim day, it is a custom to send gifts of food to friends. Allow participants to decorate a brown paper lunch bag with crayons, markers, or stickers (regular and/or foam).

**Purim Hats**   Check out Janie's Coloring Hats at ColoringHats.com for cool paper hats that can be colored and worn! Hats are sold by the bag (20 for $7.99) and by the box (100 for $24.99). Further contact information can be found in Appendix A located at the end of this book.

**Purim Noisemakers**   Here's an easy way to make a grogger (or noisemaker) for your Purim celebration and recycle at the same time! Use a simple water bottle and decorate with paint or stickers (either regular or foam variety). Fill the bottle with beans or rice and glue the lid on to prevent spillage. Now, shake and celebrate!

**Make Your Own Megilla**   The Megilla is the scroll that contains the biblical narrative of the Book of Esther. The original Megilla was printed on parchment, so why not use a brown grocery sack to imitate that type of paper? Open up the bag, lay it flat, and then divide in half longways. That way, you will have a nice long sheet for two different participants. Check out the coloring pages located at http://www.coloring.ws/esther.htm or cut out pages from a Purim coloring book. Place the pictures in order of the story. You may wish to add foam shapes, glitter glue, stickers, plastic jewels, or other similar craft items to your parchment. Once everything is dried, roll up and tie with a ribbon.

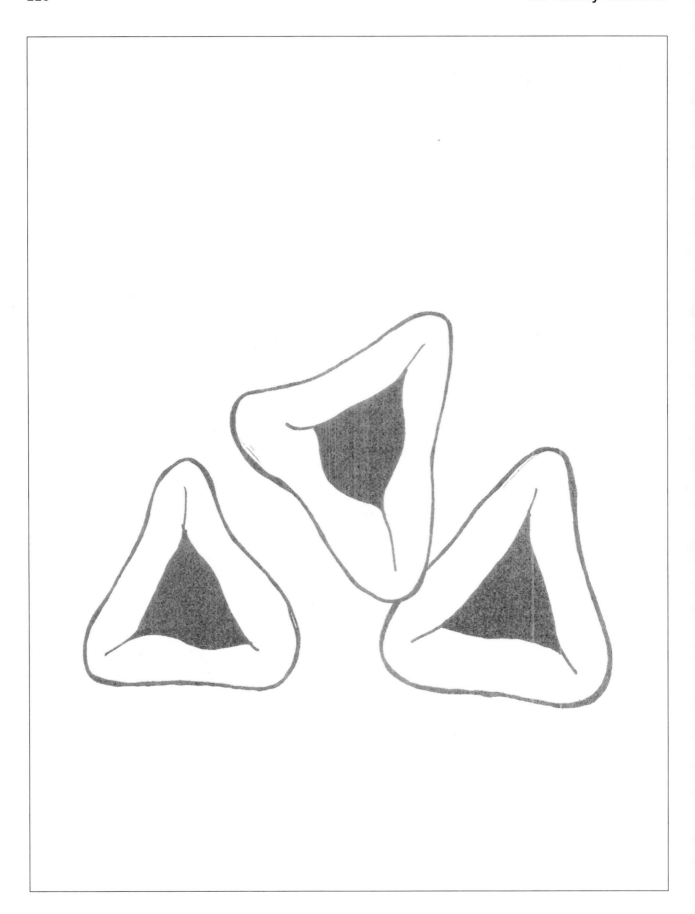

# Ramadan

*Learn all about this holiday that is so important to the Muslim faith.*

## History

Ramadan is the ninth month of the Islamic calendar. The Islamic calendar is based on the moon, or lunar calendar. The difference between the solar calendar (based on the sun) and the lunar calendar is that with the solar calendar, the months have 30 or 31 days, except for the month of February. In the lunar calendar, the months are made up of either 29 or 30 days. Therefore, the duration of Ramadan is either 29 or 30 days.

Since the Islamic calendar is lunar, Ramadan begins on a different date each year—whenever the first sliver of the crescent moon appears in the ninth month. This means that the holiday moves forward 10 to 11 days each year.

The Muslim holiday of Ramadan is a month-long observance honoring the revelation of the Holy Word to Muhammad. During this observance, Muslims fast (not eating or drinking) for the entire time that the sun is up each day. At sundown, they have a special meal called the Iftar. Once the meal is done, they go out and visit with family and friends.

During Ramadan, much time is spent with family. Those celebrating Ramadan promise not to tell lies or to gossip, and also promise not to be greedy. Also, they are asked to do as many good deeds as possible over the course of the holiday. (See Julia Jasmine's *Multicultural Holidays: Share Our Celebrations* [Teacher Created Materials, 1994].)

It is a common occurrence during Ramadan for Muslims to pray many times during the day and night. Prayers are said at least five times per day. These special prayers, called Taraweeh, are much longer than ordinary prayers.

On the twenty-seventh day of the month of Ramadan, a celebration called the Al-Qadr, or "Night of Power," is held. It is believed that on this night Allah delivered the Quran/Koran to the prophet Muhammad. The Quran/Koran says that it is on this twenty-seventh night that Allah determines the course of the world for the coming year.

After an entire month, the holiday of Ramadan ends with a feast called Eid ul-Fitr, which means "the festival of the breaking of the fast." Friends and family gather for meals. Lamb and chicken are the most common meats prepared. Larger cities may hold big celebrations, which may include dancing and singing. It is tradition in many countries that everyone, including children, gets new clothes to wear. (See Sue Fitzjohn et al.'s *Festivals Together: A Guide to Multicultural Celebration* [Hawthorn Press, 1993].)

## Poetry

"Fruity Poems," from http://www.teachersfirst.com/20/getsource.cfm?id=7964.

"I Pray to Allah," from http://www.teachersfirst.com/20/getsource.cfm?id=7964.

"It's the Day of Eid al-Fitr," from http://www.islam4kids.com/i4k/downloads/pdf/EVE_EIDFITR .pdf.

"A Ramadan Poem," from http://www.submission.org/YES/child2.html.

## Books

Addasi, Maha. *The White Nights of Ramadan*. Boyds Mills Press, 2008. ISBN: 978-1590785232.
With joyful excitement, a young girl in Kuwait tells how her family celebrates Girgian, three days under the full moon in the middle of the holy month of Ramadan: the traditions, the special clothing, foods, crafts, and the meaning of the holiday.

Aloian, Molly. *Ramadan*. Crabtree Publishing Company, 2008. ISBN: 978-0778742852.
This book is part of the Celebrations in My World series and provides the reader basic information about Ramadan.

Anderson, Sheila. *Ramadan*. Magic Wagon, 2009. ISBN: 978-1602706057.
This illustrated nonfiction book teaches young readers about the background, traditions, foods, and celebrations of the Islamic holiday.

Elferri, Efdal. *Baby Bear Discovers Ramadan*. Creative Aspirations, 2010. ISBN: 978-1450720090.
Mama Bear and Baby Bear engage in a fun dialogue about Ramadan and the essence of helping those in need.

Gilani-Williams, Fawzia. *Nabeel's New Pants*. Marshall Cavendish Children, 2010. ISBN: 978-0761456292.
Turkish shoemaker Nabeel buys Eid gifts for his family, including a burqa (a garment with a veil) for his wife, a dupalla (long scarf) for his mother, and bangles for his daughter. The shopkeeper also persuades Nabeel to buy himself new pants, but the pants are too long.

Islam, Hina. *An Eid for Everyone*. Author House, 2009. ISBN: 978-1438948454.
Eid is the name of two holidays that are celebrated by Muslims around the world.

Katz, Karen. *My First Ramadan*. Henry Holt and Company, 2007. ISBN: 978-0805078947.
It's time for Ramadan to begin. Follow along with one young boy as he observes the Muslim holy month with his family.

Mobin-Uddin, Asma. *The Best Eid Ever*. Boyds Mills Press, 2007. ISBN: 978-1590784310.
Aneesa, living in the United States, misses her parents, who are in Saudi Arabia for the pilgrimage hajj, but she enjoys celebrating Eid al-Adha with her grandmother.

Sievert, Terri. *Ramadan: Islamic Holy Month*. Capstone Press, 2006. ISBN: 978-0736869355.
This book provides a description of the Islamic holiday of Ramadan, how it started, and the ways people celebrate this cultural holiday.

Whitman, Sylvia. *Under the Ramadan Moon*. Albert Whitman and Company, 2008. ISBN: 978-0807583043.
This simple picture book celebrates the coming of Ramadan and shows a family's activities taking place "under the moon, under the moon, under the Ramadan moon."

Zucker, Jonny. *Feasting and Dates: A Ramadan and Eid-ul-Fitr Story*. Barron's Educational Series, 2004. ISBN: 978-0764126710.
Here is a simple and delightful introduction to the Islamic festival of Ramadan and Eid-ul-Fitr—suitable for even the youngest child.

---

### Older Gems, or Titles Too Good to Pass Up

Ghazi, Suhaib H. *Ramadan*. Holiday House, 1996. ISBN: 978-0823412549.
The month of Ramadan, an Islamic time of fasting, feasting, sharing, and prayer, is seen through the eyes of young Hakeem.

Marx, David F. *Ramadan*. Turtleback, 2002. ISBN: 978-0613543170.
This is a simple introduction to the traditions and festivities of the Muslim holiday.

## Activities

---

**Coloring Pages**

Consult your favorite pattern books or holiday coloring books for pages to use as coloring sheets. Be sure to search online as well. There's lots of great stuff out there!

- Ramadan Coloring Pages—Crayola's website has some great coloring pages for Ramadan. The ones that would work best for storyhour groups are "Ready for Ramadan," "Reading the Qur'an," and "Muslims Called to Prayer." These coloring sheets can be found at http://www.teachersfirst.com/20/getsource.cfm?id=7964 under the "Coloring Pages" heading.
- Mosque Coloring Page—A simple mosque coloring page that could be enlarged for use appears at http://holidaycoloringpages.org/coloringpages/Mosque/.
- More Ramadan Coloring Pages—Some great coloring pages can be found at http://www.primarygames.com/holidays/ramadan/coloring.htm. They also could be reduced and copied for the Ramadan Symbols Matching Game listed in the Games section of this chapter.

## Games

**New Clothes for Ramadan Matching Game**    Consult your favorite pattern books for all types of clothing patterns. Reproduce two of each on different colors of paper. Simplify cutting them out by cutting a shape around them, such as a square. This will make them much easier to handle once they are laminated and need to be cut out again. To play the matching game, hand out one of the pair of clothing pieces/colors to participants, and keep one for yourself, placing it in an apron pocket or container of some sort. Once pieces are given away, begin by pulling out the clothing pieces/colors you have, one by one, and placing them on your flannel/Velcro board. Allow participants to match them until all are gone.

**Ramadan Symbols Matching Game**    Use clip art from http://www.primarygames.com/holidays/ramadan/coloring.htm for this game. Follow the instructions for the New Clothes for Ramadan Matching Game. A variation of this game would be to use the Islamic die set offered by Ellison. It can be found in their Religious Studies section, and includes dies of a Kaaba, a mineret, and a mosque. Copy onto paper of different colors and laminate for durability.

## Miscellaneous

**Nonperishable Food Drive**    It is a custom during Eid al-Fitr to share food with the needy. Prior to the celebration of Ramadan, send home a flyer with your storyhour participants. The flyer should indicate that you will be conducting a food drive during the month of Ramadan. Allow storyhour families to bring in all types of canned goods and other nonperishables. At the end of the month of Ramadan, donate the food to a local food bank or soup kitchen. You also might wish to offer families incentives for donating food. For example, every can of food eliminates $1.00 of overdue library fines.

**Food Tasting**    If you live in a larger metropolitan area that has access to Middle Eastern restaurants, why not contact them to see if they will participate in a food-tasting component for your storyhour session? If you do not have access to a restaurant in your area, do some research on simple Middle Eastern foods, such as dates, hummus, and pita bread, and serve these foods to your participants.

**"Ramadan Is Come"**    The words and melody line to this simple song can be found on page 45 of *Festivals Together: A Guide to Multicultural Celebration* by Sue Fitzjohn et al. (Hawthorn Press, 1993). Teaching this to participants will help them learn about the holiday.

## Fingerplays

### Ramadan Is Here

| | |
|---|---|
| Ramadan is here. | |
| It's that time of year. | *(Point to wrist, indicating watch.)* |
| A whole month long | *(Arms show expanse.)* |
| Of prayers and songs. | *(Clasp hands, as in prayer.)* |
| We fast all day and eat at night. | *(Point to stomach and then make eating motions.)* |
| We celebrate and do right. | *(Shake head "yes.")* |
| Ramadan does not last. | *(Shake head "no.")* |
| We end with the festival of breaking the fast. | *(Clap hands on the word "breaking.")* |
| Let's come together everyone. | *(Make beckoning motion with hands.)* |
| Ramadan now is done. | |

—Kathy Buchsbaum

### Ramadan Is Here

*(This rhyme can be sung to the tune of "The Farmer in the Dell.")*

| | |
|---|---|
| Ramadan is here, Ramadan is here. | *(Clap three times.)* |
| Time to spend with family, | *(Point to wrist, indicating watch.)* |
| Ramadan is here. | *(Clap three times.)* |
| From sun up to sun down, from sun up to sun down | *(Arms make large circle overhead; move circle from left to right.)* |
| We fast and don't eat a crumb, | *(Shake head "no.")* |
| From sun up to sun down. | *(Arms make large circle overhead; move circle from left to right.)* |
| | |
| Now the month is done, now the month is done. | *(Shake head "yes.")* |
| Let's get together and feast, everyone | *(Make beckoning motion with hands; pretend to eat.)* |
| Now the month is done. | *(Shake head "yes.")* |

—Kathy Buchsbaum

---

**More Great Fingerplays**

"Ramadan Is Coming Soon," from http://www.preschoolexpress.com/holiday_station04/holiday_station_oct04.shtml.

"I Am Fasting," action rhyme, from http://members.optusnet.com.au/~umm_pub/presch.html.

"Ramadan Is Here Today," from http://members.optusnet.com.au/~umm_pub/presch.html.

---

## Musical Selections

"Ramadan" by Nancy Stewart. Available from http://www.nancymusic.com.

Since music about this holiday is so hard to come by, I have included a couple of links to videos that can be found on YouTube. While there, be sure to check the video links on the right-hand side of the page for additional videos:

- Check out the YouTube video "Ramadan El Sana Di (Ramadan This Year)" at http://www.youtube.com/watch?v=4NDDyZCxEsw. This video features live actors.
- Another YouTube video, "Ramadan Song with Zaky (Nasheed)," can be accessed at http://www.youtube.com/watch?v=QvBnv6ExLHk. This animated video includes the words on the screen as they are sung.

## Crafts

**Ramadan Calendar Chain**    This craft is available at http://www.submission.org/YES/child2.html. The idea behind it is basically making a paper chain, but with this paper chain, you will be counting down the days of Ramadan. Consequently, it will need to be done at the first of the month of the celebration or before. Determine if the length of Ramadan is 29 or 30 days. Have strips of colorful paper cut into 8-inch lengths. You can either glue them or staple them together, forming the chain. Alternate the colors in a pleasing manner. Attach them to the bottom of a shape such as a crescent moon or star. Hang the finished chain in a doorway or other area. Each day, neatly remove one of the chain links.

**Night Sky and Moon Project**    This project idea is available at http://www.submission.org/YES/child2.html. Use blue or black construction paper for a night sky background. Use a stencil or help participants trace the shape of the crescent moon. Let them color it in with white, yellow, gold, or silver markers or crayons. If they can draw stars by themselves, allow them to do so. If not, use the pre-gummed star stickers to place stars in the night sky.

**New Moon in the Sky**    This idea comes from Jean Warren's Preschool Express website at http://www.preschoolexpress.com/holiday_station04/holiday_station_oct04.shtml. It is a variation on the Night Sky and Moon Project. Participants cut the crescent moon shape out of a piece of aluminum foil and glue it to the black construction paper. Silver star stickers are then added.

**Ramadan Lamp Craft**    Instructions, example, and template for this simple paper craft of a candle and base are available from http://www.teachersfirst.com/20/getsource.cfm?id=7964. If you are not taken to the craft pages immediately, scroll to the bottom of the Ramadan page, and you will find the Ramadan Lamp Craft listed under the "Ramadan Crafts" section. You may wish to enlarge the template for little hands.

**New Clothes Collage**    This idea comes from Jean Warren's Preschool Express website at http://www.preschoolexpress.com/holiday_station04/holiday_station_oct04.shtml. Collect store advertisements and catalogs that include pictures of children wearing new clothes. Let participants cut out pictures and glue them onto a piece of construction paper to make a collage of clothes they would like to wear to an Eid al-Fitr celebration.

**Ramadan Wind Sock**    This idea comes from YemenLinks.com. You will need a cylindrical cardboard oatmeal box, construction paper, crepe paper streamers, glue, string, scissors, and a hole punch. If you cannot collect a suitable number of oatmeal boxes for participants, substitute heavy paper that you can glue or staple into a cylindrical shape. If using the oatmeal box, remove the bottom. Cover the box with construction paper in whatever color is desired. Write on the paper "Welcome Ramadan," "Ramadan," or "Blessed Ramadan." If doing this craft with preschoolers, you may choose to have these sayings already printed out on paper so that participants can simply choose one and glue it on the cylinder. Cut some crepe paper streamers and glue or staple them to one end of the wind stock. Punch four holes along the top of the cylinder. Cut two pieces of string about a foot long. Tie the strings to the wind sock (tie the opposite ends of a string to holes on opposite sides of the cylinder). Tie a longer piece of string to the smaller pieces. This string will be used to hang the wind sock.

**Mehndi Hand Design**    Perhaps you have seen hands decorated with beautiful, intricate designs. This is called mehndi. A short explanation of it appears on page 46 of *Festivals Together: A Guide to Multicultural Celebration* by Sue Fitzjohn et al. (Hawthorn Press, 1993). She suggests having biscuit hands for younger children to decorate. A recipe is given on page 48. If it is not possible to have these prepared, why not use the Open Hand or Child or Baby Handprint Ellison dies in one of the larger sizes? My library owns the Baby Handprint in the extra-large size. It is large enough for preschoolers to manipulate and decorate with markers in the mehndi fashion. Print out pictures of actual designs and display them so that participants can see what they look like.

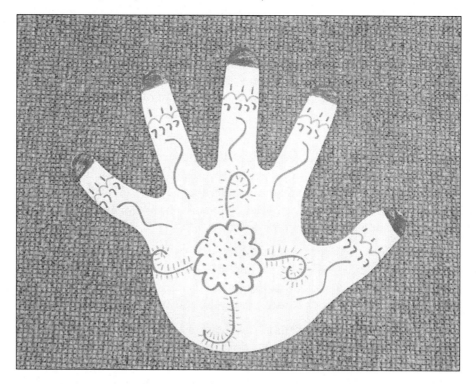

**Ramadan Fanoo**   This craft, which makes a traditional lantern, appears on page 196 of *The Festive Teacher: Multicultural Activities for Your Curriculum* by Steve Springer et al. (McGraw-Hill, 2008). I would enlarge the pattern as much as possible, making it easier for little hands to hold.

# Rosh Hashanah and Yom Kippur

*Take this opportunity to learn about Jewish New Year traditions!*

## History

Rosh Hashanah means "head of the year" in the Hebrew language. The first ten days of the Jewish month of Tishri are the High Holy Days of the Jewish religion. The first of these days is known as Rosh Hashanah. It is the Jewish New Year. Jews consider this holiday the birthday of the world. It is also the beginning of a period that lasts for ten days. This period is known as the Days of Awe. During this time, Jewish people are to ask people whom they have wronged to forgive them. The ten-day period ends with Yom Kippur or the Day of Atonement, which is considered the holiest day of the Jewish year. On this day, any Jew who is age 13 or older fasts for an entire day. They also spend the day in the synagogue praying and asking forgiveness for their sins against God. At sundown on Yom Kipper (the tenth day), Jews have a "Break Fast" where they eat bagels, fish, and other foods.

All Jewish holidays begin at sundown on the day before the holiday. On Rosh Hashanah evening, a holiday meal is enjoyed. A special bread, called challah, is eaten. Jewish people also visit the synagogue, or church, on the evening of Rosh Hashanah and again the next morning.

A tradition that is sometimes held is the ceremony called "Tashlich." Jews go to a stream or a river and toss in bread crumbs. This symbolizes ridding themselves of their sins.

At the beginning of Rosh Hashanah and at the end of Yom Kippur, a ram's horn, called a shofar, is traditionally blown. The shofar is a well-known symbol of the holidays.

Traditional foods are eaten at family dinners during this time. The fruit (most often an apple) eaten is dipped into honey to symbolize the year being full of sweetness. The challah, or eggbread, is baked in a circle to represent the cycle of the year. (See Julia Jasmine's *Multicultural Holidays: Share Our Celebrations* [Teacher Created Materials, 1994].)

## Poetry

"Rosh Hashanah," from pages 82–83 of *Every Day's a Holiday: Amusing Rhymes for Happy Times* by Dean Koontz (HarperCollins, 2003).

"Rosh Hashanah," from page 49 of *Ring Out, Wild Bells: Poems about Holidays and Seasons*, selected by Lee Bennett Hopkins (Harcourt Brace Jovanovich, 1992).

## Books

Cohen, Deborah B. *Engineer Ari and the Rosh Hashanah Ride*. Kar-Ben Publishing, 2008. ISBN: 978-0822586500.

This story is based on the trip of the first train from Jerusalem to Jaffa in 1897, shortening the time between the coast and the city from three days to three hours.

Heller, Linda. *Today Is the Birthday of the World*. Dutton Children's Books, 2009. ISBN: 978-0525479055.
>  Drawn from the liturgy of Rosh Hashanah, God is happy when his helpers are the best that they can be because "then the world is the best place that it can be and there is no better birthday present."

Holub, Joan. *Apples and Honey: A Rosh Hashanah Lift-the-Flap*. Puffin, 2003. ISBN: 978-0142501368.
>  Rosh Hashanah is here and it's the beginning of a new year. There are so many exciting things to do!

Jules, Jacqueline. *The Hardest Word: A Yom Kippur Story*. Kar-Ben Publishing, 2001. ISBN: 978-1580130288.
>  The Ziz, a clumsy but goodhearted bird of folklore, accidentally destroys a vegetable garden, and when he asks God for advice, he learns the importance of apologizing.

Jules, Jacqueline. *Noah and the Ziz*. Kar-Ben Publishing, 2005. ISBN: 978-1580131216.
>  With only a week left before the flood's arrival, Noah asks God for help in gathering the animals. His help comes in the form of the Ziz, a gigantic bird with a yellow body and red wings.

Kimmel, Eric A. *Even Higher! A Rosh Hashanah Story*. Holiday House, 2010. ISBN: 978-0823422982.
>  This beautiful Jewish folktale is about a rabbi whom the shtetl people believe performs a miracle every year before Rosh Hashanah.

Kress, Camille. *The High Holy Days*. Urj Press, 2002. ISBN: 978-0807407769.
>  This book is an introduction to the symbols and themes of the High Holy Days for the youngest child.

Kropf, Latifa Berry. *It's Shofar Time!* Kar-Ben Publishing, 2006. ISBN: 987-1580131581.
>  Children blow the shofar, create New Year's cards, bake round challah, dip apples in honey, see the Torah dressed in white, and perform Tashlich.

Morales, Melita. *Jam and Honey*. Tricycle Press, 2011. ISBN: 978-1582462992.
>  This book tells the story of a young girl and a honeybee who learn to peacefully coexist in the same garden as they go about their respective tasks.

Ofanansky, Allison. *What's the Buzz? Honey for a Sweet New Year*. Kar-Ben Publishing, 2011. ISBN: 978-0761356400.
>  This picture book provides a tour of a bee farm, and describes the role that honey plays in the celebration of Rosh Hashanah.

---

### Older Gems, or Titles Too Good to Pass Up

Gellman, Ellie. *It's Rosh Hashanah!* Kar-Ben Copies, 1985. ISBN: 978-0930494504.
>  It's a New Year. Benjy and Sarah have grown. They can do many new things this year. What new things can you do?

Goldin, Barbara D. *The World's Birthday: A Rosh Hashanah Story*. Sandpiper, 1995. ISBN: 978-0152000455.
>  Daniel wants to celebrate the Jewish New Year in a way that a child can truly comprehend—with a birthday party.

Groner, Judyth S., et. al. *The Shofar Calls to Us*. Kar-Ben Publishing, 1991. ISBN: 978-0929371610.
>  The author depicts a boy and girl celebrating the holidays and Shabbat with all five senses.

Marx, David F. *Rosh Hashanah and Yom Kippur*. Children's Press, 2000. ISBN: 978-0516263137.
>  Part of the Rookie Read-About Holidays series, this is an introduction to these Jewish holidays.

Rouss, Sylvia A. *Sammy Spider's First Rosh Hashanah*. Kar-Ben Publishing, 1996. ISBN: 978-0929371993.
>  Mother Spider explains the holiday customs and symbols to curious young Sammy.

Saypol, Judyth. *My Very Own Yom Kippur Book*. Kar-Ben Publishing, 1978. ISBN: 978-0930494056.
>  This book explains the significance of Yom Kippur, the Day of Forgiveness—the holiest day of the Jewish year.

Peppas, Lynn. *Rosh Hashanah and Yom Kippur*. Crabtree Publishing Company, 2008. ISBN: 978-0778747574.

>Rosh Hashanah is often referred to as the Jewish New Year. Millions of Jewish people all over the world celebrate this holiday.

Snyder, Laurel. *Nosh, Schlep, Schluff: Babyiddish*. Random House, 2011. ISBN: 978-0375864970.

>Illustrations and rhyming text on board book pages introduce children to Yiddish words.

Wayland, April H. *New Year at the Pier: A Rosh Hashanah Story*. Dial, 2009. ISBN: 978-0803732797.

>Izzy and his family get ready for the Jewish New Year ceremony of Tashlich.

Zucker, Jonny. *Apples and Honey: A Rosh Hashanah Story*. Frances Lincoln Children's Books, 2002. ISBN: 978-0711219298.

>A family celebrates the Jewish New Year by putting on new clothing, eating apples dipped in honey, and listening to the sounds of the shofar in the synagogue.

## Activities

> ### Coloring Pages
>
> Consult your favorite pattern books or holiday coloring books for pages to use as coloring sheets. Be sure to search online as well. There's lots of great stuff out there!

### Flannel/Velcro Board

**"Too Many Apples"**    This story can be found on pages 95–96 of *Caroline Feller Bauer's New Handbook for Storytellers with Stories, Poems, Magic, and More* by Caroline Feller Bauer (American Library Association, 1993). Turn it into a flannel/Velcro-board presentation. Since there are so many names of apple dishes to remember, use an apple cutout with the name of each item listed on it. Place them on the board as they are mentioned in the story. Or, you could pass the apples out to your participants and have them hold them so that you can see the names of the apple dishes. Then, as you tell the story, have the person holding the dish mentioned come and place it on the board. You might enjoy the treat of a real apple at the end of the story!

**"How to Make a Small House into a Large One"**    This humorous story, an old Yiddish tale, can be found on pages 351–353 of *Caroline Feller Bauer's New Handbook for Storytellers with Stories, Poems, Magic, and More* by Caroline Feller Bauer (American Library Association, 1993). A search through your favorite pattern books will yield pictures of all of the characters needed to tell the story.

**"Apple Picking"**    This flannel/Velcro-board story counts down the number of apples on a tree. It appears, complete with patterns, on pages 20–23 of *Felt Board Stories* by Liz and Dick Wilmes (Building Blocks Publications, 2001).

### Games

**Apple, Shofar, and Honey Pot Matching Game**    Since people often eat apples dipped in honey during this celebration and the shofar is an instrument that is played, use the Ellison dies for all three to cut shapes from different colors of paper. The honey pot and shofar can be located in the Religious Studies section. Laminate shapes for durability and place flannel or Velcro on the back so that the pieces will adhere to your board. Hand out one of each of the pairs to participants, putting the other of the pair into a container or an apron pocket. Play the game by placing your colors/shapes on the board, and then have the participant who has the match bring theirs up. Continue until all shapes/colors have been matched.

**Pin the Birthday Hat on the World**    Have a large laminated Earth and smaller laminated birthday hats. Play this game as you would Pin the Tail on the Donkey.

## Miscellaneous

**Blow the Shofar!**    Purchase an inexpensive shofar, such as the one offered at http://www.zionjudaica .com/Real_Looking_Plastic_Shofar-5430.asp for $5.50. Explain that this instrument is blown in the Jewish synagogue (or church) for Rosh Hashanah and Yom Kippur services. Explain that the real instrument is made from the horn of a ram, or male sheep. In ancient Israel, the shofar was used to announce events of any kind, similar to the Christian tradition of ringing bells.

**Apple Man's Secret**    During the holiday of Rosh Hashanah, it is customary to eat apples dipped in honey, symbolizing hopes for a "sweet" new year. Why not use this story? It is found on pages 6–7 of *Short-Short Stories: Simple Stories for Young Children Plus Seasonal Activities*, compiled by Jean Warren (Warren Publishing House, 1987). The highlight of the story, in whatever version you choose to use, is cutting open the apple and showing the star inside formed by the seeds!

**The Little Red House**    This is a variant of Apple Man's Secret, with the text and telling instructions found on pages 43–49 of *Easy-to-Tell Stories for Young Children* by Annette Harrison (National Storytelling Press, 1992). Yet another version can be found on pages 36–41 of *Storytime Stretchers: Tongue Twisters, Choruses, Games, and Charades* by Naomi Baltuck (August House, 2007).

**Apple Tasting**    Cut up different types of apples into bite-sized pieces. Allow participants to taste them and describe the taste as best they can (sweet, sour, mild, sharp, strong, crisp). You may wish to graph their responses, adding a math component to your program.

## Fingerplays

### Apple Dance

*(This action rhyme is sung to the tune of "The Hokey Pokey." Make an apple on a stick for each participant to dance with. You may wish to use the pattern at the end of this chapter. Laminate for durability and multiple uses. Do motions as indicated in the song.)*

>You put your apple up.
>You put your apple down.
>You put your apple up and you shake it all around
>You do the apple dance and you turn yourself around.
>That's the apple dance!
>
>You put your apple in front.
>You put your apple in back.
>You put your apple in front and you give your knees a slap.
>You do the apple dance and you turn yourself around.
>That's the apple dance!
>
>You do the apple dance, you do the apple dance.
>You do the apple dance, that's what it's all about!
>*(Repeat.)*
>
>—Kathy Buchsbaum

## Musical Selections

*Rosh Hashana Songs* CD (performed by children). Available from http://www.judaicawebstore.com/ rosh-hashana-songs-P405.aspx.
*Songs for the High Holidays* CD by Cantor Frances T. Goldman. Available from http://www.judaism.com/.

> ### More Great Fingerplays
>
> The following Rosh Hashanah and Yom Kippur fingerplays can be found in *Clap and Count: Action Rhymes for the Jewish Year* by Jacqueline Jules (Kar-Ben Copies, 2001): "This Little Shofar," "Honeybee," "Rosh Hashanah Round," "When Yom Kippur Comes," and "Two Chubby Babies."
>
> "5 Little Shofars," from TheBestKidsBooksite.com. Click on the "Fingerplays" link, locate the title in the list, and click on the "Show Me" button at the bottom.
>
> "A Sweet Treat," from page 42 of *Celebrate the Seasons: The Best of Holidays and Seasonal Celebrations—Issues 9–12, PreK–3,* edited by Donna Borst (Teaching and Learning Company, 1998).
>
> "Rosh Hashanah Happy New Year" and "Time to Say 'I'm Sorry,'" from page 35 of *The Big All-Year Book of Holidays and Seasonal Celebrations: Preschool/Kindergarten, Issues 14–18,* edited by Donna Borst (Teaching and Learning Company, 2002).

## Crafts

**Apple and Honey Craft**   Instructions and patterns appear on pages 11–13 of *Cut and Create! Holidays: Easy Step-by-Step Projects That Teach Scissor Skills* by Kim Rankin (Teaching and Learning Company, 1997). Simple shapes create an apple cut in half and a jar of honey.

**Yom Kippur Yarmulkes**   Instructions and patterns appear on pages 14–15 of *Cut and Create! Holidays: Easy Step-by-Step Projects That Teach Scissor Skills* by Kim Rankin (Teaching and Learning Company, 1997). Simple shapes can be cut from either paper or felt to make this cap.

**Apple Rubbings**   Provide participants with patterns of apples cut from poster board. Have them place these patterns under a piece of white construction paper. Allow them to use crayons to rub over the pattern of the apple.

**Apple Print Painting**   Provide participants with white construction paper, apples cut in half (so that the star shape formed by the seeds is visible), and plates with different colors of paint on them. Allow them to dip apple shapes into the paint and then press the apples onto the construction paper, making a print!

**Crown Decorating**   Check online to find a company that sells complete crown kits. These often come with everything needed to decorate your crown, including the glue. Another option is to use the King/Queen/Prince/Princess crown patterns found on page 22 of *Paper Hat Tricks I* by Patt Newbold and Anne Diebel (Paper Hat Tricks, 1994).

**Apples, Birds, and Braids**   Patterns for this craft, which uses a paper plate as a base, can be found on page 151 of *International Fall Festivals* by Marilynn G. Barr (Good Apple, 1994). A short explanation of the holiday and symbols is found on page 150.

**Jonah and the Whale**   This story is included in the readings at Yom Kippur services. Instructions and patterns for this craft appear on pages 158–159 of *International Fall Festivals* by Marilynn G. Barr (Good Apple, 1994). Use them to make a collage with construction paper and other craft supplies.

**Apple Man**   Instructions and patterns for this craft can be found on pages 52–53 of *Art Projects for All Seasons* by Karen Finch (Carson-Dellosa Publishing, 1993). The feet and hands are attached to the apple shape with accordion-folded paper strips!

**Apple Lacing Card**   The pattern for this craft can be found on page 13 of *Seasonal Cut-Ups* by Marilynn G. Barr (Monday Morning Books, 2005). Duplicate the apple pattern onto construction paper or card stock. Provide participants with crayons, hole punches, yarn, and large plastic needles. First, have them color their apples (and background, if they desire). Allow them to either straight-lace or loop-lace their yarn around the picture. These two types of lacing are explained on page 7. They may wish to leave enough yarn at the top so that this card may be hung from a doorknob. Ellison also offers a Lacing Apple die in the XL size.

**Apple Pie Craft**    This is a super-simple craft! The base is two circles, one smaller than the other. The larger circle is duplicated on brown construction paper; the slightly smaller one is duplicated on red construction paper. The brown circle is the crust for the pie and the red circle is the apple filling.

Use glue sticks to apply glue to the red construction paper circle. Center it onto the brown circle. Have small containers of apple pie spice available for participants. These are available in the spice/seasonings section or baking aisle of your local supermarket. These containers usually come with a hole-punched inside lid that allows you to shake the contents out. Do so onto the glued area. Shake off excess into a trash can. You will have a sweet-smelling apple pie to take home! A variation of this craft would be to use an apple shape, cut from an Ellison die, perhaps the largest one. Apply glue and then sprinkle on the apple pie spice. Yum!

**Star of David Hat**    See the entry in the Hanukkah chapter's Crafts section (p. 165).

**Apple Time**    This apple craft is found on pages 2 (instructions) and 4 (patterns) of *From the Hands of a Child: Special Seasonal Art Activities for Primary Children* by Anthony Flores (Fearon Teacher Aids, 1987). The leaf of the apple is the participant's hand.

**Stand-Up Apple**    Since the apple is an important fruit for this holiday, this craft really fits the bill. The apples are reproduced on heavy paper. Slits are cut into the top of one apple pattern and the bottom of the second one so that they fit together. The saying "An apple a day keeps the doctor away" appears on the leaves, but could easily be covered over when reproducing the patterns. The pattern and instructions appear on page 37 of *The Best of Holidays and Seasonal Celebrations—Issues 9–13, PreK–K*, edited by Donna Borst (Teaching and Learning Company, 2001).

**Yom Kippur Craft Kits**    The website JewishCrafts.com offers several craft kits for this holiday. Please note that the kits are sold by the dozen only:

- High Holy Day Bookmarks/Shapes and labels mount on jumbo craft sticks. Price is $.39 each.
- Judaic Sand Art—Cool pictures that you peel and sprinkle with sand. Priced at $.69 each.
- Hero Jonah—Precut foam pieces make a cute 3-D craft. Cost is $1.39 each.
- Velvet Art—Color a velvet picture with Jewish symbols. Priced at $.79 each.

**A Shofar to Sew**    This simple craft makes a shofar shape from two paper plates. Directions appear on page 19 of *Jewish Holiday Crafts for Little Hands* by Ruth E. Brinn (Kar-Ben Copies, 1993).

**Table Centerpiece**    This craft, which appears on page 27 of *Jewish Holiday Crafts for Little Hands* by Ruth E. Brinn (Kar-Ben Copies, 1993), makes a small table shape from an inverted paper cup and a large paper plate. Patterns are provided for items for the table: a round challah, kiddush cup, candlesticks, dish of honey, and bowl of apples. You may wish to enlarge them slightly before having participants color them. After participants have colored them, have them cut them out (leaving the tab attached) and glue them to the plate (tabletop).

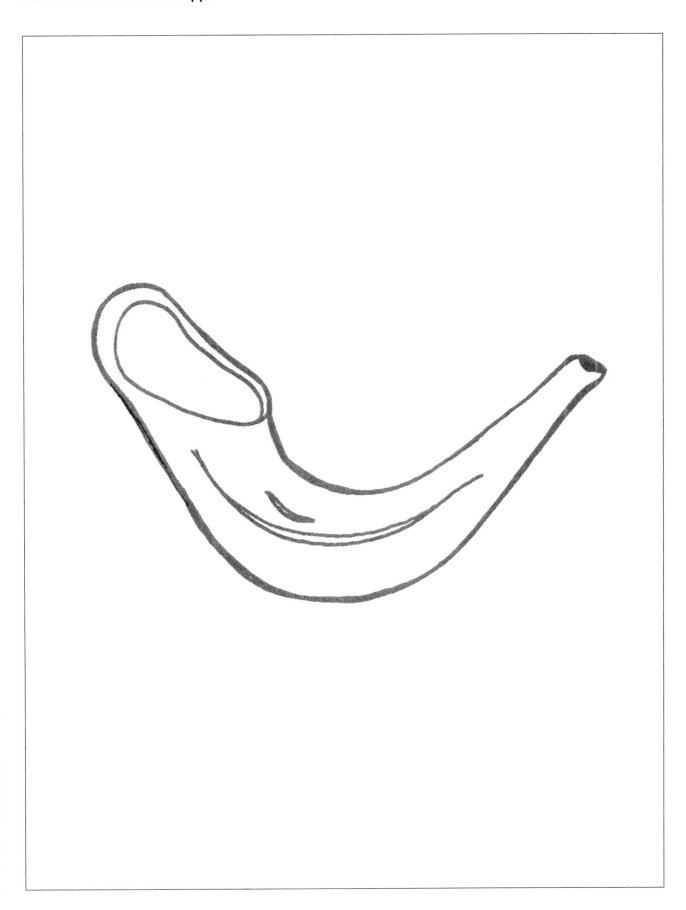

# Saint Patrick's Day

*Many people say this is the one day of the year when everyone's Irish! There are many opportunities for different types of themes with this holiday: the color green, rainbows, snakes, and, of course, leprechauns!*

## History

Saint Patrick's Day is celebrated on March 17th. People celebrate by wearing green and participating in parades, especially in large cities.

Saint Patrick is the patron saint of Ireland. Much of the history of Patrick's early life is unknown. It is known that at the age of 16, he was kidnapped from his home in the British Isles by a band of pirates and sold into slavery in Ireland. After six years of slavery, he fled back to his home in Britain. Patrick had sought religion to get him through his years of slavery, so, upon returning home, he decided to study to become a priest. He returned to Ireland after a dream convinced him that the Irish people wanted him to return to convert them to Christianity. Patrick spent approximately 30 years preaching Christianity in Ireland. He died in the fifth century on March 17th.

One legend that is told about St. Patrick is that he drove the snakes out of Ireland.

The first St. Patrick's Day celebration in the United States was held in 1737 in Boston, Massachusetts. The first official St. Patrick's Day parade was held in the 1760s in New York City. It still takes place today.

Shamrocks are known as a symbol of this holiday because Patrick used their three-leaf composition to explain the idea of the Holy Trinity. Leprechauns (small fairies) are another symbol of the holiday. They are known for keeping pots of gold. The color green is associated with St. Patrick's Day, as it is the color of Ireland. (See Edna Barth's *Shamrocks, Harps, and Shillelaghs: The Story of the St. Patrick's Day Symbols* [Seabury Press, 1977].)

## Poetry

"Green Is the Color" and "A Leprechaun's Lunch," from pages 9 and 16 of *Shamrock Days: Celebrating St. Patrick's Day with Rhymes, Songs, Projects, Games, and Snacks* by Elizabeth McKinnon (Totline Publications, 2000).

"Leprechaun Stew," from http://www.dltk-holidays.com/patrick/songs/mstew.htm.

"The Magic Wish," from page 231 of *Classroom Celebrations: The Best of Holidays and Seasonal Celebrations*, edited by Donna Borst (Teaching and Learning Company, 1996).

"Shamrocks," from page 207 of *The Preschool Calendar* by Sherrill B. Flora (T.S. Denison and Company, 1987).

"St. Patrick's Day," "The Wearin' o' the Green," and "I'll Wear a Shamrock," from http://www.the holidayspot.com/patrick/poems.htm.

"St. Patrick's Day Poems," at http://childstoryhour.com/storiesholiday3.htm offers at least eight poems to share for the St. Patrick's Day holiday.

## Books

Balian, Lorna. *Leprechauns Never Lie*. Star Bright Books, 2004. ISBN: 978-1932065374.
Kids and adults will enjoy the lessons in this tale. The illustrations are perfect, showing a mischievous leprechaun enjoying every minute of the work that Ninny Nanny is forced to undertake in her search for the gold.

Bredeson, Carmen. *St. Patrick's Day*. Children's Press, 2003. ISBN: 978-0516279213.
Part of the Rookie Read-About Holidays series, this book is a great introduction to the St. Patrick's Day holiday.

Bunting, Eve. *Green Shamrocks*. Turtleback, 2011. ISBN: 978-0606153119.
When the pot of green shamrocks that Rabbit had been growing for St. Patrick's Day goes missing, he asks all the other animals if they have seen it.

Callahan, Sean. *The Leprechaun Who Lost His Rainbow*. Albert Whitman and Company, 2009. ISBN: 978-0807544549.
It's raining, and Colleen is sad. How can her grandfather play his bagpipes in the St. Patrick's Day parade?

Holub, Joan. *Hooray for St. Patrick's Day!* Puffin, 2002. ISBN: 978-0142300619.
It's Saint Patrick's Day. Time to join in the celebration!

Robertson, Ivan. *Jack and the Leprechaun*. Turtleback, 2000. ISBN: 978-0613217880.
While visiting his cousin Sean in Ireland on St. Patrick's Day, Jack the mouse tries to catch a leprechaun for himself.

### Older Gems, or Titles Too Good to Pass Up

Blazek, Sarah. *A Leprechaun's St. Patrick's Day*. Pelican Publishing Company, 1996. ISBN: 978-1565542372.
Mischievous leprechauns plan a surprise for the St. Patrick's Day parade.

Bunting, Eve. *St. Patrick's Day in the Morning*. Clarion Books, 1980. ISBN: 978-0395290989.
Jamie, the youngest of his family, tries to find a way to prove he's not too young to march in the St. Patrick's Day parade.

dePaola, Tomie. *Jamie O'Rourke and the Big Potato*. Turtleback, 1997. ISBN: 978-0613017510.
Jamie is the laziest man in Ireland. When he catches a leprechaun, Jamie lets the leprechaun give him seed for the biggest potato ever instead of gold. That way, he will never have to garden again!

McDermott, Gerald. *Tim O'Toole and the Wee Folk*. Turtleback, 1995. ISBN: 978-0833590435.
Tim is given magical items by the wee folk, only to have them taken from him by a couple named McGoon.

Robertson, Ivan. *Jack and the Leprechaun*. Turtleback, 2000. ISBN: 978-0613217880.
While visiting his cousin Sean in Ireland on St. Patrick's Day, Jack the mouse tries to catch a leprechaun for himself.

Schertle, Alice. *Jeremy Bean's St. Patrick's Day*. Lothrop, Lee, and Shepard Books, 1987. ISBN: 978-0688048136.
Shy Jeremy Bean forgets, much to his humiliation, to wear green to school for St. Patrick's Day.

Shub, Elizabeth. *Seeing Is Believing*. Greenwillow Books, 1994. ISBN: 978-0688136475.
This story is about a young man named Tom who learns to respect magic.

Tucker, Kathy. *The Leprechaun in the Basement*. Albert Whitman and Company, 1998. ISBN: 978-0807544518.
It's St. Patrick's Day, but Michael McKeever has run out of luck. But, when he accidentally discovers a leprechaun in the basement, Michael is sure that his luck has changed!

Rockwell, Anne. *St. Patrick's Day*. HarperCollins, 2010. ISBN: 978-0060501976.
 The latest in the Rockwells' long-running holiday series, which takes place mostly in the elementary-school classroom of Mrs. Madoff.

Slater, Teddy. *The Luckiest St. Patrick's Day Ever*. Cartwheel Books, 2008. ISBN: 978-0545039437.
 Top o' the morning! It's March 17th, and the leprechauns are gathered for their favorite day of the year.

Tegen, Katherine. *The Story of the Leprechaun*. HarperCollins, 2011. ISBN: 978-0061430863.
 A leprechaun is a busy shoemaker for humans and fairies alike. When his profits cause his pot of gold to overflow, he buries it for safekeeping, but not before a greedy human spies it.

Wing, Natasha. *The Night Before St. Patrick's Day*. Grosset and Dunlap, 2009. ISBN: 978-0448448527.
 It's the night before St. Patrick's Day, and Tim and Maureen are wide awake setting traps to catch a leprechaun!

Wojciechowski, Susan. *A Fine St. Patrick's Day*. Dragonfly Books, 2008. ISBN: 978-0385736404.
 The neighboring towns of Tralee and Tralah compete each year in a St. Patrick's Day decorating contest, and each year Tralee loses. This year, however, 6-year-old Tralee resident Fiona Riley has an idea that may turn the town's luck around.

Yoon, Salina. *St. Patrick's Day Countdown*. Price Stern Sloan, 2006. ISBN: 978-0843116601.
 Five bright-green holographic shamrock tabs and fun rhyming text make this a St. Patrick's Day treat!

## Activities

### Coloring Pages

Consult your favorite pattern books or holiday coloring books for pages to use as coloring sheets. Be sure to search online as well. There's lots of great stuff out there!

- Visit http://dulemba.com/index_ColoringPages.html for author and illustrator Elizabeth O. Dulemba's great collection of holiday coloring pages! While there, sign up for her Coloring Page Tuesdays e-mails.

### Cut-and-Tell

**"Barney's Mission"**   This paper-cutting story appears on pages 27–29 of *Paper Stories* by Jean Stangl (School Specialty Children's Publishing, 1984). The end result is a shamrock. A pattern for cutting is included.

### Draw-and-Tell

**"Danny the Leprechaun"**   This draw-and-tell story, which creates a shamrock, appears on pages 96–97 of *Chalk in Hand: The Draw and Tell Book* by Phyllis Noe Pflomm (Scarecrow Press, 1986).

### Flannel/Velcro Board

**"This Little Leprechaun"**   The text to this flannel/Velcro-board presentation can be found in the March/April 1994 issue of *CopyCat Magazine* (now out of print but often available through interlibrary loan). It can be simply chanted or sung to the tune of "This Old Man." I did a Google image search and found clip art that went along with each of the places the leprechaun hides his gold (sun, shoe, beehive, bed, etc.). I printed these out and laminated them for durability. As you chant the rhyme, pause before placing the piece on the board so that the children can guess where the gold was hidden.

**"Five Little Leprechauns"**    The fingerplay rhyme for this flannel/Velcro-board adaptation can be found on page 81 of *The Best of Totline Newsletter* by Jean Warren (Warren Publishing House, 1995). On page 101 of the same book, there are patterns that go along with the rhyme. Simply color these in, cut them out, laminate for durability, and place flannel or Velcro on the back.

**"Five Little Leprechauns"**    This rhyme appears on page 195 of *Rhymes for Learning Times*, by Louise B. Scott (T.S. Denison and Company, 1983). I have adapted this rhyme as a flannel/Velcro-board presentation. You can easily find clip art for your leprechaun shapes. A magic wand is mentioned in the rhyme as well. You may wish to have a wand of some sort to add to the fun of the rhyme.

**"The Brave Little Leprechaun"**    This story can be found on page 47 of *Short-Short Stories: Simple Stories for Young Children Plus Seasonal Activities*, compiled by Jean Warren (Warren Publishing House, 1987). It can be easily used as a flannel/Velcro-board story.

**"You Can't Fool a Leprechaun"**    This poem by Cheryl Potts would make a great flannel/Velcro-board presentation. A quick search of your favorite pattern books should yield illustrations for you to use. The text is found on page 19 of *Poetry Fun by the Ton with Jack Prelutsky* by Cheryl Potts (Alleyside Press, 1995).

**"A St. Patrick's Day Elf"**    This rhyme for the flannel/Velcro board can be found on pages 195–196 of *Rhymes for Learning Times* by Louise B. Scott (T.S. Denison and Company, 1983). It should be easy to locate a hat, pants, coat, shoes, and face for your leprechaun from pattern books.

## Games

**Green Match!**    I used patterns from the March/April 1995 issue of *CopyCat Magazine* (now out of print but often available through interlibrary loan) to make my matching game. I enlarged the patterns (copying two of each), colored them, and laminated them. If you do not have access to this issue, use Google clip art to find things that are green, such as peas, celery, a shamrock, pickle, grass, etc. Print two of each picture. Laminate for durability. Pass out one of each pair to participants, keeping one for yourself in an apron pocket or container of some sort (how about a leprechaun hat?). Begin the matching game by pulling your copies of the pictures out, placing them on the flannel/Velcro board one at a time, and allowing participants to match them.

**St. Patrick's Day Match**    Patterns for a variety of St. Patrick's Day symbols (leprechaun, leprechaun's hat, pot of gold, shamrock) appear on pages 97–104 of *Holiday Patterns*, compiled by Jean Warren (Warren Publishing House, 1991). The best patterns to use are the ones that are already enclosed in a square, as this would make cutting them out simple. Follow the instructions from the other matching game listed previously in this section.

## Miscellaneous

**Green Shapes**    Cut large simple shapes out of green construction paper. I happen to have some large heavy poster board stencils that worked well for this. The shapes that I have are a teddy bear, a dog, a heart, a cat, and a balloon. Give each participant a shape. Then sing the following song (to the tune of "London Bridge"):

"If you have a green _____, green _____, green _____,
  If you have a green _____, please stand up!"

Continue with shapes until all participants are standing up. If you wish, sing the same song again, and have them sit down if they have a certain shape.

**Magic Powder**    For this activity, you will need milk and instant pistachio pudding. Be sure to have enough for your group. Consult the box for amounts needed. You will also need small Dixie cups and spoons. Make sure that there are no peanut allergies among your group before you begin. You may wish to do this activity at the beginning of your storyhour session, then place your pudding mix in the refrigerator until the end of the session so it has the chance to chill and thicken. Have the pudding mix powder in a bowl and the milk in a separate container. Use the following rhyme with this activity:

| | |
|---|---|
| Top o' the morning, children! How do you do? | As this white powder turns to green! |
| We leprechauns have fun for you. | Now each of you may have a bite, |
| Here's magic powder for us to fix. | For the color green is what we like. |
| Just add some milk and mix, mix, mix. | So, we leprechauns just want to say, |
| Then our magic will be seen, | Have a happy St. Patrick's Day! |

At the end of your session, spoon the pudding out into cups for each participant to enjoy!

**St. Patrick's Day Parade**    Let your participants wear hats that they have created from one of the craft ideas listed in the Crafts section of this chapter. Use music from the Musical Selections area and parade around your room or library. If you can pipe the music over an intercom or phone system, that would be great! Add rhythm instruments for participants to play if you wish.

**St. Patrick's Day Songs**
- The following piggyback songs (new songs sung to familiar tunes) can be found on pages 58–60 of *Holiday Piggyback Songs*, compiled by Jean Warren (Warren Publishing House, 1988): "St. Patrick's Day Is Here," "Paddy Is His Name," "I Saw a Leprechaun," and "I'm a Tiny Little Green Man."
- The songs "March 17th" and "Do You Know What a Shamrock Is?" can be found on pages 29–30 of *More Piggyback Songs*, compiled by the Totline Newsletter Staff (Warren Publishing House, 1984).
- Also, the songs "On St. Patrick's Day," "Oh, What Fun," and "Wearing Green," along with their American Sign Language motions, can be found on pages 54–55 of *Piggyback Songs to Sign* by Jean Warren and Susan Shroyer (Warren Publishing House, 1992).
- In addition, the song "I'm a Little Leprechaun" can be found on page 93 of *The Best of Totline Newsletter*, compiled by Jean Warren (Warren Publishing House, 1995).

# Fingerplays ————————————————————————————————————

## Leprechauns

### The Elf's Coat

| | |
|---|---|
| Under a toadstool, there sat a wee elf; | |
| He rocked to and fro and he sang to himself: | *(Rock body back and forth.)* |
| "A snippety-snappety, hi-diddle-dee! | |
| A clickety-clackety, one, two, three!" | *(Clap hands on each count.)* |
| He cut and he basted, this wee little elf; | |
| Because he was making a coat for himself. | *(Hold up imaginary coat.)* |
| "A snippety-snappety, hi-diddle-dee! | |
| A clickety-clackety, one, two, three!" | *(Clap hands on each count.)* |
| The little elf rocked and sang all night; | *(Rock back and forth.)* |
| He stitched and he sewed till the morning light. | |
| "A snippety-snappety, hi-diddle-dee! | |
| A clickety-clackety, one, two, three!" | *(Clap hands on each count.)* |
| He borrowed some green from the grass on the ground; | *(Cup hands.)* |
| From a nut on the tree, he borrowed some brown. | *(Put pointer finger and thumb together to form nut.)* |
| "A snippety-snappety, hi-diddle-dee! | |
| A clickety-clackety, one, two, three!" | *(Clap hands on each count.)* |

His coat was all done and he scampered away,     *(Make fingers "run.")*
Singing his song that was happy and gay.
"A snippety-snappety, hi-diddle-dee!
A clickety-clackety, one, two, three!"     *(Clap hands on each count.)*

                                      —Author unknown

### Elfman

*(You may wish to change the "elfman" to "leprechaun" here. It does not change the rhyme at the end of the line.)*

I met a little elfman
Down where the lilies blow;     *(Use thumb and pointer finger to indicate size.)*
I asked him why he was so small
And why he didn't grow.     *(Shrug shoulders, hands out at sides, palms up.)*
He slightly frowned and with his eyes
He looked me through and through.     *(Tilt head to side and look serious.)*
"I'm just as big for me," said he,
"As you are big for you."     *(Place hands on hips.)*

                                      —Author unknown

### Head and Shoulders, Knees and Toes: A St. Patrick's Day Twist!

*(Do motions as indicated on the first verse.)*

Head and shoulders, knees and toes, knees and toes,
Head and shoulders, knees and toes, knees and toes.
Eyes and ears, and mouth and nose,
Head and shoulders, knees and toes, knees and toes.
If I were a leprechaun, a leprechaun,     *(Point to self.)*
If I were a leprechaun, a leprechaun,
I'd have a pot full of gold.     *(Make large circle in front of body to represent pot.)*

If I were a leprechaun, a leprechaun!
If I was a troll, was a troll,     *(Point to self.)*
If I was a troll, was a troll,
I'd have horns and a mole on my nose.     *(Make "horns" on either side of head with index fingers; then point to nose.)*

If I was a troll, was a troll!
If I was a fairy, was a fairy,     *(Point to self.)*
If I was a fairy, was a fairy,
I'd have wings and fly through the air,     *(Put arms out to sides, flap, and move around.)*
If I was a fairy, was a fairy!
If I was a dragon, was a dragon,     *(Point to self.)*
If I was a dragon, was a dragon,
I'd have scales and fiery breath.     *(Point to skin, and blow out a big breath!)*
If I was a dragon, was a dragon!
SPOKEN: But I'm a person, so all I have is...
Head and shoulders, knees and toes, knees and toes,     *(Make motions as before.)*
Head and shoulders, knees and toes, knees and toes.
Eyes and ears, and mouth and nose,
Head and shoulders, knees and toes, knees and toes.

                                      —Kathy Buchsbaum
                                      Adapted traditional rhyme

## Miscellaneous

### The Fairies' Wash Day

*(You may wish to change "fairy" to "leprechaun" in this rhyme. It does not affect the end rhyme of the lines.)*

This is the fairies' wash day,
With acorn cups for tubs,                    *(Cup hands.)*
And tiny leaves for wash boards,             *(Show palms.)*
Each fairy rubs and rubs.                     *(Make scrubbing motion.)*
The fairy sheets so white and fine
Upon the grass are lying.                     *(Make spreading motion.)*
The spider spins a line for them,             *(Twirl finger.)*
And now the clothes are drying.

—Maude Burnham
*Rhymes for Little Hands* (Milton Bradley Company, 1910, pp. 35–36)

### Suppose

*(You could change "brownie" to "leprechaun" in this rhyme without affecting the rhyming lines.)*

Do you suppose a giant
Who is tall, tall, tall,                       *(Reach toward ceiling and stand on tiptoe.)*
Could ever be a brownie
Who is small, small, small?                   *(Crouch down on floor.)*
But the brownie who is tiny
Will try, try, try
To reach up to the giant
Who is high, high, high.                       *(Reach toward ceiling.)*

—Author unknown

### Tall and Small

*(This is a slightly different version of the previous rhyme. Again, you could substitute "leprechaun" for "elf" without affecting the rhyming lines.)*

Here is a giant who is tall, tall, tall.      *(Children stand up tall.)*
Here is an elf who is small, small, small.    *(Children slowly sink to floor.)*
The elf who is small will try, try, try       *(Children slowly rise.)*
To reach to the giant who is high, high, high. *(Children stand tall, stretch, and reach arms high.)*

—Author unknown

### An Irish Benediction

May the road rise up to meet you;             *(Make rising motion with hands.)*
May the wind be always at your back;          *(Put hands over shoulders.)*
May the sun shine warm upon your face;        *(Put hands on face.)*
May the rain fall soft upon your fields;      *(Flutter fingers down.)*
And until we meet again,                       *(Point to audience, then to self.)*
May your God hold you                          *(Extend hand, palm up.)*
In the palm of his hand.                       *(Close fingers of other hand in palm.)*

—Traditional rhyme

### Said This Little Fairy

*(You could change "fairy" to "leprechaun" in this rhyme. It does not affect the end rhymes. Hold five fingers up to begin the rhyme and point to each in succession.)*

Said this little fairy, "I'm as tired as can be."
Said this little fairy, "My eyes can hardly see."
Said this little fairy, "I'd like to go to bed."
Said this little fairy, "I want to rest my head."
Said this little fairy, "Come, climb the stairs with me."
One, two, three, four, five;               *(Point to each finger in turn.)*
They tiptoed just as still as could be.

—Author unknown

## Wearing Green

I wore a green shirt.                 *(Point to shirt.)*
I wore a green tie.                   *(Pretend to tie.)*
I wore green pants.                   *(Point to pants.)*
Can you guess why?                    *(Hold out hands in questioning manner.)*
I wore a green hat.                   *(Point to head.)*
So you can see                        *(Nod head.)*
On this Saint Patrick's Day.
You can't pinch me!                   *(Shake head "no" and pinch fingers in air.)*

—Susan M. Dailey
*A Storytime Year* (Neal-Schuman, 2001, pp. 56–57)

---

### More Great Fingerplays

"Five Fat Leprechauns," from page 13 of *Stories That Stick: Quick and Easy Storyboard Tales* by Valerie Marsh (Upstart, 2002), with patterns on page 46.

"Five Lively Leprechauns," from page 311 of *The Complete Daily Curriculum for Early Childhood* by Pam Schiller and Pat Phipps (Gryphon House, 2002).

"Do Your Ears Point Up?," an action rhyme, from page 257 of *1001 Rhymes and Fingerplays for Working with Young Children*, compiled by the Totline Staff (Warren Publishing House, 1995).

"Happy St. Patrick's Day" and "Five Little Leprechauns," from page 151 of *I'm a Little Teapot: Presenting Preschool Storytime*, compiled by Jane Cobb (Black Sheep Press, 1996).

"Five Lucky Leprechauns," from page 29 of *FingerTales* by Joan Hilyer Phelps (Upstart, 2002).

"The Little Man," from page 64 of *Seasonal Storytime Crafts* by Kathryn Totten (Upstart, 2002).

"Lazy Leprechaun," from page 64 of *Storytime Crafts* by Kathryn Totten (Alleyside Press, 1998).

"Five Clever Leprechauns," from page 21 of *52 Programs for Preschoolers: The Librarian's Year-Round Planner* by Diane Briggs (American Library Association, 1997).

"This Tiny Leprechaun" and "Five Little Leprechauns," from page 66 of *101 Fingerplays, Stories, and Songs to Use with Finger Puppets* by Diane Briggs (American Library Association, 1999).

"Five Little Shamrocks"and "My Shamrock," from page 258 of *1001 Rhymes and Fingerplays for Working with Young Children*, compiled by the Totline Staff (Warren Publishing House, 1995).

"Shamrock Search," an action rhyme, from page 224 of *Theme-A-Saurus II: The Great Big Book of More Mini Teaching Themes*, compiled by Jean Warren (Warren Publishing House, 1990).

"It's St. Patrick's Day," "Let's Wear Green," and "Can't Pinch Me," from pages 168–169 of *Great Big Holiday Celebrations* by Elizabeth McKinnon (Warren Publishing House, 1991).

"St. Patrick's Day," from page 35 of *Rhymes for Circle Time* by Louise B. Scott (Instructional Fair/T.S. Denison, 1999).

## Musical Selections

"Everybody's Irish on St. Patrick's Day" by Marla Lewis. Available from http://www.songsforteaching .com/.

"It's St. Patrick's Day" from *All Year* by Intelli-Tunes. Available from http://www.songsforteaching.com/.

"John John the Leprechaun" from *School Days* by Sharon, Lois, and Bram. Casablanca Kids. ASIN: B0001NPTNO.

"The Leprechaun" from *Start Each Day with a Song* from Music with Mar and Friends. Available from http://www.songsforteaching.com/.

"Leprechaun" from *Yes!* by Geof Johnson. Available from http://www.songsforteaching.com/.

"St. Patrick's Day" from *Happy Everything* by Dr. Jean. Melody House. ASIN: B000SM3N0E.

"Toora Loora (That's an Irish Lullaby)" from *Sleepy Time Lullabies* by Rachel Sumner. Rachel's Records. ASIN: B00003TKLL.

---

### More Great Music

The Songs for Teaching website offers two multiple-holiday CDs that include St. Patrick's Day songs, *Celebrate Holidays* and *Seasons and Celebrations*. Go to http://www.songsforteaching.com/ to access downloads of both music and printable lyrics.

---

## Crafts

**Pot O' Gold**    This craft can be found on page 236 of *The Best of Holidays and Seasonal Celebrations—Issues 1–4, PreK–K*, edited by Donna Borst and Janet Armbrust (Teaching and Learning Company, 1999). Reproduce the pattern on construction paper. To make the coins in the pot, use a glue stick and twist it slightly to make a circle shape. Use gold glitter to sprinkle onto the glue to make the coin shapes.

**Shamrock Wreath**    This craft can be found on page 41 of *March Patterns, Projects, and Plans to Perk Up Early Learning Programs* by Imogene Forte (Incentive Publications, 1990). You might want to simply use this as a coloring page. If you have an Ellison shamrock die, you can do this craft yourself by making the base of the craft a large paper plate with the middle cut out and die-cut shamrocks glued around the circle.

**Hearty Shamrock**    This simple craft uses three hearts to construct a shamrock shape. Instructions appear on page 232 of *Classroom Celebrations: The Best of Holidays and Seasonal Celebrations*, edited by Donna Borst (Teaching and Learning Company, 1996).

**Shamrock Man**    This cute craft makes a shamrock with facial features, and accordion-folded arms and legs. The hands and feet are smaller shamrocks! Instructions appear on page 10, and pattern on page 28 of *March Arts and Crafts, Grades 1–3*, edited by Susan Walker (The Education Center, 2000).

**Shamrock Crown**    This construction paper crown has shamrock shapes on its points! Instructions appear on page 12 and crown template appears on page 29 of *March Arts and Crafts, Grades 1–3*, edited by Susan Walker (The Education Center, 2000).

**Shamrock Prints**    This craft uses bell peppers cut in half and dipped in tempera paint to make prints. Instructions appear on page 38 of *Calendar Crafts: Things to Make and Do for Every Month, PreK–2*, by Carolyn Argyle (Teaching and Learning Company, 2006).

**Shamrock Leprechauns**    Instructions appear on page 39 of *Calendar Crafts: Things to Make and Do for Every Month, PreK–2*, by Carolyn Argyle (Teaching and Learning Company, 2006).

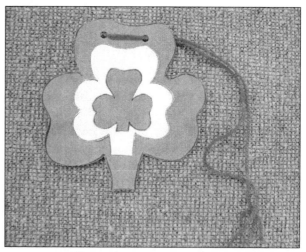

**Leprechaun Movable Puppet**   This cute leprechaun is colored, cut out, and attached with brads! The instructions show adding yarn to pull and make the puppet move, but you may wish to simplify the craft for your young participants by skipping this step. Patterns appear on pages 20–21 of *March Patterns and Projects* (Newbridge Educational, 2000).

**Shamrock Necklace**   The instructions and shamrock patterns for this necklace can be found on pages 55–56 of *Projects, Patterns and Poems for Early Education* by Marion Ruppert (Humanics Learning, 1989). The sizes of the shamrocks are graduated from small to large so they can be layered. Holes are punched and yarn is added. A similar craft could also be put together with different-sized Ellison shamrock dies.

**Shamrock Pots**   Instructions for this craft, which is a shamrock made from heart shapes and "potted" in a yogurt container, can be found on page 72 of *Arts and Crafts for All Seasons, Preschool/Kindergarten*, by the Mailbox Books Staff (The Education Center, 1999).

**Lucky Leprechaun Puppet**   The base of this craft is a paper bag. Instructions and patterns for this craft can be found on pages 80–81 of *Art Projects for All Seasons* by Karen Finch (Carson-Dellosa Publishing, 1993).

**Leprechaun Hat**   Pattern and instructions for this adorable hat can be found on page 38 of *It's Wiggle Time! Cooperative Activities to Encourage Movement* by Marilee W. Woodfield (Carson-Dellosa Publishing, 2005).

**Shamrock**   This craft makes a simple shamrock with a smiling face! Instructions and patterns for this craft can be found on pages 51–52 of *Cut and Create! for All Seasons: Easy Step-by-Step Projects That Teach Scissor Skills*, by Nancee McClure (Teaching and Learning Company, 1995).

**Shamrock Lacing Craft**   Ellison offers a shamrock lacing shape die-cut in the XL size. Cut these from card stock. Use large plastic craft needles for your yarn. As you lace, you may wish to leave enough yarn at the top so that the finished product could be hung from a doorknob! You could also add glitter to make these shamrocks really sparkle!

# Thanksgiving

*Thanksgiving is a great time of year to gather with family and friends and be thankful for all of the blessings we have! It lends itself to a variety of programming, including Pilgrims, Indians, turkeys, and Thanksgiving dinner!*

## History

The first Thanksgiving was celebrated in 1621 by the Pilgrims and Indians. This first celebration lasted several days. The Pilgrims gave thanks for the harvest that had been made possible by the Wampanoag Indians.

The Pilgrims had come to America seeking freedom from religious persecution in England. They set sail for the New World in September 1620. The ship on which they sailed was called the Mayflower. On board the ship were 44 Pilgrims who called themselves "saints" and 66 other passengers, whom the Pilgrims referred to as "strangers." The trip itself took more than 60 days to complete, and life aboard the ship was hard. Many passengers became sick and some died before land was sighted on November 10th of that year.

Once land was sighted, it was decided that some sort of an agreement had to be made between the two groups on the ship. This agreement was called the Mayflower Compact, and it unified the two groups. This unified group referred to themselves as "Pilgrims."

The Pilgrims decided to settle in Plymouth, Massachusetts, which had been named by Captain John Smith in 1614. The first winter in Plymouth was a rough one for the Pilgrims. The inclement weather hampered them in constructing houses. When spring came, the warm weather improved the health of the Pilgrims, but less than half of the original 110 who had landed had survived.

In March of 1621, an Indian named Samoset walked into the Pilgrim settlement. His greeting of "welcome" in English may have surprised the Pilgrims. He had learned the language from captains of the fishing boats that sailed off the coast. After spending the night in the settlement, he left the next day, but soon returned with another Indian named Squanto. Squanto had traveled across the ocean to England and Spain and had learned English while in England. Squanto was responsible for teaching the Pilgrims many things, among them how to plant corn in mounds with fish.

The harvest that fall was a bountiful one. The Pilgrims had much to celebrate and invited Squanto and other Indians to celebrate with them. Governor William Bradford declared a day of thanksgiving to be shared between the two groups. This celebration is thought to have taken place in mid-October.

The following year, the harvest was not as bountiful and the Pilgrims ran short on food.

The third year produced a growing season that was hot and dry and many of the crops simply died in the field. Governor Bradford ordered a day of fasting and prayer. Soon thereafter, rains came. To celebrate that year, November 29th was declared a day of thanksgiving. This date is believed to be the true beginning of our present-day Thanksgiving Day. (See Edna Barth's *Turkeys, Pilgrims, and Indian Corn: The Story of the Thanksgiving Symbols* [Seabury Press, 1975].)

The first presidential holiday proclamation ever made was by George Washington, who proclaimed November 26, 1789, a day of public thanksgiving and prayer. In 1863, President Abraham Lincoln proclaimed a national day of thanksgiving, designating the fourth Thursday of November as the holiday. (See Carol Barkin and Elizabeth James's *The Holiday Handbook* [Clarion Books, 1994].)

## Poetry

"Giving Thanks," from pages 65 of *The Big All-Year Book of Holidays and Seasonal Celebrations: Preschool/Kindergarten, Issues 14–18*, edited by Donna Borst (Teaching and Learning Company, 2002).

"Gobble Gobble," from page 119 of *Be Glad Your Nose Is on Your Face and Other Poems* by Jack Prelutsky (Greenwillow Books, 2008).

"I'm Thankful," from page 2 of *A Bad Case of the Giggles: Kids' Favorite Funny Poems* selected by Bruce Lansky (Meadowbrook Press, 1994).

"I'm Thankful," from pages 28–29 of *The New Kid on the Block* by Jack Prelutsky (Greenwillow Books, 1984).

"It's Happy Thanksgiving," "I Ate Too Much," and "Leftovers," from pages 7, 33, and 45, respectively, of *It's Thanksgiving* by Jack Prelutsky (Greenwillow Books, 1982).

"The Pilgrims Came," "Thanksgiving Time," "Turkey Time," and "The Little Girl and the Turkey," from pages 61–63 of *Month-by-Month Poetry: September, October, and November* by Marian Reiner (Scholastic Professional Books, 1999).

"Thanks for…," from page 21 of *Circle-Time Poetry Around the Year* by Jodi Simpson (Scholastic, 2005).

"Thanksgiving," from page 40 of *Autumnblings* by Douglas Florian (Greenwillow Books, 2003).

*Thanksgiving Day at Our House: Thanksgiving Poems for the Very Young* by Nancy W. Carlstrom (Simon and Schuster Books for Young Readers, 1999) offers a number of great poems for use with preschoolers.

"A Thanksgiving Thought" and "There Once Was a Turkey Named Gus," from pages 6 and 70, respectively, of *Thanksgiving: Stories and Poems* edited by Caroline Feller Bauer (HarperCollins, 1994).

"Thanksgiving Time," from page 40 of *A Child's Seasonal Treasury*, compiled and written by Betty Jones (Tricycle Press, 1996).

"Thanksgiving Turkey," from page 87 of *The Best of Holidays and Seasonal Celebrations—Issues 18–21, Grades 1–3*, edited by Donna Borst (Teaching and Learning Company, 2000).

"Thanksgiving with Grandma" and "The Wise Little Turkey," from pages 84–85 of *A School Year of Poems: 180 Favorites from Highlights* selected by Walter B. Barbe (Boyds Mills Press, 2005).

"Turkey Trot," from page 69 of *The Big All-Year Book of Holidays and Seasonal Celebrations: Preschool/Kindergarten, Issues 14–18*, edited by Donna Borst (Teaching and Learning Company, 2002).

## Books

Anderson, Derek. *Over the River: A Turkey's Tale*. Simon and Schuster Children's Publishing, 2005. ISBN: 978-0689876356.

A top-hatted father turkey, his bonnet-wearing wife, and their bespectacled chick, clutching a pilgrim doll, set out for Grandmother's house in this rendition of the classic song.

Anderson, Laurie. *Thank You, Sarah: The Woman Who Saved Thanksgiving*. Simon and Schuster Children's Publishing, 2005. ISBN: 978-0689851438.

Alarmed that the observance of Thanksgiving was dying out since many states did not observe it at all and those that did had no agreement as to a date, Sarah Hale began 38 years of letter writing in support of making it a national holiday.

Bateman, Teresa. *A Plump and Perky Turkey*. Turtleback, 2004. ISBN: 978-1417653607.

Pete, a turkey, outsmarts the townsfolk of old-time Squawk Valley as they mask their quest for a Thanksgiving entree with the premise of needing a feathered model for a themed arts-and-crafts fair.

deGroat, Diane. *We Gather Together… Now Please Get Lost*. Chronicle Books, 2001. ISBN: 978-1587170959.

> Gilbert and his class are off on a field trip to Pilgrim Town, and because he is late to school, he gets stuck with Philip the tattletale as his buddy for the day.

dePaola, Tomie. *My First Thanksgiving*. Grosset and Dunlap, 2008. ISBN: 978-0448448572.

> The traditional celebration is clearly and simply explained with spare text and dePaola's bright illustrations.

Friedman, Laurie. *Thanksgiving Rules*. Carolrhoda Books, 2009. ISBN: 978-0822579830.

> Percy Isaac Gifford, clad in his P.I.G. sweater, presents readers with a workshop on how to get the most out of Thanksgiving, complete with ten simple rules.

Hallinan, P.K. *I Am Thankful Each Day*. Ideals Publications, 2001. ISBN: 978-0824953973.

> This book introduces young children to the concept of being thankful for everything that is beautiful in our lives!

Hennessy, B.G. *One Little, Two Little, Three Little Pilgrims*. Puffin, 2001. ISBN: 978-0142300060.

> Using the "one little, two little, three little" format, pilgrim youngsters are shown engaging in a variety of activities such as caring for a pig, gathering eggs, and writing letters on a slate.

Jackson, Alison. *I Know an Old Lady Who Swallowed a Pie*. Puffin, 2002. ISBN: 978-0140565959.

> This madcap picture book stars a ravenously hungry relative who comes to Thanksgiving dinner with a pie.

Johnston, Tony. *Ten Fat Turkeys*. Turtleback, 2004. ISBN: 978-1417690602.

> Girls and boys will gobble up this hilarious story about ten goofy turkeys and their silly antics—and learn how to count backward from ten to one at the same time!

Markes, Julie. *Thanks for Thanksgiving*. HarperCollins, 2004. ISBN: 978-0060510961.

> Everyone knows that Thanksgiving is a time to give thanks. The question is, where to begin?

Melmed, Laura K. *This First Thanksgiving Day: A Counting Story*. HarperCollins, 2003. ISBN: 978-0060541842.

> Through a simple, rhyming text of 12 short poems, young readers will experience ten Wampanoag and ten Pilgrim friends getting ready for the first harvest feast in the New World.

---

### Older Gems, or Titles Too Good to Pass Up

Balian, Lorna. *Sometimes It's Turkey, Sometimes It's Feathers*. Abingdon Press, 1973. ISBN: 978-0687390745.

> When she finds a turkey egg, Mrs. Gumm decides to hatch it and have a turkey for Thanksgiving dinner.

Bunting, Eve. *A Turkey for Thanksgiving*. Clarion Books, 1991. ISBN: 978-0899197937.

> Although a paper turkey decorates Mrs. Moose's Thanksgiving table, she longs for the real thing—so her obliging husband sets out to find her one.

Kroll, Steven. *One Tough Turkey*. Holiday House, 1982. ISBN: 978-0823404575.

> This book recounts the "real story" of the first Thanksgiving when the Pilgrims pursued such tough turkeys for dinner that they had to settle for squash.

Levine, Abby. *This Is the Turkey*. Albert Whitman and Company, 2000. ISBN: 978-0807578896.

> This story is told in the pattern of "This Is the House That Jack Built." But the turkey picked out at the supermarket does not end up on the Thanksgiving dinner table!

Rockwell, Anne. *Thanksgiving Day*. HarperCollins, 1999. ISBN: 978-0060283889.

> After Charlie's teacher reads a story about the Pilgrims' first Thanksgiving, the class decides to act it out.

Milgrim, David. *Thank You, Thanksgiving.* Clarion Books, 2003. ISBN: 978-0618274666.

> As a little girl tracks through the snow to get whipped cream for the family's pumpkin pie, she stops to express her appreciation to the things around her that have given her pleasure—the clouds, the rabbits in the park, etc.

Pilkey, Dav. *'Twas the Night Before Thanksgiving.* Scholastic, 2004. ISBN: 978-0439669375.

> Patterned as a parody of the celebrated Clement Moore poem, this story of eight baby turkeys unfolds with joyous abandon and crackling vitality, as eight children embark on a Thanksgiving field trip that will change their lives forever.

Silvano, Wendi. *Turkey Trouble.* Marshall Cavendish Children, 2009. ISBN: 978-0761455295.

> As Thanksgiving approaches, Turkey fears that he will be the centerpiece of the holiday meal. Thus begins his quest for the perfect disguise so he won't be found when the time arrives. Readers will be able, after the first couple of attempted disguises, to predict who Turkey will dress up as next!

Steinberg, David. *The Turkey Ball.* Price Stern Sloan, 2005. ISBN: 978-0843114560.

> Spend the evening with some stylish turkeys at the Turkey Ball!

Wheeler, Lisa. *Turk and Runt: A Thanksgiving Comedy.* Atheneum/Richard Jackson Books, 2002. ISBN: 978-0689847615.

> Turk is the biggest, strongest, most graceful bird on Wishbone Farm. His brother Runt has figured out why people come to the farm in November, but no one wants to listen to him.

Yoon, Salina. *Five Silly Turkeys.* Price Stern Sloan, 2005. ISBN: 978-0843114164.

> From twirling on a dance floor to being chased by a bee to tanning in the sun, these are no ordinary Thanksgiving turkeys.

## Activities ———————————————————————————————————————————

> ### Coloring Pages
>
> Consult your favorite pattern books or holiday coloring books for pages to use as coloring sheets. Be sure to search online as well. There's lots of great stuff out there!
>
> - Visit http://dulemba.com/index_ColoringPages.html for author and illustrator Elizabeth O. Dulemba's great collection of holiday coloring pages. While there, sign up for her Coloring Page Tuesdays e-mails.
> - Diane deGroat has a great coloring page of Gilbert dressed in his Pilgrim finest on her website, located at http://www.dianedegroat.com/Diane_deGroat_5.html. This would be a great follow-up activity to sharing her book, located in the Books section of this chapter.

### Cut-and-Tell

**"The Pilgrims Find a Goblin"**    This great scissor tale, complete with patterns and telling instructions, can be found on pages 25–28 of *Scissor-Tales for Special Days* by Jan Grubb Philpot (Incentive Publications, 1994). The result is a turkey.

**"Little Turkey"**    This cut-and-tell story, which uses a paper plate, can be found on page 75 of *Cut and Tell: Scissor Stories for Fall* by Jean Warren (Totline Press, 1984).

### Draw-and-Tell

**"Turkey Tale"**    This draw-and-tell story can be found on pages 90–93 of *Twenty Tellable Tales: Audience Participation Folktales for the Beginning Storyteller* by Margaret Read MacDonald (H.W. Wilson, 1986).

**"A Thanksgiving Feast"**    This draw-and-tell story can be found on pages 38–39 of *Stories to Draw* by Jerry J. Mallett and Marian R. Bartch (Freline, 1982).

**"Tom Turkey"**    This appears on pages 107–108 of *Chalk in Hand: The Draw and Tell Book* by Phyllis Noe Pflomm (Scarecrow Press, 1986).

## Flannel/Velcro Board

**"Tommy Turkey"**    This story, perfect for a flannel/Velcro-board presentation, can be found on pages 119–123 of *The Everything Book for Teachers of Young Children* by Valerie Indenbaum and Marcia Shapiro (Gryphon House, 1983). Tommy is a turkey who cannot decide what color he wants to be. I can honestly say that I use this particular story every year and participants really enjoy it. Have participants join in on the "ha, ha, ha . . . ho, ho, ho . . . he, he, he" refrain! Patterns are included within the pages.

**"Running Bear's Thanksgiving"**    This is one of my all-time favorite stories to share for the Thanksgiving holiday! Running Bear has nothing to bring to the feast until he accidentally tips over his canoe! The story itself can be found on page 19 of *Short-Short Stories: Simple Stories for Young Children Plus Seasonal Activities*, compiled by Jean Warren (Warren Publishing House, 1987). I have adapted it to tell on the flannel board. A quick search of your favorite pattern books should yield the patterns you need.

**"Mixed-Up Holidays"**    This flannel/Velcro-board story in which Aunt Fanny mixes up the holidays when it is really Thanksgiving is found on pages 38–39 of *FlannelGraphs: Flannel Board Fun for Little Ones, Preschool–Grade 3*, by Jean Stangl (Fearon Teacher Aids, 1986). Patterns are found on page 72.

**"If I Knew You Were Coming!"**    Sung to the tune of the song of the same name, each verse adds something common to a Thanksgiving meal, such as mashing potatoes, baking a pie, etc. The text and patterns can be found on pages 48–51 of *Felt Board Stories* by Liz and Dick Wilmes (Building Blocks Publications, 2001).

## Games

**Feather Match**    Find a feather pattern that you like. Reproduce two feathers of the same color on colored paper. Copy as many as needed so that you have enough for your entire storyhour group. Laminate the feathers for durability. Pass out one to each participant, keeping the match for yourself. Place your feather on the flannel/Velcro board and ask for the child who has the match to bring it up! Continue until all feathers have been matched.

**Thanksgiving Match**    Patterns for a variety of Thanksgiving symbols (cornucopia, Indian boy, Pilgrim boy, Pilgrim girl, pie, turkey) appear on pages 19–30 of *Holiday Patterns*, compiled by Jean Warren (Warren Publishing House, 1991). The best patterns to use are the ones that are already enclosed in a square, as this would make cutting them out simple. Copy two of each on different colors of construction paper. Follow the instructions for the Feather Match.

## Miscellaneous

**Turkey Listening Game**    The text for this simple activity can be found on page 9 of *Holiday and Seasonal Patterns* (Edupress, 1988). The turkey pattern to color, cut out, laminate, and adhere to a paint stick can be found on page 8. I have adapted this game so that I am the only one with the turkey. I hold the turkey behind my flannel board and when the word "turkey" is mentioned in the story, I hold him up somewhere behind the board and let the participants point and say "turkey."

# Fingerplays

## Indians/Pilgrims

### Ten Little Indians

*(Count out on fingers as the rhyme progresses.)*

One little, two little, three little Indians,
Four little, five little, six little Indians,
Seven little, eight little, nine little Indians,
Ten little Indian boys.

—Traditional rhyme

### Big Indians

*(One hand represents Indians, and the other the canoe. Try to fit the number of fingers into the canoe as mentioned in the verse.)*

There were five great big Indians,
They stood so straight and tall.
They tried to fit in a little canoe,
And one of them did fall.

*(Continue with four, three, two, until…)*

There was one great big Indian,
He stood so straight and tall.
And he did fit in the little canoe,
And he paddled it right home.

—Author unknown

### Indians and Trees

This is a forest of long, long ago—
There are the trees standing all in a row.
Look very closely, what do you see? *(Hold up left hand.)*
Indians peering out—one, two, three. *(Poke three fingers of right hand through fingers of left hand.)*

Now they are hiding. The forest is still. *(Hide right fingers again.)*
Now they are hurrying over the hill.
Ever so quietly, now they are nearing *(Make fist [hill] of left hand and walk right hand over it.)*

The teepees that stand at the edge of the clearing. *(Make teepee with both hands, palms apart and fingertips up and touching.)*

—Author unknown

### Ten Little Indians

Ten little Indians standing in a line,
Ten little Indians strong, straight, and fine. *(Make all fingers stand straight.)*
Ten little Indians' tomahawks wave high, *(Pretend to wave tomahawk high over head with one hand.)*

Ten little Indians yell a war cry. Wahoo! *(Move hand back and forth in front of mouth.)*
Ten little Indians ride far out of sight, *(Put hands behind back.)*
Ten little Indians came home safe at night. *(Fingers ride back to front of body.)*
Ten little Indians to their wigwams creep, *(Put fingers straight through each other with tips up to resemble a row of wigwams.)*

Ten little Indians now are fast asleep. *(Put head on back of hands in prayer position.)*

—Author unknown

### The New Land

The Pilgrims sailed the stormy sea                    *(Wave hand like water.)*
To start a country new and free.
They met other people already there,          *(Index and middle fingers of left hand "meet"*
                                                *index and middle fingers of right hand.)*
And they had a great party on the land they    *(Spread arms wide.)*
    would share.

—Author unknown

### The Indian

This is how the Indian brave paddles his canoe,
Splash, splash, splash, splash.               *("Hold" a paddle with both hands; make two*
                                                *strokes on the right side, two on the left.)*

See how he hunts with his bow and arrow, too.
Zip, zip, zip, zip.                              *(Make action of shooting a bow and arrow.)*
Hear how he beats upon his drum.
Boom, boom, boom, boom.             *("Hold" a drum in left hand and beat with right*
                                                *hand.)*

This is how he dances when day is done.
Woo, woo, woo, woo,
Woo, woo, woo, woo.                   *(Hop twice on right foot and two times on the left,*
                                                *moving head up and down, while tapping mouth*
                                                *to make the sound.)*

—Author unknown

### Five Little Pilgrims

There were five little Pilgrims on Thanksgiving    *(Hold up five fingers and point to each in*
    Day:                                                 *succession.)*
The first one said, "I'll have cake if I may."
The second one said, "I'll have turkey roasted."
The third one said, "I'll have chestnuts toasted."
The fourth one said, "I will have pumpkin pie."
The fifth one said, "I'll have jam by and by,"
But before they had any turkey and dressing,
The Pilgrims all said a Thanksgiving blessing.    *(Fold hands, as if in prayer.)*

—Author unknown

### The Brave Little Indian (Pilgrim)

The brave little Indian (Pilgrim)              *(Puff out chest.)*
Went looking for a bear.                       *(Put hand over eyes, searching.)*
He looked in the woods                    *(Continue to search.)*
And everywhere.                          *(Spread hands to show expanse.)*
The brave little Indian                    *(Puff out chest.)*
Found a big bear—                      *(Spread hands to show height.)*
He ran like a rabbit!                     *(Run in place.)*
Oh, what a scare!                         *(Put hands on cheeks.)*

—Author unknown

**The First Thanksgiving**

Five little Pilgrims fish in the morn.     *(Hold up right hand.)*
Five little Indians help them plant corn.     *(Hold up left hand.)*
Pilgrims bring bread.     *(Move right hand closer to center.)*
Indians bring meat.     *(Move left hand closer to center.)*
Ten new friends sit down to eat.     *(Fold hands together; place in lap.)*

—Jan Irving and Robin Currie
*Mudlicious* (Libraries Unlimited, 1986, p. 171)

## Thanksgiving

**Thanksgiving Dinner**

Every day we eat our dinner.
Our table is very small.     *(Place palms of hands close together.)*
There's room for father, mother, sister,     *(Point to each finger.)*
    brother and me—that's all.
But when it's Thanksgiving Day
And the company comes,
You'd scarcely believe your eyes.     *(Rub eyes.)*
For that very same reason,
The table stretches until it is just this size!     *(Stretch arms wide.)*

—Author unknown

**Thanksgiving Feast**

*(Pretend to do things suggested.)*

Stuff the turkey,     Toss the salad,
Knead the bread,     Slice the tomatoes.
Open some beans—     Grind the cranberries,
No, corn instead.     Serve pumpkin pie.
Peel the yams,     Our Thanksgiving feast
Mash the potatoes,     Is piled a mile high!     *(Hold hand high in air.)*

—Susan M. Dailey
*A Storytime Year* (Neal-Schuman, 2001, p. 308)

**Frozen Thanksgiving Meal**

*(This action song is sung to the tune of "Mary Had a Little Lamb.")*

Let's all be a turkey fat,     *(Flap arms tucked like wings.)*
Turkey fat, turkey fat.
Let's all be a turkey fat,
For Thanksgiving Day.

FREEZE!     *(Everyone freezes in this position.)*

Let's all be a Jell-o mold,     *(Wiggle all over.)*
Jell-o mold, Jell-o mold.
Let's all be a Jell-o mold,
For Thanksgiving Day.

FREEZE!     *(Freeze in the wiggle.)*

Let's all be a dinner roll,                          *(Squat down on floor, grasp knees, and rock back and forth.)*

Dinner roll, dinner roll.
Let's all be a dinner roll,
For Thanksgiving Day.

FREEZE!                                              *(Freeze in place.)*

Let's all be a pumpkin pie,                          *(Circle face with hands; puff out cheeks.)*
Pumpkin pie, pumpkin pie.
Let's all be a pumpkin pie,
For Thanksgiving Day.

FREEZE!                                              *(Freeze in place.)*

—Jan Irving and Robin Currie
*Mudlicious* (Libraries Unlimited, 1986, pp. 172–173)

## Turkeys

### Gobble, Gobble Turkey

Gobble, gobble, turkey,
Running all around.                                  *(Run in place.)*
Gobble, gobble, turkey,
Pecking on the ground.                               *(Use one hand to peck on palm of other hand.)*
Gobble, gobble, turkey,
Standing up so straight.                             *(Stand up straight.)*
Gobble, gobble, turkey,
Running through the gate.                            *(Run in place again.)*

—Traditional rhyme

### Five Little Turkeys

Five little turkeys flew up in a tree.              *(Hold up one hand.)*
The first one said, "There's a man I see."          *(Point to thumb.)*
The second one said, "He's coming this way."        *(Point to pointer finger.)*
The third one said, "It's Thanksgiving Day."        *(Point to middle finger.)*
The fourth one said, "What's he going to do?"       *(Point to ring finger.)*
The fifth one said, "He's coming after you."        *(Point to little finger.)*
Chop went the axe before they flew away.            *(Clap hands on "chop.")*
They all were on the table on Thanksgiving Day.     *(Make table of one hand for "turkeys" and of other hand to sit.)*

—Author unknown

### Five Fat Turkeys

Five fat turkeys were sitting on a fence.           *(Hold one hand up.)*
The first one said, "I'm so immense!"               *(Point to thumb.)*
The second one said, "I can gobble at you."         *(Point to pointer finger.)*
The third one said, "I can gobble too."             *(Point to middle finger.)*
The fourth one said, "I can spread my tail."        *(Point to ring finger.)*
The fifth one said, "Don't catch it on a nail."     *(Point to little finger.)*
A farmer came along and stopped to say,             *(Raise pointer finger of other hand.)*
"Turkeys look best on Thanksgiving Day."

—Author unknown

### Mr. Turkey

| | |
|---|---|
| Mr. Turkey's tail is big and wide. | *(Spread fingers.)* |
| He swings it when he walks. | *(Swing hands.)* |
| His neck is long. | *(Stretch neck.)* |
| His chin is red. | *(Stroke chin.)* |
| And he gobbles when he talks. | *(Open and close hands and gobble.)* |

—Author unknown

### A Turkey

| | |
|---|---|
| A turkey I saw on Thanksgiving, | |
| His tail was spread so wide, | *(Put hands together, fingers spread, thumbs touching.)* |
| And he said, "Shh…don't tell that you've seen me, | *(Put finger to lips.)* |
| For I am running away to hide." | *(Use two fingers to run away.)* |

—Author unknown

### Ten Fat Turkeys

| | |
|---|---|
| Ten fat turkeys standing in a row. | |
| They spread their wings and tails just so. | *(Hold up all ten fingers spread wide.)* |
| They strut to the left. | *(Move hands in jumps to the left.)* |
| They strut to the right. | *(Move hands in jumps to the right.)* |
| They all stand up ready to fight. | *(Hold hands up.)* |
| Along comes a man with a great big gun— | *(Extend right arm and put left hand under right elbow.)* |
| Bang! You should see those turkeys run! | *(After "bang," run both hands to hide behind back.)* |

—Author unknown

### Our Turkey

| | |
|---|---|
| Our turkey is a big fat bird. | *(Hold hands far apart.)* |
| He gobbles when he talks. | *(Open and close hand to indicate gobbling.)* |
| His long red chin is drooping down. | *(Cup hand under chin.)* |
| He waddles when he walks. | *(Move hands up and down alternately, slightly apart.)* |
| His tail is like a spreading fan. | |
| On Thanksgiving Day— | *(Hold up and spread out fingers of one hand.)* |
| He spreads his tail high in the air | |
| And whoooooooosh—he flies away! | *(Shoot hand up into air.)* |

—Author unknown

### Here Is a Turkey

| | |
|---|---|
| Here is a turkey with his tail spread wide. | *(Hold up right hand with fingers spread.)* |
| He sees the farmer coming, so he's trying to hide. | *(Advance left hand.)* |
| He runs across the barnyard, wobble, wobble, wobble. | *(Move right hand from side to side.)* |
| Talking turkey talk, gobble, gobble, gobble. | *(Open and close right hand.)* |

—Author unknown

### Five Little Turkeys

*(Begin rhyme with five fingers up. Point to each in succession as the rhyme progresses.)*

Five little turkeys standing in a row.
First little turkey said, "I don't want to grow."
Second little turkey said, "Why do you say that?"

Third little turkey said, "I want to get fat."
Fourth little turkey said, "Thanksgiving is near."
Fifth little turkey said, "Yes, that's what I hear."
Then the five little turkeys that were standing
 in a row
All together said, "Come on, let's GO!"                    *(Run hand behind back.)*

                                                                                    —Author unknown

### Turkey Gobbler

I met a turkey gobbler                                  *(Point to self.)*
When I went out to play.
"Mr. Turkey Gobbler, how are you today?"               *(For turkey, use fingers and thumb of one hand to
                                                        represent mouth; move as he talks.)*

"Gobble, gobble, gobble, that I cannot say,
Don't ask me such a question on Thanksgiving Day."

                                                                                    —Author unknown

### Thanksgiving Turkey

Hobble goes the turkey,
See him strut along.                                   *(Put hands on hips, squat down, and walk "turkey"
                                                        fashion.)*

"Gobble," says the turkey.                             *(Rise up slightly; stretch neck.)*
He'll not be here long!                                *(Run and hide.)*

                                                                                    —Author unknown

### Five Fat Turkeys Are We

Five fat turkeys are we.                               *(Hold up five fingers.)*
We slept all night in a tree.                          *(Put head on hands, sleeping.)*
When the cook came around,
We couldn't be found.                                  *(Shake head "no.")*
So that's why we're here, you see.                     *(Peek head from behind hands.)*

                                                                                    —Traditional rhyme

### Turkey in the Straw

Turkey in the straw and turkey in the pan.
I am saying, "Thank you" as nicely as I can.
Turkey in the oven, turkey in the hay,
All I want is turkey on Thanksgiving Day.              *(Do the turkey walk. Hold head high and walk
                                                        with stiff legs.)*

                                                                                    —Traditional rhyme

## Miscellaneous

### I Am Thankful

*(Count on fingers the things that are listed.)*

I am thankful for pets.                                I am thankful for all the new friends that I meet.
I am thankful for school.                              I am thankful for health,
I am thankful when I can swim in a pool.               And for my family.
I am thankful for home,                                I'm especially thankful
And the food that I eat.                               That I am just ME!          *(Point to self.)*

                                                                                    —Author unknown

**Thankful**

*(This is sung to the tune of "The Muffin Man.")*

Tell me what you're thankful for,                    *(Place hands in prayer position.)*
Thankful for, thankful for.
Tell me what you're thankful for,
On this Thanksgiving Day.                             *(Ask children to suggest things that they are thankful*
                                                     *for, and add verses!)*

—Susan M. Dailey
*A Storytime Year* (Neal-Schuman, 2001, p. 308)

---

### More Great Fingerplays

"Getting Ready for the First Thanksgiving," from page 9 of *Turkey Days* by Susan O. Higgins (Totline Publications, 1999).

"It Smells Like Thanksgiving" and "Thanksgiving Time," from page 238 of *1001 Rhymes and Fingerplays for Working with Young Children*, compiled by the Totline Staff (Warren Publishing House, 1994).

"Just Like That," "Do the Turkey Hop," and "Five Little Turkeys," from pages 236–237 of *1001 Rhymes and Fingerplays for Working with Young Children*, compiled by the Totline Staff (Warren Publishing House, 1994).

---

## Musical Selections ——————————————————————————————————————

"Albuquerque Turkey," "Over the River," "Gobble! Gobble!," and "We Give Thanks" from *Happy Everything* by Dr. Jean. Melody House. ASIN: B000SM3N0E.

"Every Day Is Thanksgiving" from *Months of Music* by Karen Rupprecht and Pam Minor. Available from http://www.songsforteaching.com/.

"First Thanksgiving" from *U.S.A. Hooray!* Available from http://www.songsforteaching.com/.

"Friends and Family," "Give Thanks," and "Powwow" from *Rhythms and Rhymes for Special Times* by Jack Hartmann. Available from http://www.songsforteaching.com/.

"Give Thanks" from *Whoooo Likes Halloween?* by Pam Minor. Available from http://www.songsforteaching.com/.

"Happy Thanksgiving to All" from *Holidays and Special Times* by Greg and Steve. Youngheart. ASIN: B00000DGN5.

"I Just Want to Say Thank You" from *Holiday Songs* by Wendy Rollin. Available from http://www.songsforteaching.com/.

"Let's Have a Dinner: Thanksgiving" by Andy Glockenspiel. Available from http://www.songsforteaching.com/.

"Thank You for Thanksgiving" from *Friends* by Two of a Kind. Available from http://www.songsforteaching.com/.

"The Thanksgiving Song" from *Holly Daze* by Mary Miche. Available from http://www.songsforteaching.com/.

"Things I'm Thankful For" from *Holiday Songs and Rhythms* by Hap Palmer. Available from http://www.songsforteaching.com/.

"Turkey Hunt" and "Fly Turkey" from *Songs for All Seasons* by Geof Johnson. Available from http://www.songsforteaching.com/.

"Turkey Trot" from *All Year* by Intelli-Tunes. Available from http://www.songsforteaching.com/.

## Crafts

**Thanksgiving Turkey**    This pattern appears on page 83 of *Holidays Through the Year*, edited by Sharon Murphy (The Education Center, 1999). Allow participants to color the turkey and then add feather shapes in different colors!

**Handprint Turkeys**    Like me, you probably remember making these turkeys in grade school. Have participants (with help) trace their hands on a piece of construction paper. The thumb is, of course, the turkey's head, so draw on eyes and a mouth. Color the other fingers in to represent tail feathers. Color the palm area of the hand brown or black. Draw legs for your turkey. A simple craft, but one that will bring back great memories!

**Thanksgiving Pilgrim Hat**    Instructions and patterns can be found on pages 27–28 of *Cut and Create! Holidays: Easy Step-by-Step Projects That Teach Scissor Skills* by Kim Rankin (Teaching and Learning Company, 1997). This craft makes a nice-sized hat, complete with buckle. Add a piece of magnetic strip to the back for a holiday decoration for the refrigerator. This craft would also be easy for families to replicate to use as place cards for their Thanksgiving tables!

**Gobble! Gobble! Turkey**    Instructions for this hand and footprint turkey appear on page 17 of *The Best of The Mailbox Magazine Arts and Crafts, Grades 1–3*, edited by Karen A. Brunak (The Education Center, 1999).

**Cornucopia Craft**    Patterns for this sizeable cornucopia and fruit that can be colored and then glued together appear on pages 52–53 of *November Patterns, Projects, and Plans to Perk Up Early Learning Programs* by Imogene Forte (Incentive Publications, 1989).

**Mr. Curly Tail Turkey**    This cute craft makes a turkey whose tail feathers (made from green, yellow and orange construction paper) are curled around a pencil. You may wish to divide the patterns up and make a sheet with separate body patterns (brown paper), feet (orange paper), and the feathers (separate sheets of green, yellow, and orange paper that participants can share). Detailed instructions and patterns appear on pages 128–129 of *Calendar Crafts: Things to Make and Do for Every Month, PreK–2*, by Carolyn Argyle (Teaching and Learning Company, 2006).

**Turkey Cup-Hugger**    Pattern and instructions for this simple craft appear on page 33 of *Seasonal Storytime Crafts* by Kathryn Totten (Upstart, 2002). The turkey pattern has outstretched arms that wrap around a small Dixie cup. When I do this craft, I like to fill each small cup with candy corn once it is completed!

**Indian Corn**    Instructions and patterns for this craft can be found on pages 29–30 of *Arts and Crafts for All Seasons, Preschool/Kindergarten*, by the Mailbox Books Staff (The Education Center, 1999). The patterns provide an ear of corn shape and a husk shape that you will want to duplicate twice. The children use tempera paint in Indian corn colors (red, orange, black, and brown). Have them dip their fingers into the different colors of paint and cover the corn shape with these colors. Add the husks once the paint is dried.

**Turkey Lacing Card**    The pattern for this craft can be found on page 52 of *Seasonal Cut-Ups* by Marilynn G. Barr (Monday Morning Books, 2005). Reproduce the pattern on either construction paper or card stock. Provide participants with crayons, hole punch, yarn, and large plastic needles. Have them color their turkeys (and background, if desired). Allow them to either straight-lace or loop-lace their yarn around the picture. These two types of lacing are explained on page 7. They may wish to leave enough yarn at the top of the picture so that this craft can be hung on a doorknob!

**Cornucopia**    Instructions and patterns for this cute craft with a cornucopia and fruit with smiling faces can be found on pages 13–15 of *Cut and Create! For All Seasons: Easy Step-by-Step Projects That Teach Scissor Skills*, by Nancee McClure (Teaching and Learning Company, 1995).

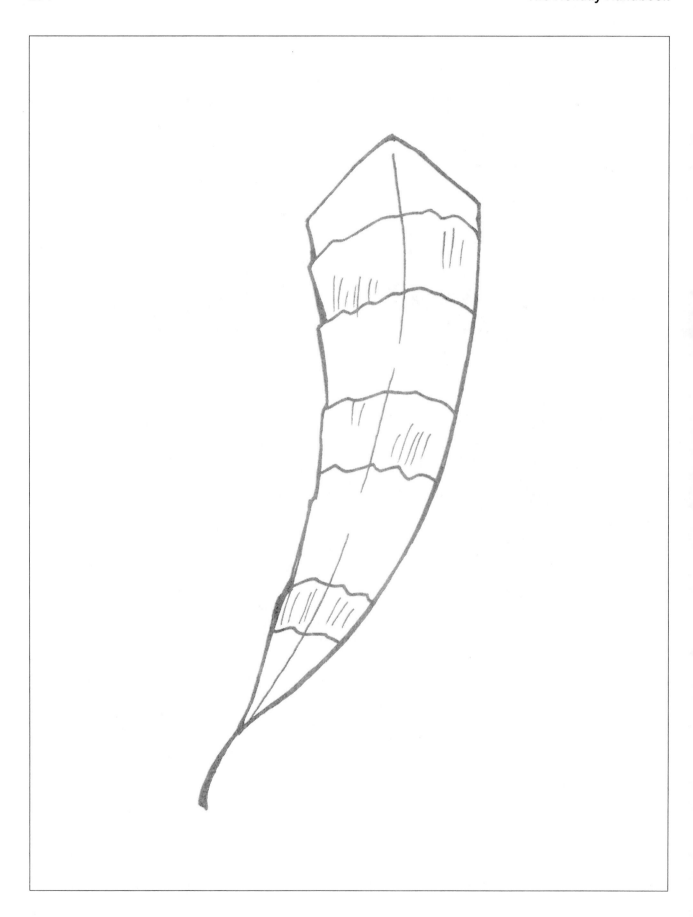

# Valentine's Day

*Hearts, cupids, and candy—it's a day to tell that someone special how much you love him or her!*

## History

The history of this holiday has many stories surrounding it. Some people think that it can be traced back to an ancient Roman festival called Lupercalia. As part of this celebration, Romans hoped that their crops would be bountiful and that their animals would be safe. Many people say that the holiday honors Saint Valentine, one of the saints in the early Christian church who died on February 14th. Still others say that the day celebrates an old English belief that birds choose their mates on the 14th of February!

It is interesting to note that for centuries, the celebration of Valentine's Day in any form was not held, due to the influence of Christianity. The church throughout the world did away with all of the festivals that were considered pagan. It was not until the 1660s in England that the celebration of Valentine's Day was reestablished. And it was well into the eighteenth century before Valentine cards made their first appearance.

Settlers to the New World brought with them their Valentine's Day customs. The holiday seems to have both waxed and waned in the late nineteenth and early twentieth centuries. In the 1920s, there were revivals of the holiday in both the United States and England that have continued into the present day. People of all ages enjoy participating in parties and the exchanging of Valentine cards, candy, and flowers. (See Edna Barth's *Hearts, Cupids, and Red Roses: The Story of the Valentine Symbols* [Houghton Mifflin/Clarion Books, 1974].)

## Poetry

"I Made My Dog a Valentine," "My Special Cake," "My Mother's Chocolate Valentine," "I Love You More Than Applesauce," and "My Father's Valentine," from pages 17, 23, 32, 36, and 42, respectively, of *It's Valentine's Day* by Jack Prelutsky (Greenwillow, 1983).

---

### Poetry Programming Ideas

"My Father's Valentine" is a great poem to illustrate as it is read. Start out with a regular-sized heart, cut lop-sided on purpose. The heart will be cut down at least four more times during the poem, ending up "not much bigger than a bean"!

"My Mother's Chocolate Valentine" is probably my all-time favorite Valentine poem! I use it every single year. The text of the poem can also be found online. I print the poem on pink paper, embellish it with Ellison die-cut hearts, and laminate for durability. I also have an actual Valentine candy box that I hold as I read the poem. At the end of the poem, I open up the box to reveal that it's empty! This always gets a laugh from kids and parents alike!

---

"The Porcupine" by Karla Kuskin, from page 6 of *Valentine's Day: Stories and Poems*, edited by Caroline Feller Bauer (HarperCollins, 1993).

"Roses Are Red," from http://www.dltk-holidays.com/valentines/m-rosesarered.htm, including a small poster-sized copy that you can print, laminate, and use for your program.

"The Valentine" by Linda G. Paulsen, from page 113 of *The Poetry Break: An Annotated Anthology with Ideas for Introducing Children to Poetry* by Caroline Feller Bauer (H.W. Wilson, 1995).

"Valentines" by Aileen Fisher, from page 174 of *The Poetry Break: An Annotated Anthology with Ideas for Introducing Children to Poetry* by Caroline Feller Bauer (H.W. Wilson, 1995).

"Warteena Weere Just Bit My Ear," from page 110 of *Something Big Has Been Here* by Jack Prelutsky (Greenwillow Books, 1990).

# Books

Bateman, Teresa. *Will You Be My Valenswine?* Albert Whitman and Company, 2005. ISBN: 978-0807591956.

> On Valentine's Day, poor Polly Piglet searches all over the barnyard, but can't find the perfect valenswine. She is just about to give up, but is it possible the right valenswine has been right under her snout all along?

Bridwell, Norman. *Clifford's First Valentine's Day*. Cartwheel Books, 2009. ISBN: 978-0545200110.

> Clifford gets into a heap of trouble as he gets covered with valentine paste, falls into a post office chute, and disappears in a mountain of mail.

Cooke, Brandy. *My Valentine*. Little Simon, 2010. ISBN: 978-1442407794.

> This sweet story all about Valentine's Day features adorable animals—a bunny, a fox, a kitten and a butterfly—celebrating this lovey-dovey holiday with flowers, chocolate, and more! This chunky, heart-shaped board book features glossy, red edges.

deGroat, Diane. *Love, Lola*. Turtleback, 2002. ISBN: 978-0613852388.

> Gilbert's sister Lola secretly delivers valentines to everyone she loves—even her brother. But the biggest surprise of all is addressed to Lola herself!

Friedman, Laurie. *Ruby Valentine Saves the Day*. Carolrhoda Books, 2010. ISBN: 978-0761342133.

> Ruby invites everyone to a grand Valentine's Day party at her mountaintop home, but when a blizzard keeps her guests away, she decides to take the carefully planned party into town.

Hudson, Eleanor. *The Best Thing about Valentine's Day*. Cartwheel Books, 2004. ISBN: 978-0439521093.

> A sweet rhyming story, narrated by a young child who loves to make cards and give them to family, friends, and classmates.

Huelin, Jodi. *Countdown to Valentine's Day*. Price Stern Sloan, 2002. ISBN: 978-0843148824.

> From 10 colored valentines to 1 special kiss, readers will be delighted as they count their way through this brightly colored paperback.

Katz, Karen. *Where Is Baby's Valentine?* Little Simon, 2006. ISBN: 978-1416909712.

> Baby made a valentine for Mommy. Where could it be?

Kroll, Steven. *The Biggest Valentine Ever*. Cartwheel Books, 2006. ISBN: 978-04397644193.

> When Mrs. Mousely asks her class to make valentines, Clayton and Desmond decide to make one together and give it to their teacher as a surprise. But things don't go as planned.

Mayer, Mercer. *Happy Valentine's Day, Little Critter!* HarperFestival, 2005. ISBN: 978-0060539739.

> It's Valentine's Day and Little Critter is celebrating. He makes an extra-special card for an extra-special valentine.

Modesitt, Jeanne. *1, 2, 3 Valentine's Day: A Counting Book*. Boyds Mills Press, 2002. ISBN: 978-1563978685.

> Mister Mouse goes house to house distributing valentines to his animal friends.

Numeroff, Laura. *Happy Valentine's Day, Mouse!* Balzer & Bray, 2009. ISBN: 978-0061804328.

> Join Mouse as he celebrates Valentine's Day with all the friends he loves.

Parish, Herman. *Amelia Bedelia's First Valentine*. Greenwillow Books, 2009. ISBN: 978-0061544583.

> Amelia Bedelia is sure she will love everything about Valentine's Day.

---

### Older Gems, or Titles Too Good to Pass Up

Bourgeois, Paulette. *Franklin's Valentines*. Turtleback, 1999. ISBN: 978-0613115575.
  The Valentine's Day party has begun at last, but Franklin lost his cards on the way to school.

Capucilli, Alyssa S. *Biscuit's Valentine's Day*. Turtleback, 2000. ISBN: 978-0613708571.
  It's Valentine's Day and Biscuit and the little girl have a lot of special deliveries to make!

Donnelly, Liza. *Dinosaur Valentine*. Scholastic, 1994. ISBN: 978-0590464159.
  A mysterious invitation to a Valentine's Day party starts an adventure between a dog and a comptosaurus.

London, Jonathan. *Froggy's First Kiss*. Turtleback, 2000. ISBN: 978-0613229890.
  Froggy falls in love with Frogilina, who reciprocates with adoring glances and treats from her lunchbox.

Spinelli, Eileen. *Somebody Loves You, Mr. Hatch*. Turtleback, 1996. ISBN: 978-0785776598.
  Colorless Mr. Hatch—who works in a shoelace factory and eats a cheese and mustard sandwich for lunch every day—is jarred by receiving a huge Valentine box of candy with a card that says only, "Somebody loves you."

---

Rey, H.A. *Happy Valentine's Day, Curious George*. HMH Books, 2011. ISBN: 978-0547131070.
  George and his friends celebrate Valentine's Day with decorating, baking, card making and some unexpected hilarity along the way!

Roberts, Bethany. *Valentine Mice!* Sandpiper, 2001. ISBN: 978-0618051526.
  Four bustling mice deliver Valentine's Day cards to animals living in a snowy forest.

Schaefer, Lola. *Guess Who? A Foldout Valentine's Adventure*. Little Simon, 2009. ISBN: 978-1416959106.
  In this adorable board book, kids can read the riddles and unfold the pages for a giant surprise!

Scotton, Rob. *Love, Splat*. HarperCollins, 2008. ISBN: 978-0007293407.
  Splat has a crush on Kitten, a fluffy white cat with pea-green eyes, but he isn't the only one!

Sutherland, Margaret. *Valentines Are for Saying I Love You*. Grosset and Dunlap, 2007. ISBN: 978-0448447025.
  In this sweet tale, a little girl makes a special valentine for everyone.

Wilson, Sarah. *Love and Kisses*. Candlewick Press, 2005. ISBN: 978-0763620110.
  Love may go a long way, but it always comes back to you. That's the message of this humorous book.

Wing, Natasha. *The Night Before Valentine's Day*. Grosset and Dunlap, 2000. ISBN: 978-0448421889.
  Kids dream of candy hearts in this takeoff of Clement C. Moore's beloved poem. The next day at school is a day of parties and games—and a surprise visitor bearing a Valentine's gift for the whole class!

## Activities ————————————————————————————————————

### Coloring Pages

Consult your favorite pattern books or holiday coloring books for pages to use as coloring sheets. Be sure to search online as well. There's lots of great stuff out there!

- Visit http://dulemba.com/index_ColoringPages.html for author and illustrator Elizabeth O. Dulemba's great collection of holiday coloring pages. While there, sign up for her Coloring Page Tuesdays e-mails.

### Cut-and-Tell

**"The Queen of Hearts: A Valentine's Day Paper Caper"**    The text, instructions, and patterns for this story are found on pages 40–42 of *Scissor-Tales for Special Days* by Jan Grubb Philpot (Incentive

Publications, 1994). The result is a Queen of Hearts with a two-piece skirt, which, when moved behind her, makes a heart!

**"V"**    This cut-and-tell story, which ends up being valentines, is found on pages 66–67 of *Paper Cutting Stories from A to Z* by Valerie Marsh (Alleyside Press, 1992).

## Draw-and-Tell

**"Claudette's Valentines"**    This draw-and-tell story can be found on pages 10–15 of *Frog's Riddle and Other Draw-and-Tell Stories* by Richard Thompson (Annick Press, 1990).

**"A Valentine"**    This draw-and-tell story, which is a valentine and some kisses, appears on page 95 of *Chalk in Hand: The Draw and Tell Book* by Phyllis Noe Pflomm (Scarecrow Press, 1986).

## Flannel/Velcro Board

**"Making Valentines"**    I do this poem as a flannel/Velcro-board activity nearly every single year! The text for this poem is provided in the Fingerplays section of this chapter. I have saved valentine cards over the years and have been able to find ones to fit every line of the poem! You may be able to pick up valentines at garage/yard sales or thrift stores. Or, have friends, neighbors, and co-workers save them for you! I have laminated them for durability and placed Velcro on the backs so that I can place them on my board.

**"Five Little Valentines"**    This rhyme is from page 251 of *1001 Rhymes and Fingerplays for Working with Young Children*, compiled by the Totline Staff (Warren Publishing House, 1994). To illustrate the rhyme, I simply take red hearts cut to the size of the middle of a heart-shaped white doily and glue them on top of it. I then laminate for durability and place Velcro on the back.

**"Hearts Everywhere"**    To illustrate this rhyme, I searched for images on Google and found pictures called for in the rhyme. I enlarged or reduced, depending on what was needed, and printed them out. I backed them on red construction paper, laminated them, and placed Velcro on the back to secure them to the board. Here is the rhyme:

|                        |                      |
| ---------------------- | -------------------- |
| Hearts on the cake,    | Hearts on the table, |
| Hearts on the box,     | Hearts on the chair, |
| Hearts on the shoes,   | Hearts on the shelf, |
| Hearts on the socks,   | Hearts everywhere!   |

When doing the rhyme, I will pause before I show the picture and let the participants see the picture and guess the word.

**"Little Valentines"**    This rhyme is from page 253 of *1001 Rhymes and Fingerplays for Working with Young Children*, compiled by the Totline Staff (Warren Publishing House, 1994). Illustrate it with five valentine hearts. Make sure the first is pink and blue. You might want to add smiling faces to the valentines as well.

**"Five Little Valentines"**    This rhyme appears in the Fingerplays section of this chapter. It also appears on page 68 of *Circle Time Book for Holidays and Seasons* by Liz and Dick Wilmes (Building Blocks Publications, 1984). The clip art that appears on that page can also be enlarged and used to illustrate your rhyme, right down to the box needed.

**"Color Valentines"**    This rhyme for the flannel/Velcro board can be found on page 115 of *The Best of Totline Flannelboards* by Kathleen Cubley (Totline Publications, 2000). The pattern to use is found on page 116. Allow participants to say the color of the valentine as it is placed on the board.

## Games

**Valentine Matching Game**    Use the patterns found on page 31 of *February Patterns and Projects* (Newbridge Educational, 2000) and reproduce them on different colors of construction paper for a valentine matching game. Great patterns (Cupid, heart, mailbox, valentine) can also be found on pages 83–90 of *Holiday Patterns*, compiled by Jean Warren (Warren Publishing House, 1991). Use the ones contained in a circle, as this will make cutting them out simple. Laminate for durability. Pass out one of the patterns to participants, keeping one for yourself and placing it in an apron pocket or container of some sort. Take out your copies, one at a time, placing them on your flannel/ Velcro board, and allowing participants to match them. Another variation on this matching game is to simply use hearts of different colors (cutting out two of each). Ellison dies work great for this purpose.

**Musical Circle of Hearts Game**    This great idea comes from BabyZone.com. Cut matching pairs of hearts from an assortment of colored construction paper. Laminate for durability. Place one heart of each pair in a box. Tape the remaining hearts to the floor in a circle. Players walk on the circle of hearts to music. When the music stops, each player must stand on one of the hearts. One heart is drawn from the box and the player standing on the matching heart gets a chance to choose a heart from the box for the next walk. Repeat as many times as participants want to play.

## Miscellaneous

**Valentine Exchange**    The week before celebrating, send home a handout for parents asking them to have valentines ready for their children to bring. Since they may not know names of all of the children in their storyhour group (and there is always the chance that new children will show up week to week), ask that they simply address their valentines "To a Friend." An activity that I do each year is to make some sort of carrier to take the valentines home that day. Of course, along with valentines, there is always candy!

An easy way to keep the cards organized is to have a designated area (such as a long table) where cards (and sometimes candy) are dropped off prior to the storyhour. Have Post-it notes handy. As each child brings in his or her cards/candy, write his or her name on a Post-it and adhere it to the table. The participants' cards are then placed there along with the names. Once they have made their valentine card carrier as a craft, each participant can go around the table and pick up a card/candy from everyone except themselves. This completely eliminates participants going around table to table passing out cards and sometimes missing someone in the confusion.

**Valentine Surprise!**    The dot-to-dot pattern for this activity can be found on page 195 of *The Best of Holidays and Seasonal Celebrations—Issues 5–8, PreK–K*, edited by Donna Borst (Teaching and Learning Company, 2000). Reproduce the pattern and laminate for durability. Using a dry-erase marker, encourage participants to say the alphabet letters with you that will complete the dot-to-dot picture. When you are finished, the picture is a heart! Note: If you clean the dry-erase marker soon after use, this activity can be reused.

**Red Shapes**    Have a variety of shapes cut from red construction paper. You may choose to do traditional shapes such as circles, squares, triangles, and rectangles, or shapes such as balloons, dogs, cats, hearts, etc. My shapes are cut from some large (8½-by-11-inch) shape stencils that I acquired years ago. In order to be sure that you have enough shapes for all participants, cut multiples of each shape. Laminate them if you choose, but I have found that mine have lasted just as well without. Pass out shapes to participants and once everyone has a shape, sing the following song (to the tune of "London Bridge"): "If you have a red triangle, red triangle, red triangle…if you have a red triangle, please stand up!" Continue until participants holding all shapes are standing. You can sing the song again if you like, having participants "please sit down" on the last line.

**"Heart Colors"**    The text of this song, sung to the tune of "The Farmer in the Dell," can be found on page 16 of *Valentine Days: Celebrating Valentine's Day with Rhymes, Songs, Projects, Games and Snacks* by Susan Olson Higgins (Totline Publications, 2000). Use this rhyme as an action song with your participants. Have hearts of all different colors cut out and pass them out to participants. Then sing the song, and when the colors are mentioned, have them hold up that particular color heart. You may wish to provide each child with two (or more) hearts for a variety of verses and colors.

# Fingerplays ——————————————————————————————————————

## Valentines

### Counting Valentines

*(This would make a great flannel/Velcro-board presentation. Have a valentine shape in each of the colors mentioned and place on the board when that color is mentioned.)*

Valentines, valentines,
How many do I see?
Valentines, valentines,
Count them with me.
I have red ones, orange ones,
Yellow ones, too.

I have green ones, purple ones,
And some that are blue.
Valentines, valentines,
How many do I see?
Count them with me!
1-2-3-4-5-6.

*(Count out the hearts and identify the colors again, perhaps as you take them off the board.)*

—Author unknown

### Making Valentines

*(This can be done as either a fingerplay or as a flannel/Velcro-board presentation. If you are lucky, you may find actual valentines that look like each of those represented. Laminate them for durability and use for flannel/Velcro board.)*

In February, what shall I do?
I'll make some valentines for you.
The first will have a Cupid's face.

*(Tilt head, questioningly.)*

*(If doing as a fingerplay, hold up one finger, and then add others as the rhyme progresses.)*

The second will be trimmed in lace.
The third will have some roses pink.
The fourth will have a verse in ink.
The fifth will have a ribbon bow.
The sixth will glisten like the snow.
The seventh will have some lines I drew.
The eighth, some flowers—just a few.
The ninth will have three little birds.
The tenth will have three little words:
I LOVE YOU!

—Author unknown

### Valentines

Valentines, valentines,
Red, white, and blue.
I'll find a nice one,
And give it to you!

*(Form heart with fingers.)*

*(Point to friend.)*

—Author unknown

### Be My Valentine

| | |
|---|---|
| Listen, Mother, | *(Point to ear.)* |
| You know what? | |
| On Valentine's Day, | |
| I love you a lot. | *(Open arms wide.)* |
| So, I'll throw a kiss | *(Throw kiss.)* |
| Mother mine. | |
| I want you for | |
| My Valentine. | *(Form heart with hands.)* |

—Author unknown

### Five Little Valentines

| | |
|---|---|
| Five little Valentines were having a race. | *(Hold up five fingers; then point to each in succession.)* |
| The first little Valentine was frilly with lace. | |
| The second little Valentine had a funny face. | |
| The third little Valentine said, "I love you." | |
| The fourth little Valentine said, "I do too." | |
| The fifth little Valentine was as sly as a fox. | |
| He ran the fastest to the Valentine box. | *(Run fingers behind back.)* |

—Author unknown

### Happy Valentines

*(Begin the rhyme with five fingers up. Take away fingers as the rhyme progresses, or simply point to each.)*

Five happy valentines
From the ten cent store.
I sent one to Mother,
Now there are four.
Four happy valentines
Pretty ones to see.
I give one to Brother,
Now there are three.
Three happy valentines,
Yellow, red, and blue.
I give one to Sister,
Now there are two.
Two happy valentines,
My, we have fun.
I give one to Daddy,
Now there is one.
One happy valentine,
The story is almost done.
I give it to Baby,
Now there are none.

—Author unknown

### How Many Valentines?

| | |
|---|---|
| Valentines, valentines, | |
| How many do you see? | |
| Valentines, valentines, | |
| Count them now with me. | |
| One for Father, | *(Hold up thumb.)* |
| One for Mother. | *(Hold up pointer finger.)* |
| One for Grandma, too. | *(Hold up middle finger.)* |
| One for Sister, | *(Hold up ring finger.)* |
| One for Brother, | *(Hold up little finger.)* |
| And here is one for YOU! | *(Make heart shape with thumbs and pointer fingers.)* |

—Author unknown

### A Mailbox Valentine

When you look in your mailbox,
What do you think you'll see?                    *(Children pretend to look in mailbox.)*
It might be a Valentine,
And it might be from me.                          *(Children point to themselves.)*

—Author unknown

### The Valentine Shop

There is the nicest valentine shop.
Before I pass, I try to stop.                     *(Put hand up in a "stop" motion.)*
Inside the shop, I always see,                    *(Point to eyes.)*
Valentines for my family.
Brothers, sisters, aunts, and cousins,            *(Count out on fingers.)*
Friends and classmates by the dozens.             *(Spread arms to show expanse.)*
A tiny one, a nickel buys.                        *(Spread hands to show tiny size.)*
A dime is for a bigger size.                      *(Extend hands farther apart.)*
A quarter for a much bigger size.                 *(Extend hands even farther apart.)*
A dollar for the biggest size.                    *(Move hands far apart.)*

—Author unknown

### Saint Valentine's Day

To every little friend I know,                    *(Move hand to show expanse.)*
A pretty valentine shall go.
To some, I'll send one like a book.               *(Put hands with palms together in front of body.)*
They'll find a message if they look.
Inside it reads, "Much love I send."              *(Open up hands, as a book.)*
Then to some other little friend,
I'll send this little heart of mine,              *(Make heart shape with hands.)*
With much love to my valentine.
I've envelopes to use for this.                   *(Make fists with hands.)*
Here write my name,                               *(Use index finger of one hand to write on palm of other.)*

There seal a kiss.                                *(Put hand to mouth; blow kiss.)*
Then when I hear the postman's ring,              *(Put hand to ear.)*
These valentines to him I'll bring.               *(Close hands into fists again.)*
I'll drop them in his bag of leather,             *(Open fists downward.)*
Then wish the postman pleasant weather            *(Salute.)*
In which to take a valentine
To you and you, dear friends of mine.             *(Point to others, then put hand on heart.)*

—Maude Burnham
*Rhymes for Little Hands* (Milton Bradley Company, 1910, pp. 77–80)

## Miscellaneous

### How Much Do You Love Me?

How much do you love me?                          *(Point to self and friend.)*
A bushel and a peck,
And a hug around the neck.                        *(Hug.)*
That's how much I love you!

—Traditional rhyme

### I Had No Money

| | |
|---|---|
| I had no money I could spend | *(Put hands out, palms up.)* |
| To show how much I loved my friend. | *(Hug self.)* |
| So I put my arms up, | *(Raise arms up, hands over head.)* |
| And smiled, you see, | *(Smile.)* |
| And the valentine will be me! | *(Touch fingers to top of head, forming heart shape with arms.)* |

—Author unknown

### A Day for Love

| | |
|---|---|
| Pretty red hearts, | *(Trace outline of heart in air with index finger.)* |
| And two-by-two. | *(Hold up two fingers for both hands.)* |
| Holding hands, | *(Clasp hands together.)* |
| And "I love you." | *(Clasp hands to heart.)* |
| Scented flowers | *(Hand "holds" flower to nose; sniff.)* |
| From garden vines. | |
| A day for love: St. Valentine's. | |

—Author unknown

### Kisses

*(This fingerplay is sung to the tune of "Frere Jacques." At the conclusion of this rhyme, hand out chocolate kisses to all participants. This would be a great song to end your storyhour with, before you go on to a craft or coloring page activity!)*

| | |
|---|---|
| I love kisses, I love kisses. | *(Begin with one hand over heart; put second hand over heart.)* |
| Yes I do, yes I do! | *(Nod head "yes.")* |
| Kiss, kiss, kiss, kiss, kiss, kiss. | |
| Kiss, kiss, kiss, kiss, kiss, kiss. | *(Make smooching noises for each of these "kisses.")* |
| For me and you. | *(Point to self, then others.)* |
| For me and you. | *(Point to self, then others.)* |

---

### More Great Fingerplays

"Happy Little Heart," from page 250 of *1001 Rhymes and Fingerplays for Working with Young Children*, compiled by the Totline Staff (Warren Publishing House, 1994).

"Love," "Time for Valentines," and "Lots of Hearts," from pages 249 and 253 of *1001 Rhymes and Fingerplays for Working with Young Children*, compiled by the Totline Staff (Warren Publishing House, 1994).

"1 Little, 2 Little, 3 Little Hearts," from page 108 of *Felt Board Fingerplays* by Liz and Dick Wilmes (Building Blocks Publications, 1997).

"Valentine Friends," from page 131 of *Great Big Holiday Celebrations* by Elizabeth McKinnon (Warren Publishing House, 1991).

"Five Little Valentines," from page 36 of *Rhymes for Circle Time* by Louise B. Scott (Instructional Fair/T.S. Denison, 1999).

"Lots of Valentines," from page 10 of *52 Programs for Preschoolers* by Diane Briggs (American Library Association, 1997).

| | |
|---|---|
| I love kisses, I love kisses. | *(Place one hand over heart, then second hand over heart.)* |
| Yes I do, yes I do! | *(Nod head "yes.")* |
| Chocolately delicious, | *(Rub tummy.)* |
| Eat them off the dishes, | *(Pretend to eat.)* |
| For me and you. | *(Point to self, then others.)* |
| For me and you. | *(Point to self, then others.)* |

—Kathy Buchsbaum

## Musical Selections

"All You Need Is Love" from *All You Need Is Love: Beatles Songs for Kids*. Music for Little People. ASIN: B00000JZAP.

"Be My Valentine" from *Rhythms and Rhymes for Special Times* by Jack Hartmann. Available from http://www.songsforteaching.com/.

"Bringing Home a Valentine" and "Will You Be My Valentine?" from *Happy Everything* by Dr. Jean. Melody House. ASIN: B000SM3N0E.

"Five Valentines" from *Months of Music* by Karen Rupprecht and Pam Minor. Available from http://www.songsforteaching.com/.

"My Forever Valentine" from *Holiday Songs* by Wendy Rollin. Available from http://www.songsforteaching.com/.

"V-A-L-E-N-T-I-N-E" from *All Year* by Intelli-Tunes. Available from http://www.songsforteaching.com/.

"Valentine's Song" from *Holiday Songs and Rhythms* by Hap Palmer. Available from http://www.songsforteaching.com/.

"The World We Love" from *Bananaphone* by Raffi. Rounder. ASIN: B0000003HW.

---

### More Great Music

The Songs for Teaching website offers two multiple-holiday CDs that include Valentine's Day songs, *Celebrate Holidays* and *Seasons and Celebrations*. Go to http://www.songsforteaching.com/ to access downloads of both music and printable lyrics.

---

## Crafts

**Guess Who Valentine Mask**    The base of this cute craft is a large heart mask shape that is reproduced on card stock, decorated, and then attached to a craft stick or dowel so that it can be held in front of the face! Instructions appear on page 13 and the pattern on page 26 of *February Arts and Crafts, Grades 1–3*, edited by Susan Walker (The Education Center, 2000).

**Valentine Mailbag**    This craft has hearts of various sizes attached to a paper bag that form a heart "person." Legs and arms are constructed by accordion-folding paper strips. Instructions appear on page 24 of *February Patterns and Projects* (Newbridge Educational, 2000). This would be a great craft for participants to make to take home valentines!

**Valentine Rabbits**    This darling rabbit is made out of heart shapes, with ears and whiskers added! Detailed instructions and patterns appear on pages 21–22 of *Calendar Crafts: Things to Make and Do for Every Month, PreK–2*, by Carolyn Argyle (Teaching and Learning Company, 2006).

**Paper Plate Valentine Pockets**    This craft makes a holder out of two paper plates, perfect for participants to use to take home their valentines! Instructions appear on page 23 of *Calendar Crafts: Things to Make and Do for Every Month, PreK–2*, by Carolyn Argyle (Teaching and Learning Company, 2006).

**Valentine Bags**    The base of this simple craft is red or white paper bags that participants decorate with crayons or markers and valentine stickers. It can be used to collect and take home valentines! Instructions appear on page 28 of *Calendar Crafts: Things to Make and Do for Every Month, PreK–2*, by Carolyn Argyle (Teaching and Learning Company, 2006).

**Heart Rubbings**    Prior to doing this craft, cut out hearts of various sizes from poster board. Cut out the same number to be placed at each individual table in your area, and then put them in a baggie. Provide participants with white construction paper and crayons. Allow them to place the hearts underneath the construction paper and rub a crayon over the top. Hearts appear like magic! A nice variation of this craft would be to use sandpaper instead of poster board. This would give the rubbing a nice textured look. Oriental Trading Company also sells a set of eight heart rubbing plates for $4.99. These are more intricate in their design. If participants are very young, you may want to stick with just the plain poster board or sandpaper hearts. Once the craft is finished, the heart patterns can be stored in the baggie until the next use!

**Conversation Hearts Valentine Bag**    *CopyCat Magazine*, in its January/February 1996 issue (now out of print but often available through interlibrary loan), had a great full-page pattern set of Conversation Heart shapes that appeared on page 34. I copied this page and added slogans to each of the hearts by simply going into Word and typing out in a decent-sized font the following sayings: Stuck on You, Be My Friend, So Fine, I Love You, Smile!, Love Bug, Be Kind, Friends Forever, Hugs, Love, Be Mine, and U R Nice. Once these were typed out, I printed them and cut and taped them to the inside areas of the heart shapes. Once printed out, they looked just like the Conversation Hearts! Each participant received a page of these hearts, which they then colored, cut out, and pasted to a lunch-sized paper bag. I used the regular brown ones, but white ones would work great as well. When finished, participants used these bags to gather their valentines from their card exchange!

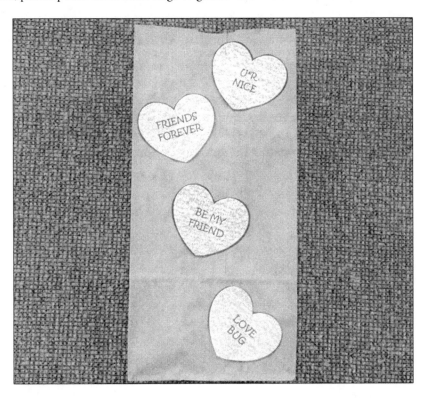

**Valentine Pouches**    The base of this simple craft is a manila envelope that is decorated. Instructions for this craft can be found on page 53 of *Quick Tricks for Holidays* by Annalisa McMorrow (Monday Morning Books, 2001). Use this pouch to carry home valentines!

**Valentine Pal**    Instructions and patterns for this craft can be found on pages 76–77 of *Art Projects for All Seasons* by Karen Finch (Carson-Dellosa Publishing, 1993). The large heart shape that forms the body has features drawn on. The hands and feet are attached by accordion-folded paper strips.

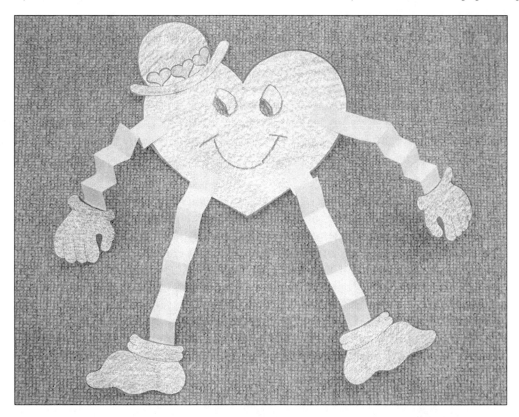

**Heart Lacing Card**    The pattern for this craft can be found on page 28 of *Seasonal Cut-Ups* by Marilynn G. Barr (Monday Morning Books, 2005). Duplicate the pattern on either construction paper or card stock. Provide participants with crayons, hole punch, yarn, and large plastic needles. Have them color the heart (and the background, if desired). Allow them to either straight-lace or loop-lace their yarn around the picture. These two types of lacing are explained on page 7. They may wish to leave enough yarn at the top so that the craft can be hung on a doorknob.

# Veterans Day and Memorial Day

*I have grouped these two holidays together, as they both deal with patriotism and the honoring of soldiers who are serving and who have served our country.*

## History

Memorial Day is observed as a public holiday on the last Monday in May. It is also known as Decoration Day. It was first observed in 1868, honoring those brave soldiers who had fought on both sides in the Civil War, by holding parades, decorating graves, and public speeches. Today it is a day to remember and honor all of those who have died in battle. The American Legion, a patriotic veterans' organization, can be seen on this holiday selling small artificial red poppies. This raises money to help disabled veterans.

Memorial Day has also come to be known as a day when family members who have passed on are remembered by having decorations placed on their graves. Many people hang the American flag at their home or business. This holiday is also a time for picnics or cookouts with family and friends.

Veterans Day is observed on November 11th. It is the date for the yearly celebration of the holiday that honors the men and women who have served in the United States armed forces. Parades are held and special ceremonies and speeches are usually given.

World War I ended on November 11th, during the eleventh hour of the eleventh day of the eleventh month of 1918. This was the day that the agreement was signed between the Allies and the Central Powers, ending the First World War. This day was originally called Armistice Day. It has also been known as Remembrance Day, and is still known as that in Canada and England. (See Julia Jasmine's *Multicultural Holidays: Share Our Celebrations* [Teacher Created Materials, 1994].)

## Poetry

"Memorial Day," from page 46 of *Every Day's a Holiday: Amusing Rhymes for Happy Times* by Dean Koontz (HarperCollins, 2003).

"They Keep Us Free," from http://www.apples4theteacher.com/holidays/memorial-day/kids-poems-rhymes/they-keep-us-free.html.

"Veteran's Day" by Cheryl Dyson, from http://www.apples4theteacher.com/holidays/veterans-day/poems-rhymes/veterans-day.html.

## Books

Bunting, Eve. *My Red Balloon*. Boyds Mills Press, 2005. ISBN: 978-1590782637.
A young, blond preschooler, Bobby, cannot wait for a huge aircraft carrier to dock; Daddy's ship is coming home after many months at sea.

Catalanotto, Peter. *The Veteran's Day Visitor*. Henry Holt and Company, 2008. ISBN: 978-0805078404.
Pop-Pop is shocked when he hears Emily and her friend Vinni don't know what a veteran is, so he volunteers to visit their school and tell the students about Veterans Day.

Cotton, Jacqueline S. *Memorial Day*. Children's Press, 2002. ISBN: 978-0516273693.
This book introduces the history of Memorial Day and explains how it is observed today.

Cotton, Jacqueline S. *Veteran's Day*. Children's Press, 2002. ISBN: 978-0516274997.
This book explains the history of Veterans Day and suggests ways to honor veterans on this special day, such as flying the flag, attending parades, buying poppies, and visiting hospitals.

Douglas, Lloyd J. *Let's Get Ready for Memorial Day*. Children's Press, 2003. ISBN: 978-0516243559.
This book offers an introduction to the holiday and explains its significance.

Ferguson-Cohen, Michelle. *Daddy, You're My Hero!* Little Red-Haired Girl Publishers, 2003. ISBN: 978-0972926447.
This book encourages discussion about and pride in the service of a military parent.

Golding, Theresa. *Memorial Day Surprise*. Boyds Mills Press, 2004. ISBN: 978-1590780480.
When Marco attends a Memorial Day parade, he is surprised to see a familiar face among the veterans.

Hallowell, Kirsten. *Daddy Is a Soldier*. Trafford Publishing, 2004. ISBN: 978-1412018536.
A perfect book for children with parents in the military, the story is told by a little boy who is proud of his dad's job even though it takes him away from home.

Hardin, Melinda. *Hero Dad*. Marshall Cavendish Children's Books, 2010. ISBN: 978-0761457138.
A child demonstrates that while Dad differs from a traditional superhero, as an American soldier, he is a superhero of a different kind.

Henry, Heather F. *Pepper's Purple Heart: A Veteran's Day Story*. Cubbie Blue Publishing, 2003. ISBN: 978-0970634108.
Claire and Robbie learn why we honor veterans on Veterans Day. Claire also learns responsibility after her neighbor rescues her puppy, Pepper.

Rissman, Rebecca. *Veteran's Day*. Heinemann Educational Books, 2010. ISBN: 978-1432940720.
This book introduces readers to what it means to celebrate Veterans Day, and shows them why this holiday is so special.

Scillian, Devin. *H Is for Honor: A Military Family Alphabet*. Sleeping Bear Press, 2006. ISBN: 978-1585362929.
Children will discover why drill sergeants have to be so tough, what it means to be patriotic, and why we need Special Forces such as the Navy SEALS, the Green Berets, and the Army Rangers.

---

### Older Gems, or Titles Too Good to Pass Up

Bangs, Edward. *Steven Kellogg's Yankee Doodle*. Parents Magazine Press, 1976. ISBN: 978-0819308337.
An illustrated version of the well-known song of the American Revolution.

Emberley, Ed. *Drummer Hoff*. Turtleback, 1972. ISBN: 978-0613880763.
A tale of seven soldiers who build a magnificent cannon and Drummer Hoff, who fires it.

Frost, Helen. *Memorial Day*. Capstone Press, 2000. ISBN: 978-0736887281.
This book offers a brief history of the holiday and why it is celebrated.

Hoff, Syd. *Captain Cat*. HarperCollins, 1994. ISBN: 978-0064441766.
The story of a striped feline who strays onto an army base and steps right into military life.

McKinley, Robin. *My Father Is in the Navy*. Greenwillow Books, 1992. ISBN: 978-0688106393.
When Sara hears that her father is coming home from the Navy, she is scarcely excited—she does not remember him.

Scott, Geoffrey. *Memorial Day*. Carolrhoda Books, 1983. ISBN: 978-0876142196.
This book explains why and how we celebrate Memorial Day, the last Monday in May, a day set aside to honor those who have fought and died in the nation's wars.

Spicer, Maggee. *When They Are Up…* Fitzhenry and Whiteside, 2003. ISBN: 978-1550417074.
Based on the beloved nursery song, this charming romp presents various ideas for what the Grand Old Duke of York's 10,000 men do "when they are up," down, and in between.

Spinelli, Eileen. *While You Were Away.* Hyperion Books for Children, 2008. ISBN: 978-1423113519.
Three children anticipate happy reunions with their parents who are on active military duty abroad.

Walker, Robert. *Veteran's Day.* Crabtree Publishing Company, 2010. ISBN: 978-0778747673.
Part of the Celebrations in My World series, this title focuses on the importance of the Veterans Day holiday.

## Activities

---

### Coloring Pages

Consult your favorite pattern books for pages to use as coloring sheets. Be sure to search online as well. There's lots of great stuff out there!

- Visit http://dulemba.com/index_ColoringPages.html for author and illustrator Elizabeth O. Dulemba's great collection of holiday coloring pages. Under her Patriotic section is one titled "Veteran's Day Tribute." While there, sign up for her Coloring Page Tuesdays e-mails.
- EnchantedLearning.com has some great coloring pages.
- Medal of Honor—Page 245 of *The Festive Teacher: Multicultural Activities for Your Curriculum* by Steve Springer et al. (McGraw-Hill, 2008) has a great full-page picture of a medal that could be used as a coloring sheet.
- Veteran's Day Coloring Page—Visit http://www.first-school.ws/t/cp_seasonal/us_veteran .html for a great coloring page.

---

### Cut-and-Tell

**"A New Flag"** This cut-and-tell story plus patterns can be found on pages 32–35 of *Paper-Cutting Stories for Holidays and Special Events* by Valerie Marsh (Alleyside Press, 1994). The end result is a flag.

### Games

**Patriotic Match** Use Ellison die-cuts from their Patriotic set (found in the Social Studies section of their catalog). Cut two of each pattern from red, white, and blue construction paper. If this does not give you an amount large enough to use with your group, use other colors as well. To play this matching game, hand out one of the pair of patterns to each participant and keep the matching piece and place in a container or apron pocket. Once all participants have a pattern, begin the game by pulling colors from your pocket one at a time and placing them on a flannel/Velcro board. Have the participant who has the match bring up his or her piece and place it next to yours. Continue until all patterns/colors have been matched.

**Pin the Medal on the Soldier** Before playing this game, explain to participants how soldiers may receive medals for brave things that they have done while in service to our country. On a piece of poster board, have a drawing of a soldier, possibly from the waist up. You may wish to use the veteran found at http://www.dltk-holidays.com/remembrance/posters/index.htm. He can be printed in either color or black and white. If printed in black and white, you could use an overhead projector to trace the shape onto your poster board. Laminate for durability. Use the Award #1B Ellison die-cut in the small size if available to make your medals. As an alternative, there is also a medal pattern found at the same site. Place tape on the backs of the medals. Blindfold participants and let them try to place the medals on the soldier's chest.

**Medal/Award Matching Game**    Use the Award #1B Ellison die-cut in the large size or the medal pattern found at http://www.dltk-holidays.com/remembrance/posters/index.htm to cut medals from different colors of paper (two of each color). Laminate for durability and then put flannel or Velcro on the backs of each. To play this game, pass out one of each of the different colors to participants, keeping the other of the pair for yourself and placing them either in a container of some sort or an apron pocket. Once each participant has a color, begin the game by pulling the colors from your pocket one at a time and placing them on your board. Have the participant who has the match bring his or hers up and place it next to yours. Continue until all of the colors have been matched.

**Poppy Match**    Use the Flower #1B Generic Ellison die-cut in the large size, as it most closely resembles a poppy shape. Using colored paper, cut two of each color. Laminate the flowers for durability and place a piece of flannel or Velcro on the back. Follow the instructions for the Medal/Award Matching Game.

**Memorial Day Matching Game**    Consult sources of clip art to find items that would work for Memorial Day: flag, poppy, perhaps a soldier's helmet. Enlarge or reduce them to a decent size and copy two of them onto paper. Use this pattern to copy onto different colors of construction paper. You may wish to simplify cutting them out by simply making a shape around the object, such as a circle or square. Laminate for durability. Follow the rules of the other matching games listed in this section.

## Miscellaneous

**Veteran's Day Guest Speaker**    If you have participants who have parents serving in the military who are available to visit your program, why not invite them to speak? Have them bring (or wear) their uniform and bring in other items that may interest participants.

**Veterans Day Parade**    Everyone loves marching songs! Find some patriotic music (check out the *Patriotic Songs of the U.S.A.* CD listed in the Musical Selections section of this chapter) and have your own parade. Provide flags for participants, and/or use your drums, tambourines, and other percussion instruments. If you are able to broadcast your music over a PA or phone system, parade all around your library! If you want to use flags other than just the American flag, EnchantedLearning.com has great color reproductions of the Air Force, Army, Marine, Navy, and Coast Guard flags available. The website has a membership cost of $20.00 per year, but this is a nominal price to pay for the great items available to you!

**Children's Songs for Veterans Day**    Several piggyback songs (songs sung to familiar tunes) can be found at http://www.theholidayzone.com/veterans/songs.html:

- "History" (sung to the tune of "Twinkle, Twinkle Little Star")
- "Oh Veterans" (sung to the tune of "Oh Christmas Tree")
- "Veteran's Day" (sung to the tune of "Jingle Bells")
- "Veterans, We Thank You" (sung to the tune of "Three Blind Mice")

**Camouflage Paper Doll "Friends"**    These paper dolls would be great to use for display on your flannel/Velcro board in order to explain to participants about military clothing. The patterns can be found at http://www.makingfriends.com/friends/f+camouflage.htm.

## Fingerplays ———————————————————————————————

### Five Little Soldiers

| | |
|---|---|
| Five little soldiers standing in a row. | *(Hold up five fingers of right hand.)* |
| Three stood straight and two stood so. | *(Put right thumb and pinkie down.)* |
| Along came the captain, and what do you think? | |
| Those soldiers jumped up, quick as a wink! | *(Release thumb and pinkie to stand.)* |

—Traditional rhyme

## Ten Little Soldiers

| | |
|---|---|
| Ten little soldiers standing in a row. | *(Hold up both hands, fingers up straight.)* |
| When they see the captain, they bow just so. | *(Bend all fingers down.)* |
| They march to the left. | *(March fingers left.)* |
| They march to the right. | *(March fingers right.)* |
| And then they shut their eyes, | |
| And they sleep all night. | *(Fold fingers into fists.)* |

—Traditional rhyme

## Ten Little Soldiers

| | |
|---|---|
| Ten little soldiers stand up straight. | *(Hold up ten fingers.)* |
| Ten little soldiers make a gate. | *(Move hands together so that thumbs are touching.)* |
| Ten little soldiers make a ring. | *(Touch thumbs and little fingers together, making a circle.)* |
| Ten little soldiers bow to the king. | *(Bend fingers down.)* |
| Ten little soldiers dance all day. | *(Wiggle all fingers.)* |
| Ten little soldiers hide away. | *(Hide hands behind back.)* |

—Traditional rhyme

## The Noble Duke of York

*(Sing this traditional rhyme.)*

| | |
|---|---|
| The noble Duke of York, | |
| He had ten thousand men. | |
| He marched them up the hill, | *(March in place.)* |
| And he marched them down again. | *(Continue marching.)* |
| And when they're up, they're up | *(Stand on tiptoes.)* |
| And when they're down, they're down. | *(Crouch down.)* |
| And when they're only halfway up, | *(Stand halfway up.)* |
| They're neither up nor down! | |

—Traditional rhyme

## We Love Veterans

*(This action song is sung to the tune of "Frere Jacques.")*

| | |
|---|---|
| We love veterans, | *(Place one hand over heart.)* |
| We love veterans. | *(Place other hand over heart.)* |
| Yes, we do, | *(Shake head.)* |
| Yes, we do! | |
| Veterans, we salute you, | *(Salute with one hand.)* |
| Veterans, we salute you. | *(Switch and salute with other hand.)* |
| We love you, | *(Place hands over heart.)* |
| Yes, we do! | *(Shake head "yes.")* |

—Barbara Scott

## The Soldiers

| | |
|---|---|
| Here are the soldiers who would fight | *(Hold up both hands, ten fingers up.)* |
| For their country and the right. | |
| Here is the fort that towers high, | *(Hold hands in front of body, palms facing in, fingertips touching.)* |
| Here's their flag up in the sky. | *(Make same motion as above, but hold up one thumb in the air to represent flag on pole.)* |

---

**More Great Fingerplays**

"Veteran's March," an action song, at http://www.lessonplanspage.com/MusicVeteransDayMarchK2.htm. This site suggests having participants hold flags as they march in a circle!

"Marching Flags," an action rhyme, by Jean Warren from page 59 of *Busy Bees Summer: Fun for Two's and Three's* by Elizabeth McKinnon and Gayle Bittinger (Warren Publishing House, 1995). This rhyme could be adapted to say "Oh, when the veterans go marching by" instead of "Oh when the flags go marching by"; "How we love to see their uniforms (or medals, or see them salute)" instead of "How we love to see the colors." Participants could march as they sing the song.

"Happy Independence Day" by Barbara Paxson from page 265 of *1001 Rhymes and Fingerplays for Working with Young Children*, compiled by the Totline staff (Warren Publishing House, 1994). The title could be revised to "Happy Veterans Day" or "Happy Memorial Day." This change could also be reflected in the last line of the rhyme.

---

Grimly peeping through the wall
Are the cannon large and small.

When the shadows slowly creep,
Soldiers in their camp tents sleep.
Through the night each sentinel
At his post cries, "All is well!"
When the soldiers, one and all,
Hear the bugle's early call;
Quickly then, they stand so fine
In a straight and even line.

*(Hold out index and middle fingers in each hand together to represent cannons.)*

*(Cup hands, palms down, to represent tents.)*

*(Cup hands around mouth.)*

*(Put hand to ear, listening.)*

*(Hold up both hands, ten fingers up.)*

—Maude Burnham
*Rhymes for Little Hands* (Milton Bradley Company, 1910, pp. 150–152)

## Musical Selections ————————————————————————————————————

*Holding the Flag: A Tribute to Veterans* CD by the U.S. Military Band of the Air Force, Army, Coast
 Guard, Marines, and Navy. This CD is chock-full of patriotic music perfect for marching or
 accompanying with rhythm band instruments!
*Patriotic Songs and Marches* CD. Available from http://www.kimboed.com/.
*Patriotic Songs of the U.S.A.* CD. Available from http://www.melodyhousemusic.com/.
"Veteran's Day" from *Happy Everything* by Dr. Jean. Melody House. ASIN: B000SM3N0E.

## Crafts ————————————————————————————————————————————

**Remembrance Day Bingo Dauber Art**    Instructions and templates for this craft can be found at http://www.dltk-holidays.com/remembrance/mdaubers.htm. The finished shape is a poppy, a flower associated with the holiday. Templates included are for both a single poppy and for a poppy wreath.

**Lest We Forget Refrigerator Magnet**    Instructions and templates for this craft can be found at http://www.dltk-holidays.com/remembrance/mlestweforget.html. Templates can be printed out in either black and white or color.

**Remembrance Day Hands Wreath**    Instructions for the wreath appear at http://www.dltk-holidays .com/remembrance/mremembrancehands.html. This site also has both color and black-and-white patterns for poppies that can be added to this hand wreath, if desired.

**Heart Poppy Paper Craft**    Instructions and templates for this craft appear at http://www.dltk-holidays .com/remembrance/mvflower.html. Templates appear in both color and black and white. Since the patterns are large and would be easy for young hands to color and cut out, the black-and-white templates would be preferable.

**Flag Lacing Card**    The pattern for this craft can be found on page 23 of *Seasonal Cut-Ups* by Marilynn G. Barr (Monday Morning Books, 2005). Copy the pattern onto construction paper or card stock. Provide participants with crayons, hole punch, yarn, and large plastic needles. Have them color their flags (and background, if desired). Allow them to either straight-lace or loop-lace their yarn around the picture. These two types of lacing are explained on page 7. They may wish to leave enough yarn at the top so that the completed craft can be hung on a doorknob. Give this craft to a friend or relative who is a veteran to thank them for their service to our country!

**Patriotic Parade Stick**    This great idea comes from http://www.ehow.com/list_6391301_ preschool-art-activities-veterans-day.html. Using red, white, and blue paint and star stickers, have participants decorate empty paper towel tubes. Create streamers by cutting red, white, and blue crepe paper into 5-inch strips. Have them glue or staple the streamers to the top of the paper towel tubes.

**Fingerprint Poppies**    This cute idea also comes from http://www.ehow.com/list_6391301_preschool-art-activities-veterans-day.html. The red poppy is a symbol of remembrance for veterans all over the world. Have participants dip their thumbs into red finger paint and stamp four thumb prints in a square formation on a piece of white paper. Have them place their index fingers into green finger paint and stamp the green paint in the center of the poppy. Participants can create as many or as few poppies as they would like!

**Star Sticks**    Another idea from http://www.ehow.com/list_6391301_preschool-art-activities-veterans-day.html: Help participants create a five-pointed star by gluing six craft sticks into a star formation (two triangles overlapped, one upside down). Once stars are assembled, allow participants to decorate them using red, white, and blue paint or markers, and silver and gold glitter. Tie a piece of string or yarn to the star, so that it can be hung.

**Patriotic Necklaces**    Make a patriotic necklace by stringing red, white, and blue beads onto lanyards. Your local craft store should be able to supply you with what is needed. Another source of materials for this craft is OrientalTrading.com. You can make bracelets as well!

**Heart Poppies**    This craft can be found at http://www.kinderart.com/seasons/heart poppies.shtml. The heart pattern can be printed from this site, or you can use one of your own. Participants should make four small hearts from red construction paper. Once the hearts are cut, they should be arranged to create a poppy shape. Cut a small circle from green construction paper and place it in the middle of the poppy.

**Patriotic Door Hanger**    Use the Ellison door hanger pattern as the base of this craft. Use the USA die-cut and tiny Primitive Stars die-cut. Cut out the star shapes from red, white, and blue construction paper. Center the USA logo in the middle

of the door hanger and paste the red, white, and blue stars all around. You could also use the eagle's head die-cut and paste the stars around it.

**Memorial Day Booklet**    This eight-page mini-book can be colored, cut out, and folded. The pattern is in PDF form at http://www .education world.com/a_lesson/worksheets/ TCM/pdfs/020524pt.pdf.

While this appendix is not exhaustive, the following is a representative list of companies from which you can purchase basic craft supplies, such as glue, scissors, and paper, and items such as flannel boards, markers, etc. In addition, specialty companies are listed. Contact information for each company is included.

**ABC School Specialty**
P.O. Box 1579
Appleton, WI 54912-1579
Telephone: 1-888-388-3224
Fax: 1-888-388-6344
http://store.schoolspecialtyonline.net/

This site offers a great combination flannel/dry-erase board (one side is a blue flannel-board background, the other a dry-erase board), as well as magnetic boards. They also carry a 3-in-1 portable easel that provides a magnet board, a 2-sided white-board, and a flannel board. They also offer many varied art supplies.

**Accu-Cut Systems**
1035 East Dodge Street
Fremont, NV 68025
Telephone: 1-800-288-1670
Fax: 1-800-369-1332
http://www.accucuteducation.com/

Although I reference the Ellison machine and dies many times in this book, I have used the Accu-Cut machine and it is a wonderful system as well. Request a catalog from them or view their die-cut selection online. Check out their selection of holiday and Jewish dies (under the Religion tab). They also offer a Multicultural set that includes an African boy and girl, an Asian boy, and a South American girl.

**Act II Books and Puppets**
111 Anthes Avenue, Unit B
P.O. Box 1593
Langley, WA 98260
Telephone: 1-360-221-4442

Fax: 1-360-364-0044
http://www.kidsbooksandpuppets.com/

This company carries Folkmanis puppets at up to 20–25 percent off retail price. They also carry many hard-to-find or discontinued puppets. Check out their Large Red Dragon Puppet (one of Folkmanis's puppets that has been discontinued) for your Chinese New Year program. They also carry a large line of costume and dress-up hats that would add a nice touch to your programs.

**Becker's School Supplies**
1500 Melrose Highway
Pennsauken, NJ 08110-1410
Telephone: 1-800-523-1490
Fax: 1-856-792-4500
http://www.shopbecker.com/

In addition to basic craft supplies, this company also offers multicultural puppets, a storytelling glove (holds puppets with Velcro backing), flannel boards, a portable easel that easily transforms into a magnetic/flannel/whiteboard, other portable multipurpose tabletop easels, chalkboards, dry-erase markers, jumbo ink pads, multicultural markers (includes eight skin colors), craft sticks, chenille stems (pipe cleaners), Global Village craft papers (papers designed to look like authentic textiles), face pads, paper doll pads, and skin tone paper for multicultural projects.

**Book Props, LLC**
1120 McVey Avenue
Lake Oswego, OR 97034
Telephone: 1-800-636-5314

Fax: 1-503-636-8724
http://www.bookprops.com/Site_1/Home.html

Book Props are handmade, beautifully detailed, interactive sets that add depth and visual excitement to storytelling in classroom and library group settings. Their Show-A-Tale aprons and banners, with Velcro-sticking ability, are the preferred method for presenting their stories. The company uses a variety of durable fabrics. The individual pieces are sewn, silk-screened, sometimes stuffed, and hand-painted. They do not copy illustrations from the stories that they offer, but offer their reinterpretation of the characters. Sets are pricey, ranging from $200.00 to $305.00.

### Brodart

P.O. Box 300
McElhattan, PA 17748
Telephone: 1-888-820-4377
Fax: 1-800-283-6087
http://www.shopbrodart.com/

Brodart offers a variety of flannel-board units, a Holiday Flannelboard Storytelling package that includes four stories (The Orange Ghost, The Thanksgiving Story, The Night Before Christmas, and The Enormous Easter Egg), and a storytelling apron. They also offer a line of plush puppets, among them an adorable Folkmanis groundhog and a beautiful Folkmanis peacock (great for that Diwali program).

### Childcraft School Specialty

P.O. Box 1579
Appleton, WI 54912-1579
Telephone: 1-888-388-3224
Fax: 1-888-388-6344
http://www.childcraft.com/

This company offers basic craft supplies from fun foam to craft sticks, glue to paper. They also offer world patterns paper packs, economy marker boards and dry-erase boards, jumbo stampers, and flexible magnetic tape. Be sure to check their section of Clearance Specials in the back of the catalog.

### Constructive Playthings

13201 Arrington Road
Grandview, MO 64030
Telephone: 1-800-448-1412
Fax: 1-816-761-9295
http://www.constructiveplaythings.com/

Basic craft supplies are offered here, as well as washable multicultural paints, skin-tone construction paper (ten shades), multicultural crayons (eight skin-tone shades), a Tell-A-Story apron (Velcro-backed items can be attached), magnetic boards, flannel boards, and dry-erase markers.

### The Craft Shop

699 E. 2nd Street
Brooklyn, NY 11218
Telephone: 1-866-422-7238 or 1-718-431-0301
Fax: 1-718-436-5815
http://www.thecraftshoponline.com/

Click on the "Judaica" link on the left-hand list. Then click on the "Teachers Aid" link. Under the "Specialty Items" link, you will find a variety of Chanukah and Rosh Hashanah kits both for flannel boards and magnet boards. This site also sells portable flannel boards. Kits for other Jewish holidays are also available.

### Creative Diversity

P.O. Box 11927
Winston-Salem, NC 27116
Telephone: 1-800-624-7968
Fax: 1-800-410-7282
http://www.hatchearlychildhood.com//Catalog.aspx?cl
=ShopCreativeDiversityCatalog

This company, now part of Hatch, offers sets of African, Asian, and Hispanic play foods ($14.99 to $17.99 per set). In addition, they also sell World Textile Craft Paper collections, Self Expressions Human Paper Shades kits ($13.99 for 40 full bodies, 50 faces, 35 hands, and 35 feet), eyeball stickers (in a variety of ethnic shapes), multicultural tissue paper, foot shapes (in eight different skin tones), the Multicultural Kids Life-Size paper craft paper, skin tone craft papers, Handlet Padlet (hands in eight rich skin tones), Card Characters (eight skin tones), and Face Pads. They also carry multicultural washable tempera paint (in eight skin tones), and multicultural crayons and markers. They also offer African mask kits.

### Culture for Kids Catalog

Culture for Kids
4480 Lake Forest Drive, Suite 302
Cincinnati, OH 45242
Telephone: 1-513-563-3100, x0
Fax: 1-513-563-3105
http://www.cultureforkids.com/

This is a great source of books, CDs, craft kits, and even decorations that will add pizzazz to your programming.

You can even purchase a wooden "make your own sushi" kit.

### DEMCO
P.O. Box 7488
Madison, WI 53707
Telephone: 1-800-962-4463
Fax: 1-800-245-1329
http://www.demco.com/

DEMCO offers a variety of arts and crafts materials, from crayons and markers to accessories such as chenille stems and pom-poms. They also offer a variety of tabletop easels, including a couple of easels that offer flannel-board, magnetic-board, and marker-board capabilities. In addition, they also offer dry erase and chalkboards in smaller lap-size boards.

### Discount School Supply
P.O. Box 6013
Carol Stream, IL 60197-6013
Telephone: 1-800-627-2829
Fax: 1-800-879-3753
http://www.DiscountSchoolSupply.com/

All kinds of craft materials and supplies are available here, as well as World Colors Construction Paper (ten different colors in a package of 50 sheets), and adhesive magnetic tape.

### Ellison
25862 Commercentre Drive
Lake Forest, CA 92630-8804
Telephone: 1-800-253-2238
Fax: 1-800-253-2240
http://www.ellisoneducation.com/

This is the go-to source for die-cut patterns to use for name tags for your programming, as well as for cutting out patterns for matching games. The selection is amazing. Check out their Jewish and Islamic sets under the Religious Studies section. Note: If your library does not personally own an Ellison die, that doesn't mean it is not within reach. Check with your local schools or your library co-op or regional system. Many times they will lend dies for use. A new feature of the company's website is that catalogs can be viewed online. Take a look at the specialty catalogs for both Islamic and Judaic offerings.

### The Felt Source
c/o S&P Distributors
31256 Corte Talvera

Temecula, CA 92592-5469
Telephone: 1-877-463-1053
Fax: 1-877-463-1053
http://www.thefeltsource.com/

This company offers a wide variety of tabletop and larger flannel boards and combination boards. A shelf area between the boards allows for storage of markers, eraser, and the like. They also offer a large variety of flannel-board sets and stories. They are also a distributor of Betty Lukens and Little Folks Visual sets.

### Folkmanis Puppets
1219 Park Avenue
Emeryville, CA 94608
Telephone: 1-800-654-8922
Fax: 1-510-654-7756
http://www.folkmanis.com/

Folkmanis has been producing quality puppets since 1976. Click on the "Find a Store" tab on the homepage to enter your zip code and find a store near you that carries this great line of puppets. There is also a link to a list of online retailers. If you are ever in Emeryville, California, the company has a store there that sells factory seconds of their puppets at reduced prices.

### Gaylord
P.O. Box 4901
Syracuse, NY 13221-4901
Telephone: 1-800-962-9580
Fax: 1-800-272-3412
http://www.gaylord.com/

Gaylord offers a small selection of hand and glove puppets, a portable flannel board, and some nice sturdy combination easels with flannel, magnetic, and dry-erase boards. Gaylord offers some limited craft supplies as well.

### Genesisarts
P.O. Box 45614
Los Angeles, CA 90045
Telephone: 1-888-895-4691
Fax: Same as above
http://www.genesisartsfeltstory.com/
http://www.genesisartsandbooks.com/

Wow! Betty Yip originally started selling on eBay in 2003. She offers all sorts of reasonably priced felt story kits, including seasonal stories. She even entertains requests for making special flannel-board stories. While there is a physical address listed, it is for business contact only. All of this company's business is conducted online.

The second website listed also offers a selection of children's books, DVDs, and audiobooks.

### Glitterful Felt Stories
Telephone: 1-949-633-4170
Fax: 1-949-305-4384
http://www.Glitterfulfeltstories.com/

Shelby Barone offers felt board, felt-board stories based on books, glove and puppet stories, hand and finger puppets, and stories for holidays. For Kwanzaa, she offers: Kwanzaa Kinara song set, K-W-A-N-Z-A-A song set, and Kwanzaa's Here and Kwanzaa Candles sets. For Hanukkah: Five Little Latkes set, Hanukkah Menorah song set, I'm a Little Dreidel set, and Large Hanukkah Menorah set. All of her sales are done online.

### Guildcraft Arts and Crafts
100 Fire Tower Drive
Tonawanda, NY 14150
Telephone: 1-800-345-5563
Fax: 1-800-550-3555
http://www.Guildcraftinc.com/

This is a great source for basic craft supplies. It is also a source for beads and plastic lanyard, paper and foam crowns, and flexible magnetic tape. Also available are large flag shapes (14 by 16 inches) that are ready to decorate, paper, and a number of multicultural crafts. Many of the crafts come in prepackaged kits and are priced accordingly. Please note that many of the crafts available are not recommended for children under three years of age.

Another great item available from this company is something called a Tracer Projector. If you do not have access to an overhead projector, this handy machine sits on top of a photo or drawing that is 5 by 5 inches and magnifies it up to 10 times. At the price of $79.95, it may fill the same need as that of a more costly overhead projector.

### Hancock Fabrics
3406 West Main Street
Tupelo, MS 38801
Telephone: 1-877-322-7427
http://www.hancockfabrics.com/

Click on the Crafts tab located on the right-hand side of the homepage. Then, under the pull-down menu, click on Kids' Crafts. They offer a nice selection of beads and accessories, as well as glitter pens and some cool-looking bullet-tip and broad-line dry-erase markers for drawing. They also offer henna art kits.

### Hatch
P.O. Box 11927
Winston-Salem, NC 27116
Telephone: 1-800-624-7968
Fax: 1-800-410-7282
http://www.hatchearlychildhood.com/

In addition to many basic craft supplies, this company offers Hispanic and multicultural play food sets, Color of My Friends washable tempera paints (eight colors), Around the World Specialty paper package, multicultural construction paper, Multicultural Kids life-size craft paper in eight skin tones, and face pads (in eight skin tones/50 sheets per pad).

### Highsmith
P.O. Box 7820
Madison, WI 53707-7820
Telephone: 1-800-558-2110
Fax: 1-800-835-2329
http://www.Highsmith.com/

Highsmith offers a wide variety of flannel boards, magnet boards and combination boards.

### Janie's Coloring Hats
86 Auerbach Lane
Lawrence, NY 11559
Telephone: 1-516-374-7228
Fax: 1-516-374-7066
http://www.coloringhats.com/

What a cool site and what a great idea. This site will provide you with paper coloring hats for all of the Jewish holidays and other holidays around the world as well. Hats are sold by the bag (20/$7.99), by the box (100/$24.99) and even by the case (1000/$189.99).

### JoAnn Fabric and Craft Stores
http://www.joann.com/

It is likely that there is a JoAnn Fabric store in your area. In checking under the Kids Crafts tab on the homepage, they offer a nice selection of pony beads, as well as a great selection of basic art and craft supplies.

### Judaica for Kids
3044 Old Denton Road
Ste. 111, PMB 199
Carrollton, TX 75007
Telephone: 214-850-6267
Fax: 1-972-394-3356
http://www.judaicaforkids.com/

This company offers the complete package of all things for Jewish families, from books to craft kits, to party supplies to DVDs and music.

## Just for the Mitzvah
625 N.E. 173rd Terrace
N. Miami Beach, FL 33162
Telephone: 1-888-4-THE-MIT
Fax: 1-305-947-5563
http://www.jewishcrafts.com/

This company presents a wide variety of craft kits for all Jewish holidays. Full-color examples appear on the company's website. All items are sold by dozens only. Each project contains step-by-step instructions and multipurpose materials, such as precut wood, craft board, and felt components.

## Kaplan Early Learning Company
1310 Lewisville-Clemmons Road
Lewisville, NC 27023
Telephone: 1-800-334-2014
Fax: 1-800-452-7526
http://www.kaplanco.com/

Check out the selection available under the Puppets and Accessories tab on the left-hand side of the home-page. This company offers a nice selection of hand and glove puppets, as well as sets of multicultural families. Also available from this company is the Monkey Mitt, complete with five sets of small puppets for use with it.

## Kimbo Educational
P.O. Box 477
Long Branch, NJ 07740-0477
Telephone: 1-800-631-2187
Fax: 1-732-870-3340
http://www.kimboed.com/

A wonderful selection of all kinds of children's music CDs. You will find music for use with beanbags, rhythm sticks, ribbon sticks, and lots of just plain fun music to groove to. This company also offers downloads of CDs and DVDs on the website.

## Kipp Brothers Toys and Novelties
491 Muskegon Drive
Greenfield, IN 46140
Telephone: 1-800-428-1153
Fax: 1-800-832-5477
http://www.kipptoys.com/

Easter and St. Patrick's Day items are available, as well as a great line of hats and headwear that will work well for programming.

## Lakeshore Learning Materials
2695 Dominguez Street
Carson, CA 90895
Telephone: 1-800-421-5354
Fax: 1-800-537-5403
http://www.lakeshorelearning.com/

In addition to lots of basic craft supplies, this company offers washable People Colors liquid tempera paint (eight shades), jumbo ink pads, People Shapes project kits ($29.95 for 24 people shapes and everything needed to decorate them; an additional 24 shapes can be purchased for $6.95), a storytelling glove and lapboard, and a tabletop storytelling board and storytelling easel.

## The Library Store
301 East South Street
P.O. Box 964
Tremont, IL 61568
Telephone: 1-800-548-7204
Fax: 1-800-320-7706
http://www.thelibrarystore.com/

This company offers several flannel/magnetic/dry-erase boards for use.

## Little Folk Visuals
P.O. Box 14243
Palm Desert, CA 92255
Telephone: 1-800-537-7227
Fax: 1-760-360-0225
http://www.littlefolkvisuals.com/

This company offers flannel/felt-board kits of bilingual rhymes, a cute birthday cake and candles, sets of multicultural families, and children and faces of the world sets. They also offer felt boards. Their catalogs are available on their site in PDF form.

## Manhattan Toy
http://www.manhattantoy.com/

This company offers a decent-sized selection of hand and finger puppets. And remember *Fraggle Rock*? They offer character puppets.

## Melody House
819 N.W. 92nd Street
Oklahoma City, OK 73114
Telephone: 1-800-234-9228
Fax: 1-405-840-3384
http://www.melodyhousemusic.com/

A great source for music CDs, Monkey Mitt storytelling sets, storytelling boards and props, storytelling apron, rhythm instruments, rhythm sticks, ribbon wands, and scarves.

## Merry Makers

3640 Grand Avenue, Suite 200
Oakland, CA 94610
Telephone: 1-888-989-0454
Fax: 1-510-451-2174
http://www.merrymakersinc.com/

Merry Makers was founded in 1993 with the goal of providing dolls and toys based on children's books, museum collections, and other characters for customers the world over. Their catalog (and supplements) is available online in PDF format. Check out Splat the Cat with holiday accessories, and the Abraham Lincoln and George Washington finger puppets.

## Mimi's Motifs

P.O. Box 3234
Visalia, CA 93278
Telephone: 1-877-367-6464
Fax: 1-559-625-1351
http://www.mimismotifs.com/index.html

What a treasure trove of items. Mimi offers zip-up carry-along activity books, wall hangings, reversible storytelling dolls, hand and finger puppets, and religious/holiday items such as an Aleph Bet wall hanging and dreidel game. Her adorable finger puppets are hand-crocheted. Check out the Melville Dewey hand puppet.

## Music for Little People

30 Amberwood Parkway
Ashland, OH 44805
Telephone: 1-800-409-2457
Fax: 1-419-281-6883
http://www.musicforlittlepeople.com/

This company offers a diverse mix of music CDs (holiday music, selected artists such as Dan Zane and Laurie Berkner), and a great mix of multicultural music, such as Uni Verse of Song/Spanish, songs performed in English and Spanish. Check out their World Rhythm instrument set.

## Music in Motion

P.O. Box 869231
Plano, TX 75086-9231
Telephone: 1-800-807-3520
Fax: 1-972-943-8906
http://www.musicmotion.com/

A great selection of everything musical awaits you here. Check out their cultural instruments sets, music and movement items such as scarves, beanbags and ribbon wands, hats and props, and a nice selection of CDs. Their latest catalog is available for download on their website.

## Oriental Trading Company

P.O. Box 2308
Omaha, NE 68103-2308
Telephone: 1-800-348-6483
Fax: 1-800-327-8904
http://www.orientaltrading.com/

Oriental Trading seems to have it all. This company offers several different catalogs. Their Party catalog has all sorts of neat items. The Birthday Cake with Candles Hat (for $5.99) makes a great wearable for your birthday program. They have an Easter section with baskets and eggs. The St. Patrick's section boasts everything from necklaces to a CD of party music. Their large Chinese New Year section offers everything you can think of to decorate for your program and provide giveaways. In their regular catalog, the Fiesta Fun section has an inflatable cactus ring-toss game that you might want to incorporate into your Cinco de Mayo program. Their Patriotic area has small flags to purchase, as well as glitter tattoos (think program giveaways). Their Hands-On Fun catalog has lots of craft kits available for holidays. You name the holiday—there are probably kits available for purchase. The holiday sections offer items such as an inflatable Valentine Octopus Ring-Toss game. In addition, Oriental Trading offers many basic craft materials. I was very impressed with the variety of items for Chinese New Year in the Hands-On Fun catalog. Oriental Trading is also a source for puppets and festive hats that can be used in your programs. Also, the smaller seasonal catalogs that the company sends out periodically have great decorations and crafts for holidays.

## OyToys

8601 Dunwoody Place
Suite 440
Atlanta, GA 30350
Telephone: 1-866-694-1373
Fax: 1-205-449-2062
http://www.oytoys.com/

This company specializes in all things Jewish. Check out their holiday section with all sorts of items for all Jewish holidays, such as menorahs, books, holiday CDs, dreidels, games, shofars, stickers, foam shapes, etc. The selection of items is tremendous. This company also offers chocolate gelt and other holiday treats.

## The Puppet Store
888 Newark Avenue, Suite #544
Jersey City, NJ 07306
Telephone: 1-800-571-8845
http://www.thepuppetstore.com/

This company offers a full supply of full- and half-body puppets as well as hand and glove puppets. They even offer marionette puppets. Currently, they have a stock of more than 400 puppets available.

## Puppet Super Store
8971 Lanier Way
Sacramento, CA 95826
Telephone: 1-916-706-1401
Fax: 1-831-597-5100
http://www.puppetsuperstore.com/shoppingcart/index.php?p=home

This company offers a wide variety of hand, finger, full and half-body puppets, as well as marionettes, plush toys, retired Folkmanis puppets, character puppets, and even puppet stages.

## Puppets at Half Price
A Division of The Book Fair, Inc.
1872 Johns Drive
Glenview, IL 60025
Telephone: 1-847-965-1466
Fax: 1-847-966-2665
http://www.puppetsathalfprice.com/index.htm

Established in 1982, The Book Fair is a family-owned business selling books, puppets, and other educational products all at half-price. They offer finger puppets, hand puppets, plush items, book and puppet sets, and book and plush sets.

## Rhode Island Novelty
5 Industrial Road
Cumberland, RI 02864
Telephone: 1-800-528-5599
Fax: 1-800-448-1775
http://www.rinovelty.com/

Hats, finger puppets, paper fans, and parasols for Chinese New Year, and additional goodies that will add pizzazz to your programming are available here.

## S&S Worldwide
P.O. Box 513
75 Mill Street

Colchester, CT 06415-0513
Telephone: 1-800-288-9941
Fax: 1-800-566-6678
http://www.ssww.com/

This company offers basic craft supplies, from glue to scissors to beads and pom-poms. They also offer multicultural tempera paint (eight different tones), African and Hispanic textile print paper, and jumbo ink pads. They also have specific craft sections for holidays such as Hanukkah and Kwanzaa.

## SmileMakers
P.O. Box 2543
Spartanburg, SC 29304
Telephone: 1-888-800-7645
Fax: 1-877-567-7645
http://www.smilemakers.com/

SmileMakers isn't just a sticker company. They offer craft sticks, chenille stems, and assorted craft items. They offer skin-toned craft paper in eight flesh tones. Things that I was pleasantly surprised to find in their catalog: often hard-to-find white paper bags (100 bags for $13.99) and round doilies (100 for $4.99).

## Songs for Teaching
6632 Telegraph Road #242
Bloomfield Hills, MI 48301
Telephone: 1-800-649-5514
Fax: 1-866-769-8528
http://www.songsforteaching.com/

This company is a great source for ordering music both in hard copy and as downloads. They offer thousands of children's songs, lyrics, sound clips, and teaching suggestions.

## Talk Islam Online Store
c/o Online-Islamic-Store.com
P.O. Box 2667
Columbia, MD 21045
Telephone: 1-800-478-1164
Fax: 1-410-362-9696
http://www.onlineislamicstore.com/

Click on the Kids' Books tab at the top of the page, then on "Muslim Poems, Rhymes, Plays, and Activity Books" and "Poems, Rhymes, Plays, Puzzles, and Activity Books" links. Nursery rhyme books are available as well as coloring books that could provide coloring pages for programs. Click on the Toys tab and check out the Arabic Alphabet and Numbers Magnet Boards and the mosque building blocks sets.

**Teachers' Discount**
P.O. Box 1579
Appleton, WI 54912-1579
Telephone: 1-800-470-7616
Fax: 1-800-470-7620
http://www.tdbestprice.com/

Lots of basic craft supplies are offered here. Also available are Handlet Padlets, Paper Doll Pads, Card Characters, Face Pads, and Foot Shape Paper in varying skin tones, Monkey Mitt (furry mitt with Velcro pads on each finger, perfect for illustrating fingerplays with small characters), flannel boards, magnetic boards, dry-erase boards (some multipurpose), Jumbo Stamp Pads, and a Creative Pockets apron (with several useful pockets).

**U.S. Toy Company**
13201 Arrington Road
Grandview, MO 64030-2886
Telephone: 1-800-832-0224
Fax: 1-816-761-9295
http://www.ustoy.com/

This company has a nice selection of St. Patrick's Day items (the leprechaun costume set is especially cute), Chinese New Year, and birthday party items (including piñatas), as well as a nice selection of hats.

# Barbara's Gallery of Holiday Storytime Crafts

## April Fools' Day

Largest Tie Ever!

## Arbor Day, Earth Day, and Tu B'Shevat

Easy Shapes Trees and Leaf Rubbings

## Birthdays

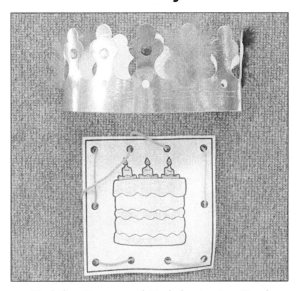

Birthday Crown and Birthday Lacing Card

## Chinese New Year

Chinese Zodiac Wreath and Chinese New Year Dragon

## Christmas

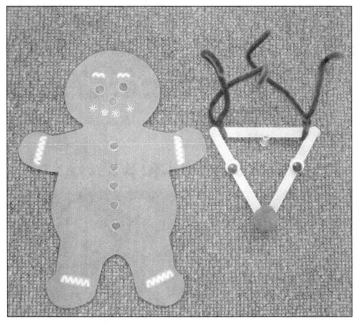

Gingerbread Man and Craft Stick Reindeer

## Cinco de Mayo

Let's Make Tacos! and Cinco de Mayo Sombrero

## Columbus Day

Sail On, Columbus and Columbus Puppet

# Diwali/Divali

Flower Garland and Bengal Tiger

# Easter

Bunny Card and Baby Chick Surprise Egg

# Father's Day and Mother's Day

Flower Wreath and Baseball Photo Frame

# Fourth of July/Independence Day and Flag Day

Fourth of July Star Man and Star Wreath

# Grandparents Day

Grandparents Day Bookmark

# Groundhog Day

Furry Weatherman and Groundhog Paper Bag Puppet

# Halloween

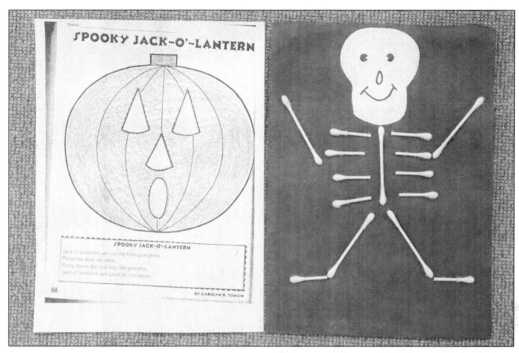

Spooky Jack-O'-Lantern and Easy Skeleton

## Hanukkah

Star of David and Hanukkah Handprint Menorah

## Kwanzaa

Kwanzaa Place Mat and Kwanzaa Candle

## Martin Luther King Day

Peace Dove and Shake Hands!

## May Day

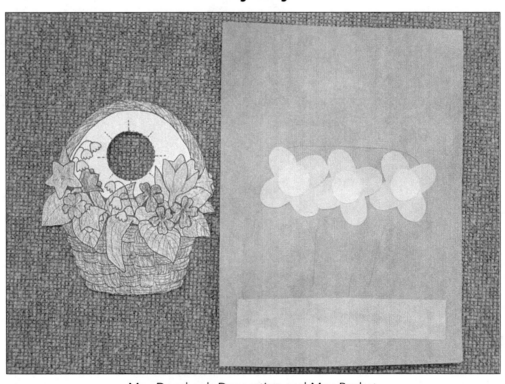

May Doorknob Decoration and May Basket

## New Year's Day

Tambourine and New Year's Noisemaker

## Passover

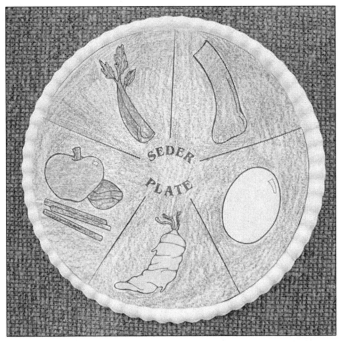

Seder Plate

## Presidents' Day

Lincoln Penny Pendant and Abe and George Wreath

# Purim

Purim Masks and Let's Make a Crown!

# Ramadan

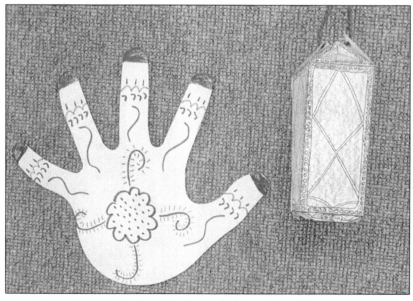

Mehndi Hand Design and Ramadan Fanoo

## Rosh Hashanah and Yom Kippur

Apple Pie and Stand-Up Apple

## Saint Patrick's Day

Leprechaun Movable Puppet and Shamrock Necklace

## Thanksgiving

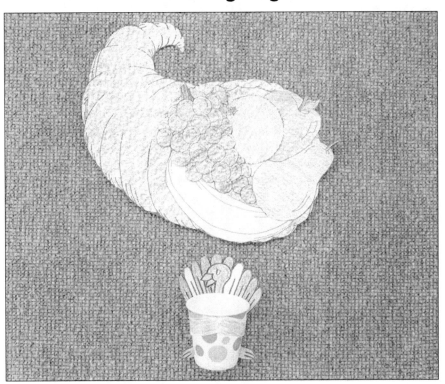

Cornucopia and Turkey Cup-Hugger

# Valentine's Day

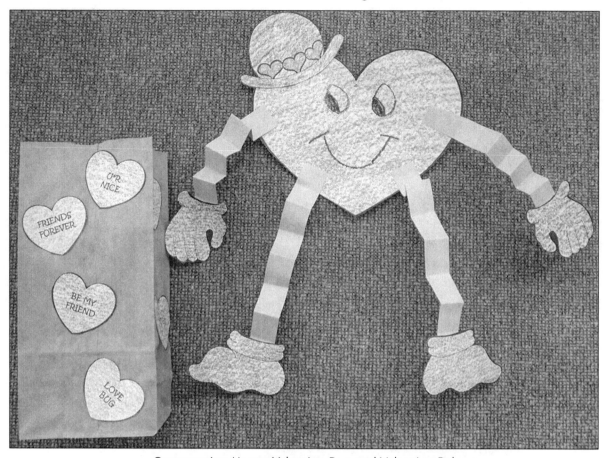

Conversation Hearts Valentine Bag and Valentine Pal

# Veterans Day and Memorial Day

Heart Poppy and Patriotic Door Hanger

# About the Author

Barbara Scott has been Children's Librarian at the Bucyrus Public Library in Bucyrus Ohio for 26 years. During that time, she has been responsible for creating preschool storytimes, as well as administering the state summer reading program and ordering materials for the Children's Department. In addition, she has been active over the years in the Ohio Library Council, serving on various committees. She holds a Bachelor of Science degree from the University of Rio Grande, where she double-majored in Library Science and English.

She is the proud mother of two children, Brandon (B.J.) and Sarah.

She loves scouring thrift stores and antique malls in search of midcentury modern items from the 1960s, 1970s, and 1980s. She collects vintage holiday items, especially Christmas ones.

CPSIA information can be obtained at www.ICGtesting.com
Printed in the USA
BVOW051807290312

286315BV00004BA/1/P